THE
LINCOLN-DOUGLAS DEBATES

ABRAHAM LINCOLN
AND
STEPHEN A. DOUGLAS

DOVER PUBLICATIONS, INC.
Mineola, New York

Copyright

Bibliographical Note

This Dover edition, first published in 2004, is an unabridged republication of two speeches and seven debates originally published in *The Political Debates between Abraham Lincoln and Stephen A. Douglas,* published by G. P. Putnam's Sons, New York and London, 1913. A new Introduction has been specially prepared for the Dover edition.

Library of Congress Cataloging-in-Publication Data

Lincoln, Abraham, 1809–1865.
    The Lincoln-Douglas debates / Abraham Lincoln and Stephen A. Douglas.
        p. cm.
    A selection of two speeches and seven debates originally published in The political debates between Abraham Lincoln and Stephen A. Douglas in the senatorial campaign of 1858 in Illinois.
    ISBN 0-486-43543-1 (pbk.)
        1. United States—Politics and government—1857–1861. 2. Lincoln-Douglas debates, 1858. I. Douglas, Stephen Arnold, 1813–1861. II. Lincoln, Abraham, 1809–1865. Political debates between Abraham Lincoln and Stephen A. Douglas in the senatorial campaign of 1858 in Illinois. III. Title.

E457.4.L77 2004
324.9773'03—dc22

                                                                                2004043898

Manufactured in the United States of America
Dover Publications, Inc., 31 East 2nd Street, Mineola, N.Y. 11501

Contents

Introduction

One of the most significant and far-reaching political events in United States history, the Lincoln-Douglas debates of 1858 sharpened and brought to a head a number of crucial questions concerning slavery, states' rights, the legal status of blacks, the effects of the Dred Scott decision, and other issues. Although it is difficult today to believe that less than a century and a half ago, men of goodwill on both sides were debating the legality and desirability of enslaving other human beings, such was indeed the case.

The debates were held as part of the campaign for the Illinois senatorial seat in 1858, pitting the two-term incumbent, Democrat Stephen A. Douglas, against the lesser-known Abraham Lincoln, a successful lawyer and state politician, and the Republican candidate. Held in seven congressional districts around the state, the debates (somewhat reluctantly agreed to by Douglas) focused on issues of critical importance to the country, resulting in close attention by the public and the media. Indeed, some thought the future of the nation rested on the outcome. "The battle of the Union is to be fought in Illinois," declared one Washington newspaper.

In a sense Lincoln helped lay the groundwork for debate of the slavery question with his famous "House Divided" speech (p. 1), given in Springfield on June 17, 1858. In that address, he warned that the nation could not survive as half-free and half-slave ("A house divided against itself cannot stand."). Moreover, he charged that Douglas's "popular sovereignty" position— allowing the states to decide the slavery issue for themselves— fostered the spread of slavery both in the states and in the western territories the United States had acquired from Mexico. Although Douglas did not like slavery, he liked even less the idea of the federal government telling states what they could or could not do. As an early advocate of states' rights, he felt deeply that the people of each state or territory should have the right to decide whether or not slavery was right for them.

Lincoln opposed slavery both on moral grounds ("If slavery is not wrong, nothing is wrong."), and political grounds, pointing out that the Declaration of Independence declared that all men are created equal. Surprisingly enough, Lincoln did not consider the black man his social or intellectual equal, but thought he was entitled to equal protection under the law. He saw it as a basic issue of good versus evil, right versus wrong, and he accused his opponent of upholding a wrong.

In his speech in Chicago on July 9, 1858 (p. 10), Douglas accused Lincoln of fomenting civil war by insisting that the states must be either all free or all slave. He was disturbed by Lincoln's attempt to settle a controversial moral issue by political means, warning that it could lead to a conflict between the states. He also defended the principle of self-government for states and territories, declaring that "uniformity in local and domestic affairs would be destructive of State rights, of State sovereignty, of personal liberty and personal freedom." He further took Lincoln to task for the latter's criticism of the Dred Scott decision, in which the Supreme Court decided that all people of African ancestry—slaves as well as those who were free—could never become citizens of the United States and therefore could not sue in federal court. As part of the decision, the court also ruled that the federal government did not have the power to prohibit slavery in its territories.

For his part, Douglas maintained that a slave (or an Indian) was not the equal of a white man. "I am opposed to giving him a voice in the adminstration of the government. I would extend to the negro, and the Indian, and to all dependent races every right, every privilege, and every immunity consistent with the safety and welfare of the white races; but equality they never should have, either political or social, or in any other respect whatever."

The debates began in earnest on August 21, 1858, in Ottawa, Illinois (p. 26). The question of the extension of slavery into the territories dominated the seven debates. At Freeport, in August, Lincoln asked whether it was possible for the people of a United States territory to exclude slavery from its limits before the formation of a state constitution. Douglas replied that it was up to the people of the territory to allow or ban slavery from that region. This argument was based on Douglas' belief that popular sovereignty was compatible with the Dred Scott decision, which ruled that the people of a territory could not exclude slavery. (In a bit of fudging, Douglas said they could do it by means of local legislation.) Known today as the "Freeport Doctrine" ("Slavery cannot exist a day in the midst of an unfriendly people with unfriendly laws."), Douglas's opinion caused great controversy throughout America.

During the third debate in Jonesboro on September 15 (p. 109), Douglas accused Lincoln of conspiring with Lyman Trumball, a Democrat who supported Lincoln and the Republican cause, to abolitionize both parties. Knowing there was little chance of gaining much support among the proslavery advocates in attendance, Lincoln wisely refused to respond and again questioned Douglas's "Freeport Doctrine."

The debates continued on through the fall, with both candidates trying to delineate their own positions, repudiate the accusations, unfair or otherwise, of the opponent, and appeal to the populace for support.

In the fourth debate, at Charleston, Lincoln unequivocally stated that he was "not in favor of making voters or jurors of negroes, nor of qualifying them to hold office, nor to intermarry with white people." Moreover, he opined that the physical differences between the white and black races forbade them from living together on terms of social and political equality. Despite this inequality, however, he did not believe that because the white man is to hold the superior position, the negro should therefore be denied everything. As Lincoln's speech was given in the southern part of the state, Douglas accused his opponent of pandering to the proslavery South, and that Lincoln took a different tack on "equality" when addressing audiences in the Abolitionist North.

October found the two debating at Galesburgh (p. 207), at which forum Douglas took the opportunity to stress his belief in the principle that underlay the Missouri Compromise and the Kansas-Nebraska Act (which Douglas introduced), i.e. "the great fundamental principle that the people of each State and Territory of this Union have the right, and ought to be permitted to exercise the right, of regulating their own domestic concerns in their own way, subject to no other limitation or restriction than that which the Constitution of the United States imposes upon them."

Douglas also declared Lincoln's claim that the white and the black man are made equal by the Declaration of Independence and divine providence "a monstrous heresy," claiming that Jefferson had only white men in mind when composing the Declaration. He further pointed out that Jefferson and all the signers of the Declaration owned slaves, and none of them freed their slaves afterward. In response, Lincoln affirmed that nowhere in the Constitution is it stated that a slave is the property of his owner.

In the sixth debate, at Quincy on October 13 (p. 249), Lincoln returned to the theme of the rights of the black man, declaring that the Declaration of Independence guaranteed him the rights of life, liberty, and the pursuit of happiness, just as it did white men. And while the black man might not be his [Lincoln's] social, intellectual, or moral equal, he nevertheless insisted that in the black man's "right to eat the bread without the leave of any body else which his own hand earns, he is my equal and the equal of Judge Douglas, and the equal of every other man."

Douglas continued to accuse Lincoln of inconsistency, claiming that he embraced one set of principles when speaking in Abolitionist counties and another set of principles when addressing anti-Abolitionist groups. He also attacked Lincoln's policy of limiting the spread of slave states, with its ultimate aim of abolishing slavery altogether. For Douglas, the question was not whether slavery was right or wrong, but whether states had the right to decide the question for themselves. For his part,

Lincoln had accused Douglas of being part of a conspiracy to make slavery national, and on this occasion refused to withdraw the charge unless it could be proved false.

The final debate took place at Alton on October 15, 1858 (p. 293). In it Douglas again attacked three central propositions that Lincoln favored and that he [Douglas] opposed: First, that the country could not permanently survive divided into free and slave states, but must be one or the other. Second, Lincoln's criticism of the Dred Scott decision for depriving blacks of the rights and benefits guaranteed under the Constitution to the citizens of each state; and third, Lincoln's assertion that the distinctions between this man and that man, this race and the other race, must be discarded. For Lincoln the country had to stand by the Declaration of Independence, which declared all men created equal.

In his reply, addressing the moral issue of slavery, Lincoln rose to the heights of eloquence in his condemnation: "That is the real issue. That is the issue that will continue in this country when these poor tongues of Judge Douglas and myself shall be silent. It is the eternal struggle between these two principles— right and wrong—throughout the world. They are the two principles that have stood face to face from the beginning of time; and will ever continue to struggle. The one is the common right of humanity and the other the divine right of kings. It is the same principle in whatever shape it develops itself. It is the same spirit that says, 'You work and toil and earn bread, and I'll eat it.' No matter in what shape it comes, whether from the mouth of a king who seeks to bestride the people of his own nation and live by the fruit of their labor, or from one race of men as an apology for enslaving another race, it is the same tyrannical principle."

In the election that followed, in November of 1858, Lincoln won the popular vote by more than 4,000 votes. However, at the time senators were chosen by state legislatures (changed by the Seventeenth Amendment in 1913), without regard to the popular vote. In the legislature, Lincoln received forty-six votes compared to Douglas's fifty-four, and thereby lost the election. He responded with the famous quip, "I am too big to cry about it, but it hurts too awful bad to laugh!"

Despite the loss, Lincoln emerged from the debates as a renowned orator and respected individual, a man who had made a deep impression on his countrymen. Just two years later, Lincoln garnered the Republican nomination for president and won the general election, defeating Douglas and two other candidates by a large majority of electoral votes.

Speech of Abraham Lincoln
SPRINGFIELD, JUNE 17, 1858

[The following speech was delivered at Springfield, Ill., at the close of the Republican State Convention held at that time and place, and by which Convention Mr. LINCOLN had been named as their candidate for United States Senator. Mr. DOUGLAS was not present.]

MR. PRESIDENT AND GENTLEMEN OF THE CONVENTION: If we could first know where we are, and whither we are tending, we could better judge what to do, and how to do it. We are now far into the fifth year since a policy was initiated with the avowed object and confident promise of putting an end to slavery agitation. Under the operation of that policy, that agitation has not only not ceased, but has constantly augmented. In my opinion, it will not cease until a crisis shall have been reached and passed. "A house divided against itself cannot stand." I believe this government cannot endure permanently half slave and half free. I do not expect the Union to be dissolved; I do not expect the house to fall; but I do expect it will cease to be divided. It will become all one thing, or all the other. Either the opponents of slavery will arrest the further spread of it, and place it where the public mind shall rest in the belief that it is in the course of ultimate extinction, or its advocates will push it forward till it shall become alike lawful in all the States, old as well as new, North as well as South.

Have we no tendency to the latter condition?

Let any one who doubts, carefully contemplate that now almost complete legal combination—piece of machinery, so to speak—compounded of the Nebraska doctrine and the Dred Scott decision. Let him consider, not only what work the machinery is adapted to do, and how well adapted, but also let him study the history of its construction, and trace, if he can, or rather fail, if he can, to trace the evidences of design, and concert of action, among its chief architects, from the beginning.

The new year of 1854 found slavery excluded from more than half the States by State Constitutions, and from most of the National territory by Congressional prohibition. Four days later, commenced the struggle which ended in repealing that Congressional prohibition. This opened all the National territory to slavery, and was the first point gained.

But, so far, Congress only had acted, and an indorsement by the people, real or apparent, was indispensable to save the point already gained, and give chance for more.

This necessity had not been overlooked, but had been provided for, as well as might be, in the notable argument of "squatter sovereignty," otherwise called "sacred right of self-government," which latter phrase, though expressive of the only rightful basis of any government, was so perverted in this attempted use of it as to amount to just this: That if any *one* man choose to enslave *another,* no *third* man shall be allowed to object. That argument was incorporated into the Nebraska Bill itself, in the language which follows: "It being the true intent and meaning of this Act not to legislate slavery into any Territory or State, nor to exclude it therefrom, but to leave the people thereof perfectly free to form and regulate their domestic institutions in their own way, subject only to the Constitution of the United States." Then opened the roar of loose declamation in favor of "squatter sovereignty," and "sacred right of self-government." "But," said opposition members, "let us amend the bill so as to expressly declare that the people of the Territory may exclude slavery." "Not we," said the friends of the measure, and down they voted the amendment.

While the Nebraska Bill was passing through Congress, a *law case,* involving the question of a negro's freedom, by reason of his owner having voluntarily taken him first into a free State, and then into a territory covered by the Congressional prohibition, and held him as a slave for a long time in each, was passing through the United States Circuit Court for the District of Missouri; and both Nebraska Bill and lawsuit were brought to a decision in the same month of May, 1854. The negro's name was "Dred Scott," which name now designates the decision finally made in the case. Before the then next Presidential election, the law case came to, and was argued in, the Supreme Court of the United States; but the decision of it was deferred until after the election. Still, before the election, Senator Trumbull, on the floor of the Senate, requested the leading advocate of the Nebraska Bill to state *his opinion* whether the people of a Territory can constitutionally exclude slavery from their limits; and the latter answers: "That is a question for the Supreme Court."

The election came. Mr. Buchanan was elected, and the indorsement, such as it was, secured. That was the second point gained. The indorsement, however, fell short of a clear popular majority by nearly four hundred thousand votes, and so, perhaps, was not overwhelmingly reliable and satisfactory. The outgoing President, in his last annual message, as impressively as possible echoed back upon the people the weight and authority of the indorsement. The Supreme Court met again, did not announce their decision, but ordered a reargument. The Presidential inauguration came, and still no decision of the court; but the incoming President, in his inaugural address, fervently exhorted the people to abide by the forthcoming decision, whatever it might be. Then, in a few days, came the decision.

The reputed author of the Nebraska Bill finds an early occasion to make a speech at this capital indorsing the Dred Scott decision, and vehemently denouncing all opposition to it. The new President, too, seizes the early occasion of the Silliman letter to indorse and strongly construe that decision, and to express his astonishment that any different view had ever been entertained!

At length a squabble springs up between the President and the author of the Nebraska Bill, on the mere question of *fact,* whether the Lecompton Constitution was or was not in any just sense made by the people of Kansas; and in that quarrel the latter declares that all he wants is a fair vote for the people, and that he cares not whether slavery be voted *down* or voted *up*. I do not understand his declaration, that he cares not whether slavery be voted down or voted up, to be intended by him other than as an apt definition of the policy he would impress upon the public mind,—the principle for which he declares he has suffered so much, and is ready to suffer to the end. And well may he cling to that principle! If he has any parental feeling, well may he cling to it. That principle is the only shred left of his original Nebraska doctrine. Under the Dred Scott decision "squatter sovereignty" squatted out of existence, tumbled down like temporary scaffolding; like the mould at the foundry, served through one blast, and fell back into loose sand; helped to carry an election, and then was kicked to the winds. His late joint struggle with the Republicans, against the Lecompton Constitution, involves nothing of the original Nebraska doctrine. That struggle was made on a point—the right of a people to make their own constitution—upon which he and the Republicans have never differed.

The several points of the Dred Scott decision, in connection with Senator Douglas's "care not" policy, constitute the piece of machinery, in its present state of advancement. This was the third point gained. The working points of that machinery are:

Firstly, That no negro slave, imported as such from Africa, and no descendant of such slave, can ever be a citizen of any State, in the sense of that term as used in the Constitution of the United States. This point is made in order to deprive the negro, in every possible event, of the benefit of that provision of the United States Constitution which declares that "The citizens of each State shall be entitled to all privileges and immunities of citizens in the several States."

Secondly, That, "subject to the Constitution of the United States," neither Congress nor a Territorial Legislature can exclude slavery from any United States Territory. This point is made in order that individual men may fill up the Territories with slaves, without danger of losing them as property, and thus to enhance the chances of permanency to the institution through all the future.

Thirdly, That whether the holding a negro in actual slavery in a free State makes him free, as against the holder, the United States courts will not decide, but will leave to be decided by the courts of any slave State the negro may be forced into by the master. This point is made, not to be pressed immediately; but, if acquiesced in for a while, and apparently indorsed by the people at an election, then to sustain the logical conclusion that what Dred Scott's master might lawfully do with Dred Scott, in the free State of Illinois, every other master may lawfully do with any other one, or one thousand slaves, in Illinois, or in any other free State.

Auxiliary to all this, and working hand in hand with it, the Nebraska doctrine, or what is left of it, is to educate and mould public opinion, at least Northern public opinion, not to care whether slavery is voted down or voted up. This shows exactly where we now are; and partially, also, whither we are tending.

It will throw additional light on the latter, to go back and run the mind over the string of historical facts already stated. Several things will now appear less dark and mysterious than they did when they were transpiring. The people were to be left "perfectly free," "subject only to the Constitution." What the Constitution had to do with it, outsiders could not then see. Plainly enough now,—it was an exactly fitted niche, for the Dred Scott decision to afterward come in, and declare the perfect freedom of the people to be just no freedom at all. Why was the amendment, expressly declaring the right of the people, voted down? Plainly enough now,—the adoption of it would have spoiled the niche for the Dred Scott decision. Why was the court decision held up? Why even a Senator's individual opinion withheld, till after the Presidential election? Plainly enough now,—the speaking out then would have damaged the "perfectly free" argument upon which the election was to be carried. Why the outgoing President's felicitation on the indorsement? Why the delay of a reargument? Why the incoming President's advance exhortation in favor of the decision? These things look like the cautious patting and petting of a spirited horse preparatory to mounting him, when it is dreaded that he may give the rider a fall. And why the hasty after-indorsement of the decision by the President and others?

We cannot absolutely know that all these exact adaptations are the result of preconcert. But when we see a lot of framed timbers, different portions of which we know have been gotten out at different times and places and by different workmen,— Stephen, Franklin, Roger, and James, for instance,—and when we see these timbers joined together, and see they exactly make the frame of a house or a mill, all the tenons and mortises exactly fitting, and all the lengths and proportions of the different pieces exactly adapted to their respective places, and not a piece too many or too few,—not omitting even scaffolding,—or, if a single piece be lacking, we see the place in the frame exactly fitted and prepared yet to bring such piece in,—in such a case, we find it impossible not to believe that Stephen and Franklin and Roger and James all understood one another from the beginning, and all worked upon a common plan or draft drawn up before the first blow was struck.

It should not be overlooked that by the Nebraska Bill the people of a *State* as well as Territory were to be left "perfectly free," "subject only to the Constitution." Why mention a State? They were legislating for Territories, and not for or about States. Certainly the people of a State are and ought to be subject to the Constitution of the United States; but why is mention of this lugged into this merely Territorial law? Why are the people of a Territory and the people of a State therein lumped together, and their relation to the Constitution therein treated as being precisely the same? While the opinion of the court, by Chief Justice Taney, in the Dred Scott case, and the separate opinions of all the concurring Judges, expressly declare that the Constitution of the United States neither permits Congress nor a Territorial Legislature to exclude slavery from any United States Territory, they all omit to declare whether or not the same Constitution permits a State, or the people of a State, to exclude it. *Possibly,* this is a mere omission; but who can be quite sure, if McLean or Curtis had sought to get into the opinion a declaration of unlimited power in the people of a State to exclude slavery from their limits, just as Chase and Mace sought to get such declaration, in behalf of the people of a Territory, into the Nebraska Bill,—I ask, who can be quite sure that it would not have been voted down in the one case as it had been in the other? The nearest approach to the point of declaring the power of a State over slavery is made by Judge Nelson. He approaches it more than once, using the precise idea, and almost the language, too, of the Nebraska Act. On one occasion, his exact language is, "Except in cases where the power is restrained by the Constitution of the United States, the law of the State is supreme over the subject of slavery within its jurisdiction." In what cases the power of the States is so restrained by the United States Constitution, is left an open question, precisely as the same question, as to the restraint on the power of the Territories, was left open in the Nebraska Act. Put this and that together, and we have another nice little niche, which we may, ere long, see filled with another Supreme Court decision, declaring that the Constitution of the United States does not permit a *State* to exclude slavery from its limits. And this may especially be expected if the doctrine of "care not whether slavery be voted down or voted up" shall gain upon the public mind sufficiently to give promise that such a decision can be maintained when made.

Such a decision is all that slavery now lacks of being alike lawful in all the States. Welcome or unwelcome, such decision is probably coming, and will soon be upon us, unless the power of the present political dynasty shall be met and overthrown. We shall lie down pleasantly dreaming that the people of Missouri are on the verge of making their State free, and we shall awake to the reality instead that the Supreme Court has made Illinois a slave State. To meet and overthrow the power of that dynasty is the work now before all those who would prevent that consummation. That is what we have to do. How can we best do it?

There are those who denounce us openly to their own friends, and yet whisper to us softly that Senator Douglas is the aptest instrument there is with which to effect that object. They wish us to *infer* all, from the fact that he now has a little quarrel with the present head of the dynasty, and that he has regularly voted with us on a single point, upon which he and we have never differed. They remind us that he is a great man, and that the largest of us are very small ones. Let this be granted. But "a living dog is better than a dead lion." Judge Douglas, if not a dead lion, for this work is at least a caged and toothless one. How can he oppose the advances of slavery? He don't care anything about it. His avowed mission is impressing the "public heart" to *care nothing about it*. A leading Douglas Democratic newspaper thinks Douglas's superior talent will be needed to resist the revival of the African slave trade. Does Douglas believe an effort to revive that trade is approaching? He has not said so. Does he really think so? But if it is, how can he resist it? For years he has labored to prove it a sacred right of white men to take negro slaves into the new Territories. Can he possibly show that it is less a sacred right to buy them where they can be bought cheapest? And unquestionably they can be bought cheaper in Africa than in Virginia. He has done all in his power to reduce the whole question of slavery to one of a mere right of property; and, as such, how can he oppose the foreign slave trade,—how can he refuse that trade in that "property" shall be "perfectly free,"—unless he does it as a protection to the home production? And as the home producers will probably not ask the protection, he will be wholly without a ground of opposition.

Senator Douglas holds, we know, that a man may rightfully be wiser to-day than he was yesterday; that he may rightfully change when he finds himself wrong. But can we, for that reason, run ahead, and infer that he will make any particular change, of which he himself has given no intimation? Can we safely base our action upon any such vague inference? Now, as ever, I wish not to misrepresent Judge Douglas's position, question his motives, or do aught that can be personally offensive to him. Whenever, if ever, he and we can come together on principle so that our cause may have assistance from his great ability, I hope to have interposed no adventitious obstacles. But clearly he is not now with us; he does not pretend to be,—he does not promise ever to be.

Our cause, then, must be intrusted to, and conducted by, its own undoubted friends,—those whose hands are free, whose hearts are in the work, who *do care* for the result. Two years ago the Republicans of the nation mustered over thirteen hundred thousand strong. We did this under the single impulse of resistance to a common danger, with every external circumstance against us. Of strange, discordant, and even hostile elements we gathered from the four winds, and formed and fought the battle through, under the constant hot fire of a disciplined, proud, and pampered enemy. Did we brave all then to falter now,—now, when that same enemy is wavering, dissevered, and belligerent? The result is not doubtful. We shall not fail; if we stand firm, we *shall not fail*. Wise counsels may accelerate, or mistakes delay it, but, sooner or later, the victory is sure to come.

Speech of Senator Douglas

On the Occasion of his Public Reception at Chicago, Friday Evening, July 9, 1858. (Mr. Lincoln was present.)

Mr. Douglas said,—

MR. CHAIRMAN AND FELLOW-CITIZENS: I can find no language which can adequately express my profound gratitude for the magnificent welcome which you have extended to me on this occasion. This vast sea of human faces indicates how deep an interest is felt by our people in the great questions which agitate the public mind, and which underlie the foundations of our free institutions. A reception like this, so great in numbers that no human voice can be heard to its countless thousands,—so enthusiastic that no one individual can be the object of such enthusiasm,—clearly shows that there is some great principle which sinks deep in the heart of the masses, and involves the rights and the liberties of a whole people, that has brought you together with a unanimity and a cordiality never before excelled, if, indeed, equalled, on any occasion. I have not the vanity to believe that it is any personal compliment to me.

It is an expression of your devotion to that great principle of self-government, to which my life for many years past has been, and in the future will be, devoted. If there is any one principle dearer and more sacred than all others in free governments, it is that which asserts the exclusive right of a free people to form and adopt their own fundamental law, and to manage and regulate their own internal affairs and domestic institutions.

When I found an effort being made during the recent session

of Congress to force a constitution upon the people of Kansas against their will, and to force that State into the Union with a constitution which her people had rejected by more than ten thousand, I felt bound as a man of honour and a representative of Illinois, bound by every consideration of duty, of fidelity, and of patriotism, to resist to the utmost of my power the consummation of that fraud. With others, I did resist it, and resisted it successfully until the attempt was abandoned. We forced them to refer that constitution back to the people of Kansas, to be accepted or rejected as they shall decide at an election which is fixed for the first Monday in August next. It is true that the mode of reference, and the form of the submission, was not such as I could sanction with my vote, for the reason that it discriminated between free States and slave States; providing that if Kansas consented to come in under the Lecompton Constitution it should be received with a population of thirty-five thousand; but that if she demanded another constitution, more consistent with the sentiments of her people and their feelings, that it should not be received into the Union until she had 93,420 inhabitants. I did not consider that mode of submission fair, for the reason that any election is a mockery which is not free, that any election is a fraud upon the rights of the people which holds out inducements for affirmative votes, and threatens penalties for negative votes. But whilst I was not satisfied with the mode of submission, whilst I resisted it to the last, demanding a fair, a just, a free mode of submission, still, when the law passed placing it within the power of the people of Kansas at that election to reject the Lecompton Constitution, and then make another in harmony with their principles and their opinions, I did not believe that either the penalties on the one hand, or the inducements on the other, would force that people to accept a constitution to which they are irreconcilably opposed. All I can say is, that if their votes can be controlled by such considerations all the sympathy which has been expended upon them has been misplaced, and all the efforts that have been made in defence of their right to self-government have been made in an unworthy cause.

Hence, my friends, I regard the Lecompton battle as having

been fought, and the victory won, because the arrogant demand for the admission of Kansas under the Lecompton Constitution unconditionally, whether her people wanted it or not, has been abandoned, and the principle which recognizes the right of the people to decide for themselves has been submitted in its place.

Fellow-citizens, while I devoted my best energies—all my energies, mental and physical—to the vindication of the great principle, and whilst the result has been such as will enable the people of Kansas to come into the Union with such a constitution as they desire, yet the credit of this great moral victory is to be divided among a large number of men of various and different political creeds. I was rejoiced when I found in this great contest the Republican party coming up manfully and sustaining the principle that the people of each Territory, when coming into the Union, have the right to decide for themselves whether slavery shall or shall not exist within their limits. I have seen the time when that principle was controverted. I have seen the time when all parties did not recognize the right of a people to have slavery or freedom, to tolerate or prohibit slavery as they deemed best, but claimed that power for the Congress of the United States, regardless of the wishes of the people to be affected by it; and when I found upon the Crittenden-Montgomery bill the Republicans and Americans of the North, and I may say, too, some glorious Americans and old-line Whigs from the South, like Crittenden and his patriotic associates, joined with a portion of the Democracy to carry out and vindicate the right of the people to decide whether slavery should or should not exist within the limits of Kansas, I was rejoiced within my secret soul, for I saw an indication that the American people, when they came to understand the principle, would give it their cordial support.

The Crittenden-Montgomery bill was as fair and as perfect an exposition of the doctrine of popular sovereignty as could be carried out by any bill that man ever devised. It proposed to refer the Lecompton Constitution back to the people of Kansas, and give them the right to accept or reject it as they pleased, at a fair election, held in pursuance of law, and in the event of their rejecting it, and forming another in its stead, to permit them to come into the Union on an equal footing with the original States. It was fair and just in all of its provisions. I gave it my cordial support, and was rejoiced when I found that it passed the House of Representatives, and at one time I entertained high hope that it would pass the Senate.

I regard the great principle of popular sovereignty as having been vindicated and made triumphant in this land as a permanent rule of public policy in the organization of Territories and the admission of new States. Illinois took her position upon this principle many years ago. You all recollect that in 1850, after the passage of the Compromise measures of that year, when I returned to my home there was great dissatisfaction expressed at my course in supporting those measures. I appeared before the people of Chicago at a mass meeting, and vindicated each and every one of those measures; and by reference to my speech on that occasion, which was printed and circulated broadcast throughout the State at the time, you will find that I then and there said that those measures were all founded upon the great principle that every people ought to possess the right to form and regulate their own domestic institutions in their own way, and that, that right being possessed by the people of the States, I saw no reason why the same principle should not be extended to all of the Territories of the United States. A general election was held in this State a few months afterwards, for members of the Legislature, pending which all these questions were thoroughly canvassed and discussed, and the nominees of the different parties instructed in regard to the wishes of their constituents upon them. When that election was over, and the Legislature assembled, they proceeded to consider the merits of those Compromise measures, and the principles upon which they were predicated. And what was the result of their action? They passed resolutions, first repealing the Wilmot Proviso instructions, and in lieu thereof adopted another resolution, in which they declared the great principle which asserts the right of the people to make their own form of government and establish their own institutions. That resolution is as follows:

Resolved, That our liberty and independence are based upon the right of the people to form for themselves such a government as they may choose; that this great principle, the birthright of freemen, the gift of Heaven, secured to us by the blood of our ancestors, ought to be secured to future generations, and no limitation ought to be applied to this power in the organization of any Territory of the United States, of either Territorial Government or State Constitution, provided the Government so established shall be republican, and in conformity with the Constitution of the United States.

That resolution, declaring the great principle of self-government as applicable to the Territories and new States, passed the House of Representatives of this State by a vote of sixty-one in the affirmative, to only four in the negative. Thus you find that an expression of public opinion—enlightened, educated, intelligent public opinion—on this question, by the representatives of Illinois in 1851, approaches nearer to unanimity than has ever been obtained on any controverted question. That resolution was entered on the journal of the Legislature of the State of Illinois, and it has remained there from that day to this, a standing instruction to her Senators, and a request to her Representatives, in Congress to carry out that principle in all future cases. Illinois, therefore, stands pre-eminent as the State which stepped forward early and established a platform applicable to this slavery question, concurred in alike by Whigs and Democrats, in which it was declared to be the wish of our people that thereafter the people of the Territories should be left perfectly free to form and regulate their domestic institutions in their own way, and that no limitation should be placed upon that right in any form.

Hence what was my duty in 1854, when it became necessary to bring forward a bill for the organization of the Territories of Kansas and Nebraska? Was it not my duty, in obedience to the Illinois platform, to your standing instructions to your Senators, adopted with almost entire unanimity, to incorporate in that bill the great principle of self-government, declaring that it was "the true intent and meaning of the Act not to legislate slavery into any State or Territory, or to exclude it therefrom, but to leave the people thereof perfectly free to form and regulate their domestic institutions in their own way, subject only to the Constitution of the United States"? I did incorporate that principle in the Kansas-Nebraska Bill, and perhaps I did as much as any living man in the enactment of that bill, thus establishing the doctrine in the public policy of the country. I then defended that principle against assaults from one section of the Union. During this last winter it became my duty to vindicate it against assaults from the other section of the Union. I vindicated it boldly and fearlessly, as the people of Chicago can bear witness, when it was assailed by Free-soilers; and during this winter I vindicated and defended it as boldly and fearlessly when it was attempted to be violated by the almost united South. I pledged myself to you on every stump in Illinois in 1854, I pledged myself to the people of other States north and south, wherever I spoke; and in the United States Senate and elsewhere, in every form in which I could reach the public mind or the public ear, I gave the pledge that I, so far as the power should be in my hands, would vindicate the principle of the right of the people to form their own institutions, to establish free States or slave States as they chose, and that that principle should never be violated either by fraud, by violence, by circumvention, or by any other means, if it was in my power to prevent it. I now submit to you, my fellow-citizens, whether I have not redeemed that pledge in good faith. Yes, my friends, I have redeemed it in good faith; and it is a matter of heartfelt gratification to me to see these assembled thousands here to-night bearing their testimony to the fidelity with which I have advocated that principle, and redeemed my pledges in connection with it.

I will be entirely frank with you. My object was to secure the right of the people of each State and of each Territory, north or south, to decide the question for themselves, to have slavery or not, just as they chose; and my opposition to the Lecompton Constitution was not predicated upon the ground that it was a pro-slavery constitution, nor would my action have been different had it been a Free-soil constitution. My speech against the Lecompton fraud was made on the 9th of December, while the vote on the slavery clause in that constitution was not taken until the 21st of the same month, nearly two weeks after. I made my speech against the Lecompton monstrosity solely on the ground that it was a violation of the fundamental principles of free government; on the ground that it was not the act and deed of the people of Kansas; that it did not embody their will; that they were averse to it; and hence I denied the right of Congress to force it upon them, either as a free State or a slave State. I deny the right of Congress to force a slaveholding State upon an unwilling people. I deny their right to force a free State upon an unwilling people. I deny their right to force a good thing upon a people who are unwilling to receive it. The great principle is the right of every community to judge and decide for itself whether a thing is right or wrong, whether it would be good or evil for them to adopt it; and the right of free action, the right of free thought, the right of free judgment, upon the question is dearer to every true American than any other under a free government. My objection to the Lecompton contrivance was that it undertook to put a constitution on the people of Kansas against their will, in opposition to their wishes, and thus violated the great principle upon which all our institutions rest. It is no answer to this argument to say that slavery is an evil, and hence should not be tolerated. You must allow the people to decide for themselves whether it is a good or an evil. You allow them to decide for themselves whether they desire a Maine liquor law or not; you allow them to decide for themselves what kind of common schools they will have, what system of banking they will adopt, or whether they will adopt any at all; you allow them to decide for themselves the relations between husband and wife, parent and child, guardian and ward,—in fact, you allow them to decide for themselves all other questions: and why not upon this question? Whenever you put a limitation upon the right of any people to decide what laws they want, you have destroyed the fundamental principle of self-government.

In connection with this subject, perhaps, it will not be improper for me on this occasion to allude to the position of those who have chosen to arraign my conduct on this same subject. I have observed from the public prints that but a few days ago the Republican party of the State of Illinois assembled in Convention at Springfield, and not only laid down their platform, but nominated a candidate for the United States Senate, as my successor. I take great pleasure in saying that I have known, personally and intimately, for about a quarter of a century, the worthy gentleman who has been nominated for my place, and I will say that I regard him as a kind, amiable, and intelligent gentleman, a good citizen and an honorable opponent; and whatever issue I may have with him will be of principle, and not involving personalities. Mr. Lincoln made a speech before that Republican Convention which unanimously nominated him for the Senate,—a speech evidently well prepared and carefully written,—in which he states the basis upon which he proposes to carry on the campaign during this summer. In it he lays down two distinct propositions which I shall notice, and upon which I shall take a direct and bold issue with him.

His first and main proposition I will give in his own language, Scripture quotations and all [laughter]; I give his exact language: "'A house divided against itself cannot stand.' I believe this government cannot endure, permanently, half *slave* and half *free*. I do not expect the Union to be *dissolved,* I do not expect the house to *fall;* but I do expect it to cease to be divided. It will become *all* one thing, or *all* the other."

In other words, Mr. Lincoln asserts, as a fundamental principle of this government, that there must be uniformity in the local laws and domestic institutions of each and all the States of the Union; and he therefore invites all the non-slaveholding States to band together, organize as one body, and make war upon slavery in Kentucky, upon slavery in Virginia, upon the Carolinas, upon slavery in all of the slaveholding States in this Union, and to persevere in that war until it shall be exterminated. He then notifies the slaveholding States to stand together as a unit and make an aggressive war upon the free States of this Union with a view of establishing slavery in them all; of forcing it upon Illinois, of forcing it upon New York, upon New England, and upon every other free State, and that they shall keep up the warfare until it has been formally established in them all. In other words, Mr. Lincoln advocates boldly and clearly a war of sections, a war of the North against the South, of the free States against the slave States,—a war of extermination, to be continued relentlessly until the one or the other shall be subdued, and all the States shall either become free or become slave.

Now, my friends, I must say to you frankly that I take bold, unqualified issue with him upon that principle. I assert that it is neither desirable nor possible that there should be uniformity in the local institutions and domestic regulations of the different States of the Union. The framers of our government never contemplated uniformity in its internal concerns. The fathers of the Revolution and the sages who made the Constitution well understood that the laws and domestic institutions which would suit the granite hills of New Hampshire would be totally unfit for the rice plantations of South Carolina; they well understood that the laws which would suit the agricultural districts of Pennsylvania and New York would be totally unfit for the large mining regions of the Pacific, or the lumber regions of Maine. They well understood that the great varieties of soil, of production, and of interests in a republic as large as this, required different local and domestic regulations in each locality, adapted to the wants and interests of each separate State; and for that reason it was provided in the Federal Constitution that the thirteen original States should remain sovereign and supreme within their own limits in regard to all that was local and internal and domestic, while the Federal Government should have certain specified powers which were general and national, and could be exercised only by Federal authority.

The framers of the Constitution well understood that each locality, having separate and distinct interests, required separate and distinct laws, domestic institutions, and police regulations adapted to its own wants and its own condition; and they acted on the presumption, also, that these laws and institutions would be as diversified and as dissimilar as the States would be numerous, and that no two would be precisely alike, because the interests of no two would be precisely the same. Hence I assert that the great fundamental principle which underlies our complex system of State and Federal governments contemplated diversity and dissimilarity in the local institutions and domestic affairs of each and every State then in the Union, or thereafter to be admitted into the Confederacy. I therefore conceive that my friend Mr. Lincoln has totally misapprehended the great principles upon which our government rests. Uniformity in local and domestic affairs would be destructive of State rights, of State sovereignty, of personal liberty and personal freedom. Uniformity is the parent of despotism the world over, not only in politics, but in religion. Wherever the doctrine of uniformity is proclaimed, that all the States must be free or all slave, that all labor must be white or all black, that all the citizens of the different States must have the same privileges or be governed by the same regulations, you have destroyed the greatest safeguard which our institutions have thrown around the rights of the citizen.

How could this uniformity be accomplished, if it was desirable and possible? There is but one mode in which it could be obtained, and that must be by abolishing the State legislatures, blotting out State sovereignty, merging the rights and sovereignty of the States in one consolidated empire, and vesting Congress with the plenary power to make all the police regulations, domestic and local laws, uniform throughout the limits of the Republic. When you shall have done this, you will have uniformity. Then the States will all be slave or all be free; then negroes will vote everywhere or nowhere; then you will have a Maine liquor law in every State or none; then you will have uniformity in all things, local and domestic, by the authority of the Federal Government. But when you attain that uniformity, you will have converted these thirty-two sovereign, independent States into one consolidated empire, with the uniformity of despotism reigning triumphant throughout the length and breadth of the land.

From this view of the case, my friends, I am driven irresistibly to the conclusion that diversity, dissimilarity, variety, in all our local and domestic institutions is the great safeguard of our liberties, and that the framers of our institutions were wise, sagacious, and patriotic when they made this government a confederation of sovereign States, with a legislature for each, and conferred upon each legislature the power to make all local and domestic institutions to suit the people it represented, without interference from any other State or from the general Congress of the Union. If we expect to maintain our liberties, we must preserve the rights and sovereignty of the States; we must maintain and carry out that great principle of self-government incorporated in the Compromise measures of 1850, indorsed by the Illinois Legislature in 1851, emphatically embodied and carried out in the Kansas-Nebraska Bill, and vindicated this year by the refusal to bring Kansas into the Union with a constitution distasteful to her people.

The other proposition discussed by Mr. Lincoln in his speech consists in a crusade against the Supreme Court of the United States on account of the Dred Scott decision. On this question also I desire to say to you unequivocally that I take direct and distinct issue with him. I have no warfare to make on the Supreme Court of the United States, either on account of that or any other decision which they have pronounced from that bench. The Constitution of the United States has provided that the powers of government (and the constitution of each State has the same provision) shall be divided into three departments,—executive, legislative, and judicial. The right and the province of expounding the Constitution and construing the law is vested in the judiciary established by the Constitution. As a lawyer, I feel at liberty to appear before the court and controvert any principle of law while the question is pending before the tribunal; but when the decision is made, my private opinion, your opinion, all other opinions, must yield to the majesty of that authoritative adjudication. I wish you to bear in mind that this involves a great principle, upon which our rights, our liberty, and our property all depend. What security have you for your property, for your reputation, and for your personal rights, if the courts are not upheld, and their decisions respected when once fairly rendered by the highest tribunal known to the Constitution? I do not choose, therefore, to go into any argument with Mr. Lincoln in reviewing the various decisions which the Supreme Court has made, either upon the Dred Scott case or any other. I have no idea of appealing from the decision of the Supreme Court upon a constitutional question to the decisions of a tumultuous town meeting. I am aware that once an eminent lawyer of this city, now no more, said that the State of Illinois had the most perfect judicial system in the world, subject to but one exception, which could be cured by a slight amendment, and that amendment was to so change the law as to allow an appeal from the decisions of the Supreme Court of Illinois, on all constitutional questions, to justices of the peace.

My friend Mr. Lincoln, who sits behind me, reminds me that that proposition was made when I was judge of the Supreme Court. Be that as it may, I do not think that fact adds any greater weight or authority to the suggestion. It matters not with me who was on the bench, whether Mr. Lincoln or myself, whether a Lockwood or a Smith, a Taney or a Marshall; the decision of the highest tribunal known to the Constitution of the country must be final till it has been reversed by an equally high authority. Hence, I am opposed to this doctrine of Mr. Lincoln by which he proposes to take an appeal from the decision of the Supreme Court of the United States, upon this high constitutional question, to a Republican caucus sitting in the country. Yes, or any other caucus or town meeting, whether it be Republican, American, or Democratic. I respect the decisions of that august tribunal; I shall always bow in deference to them. I am a law-abiding man. I will sustain the Constitution of my country as our fathers have made it. I will yield obedience to the laws, whether I like them or not, as I find them on the statute book. I will sustain the judicial tribunals and constituted authorities in all matters within the pale of their jurisdiction as defined by the Constitution.

But I am equally free to say that the reason as signed by Mr. Lincoln for resisting the decision of the Supreme Court in the Dred Scott case does not in itself meet my approbation. He objects to it because that decision declared that a negro descended from African parents, who were brought here and sold as slaves, is not and cannot be a citizen of the United States. He says it is wrong because it deprives the negro of the benefits of that clause of the Constitution which says that citizens of one State shall enjoy all the privileges and immunities of citizens of the several States; in other words, he thinks it wrong because it deprives the negro of the privileges, immunities, and rights of citizenship, which pertain, according to that decision, only to the white man. I am free to say to you that in my opinion this government of ours is founded on the white basis. It was made by the white man, for the benefit of the white man, to be administered by white men, in such manner as they should determine. It is also true that a negro, an Indian, or any other man of inferior race to a white man should be permitted to enjoy, and humanity requires that he should have, all the rights, privileges, and immunities which he is capable of exercising consistent with the safety of society. I would give him every right and every privilege which his capacity would enable him to enjoy, consistent with the good of the society in which he lived. But you ask me, What are these rights and these privileges? My answer is, that each State must decide for itself the nature and extent of these rights. Illinois has decided for herself. We have decided that the negro shall not be a slave, and we have at the same time decided that he shall not vote, or serve on juries, or enjoy political privileges. I am content with that system of policy which we have adopted for ourselves. I deny the right of any other State to complain of our policy in that respect, or to interfere with it, or to attempt to change it. On the other hand, the State of Maine has decided that in that State a negro man may vote on an equality with the white man. The sovereign power of Maine had the right to prescribe that rule for herself. Illinois has no right to complain of Maine for conferring the right of negro suffrage, nor has Maine any right to interfere with or complain of Illinois because she has denied negro suffrage.

The State of New York has decided by her constitution that a negro may vote, provided that he own $250 worth of property, but not otherwise. The rich negro can vote, but the poor one cannot. Although that distinction does not commend itself to my judgment, yet I assert that the sovereign power of New York had a right to prescribe that form of the elective franchise. Kentucky, Virginia, and other States have provided that negroes, or a certain class of them in those States, shall be slaves, having neither civil nor political rights. Without indorsing the wisdom of that decision, I assert that Virginia has the same power, by virtue of her sovereignty, to protect slavery within her limits as Illinois has to banish it forever from our own borders. I assert the right of each State to decide for itself on all these questions, and I do not subscribe to the doctrine of my friend Mr. Lincoln, that uniformity is either desirable or possible. I do not acknowledge that the States must all be free or must all be slave.

I do not acknowledge that the negro must have civil and political rights everywhere or nowhere. I do not acknowledge that the Chinese must have the same rights in California that we would confer upon him here. I do not acknowledge that the coolie imported into this country must necessarily be put upon an equality with the white race. I do not acknowledge any of these doctrines of uniformity in the local and domestic regulations in the different States.

Thus you see, my fellow-citizens, that the issues between Mr. Lincoln and myself, as respective candidates for the United States Senate, as made up, are direct, unequivocal, and irreconcilable. He goes for uniformity in our domestic institutions, for a war of sections, until one or the other shall be subdued. I go for the great principle of the Kansas-Nebraska Bill,—the right of the people to decide for themselves.

On the other point, Mr. Lincoln goes for a warfare upon the Supreme Court of the United States because of their judicial decision in the Dred Scott case. I yield obedience to the decisions in that court,—to the final determination of the highest judicial tribunal known to our Constitution. He objects to the Dred Scott decision because it does not put the negro in the possession of the rights of citizenship on an equality with the white man. I am opposed to negro equality. I repeat that this nation is a white people,—a people composed of European descendants, a people that have established this government for themselves and their posterity,—and I am in favor of preserving, not only the purity of the blood, but the purity of the government from any mixture or amalgamation with inferior races. I have seen the effects of this mixture of superior and inferior races, this amalgamation of white men and Indians and negroes; we have seen it in Mexico, in Central America, in South America, and in all the Spanish-American States; and its result has been degeneration, demoralization, and degradation below the capacity for self-government.

I am opposed to taking any step that recognizes the negro man or the Indian as the equal of the white man. I am opposed to giving him a voice in the administration of the government. I would extend to the negro and the Indian and to all dependent races every right, every privilege, and every immunity consistent with the safety and welfare of the white races; but equality they never should have, either political or social, or in any other respect whatever.

My friends, you see that the issues are distinctly drawn. I stand by the same platform that I have so often proclaimed to you and to the people of Illinois heretofore. I stand by the Democratic organization, yield obedience to its usages, and support its regular nominations. I indorse and approve the Cincinnati platform, and I adhere to and intend to carry out, as part of that platform, the great principle of self-government, which recognizes the right of the people in each State and Territory to decide for themselves their domestic institutions. In other words, if the Lecompton issue shall arise again, you have only to turn back and see where you have found me during the last six months, and then rest assured that you will find me in the same position, battling for the same principle, and vindicating it from assault from whatever quarter it may come, so long as I have the power to do it.

Fellow-citizens, you now have before you the outlines of the propositions which I intend to discuss before the people of Illinois during the pending campaign. I have spoken without preparation and in a very desultory manner, and may have omitted some points which I desired to discuss, and may have been less explicit on others than I could have wished. I have made up my mind to appeal to the people against the combination which has been made against me. The Republican leaders have formed an alliance—an unholy, unnatural alliance—with a portion of the unscrupulous Federal office-holders. I intend to fight that allied army wherever I meet them. I know they deny the alliance, while avoiding the common purpose; but yet these men who are trying to divide the Democratic party for the purpose of electing a Republican Senator in my place are just as much the agents, the tools, the supporters of Mr. Lincoln as if they were avowed Republicans, and expect their reward for their services when the Republicans come into power. I shall deal with these allied forces just as the Russians dealt with the Allies at Sebastopol. The Russians, when they fired a broadside at the common enemy, did not stop to inquire whether it hit a Frenchman, an Englishman, or a Turk, nor will I stop, nor shall I stop to inquire whether my blows hit the Republican leaders or their allies, who are holding the Federal offices and yet acting in concert with the Republicans to defeat the Democratic party and its nominees. I do not include all of the Federal office-holders in this remark. Such of them as are Democrats and show their Democracy by remaining inside of the Democratic organization and supporting its nominees, I recognize as Democrats; but those who, having been defeated inside of the organization, go outside and attempt to divide and destroy the party in concert with the Republican leaders, have ceased to be Democrats, and belong to the allied army, whose avowed object is to elect the Republican ticket by dividing and destroying the Democratic party.

My friends, I have exhausted myself, and I certainly have fatigued you, in the long and desultory remarks which I have made. It is now two nights since I have been in bed, and I think I have a right to a little sleep. I will, however, have an opportunity of meeting you face to face, and addressing you on more than one occasion before the November election. In conclusion, I must again say to you, justice to my own feelings demands it, that my gratitude for the welcome you have extended to me on this occasion knows no bounds, and can be described by no language which I can command. I see that I am literally at home when among my constituents. This welcome has amply repaid me for every effort that I have made in the public service during nearly twenty-five years that I have held office at your hands. It not only compensates me for the past, but it furnishes an inducement and incentive for future efforts which no man, no matter how patriotic, can feel who has not witnessed the magnificent reception you have extended to me to-night on my return.

First Joint Debate
OTTAWA, AUGUST 21, 1858

Mr. Douglas's Speech

LADIES AND GENTLEMEN: I appear before you to-day for the purpose of discussing the leading political topics which now agitate the public mind. By an arrangement between Mr. Lincoln and myself we are present here to-day for the purpose of having a joint discussion, as the representatives of the two great political parties of the State and Union, upon the principles in issue between those parties; and this vast concourse of people shows the deep feeling which pervades the public mind in regard to the questions dividing us.

Prior to 1854 this country was divided into two great political parties, known as the Whig and Democratic parties. Both were national and patriotic, advocating principles that were universal in their application. An old line Whig could proclaim his principles in Louisiana and Massachusetts alike. Whig principles had no boundary sectional line; they were not limited by the Ohio River, nor by the Potomac, nor by the line of the free and slave States, but applied and were proclaimed wherever the Constitution ruled or the American flag waved over the American soil. So it was, and so it is with the great Democratic party, which, from the days of Jefferson until this period, has proven itself to be the historic party of this nation. While the Whig and Democratic parties differed in regard to a bank, the tariff, distribution, the specie circular, and the sub-treasury, they agreed on the great slavery question which now agitates the Union. I say that the Whig party and the Democratic party agreed on this slavery question, while they differed on those matters of expediency to which I have referred. The Whig party and the Democratic party jointly adopted the Compromise measures of 1850 as the basis of a proper and just solution of this slavery question in all its forms. Clay was the great leader, with Webster on his right and Cass on his left, and sustained by the patriots in the Whig and Democratic ranks who had devised and enacted the Compromise measures of 1850.

In 1851 the Whig party and the Democratic party united in Illinois in adopting resolutions indorsing and approving the principles of the Compromise measures of 1850, as the proper adjustment of that question. In 1852, when the Whig party assembled in convention at Baltimore for the purpose of nominating a candidate for the presidency, the first thing it did was to declare the Compromise measures of 1850, in substance and in principle, a suitable adjustment of that question. [Here the speaker was interrupted by loud and long-continued applause.] My friends, silence will be more acceptable to me in the discussion of these questions than applause. I desire to address myself to your judgment, your understanding, and your consciences, and not to your passions or your enthusiasm. When the Democratic Convention assembled in Baltimore in the same year, for the purpose of nominating a Democratic candidate for the presidency, it also adopted the Compromise measures of 1850 as the basis of Democratic action. Thus you see that up to 1853–'54, the Whig party and the Democratic party both stood on the same platform with regard to the slavery question. That platform was the right of the people of each State and each Territory to decide their local and domestic institutions for themselves, subject only to the Federal Constitution.

During the session of Congress of 1853–'54, I introduced into the Senate of the United States a bill to organize the Territories of Kansas and Nebraska on that principle which had been adopted in the Compromise measures of 1850, approved by the Whig party and the Democratic party in Illinois in 1851, and indorsed by the Whig party and the Democratic party in National Convention in 1852. In order that there might be no misunderstanding in relation to the principle involved in the Kansas and Nebraska Bill, I put forth the true intent and meaning of this Act in these words: "It is the true intent and meaning of this Act not to legislate slavery into any State or Territory, or to exclude it therefrom, but to leave the people thereof perfectly free to form and regulate their domestic institutions in their own way, subject only to the Federal Constitution." Thus you see that up to 1854, when the Kansas and Nebraska Bill was brought into Congress for the purpose of carrying out the principles which both parties had up to that time indorsed and approved, there had been no division in this country in regard to that principle except the opposition of the Abolitionists. In the House of Representatives of the Illinois Legislature, upon a resolution asserting that principle, every Whig and every Democrat in the House voted in the affirmative, and only four men voted against it, and those four were old line Abolitionists.

In 1854, Mr. Abraham Lincoln and Mr. Trumbull entered into an arrangement, one with the other, and each with his respective friends, to dissolve the old Whig party on the one hand, and to dissolve the old Democratic party on the other, and to connect the members of both into an Abolition party, under the name and disguise of a Republican party. The terms of that arrangement between Mr. Lincoln and Mr. Trumbull have been published to the world by Mr. Lincoln's special friend James H. Matheny, Esq., and they were, that Lincoln should have Shields's place in the United States Senate, which was then about to become vacant, and that Trumbull should have my seat when my term expired. Lincoln went to work to Abolitionize the old Whig party all over the State, pretending that he was then as good a Whig as ever; and Trumbull went to work in his part of the State preaching Abolitionism in its milder and lighter form, and trying to Abolitionize the Democratic party, and bring old Democrats handcuffed and bound hand and foot into the Abolition camp. In pursuance of the arrangement, the parties met at Springfield in October, 1854, and proclaimed their new platform. Lincoln was to bring into the Abolition camp the old line Whigs, and transfer them over to Giddings, Chase, Fred Douglass, and Parson Lovejoy, who were ready to receive them and christen them in their new faith. They laid down on that occasion a platform for their new Republican party, which was to be thus constructed. I have the resolutions of their State

Convention then held, which was the first mass State Convention ever held in Illinois by the Black Republican party, and I now hold them in my hands, and will read a part of them, and cause the others to be printed. Here are the most important and material resolutions of this Abolition platform:

"1. *Resolved,* That we believe this truth to be self-evident, that when parties become subversive of the ends for which they are established, or incapable of restoring the government to the true principles of the Constitution, it is the right and duty of the people to dissolve the political bands by which they may have been connected therewith, and to organize new parties, upon such principles and with such views as the circumstances and exigencies of the nation may demand.

"2. *Resolved,* That the times imperatively demand the reorganization of parties, and, repudiating all previous party attachments, names and predilections, we unite ourselves in defence of the liberty and Constitution of the country, and will hereafter co-operate as the Republican party, pledged to the accomplishment of the following purposes: To bring the administration of the government back to the control of first principles; to restore Nebraska and Kansas to the position of free Territories; that, as the Constitution of the United States vests in the States, and not in Congress, the power to legislate for the extradition of fugitives from labor, to repeal and entirely abrogate the Fugitive Slave law; to restrict slavery to those States in which it exists; to prohibit the admission of any more slave States into the Union; to abolish slavery in the District of Columbia; to exclude slavery from all the Territories over which the General Government has exclusive jurisdiction; and to resist the acquirement of any more Territories, unless the practice of slavery therein forever shall have been prohibited.

"3. *Resolved,* That in furtherance of these principles we will use such constitutional and lawful means as shall seem best adapted to their accomplishment, and that we will support no man for office, under the General or State Government, who is not positively and fully committed to the support of these principles, and whose personal character and conduct is not a guarantee that he is reliable, and who shall not have abjured old party allegiance and ties."

Now, gentlemen, your Black Republicans have cheered every one of those propositions, and yet I venture to say that you cannot get Mr. Lincoln to come out and say that he is now in favor of each one of them. That these propositions, one and all, constitute the platform of the Black Republican party of this day, I have no doubt; and when you were not aware for what purpose I was reading them, your Black Republicans cheered them as good Black Republican doctrines. My object in reading these resolutions was to put the question to Abraham Lincoln this day, whether he now stands and will stand by each article in that creed and carry it out. I desire to know whether Mr. Lincoln to-day stands, as he did in 1854, in favor of the unconditional repeal of the Fugitive Slave law. I desire him to answer whether he stands pledged to-day, as he did in 1854, against the admission of any more slave States into the Union, even if the people want them. I want to know whether he stands pledged against the admission of a new State into the Union with such a constitution as the people of that State may see fit to make. I want to know whether he stands to-day pledged to the abolition of slavery in the District of Columbia. I desire him to answer whether he stands pledged to the prohibition of the slave trade between the different States. I desire to know whether he stands pledged to prohibit slavery in all the Territories of the United States, north as well as south of the Missouri Compromise line. I desire him to answer whether he is opposed to the acquisition of any more territory, unless slavery is prohibited therein. I want his answer to these questions. Your affirmative cheers in favor of this Abolition platform is not satisfactory. I ask Abraham Lincoln to answer these questions, in order that, when I trot him down to lower Egypt, I may put the same questions to him. My principles are the same everywhere. I can proclaim them alike in the North, the South, the East, and the West. My principles will apply wherever the Constitution prevails and the American flag waves. I desire to know whether Mr. Lincoln's principles will bear transplanting from Ottawa to Jonesboro? I put these questions to him to-day distinctly and ask an answer. I have a right to an answer, for I quote from the platform of the Republican party, made by himself and others at the time that party was formed, and the bargain made by Lincoln to dissolve and kill the old Whig party, and transfer its members, bound hand and foot, to the Abolition party, under the direction of Giddings and Fred Douglass. In the remarks I have made on this platform, and the position of Mr.

Lincoln upon it, I mean nothing personally disrespectful or unkind to that gentleman. I have known him for nearly twenty-five years. There were many points of sympathy between us when we first got acquainted. We were both comparatively boys, and both struggling with poverty in a strange land. I was a school-teacher in the town of Winchester, and he a flourishing grocery-keeper in the town of Salem. He was more successful in his occupation than I was in mine, and hence more fortunate in this world's goods. Lincoln is one of those peculiar men who perform with admirable skill everything which they undertake. I made as good a school-teacher as I could, and when a cabinet-maker I made a good bedstead and tables, although my old boss said I succeeded better with bureaus and secretaries than anything else; but I believe that Lincoln was always more successful in business than I, for his business enabled him to get into the Legislature. I met him there, however, and had a sympathy with him, because of the up-hill struggle we both had in life. He was then just as good at telling an anecdote as now. He could beat any of the boys wrestling, or running a foot-race, in pitching quoits or tossing a copper; could ruin more liquor than all the boys of the town together; and the dignity and impartiality with which he presided at a horse-race or fist-fight excited the admiration and won the praise of everybody that was present and participated. I sympathized with him because he was struggling with difficulties and so was I. Mr. Lincoln served with me in the Legislature in 1836, when we both retired, and he subsided, or became sub-merged, and he was lost sight of as a public man for some years. In 1846, when Wilmot introduced his celebrated proviso, and the Abolition tornado swept over the country, Lincoln again turned up as a member of Congress from the Sangamon district. I was then in the Senate of the United States, and was glad to welcome my old friend and companion. Whilst in Congress, he distinguished himself by his opposition to the Mexican war, tak-ing the side of the common enemy against his own country; and when he returned home he found that the indignation of the people followed him everywhere, and he was again submerged, or obliged to retire into private life, forgotten by his former friends. He came up again in 1854, just in time to make this

Abolition or Black Republican platform, in company with Giddings, Lovejoy, Chase, and Fred Douglass, for the Republican party to stand upon. Trumbull, too, was one of our own contemporaries. He was born and raised in old Connecticut, was bred a Federalist, but, removing to Georgia, turned Nullifier when Nullification was popular, and as soon as he disposed of his clocks and wound up his business, migrated to Illinois, turned politician and lawyer here, and made his appearance in 1841 as a member of the Legislature. He became noted as the author of the scheme to repudiate a large portion of the State debt of Illinois, which, if successful, would have brought infamy and disgrace upon the fair escutcheon of our glorious State. The odium attached to that measure consigned him to oblivion for a time. I helped to do it. I walked into a public meeting in the hall of the House of Representatives, and replied to his repudiating speeches, and resolutions were carried over his head denouncing repudiation, and asserting the moral and legal obligation of Illinois to pay every dollar of the debt she owed, and every bond that bore her seal. Trumbull's malignity has followed me since I thus defeated his infamous scheme.

These two men having formed this combination to Abolitionize the old Whig party and the old Democratic party, and put themselves into the Senate of the United States, in pursuance of their bargain, are now carrying out that arrangement. Matheny states that Trumbull broke faith; that the bargain was that Lincoln should be the Senator in Shields's place, and Trumbull was to wait for mine; and the story goes that Trumbull cheated Lincoln: having control of four or five Abolitionized Democrats who were holding over in the Senate, he would not let them vote for Lincoln, and which obliged the rest of the Abolitionists to support him in order to secure an Abolition Senator. There are a number of authorities for the truth of this besides Matheny, and I suppose that even Mr. Lincoln will not deny it.

Mr. Lincoln demands that he shall have the place intended for Trumbull, as Trumbull cheated him and got his, and Trumbull is stumping the State traducing me for the purpose of securing the position for Lincoln, in order to quiet him. It was in consequence of this arrangement that the Republican Convention was empanelled to instruct for Lincoln and nobody else, and it was on this account that they passed resolutions that he was their first, their last, and their only choice. Archy Williams was nowhere, Browning was nobody, Wentworth was not to be considered; they had no man in the Republican party for the place except Lincoln, for the reason that he demanded that they should carry out the arrangement.

Having formed this new party for the benefit of deserters from Whiggery, and deserters from Democracy, and having laid down the Abolition platform which I have read, Lincoln now takes his stand and proclaims his Abolition doctrines. Let me read a part of them. In his speech at Springfield to the convention which nominated him for the Senate, he said:

"In my opinion it will not cease until a crisis shall have been reached and passed. 'A house divided against itself cannot stand.' I believe this government *cannot endure permanently half slave and half free*. I do not expect the Union to be dissolved,—I do not expect the house to fall; *but I do expect it will cease to be divided.* It will become all one thing, or all the other. Either the opponents of slavery *will arrest the further spread of it,* and place it where the public mind shall rest in the belief *that it is in the course of ultimate extinction,* or its advocates *will push it forward till it shall become alike lawful in all the States,*—old as well as new, North as well as South."

["Good," "Good," and cheers.]

I am delighted to hear you Black Republicans say "good." I have no doubt that doctrine expresses your sentiments, and I will prove to you now, if you will listen to me, that it is revolutionary, and destructive of the existence of this government. Mr. Lincoln, in the extract from which I have read, says that this government cannot endure permanently in the same condition in which it was made by its framers,—divided into free and slave States. He says that it has existed for about seventy years thus divided, and yet he tells you that it cannot endure permanently on the same principles and in the same relative condition in which our fathers made it. Why can it not exist divided into free and slave States? Washington, Jefferson, Franklin, Madison,

Hamilton, Jay, and the great men of that day, made this government divided into free and slave States, and left each State perfectly free to do as it pleased on the subject of slavery. Why can it not exist on the same principles on which our fathers made it? They knew when they framed the Constitution that in a country as wide and broad as this, with such a variety of climate, production, and interest, the people necessarily required different laws and institutions in different localities. They knew that the laws and regulations which would suit the granite hills of New Hampshire would be unsuited to the rice plantations of South Carolina, and they therefore provided that each State should retain its own Legislature and its own sovereignty, with the full and complete power to do as it pleased within its own limits, in all that was local and not national. One of the reserved rights of the States was the right to regulate the relations between master and servant on the slavery question. At the time the Constitution was framed, there were thirteen States in the Union, twelve of which were slaveholding States and one a free State. Suppose this doctrine of uniformity preached by Mr. Lincoln, that the States should all be free or all be slave, had prevailed, and what would have been the result? Of course, the twelve slaveholding States would have overruled the one free State, and slavery would have been fastened by a constitutional provision on every inch of the American Republic, instead of being left, as our fathers wisely left it, to each State to decide for itself. Here I assert that uniformity in the local laws and institutions of the different States is neither possible nor desirable. If uniformity had been adopted when the government was established, it must inevitably have been the uniformity of slavery everywhere, or else the uniformity of negro citizenship and negro equality everywhere.

We are told by Lincoln that he is utterly opposed to the Dred Scott decision, and will not submit to it, for the reason that he says it deprives the negro of the rights and privileges of citizenship. That is the first and main reason which he assigns for his warfare on the Supreme Court of the United States and its decision. I ask you, are you in favor of conferring upon the negro the rights and privileges of citizenship? Do you desire to strike out

of our State Constitution that clause which keeps slaves and free
negroes out of the State, and allow the free negroes to flow in,
and cover your prairies with black settlements? Do you desire to
turn this beautiful State into a free negro colony, in order that
when Missouri abolishes slavery she can send one hundred
thousand emancipated slaves into Illinois, to become citizens
and voters, on an equality with yourselves? If you desire negro
citizenship, if you desire to allow them to come into the State
and settle with the white man, if you desire them to vote on an
equality with yourselves, and to make them eligible to office, to
serve on juries, and to adjudge your rights, then support Mr.
Lincoln and the Black Republican party, who are in favor of the
citizenship of the negro. For one, I am opposed to negro citizenship in any and every form. I believe this government was
made on the white basis. I believe it was made by white men, for
the benefit of white men and their posterity forever, and I am in
favor of confining citizenship to white men, men of European
birth and descent, instead of conferring it upon negroes,
Indians, and other inferior races.

Mr. Lincoln, following the example and lead of all the little
Abolition orators, who go around and lecture in the basements
of schools and churches, reads from the Declaration of
Independence that all men were created equal, and then asks,
How can you deprive a negro of that equality which God and
the Declaration of Independence award to him? He and they
maintain that negro equality is guaranteed by the laws of God,
and that it is asserted in the Declaration of Independence. If
they think so, of course they have a right to do so, and so vote. I
do not question Mr. Lincoln's conscientious belief that the
negro was made his equal, and hence is his brother, but for my
own part, I do not regard the negro as my equal, and positively
deny that he is my brother, or any kin to me whatever. Lincoln
has evidently learned by heart Parson Lovejoy's catechism. He
can repeat it as well as Farnsworth, and he is worthy of a medal
from Father Giddings and Fred Douglass for his Abolitionism.
He holds that the negro was born his equal and yours, and that
he was endowed with equality by the Almighty, and that no
human law can deprive him of these rights, which were guaran-

teed to him by the Supreme Ruler of the Universe. Now I do not believe that the Almighty ever intended the negro to be the equal of the white man. If He did, He has been a long time demonstrating the fact. For thousands of years the negro has been a race upon the earth, and during all that time, in all latitudes and climates, wherever he has wandered or been taken, he has been inferior to the race which he has there met. He belongs to an inferior race, and must always occupy an inferior position. I do not hold that because the negro is our inferior that therefore he ought to be a slave. By no means can such a conclusion be drawn from what I have said. On the contrary, I hold that humanity and Christianity both require that the negro shall have and enjoy every right, every privilege, and every immunity consistent with the safety of the society in which he lives. On that point, I presume, there can be no diversity of opinion. You and I are bound to extend to our inferior and dependent beings every right, every privilege, every facility and immunity consistent with the public good.

The question then arises, What rights and privileges are consistent with the public good? This is a question which each State and each Territory must decide for itself. Illinois has decided it for herself. We have provided that the negro shall not be a slave and we have also provided that he shall not be a citizen, but protect him in his civil rights, in his life, his person and his property, only depriving him of all political rights whatsoever, and refusing to put him on an equality with the white man. That policy of Illinois is satisfactory to the Democratic party and to me; and if it were to the Republicans, there would then be no question upon the subject. But the Republicans say that he ought to be made a citizen, and when he becomes a citizen he becomes your equal, with all your rights and privileges. They assert the Dred Scott decision to be monstrous because it denies that the negro is or can be a citizen under the Constitution. Now, I hold that Illinois had a right to abolish and prohibit slavery as she did, and I hold that Kentucky has the same right to continue and protect slavery that Illinois had to abolish it. I hold that New York had as much right to abolish slavery as Virginia has to continue it, and that each and every State of this Union is a sovereign power, with the right to do as it pleases upon this question of slavery, and upon all its domestic institutions. Slavery is not the only question which comes up in this controversy. There is a far more important one to you, and that is,—What shall be done with the free negro? We have settled the slavery question as far as we are concerned; we have prohibited it in Illinois forever; and in doing so, I think we have done wisely, and there is no man in the State who would be more strenuous in his opposition to the introduction of slavery than I would. But when we settled it for ourselves, we exhausted all our power over that subject. We have done our whole duty, and can do no more. We must leave each and every other State to decide for itself the same question. In relation to the policy to be pursued toward the free negroes, we have said that they shall not vote; whilst Maine, on the other hand, has said that they shall vote. Maine is a sovereign State, and has the power to regulate the qualifications of voters within her limits. I would never consent to confer the right of voting and of citizenship upon a negro; but still I am not going to quarrel with Maine for differing from me in opinion. Let Maine take care of her own negroes, and fix the qualifications of her own voters to suit herself, without interfering with Illinois, and Illinois will not interfere with Maine. So with the State of New York. She allows the negro to vote, provided he owns two hundred and fifty dollars' worth of property but not otherwise. While I would not make any distinction whatever between a negro who held property and one who did not, yet if the sovereign State of New York chooses to make that distinction, it is her business and not mine, and I will not quarrel with her for it. She can do as she pleases on this question if she minds her own business, and we will do the same thing. Now, my friends, if we will only act conscientiously and rigidly upon this great principle of popular sovereignty, which guarantees to each State and Territory the right to do as it pleases on all things, local and domestic, instead of Congress interfering, we will continue at peace one with another. Why should Illinois be at war with Missouri, or Kentucky with Ohio, or Virginia with New York, merely because their institutions differ? Our fathers intended that our institutions should differ. They knew that the North and the South, having different climates, productions, and interests, required different institutions. This doctrine of Mr. Lincoln, of uniformity among the institutions of the different States, is a new doctrine, never dreamed of by Washington, Madison, or the framers of this government. Mr. Lincoln and the Republican party set themselves up as wiser than these men who made this government, which has flourished for seventy years under the principle of popular sovereignty, recognizing the right of each State to do as it pleased. Under that principle, we have grown from a nation of three or four millions to a nation of about thirty millions of people; we have crossed the Alleghany Mountains and filled up the whole Northwest, turning the prairie into a garden, and building up churches and schools, thus spreading civilization and Christianity where before there was nothing but savage barbarism. Under that principle we have become, from a feeble nation, the most powerful on the face of the earth; and if we only adhere to that principle, we can go forward increasing in territory, in power, in strength, and in glory until the Republic of America shall be the North Star that shall guide the friends of freedom throughout the civilized world. And why can we not adhere to the great principle of self-government, upon which our institutions were originally based? I believe that this new doctrine preached by Mr. Lincoln and his party will dissolve the Union if it succeeds. They are trying to array all the Northern States in one body against the South, to excite a sectional war between the free States and the slave States, in order that the one or the other may be driven to the wall.

I am told that my time is out. Mr. Lincoln will now address you for an hour and a half, and I will then occupy an half hour in replying to him.

Mr. Lincoln's Reply

MY FELLOW-CITIZENS: When a man hears himself somewhat misrepresented, it provokes him,—at least, I find it so with myself; but when misrepresentation becomes very gross and palpable, it is more apt to amuse him. The first thing I see fit to notice is the fact that Judge Douglas alleges, after running through the history of the old Democratic and the old Whig parties, that Judge Trumbull and myself made an arrangement in 1854, by which I was to have the place of General Shields in the United States Senate, and Judge Trumbull was to have the place of Judge Douglas. Now, all I have to say upon that subject is that I think no man—not even Judge Douglas—can prove it, *because it is not true*. I have no doubt he is *"conscientious"* in saying it. As to those resolutions that he took such a length of time to read, as being the platform of the Republican party in 1854, I say I never had anything to do with them, and I think Trumbull never had. Judge Douglas cannot show that either of us ever did have anything to do with them. I believe *this* is true about those resolutions: There was a call for a convention to form a Republican party at Springfield, and I think that my friend Mr. Lovejoy, who is here upon this stand, had a hand in it. I think this is true, and I think if he will remember accurately he will be able to recollect that he tried to get me into it, and I would not go in. I believe it is also true that I went away from Springfield when the convention was in session, to attend court in Tazewell County. It is true they did place my name, though without authority, upon the committee, and afterward wrote me to attend the meeting of the committee; but I refused to do so, and I never had anything to do with that organization. This is the plain truth about all that matter of the resolutions.

Now, about this story that Judge Douglas tells of Trumbull bargaining to sell out the old Democratic party, and Lincoln agreeing to sell out the old Whig party, I have the means of *knowing* about that: Judge Douglas cannot have; and I know there is no substance to it whatever. Yet I have no doubt he is *"conscientious"* about it. I know that after Mr. Lovejoy got into the Legislature that winter, he complained of me that I had told all the old Whigs of his district that the old Whig party was good enough for them, and some of them voted against him because I told them so. Now, I have no means of totally disproving such charges as this which the Judge makes. A man cannot prove a negative; but he has a right to claim that when a man makes an affirmative charge, he must offer some proof to show the truth

of what he says. I certainly cannot introduce testimony to show
the negative about things, but I have a right to claim that if a
man says he *knows* a thing, then he must show *how* he knows it.
I always have a right to claim this, and it is not satisfactory to me
that he may be "conscientious" on the subject.

Now, gentlemen, I hate to waste my time on such things; but
in regard to that general Abolition tilt that Judge Douglas
makes, when he says that I was engaged at that time in selling
out and Abolitionizing the old Whig party, I hope you will permit me to read a part of a printed speech that I made then at
Peoria, which will show altogether a different view of the position I took in that contest of 1854.

A Voice: "Put on your specs."

Mr. Lincoln: Yes, sir, I am obliged to do so; I am no longer
a young man.

"This is the *repeal* of the Missouri Compromise.[1] The foregoing history may not be precisely accurate in every particular, but I am sure it
is sufficiently so for all the uses I shall attempt to make of it, and in it
we have before us the chief materials enabling us to correctly judge
whether the repeal of the Missouri Compromise is right or wrong.

"I think, and shall try to show, that it is wrong—wrong in its direct
effect, letting slavery into Kansas and Nebraska, and wrong in its
prospective principle, allowing it to spread to every other part of the
wide world where men can be found inclined to take it.

"This *declared* indifference, but, as I must think, covert *real* zeal for
the spread of slavery, I cannot but hate. I hate it because of the monstrous injustice of slavery itself. I hate it because it deprives our republican example of its just influence in the world,—enables the enemies
of free institutions, with plausibility, to taunt us as hypocrites; causes
the real friends of freedom to doubt our sincerity, and especially
because it forces so many really good men amongst ourselves into an
open war with the very fundamental principles of civil liberty, criticis-
ing the Declaration of Independence, and insisting that there is no
right principle of action but *self-interest*.

"Before proceeding, let me say I think I have no prejudice against

[1]This extract from Mr. Lincoln's Peoria speech of 1854 was read by him in the
Ottawa debate, but was not reported fully or accurately in either the *Times* or
Press and Tribune. It is inserted now as necessary to a complete report of the
debate.

the Southern people. They are just what we would be in their situation. If slavery did not now exist among them, they would not introduce it. If it did now exist among us, we should not instantly give it up. This I believe of the masses north and south. Doubtless there are individuals on both sides who would not hold slaves under any circumstances; and others who would gladly introduce slavery anew, if it were out of existence. We know that some Southern men do free their slaves, go north, and become tip-top Abolitionists; while some Northern ones go south and become most cruel slave-masters.

"When Southern people tell us they are no more responsible for the origin of slavery than we, I acknowledge the fact. When it is said that the institution exists, and that it is very difficult to get rid of it, in any satisfactory way, I can understand and appreciate the saying. I will not blame them for not doing what I should not know how to do myself. If all earthly power were given me, I should not know what to do, as to the existing institution. My first impulse would be to free all the slaves and send them to Liberia,—to their own native land. But a moment's reflection would convince me that whatever of high hope (as I think there is), there may be in this in the long run, its sudden execution is impossible. If they were all landed there in a day, they would all perish in the next ten days; and there are not surplus shipping and surplus money enough in the world to carry them there in many times ten days. What then? Free them all and keep them among us as underlings? Is it quite certain that this betters their condition? I think I would not hold one in slavery, at any rate; yet the point is not clear enough to me to denounce people upon. What next? Free them, and make them politically and socially our equals? My own feelings will not admit of this; and if mine would, we well know that those of the great mass of white people will not. Whether this feeling accords with justice and sound judgment, is not the sole question, if, indeed, it is any part of it. A universal feeling, whether well or ill founded, cannot be safely disregarded. We cannot, then, make them equals. It does seem to me that systems of gradual emancipation might be adopted; but for their tardiness in this I will not undertake to judge our brethren of the South.

"When they remind us of their constitutional rights, I acknowledge them, not grudgingly, but fully and fairly; and I would give them any legislation for the reclaiming of their fugitives, which should not, in its stringency, be more likely to carry a free man into slavery than our ordinary criminal laws are to hang an innocent one.

"But all this, to my judgment, furnishes no more excuse for permitting slavery to go into our own free territory than it would for reviving the African slave-trade by law. The law which forbids the bringing of slaves *from* Africa, and that which has so long forbid the taking of them *to* Nebraska, can hardly be distinguished on any moral principle; and the repeal of the former could find quite as plausible excuses as that of the latter."

I have reason to know that Judge Douglas *knows* that I said this. I think he has the answer here to one of the questions he put to me. I do not mean to allow him to catechise me unless he pays back for it in kind. I will not answer questions one after another, unless he reciprocates; but as he has made this inquiry, and I have answered it before, he has got it without my getting anything in return. He has got my answer on the Fugitive Slave law.

Now, gentlemen, I don't want to read at any greater length; but this is the true complexion of all I have ever said in regard to the institution of slavery and the black race. This is the whole of it; and anything that argues me into his idea of perfect social and political equality with the negro is but a specious and fantastic arrangement of words, by which a man can prove a horse-chestnut to be a chestnut horse. I will say here, while upon this subject, that I have no purpose, directly or indirectly, to interfere with the institution of slavery in the States where it exists. I believe I have no lawful right to do so, and I have no inclination to do so. I have no purpose to introduce political and social equality between the white and the black races. There is a physical difference between the two which, in my judgment, will probably forever forbid their living together upon the footing of perfect equality; and inasmuch as it becomes a necessity that there must be a difference, I, as well as Judge Douglas, am in favor of the race to which I belong having the superior position. I have never said anything to the contrary, but I hold that, notwithstanding all this, there is no reason in the world why the negro is not entitled to all the natural rights enumerated in the Declaration of Independence,—the right to life, liberty, and the pursuit of happiness. I hold that he is as much entitled to these as the white man. I agree with Judge Douglas he is not my equal in many respects,—certainly not in color, perhaps not in moral or intellectual endowment. But in the right to eat the bread, without the leave of anybody else, which his own hand earns, *he is my equal, and the equal of Judge Douglas, and the equal of every living man.*

Now I pass on to consider one or two more of these little follies. The Judge is wofully at fault about his early friend Lincoln being a "grocery-keeper." I don't know as it would be a great sin, if I had been; but he is mistaken. Lincoln never kept a grocery anywhere in the world. It is true that Lincoln did work the latter part of one winter in a little stillhouse, up at the head of a hollow. And so I think my friend the Judge is equally at fault when he charges me at the time when I was in Congress of having opposed our soldiers who were fighting in the Mexican war. The Judge did not make his charge very distinctly, but I can tell you what he can prove, by referring to the record. You remember I was an old Whig, and whenever the Democratic party tried to get me to vote that the war had been righteously begun by the President, I would not do it. But whenever they asked for any money, or landwarrants, or anything to pay the soldiers there, during all that time, I gave the same vote that Judge Douglas did. You can think as you please as to whether that was consistent. Such is the truth; and the Judge has the right to make all he can out of it. But when he, by a general charge, conveys the idea that I withheld supplies from the soldiers who were fighting in the Mexican war, or did anything else to hinder the soldiers, he is, to say the least, grossly and altogether mistaken, as a consultation of the records will prove to him.

As I have not used up so much of my time as I had supposed, I will dwell a little longer upon one or two of these minor topics upon which the Judge has spoken. He has read from my speech in Springfield, in which I say that "a house divided against itself cannot stand." Does the Judge say it *can* stand? I don't know whether he does or not. The Judge does not seem to be attending to me just now, but I would like to know if it is his opinion that a house divided against itself *can stand.* If he does, then there is a question of veracity, not between him and me, but between the Judge and an Authority of a somewhat higher character.

Now, my friends, I ask your attention to this matter for the purpose of saying something seriously. I know that the Judge may readily enough agree with me that the maxim which was put forth by the Saviour is true, but he may allege that I misapply it; and the Judge has a right to urge that, in my application, I do misapply it, and then I have a right to show that I do *not* misapply it. When he undertakes to say that because I think this nation, so far as the question of slavery is concerned, will all become one thing or all the other, I am in favor of bringing about a dead uniformity in the various States, in all their institutions, he argues erroneously. The great variety of the local institutions in the States, springing from differences in the soil, differences in the face of the country, and in the climate, are bonds of Union. They do not make "a house divided against itself," but they make a house united. If they produce in one section of the country what is called for by the wants of another section, and this other section can supply the wants of the first, they are not matters of discord, but bonds of union, true bonds of union. But can this question of slavery be considered as among *these* varieties in the institutions of the country? I leave it to you to say whether, in the history of our government, this institution of slavery has not always failed to be a bond of union, and, on the contrary, been an apple of discord and an element of division in the house. I ask you to consider whether, so long as the moral constitution of men's minds shall continue to be the same, after this generation and assemblage shall sink into the grave, and another race shall arise, with the same moral and intellectual development we have,—whether, if that institution is standing in the same irritating position in which it now is, it will not continue an element of division? If so, then I have a right to say that, in regard to this question, the Union is a house divided against itself; and when the Judge reminds me that I have often said to him that the institution of slavery has existed for eighty years in some States, and yet it does not exist in some others, I agree to the fact, and I account for it by looking at the position in which our fathers originally placed it—restricting it from the new Territories where it had not gone, and legislating to cut off its source by the abrogation of the slave-trade, thus putting the seal of legislation *against its spread*. The public mind *did* rest in the belief that it was in the course of ultimate extinction. But lately, I think—and in this I charge nothing on the Judge's motives—lately, I think that he, and those acting with him, have placed that institution on a new basis, which looks to the *perpetuity and nationalization of slavery*. And while it is placed upon this new basis, I say, and I have said, that I believe we shall not have peace upon the question until the opponents of slavery arrest the further spread of it, and place it where the public mind shall rest in the belief that it is in the course of ultimate extinction; or, on the other hand, that its advocates will push it forward until it shall become alike lawful in all the States, old as well as new, North as well as South. Now, I believe if we could arrest the spread, and place it where Washington and Jefferson and Madison placed it, it *would be* in the course of ultimate extinction, and the public mind *would,* as for eighty years past, believe that it was in the course of ultimate extinction. The crisis would be past, and the institution might be let alone for a hundred years, if it should live so long, in the States where it exists; yet it would be going out of existence in the way best for both the black and the white races.

A voice: "Then do you repudiate popular sovereignty?"

MR. LINCOLN: Well, then, let us talk about popular sovereignty! What is popular sovereignty? Is it the right of the people to have slavery or not have it, as they see fit, in the Territories? I will state—and I have an able man to watch me—my understanding is that popular sovereignty, as now applied to the question of slavery, does allow the people of a Territory to have slavery if they want to, but does not allow them *not* to have it if they *do not* want it. I do not mean that if this vast concourse of people were in a Territory of the United States, any one of them would be obliged to have a slave if he did not want one; but I do say that, as I understand the Dred Scott decision, if any one man wants slaves, all the rest have no way of keeping that one man from holding them.

When I made my speech at Springfield, of which the Judge

complains, and from which he quotes, I really was not thinking of the things which he ascribes to me at all. I had no thought in the world that I was doing anything to bring about a war between the free and slave States. I had no thought in the world that I was doing anything to bring about a political and social equality of the black and white races. It never occurred to me that I was doing anything or favoring anything to reduce to a dead uniformity all the local institutions of the various States. But I must say, in all fairness to him, if he thinks I am doing something which leads to these bad results, it is none the better that I did not mean it. It is just as fatal to the country, if I have any influence in producing it, whether I intend it or not. But can it be true that placing this institution upon the original basis—the basis upon which our fathers placed it—can have any tendency to set the Northern and the Southern States at war with one another, or that it can have any tendency to make the people of Vermont raise sugar-cane, because they raise it in Louisiana, or that it can compel the people of Illinois to cut pine logs on the Grand Prairie, where they will not grow, because they cut pine logs in Maine, where they do grow? The Judge says this is a new principle started in regard to this question. Does the Judge claim that he is working on the plan of the founders of government? I think he says in some of his speeches—indeed, I have one here now—that he saw evidence of a policy to allow slavery to be south of a certain line, while north of it it should be excluded, and he saw an indisposition on the part of the country to stand upon that policy, and therefore he set about studying the subject upon *original principles,* and upon *original principles* he got up the Nebraska Bill! I am fighting it upon these "original principles,"—fighting it in the Jeffersonian, Washingtonian, and Madisonian fashion.

Now, my friends, I wish you to attend for a little while to one or two other things in that Springfield speech. My main object was to show, so far as my humble ability was capable of showing, to the people of this country what I believed was the truth,—that there was a *tendency,* if not a conspiracy, among those who have engineered this slavery question for the last four or five years, to make slavery perpetual and universal in this nation.

Having made that speech principally for that object, after arranging the evidences that I thought tended to prove my proposition, I concluded with this bit of comment:

"We cannot absolutely know that these exact adaptations are the result of preconcert; but when we see a lot of framed timbers, different portions of which we know have been gotten out at different times and places, and by different workmen—Stephen, Franklin, Roger, and James, for instance,—and when we see these timbers joined together, and see they exactly make the frame of a house or a mill, all the tenons and mortises exactly fitting, and all the lengths and proportions of the different pieces exactly adapted to their respective places, and not a piece too many or too few,—not omitting even the scaffolding,—or if a single piece be lacking, we see the place in the frame exactly fitted and prepared yet to bring such piece in,—in such a case we feel it impossible not to believe that Stephen and Franklin and Roger and James all understood one another from the beginning, and all worked upon a common plan or draft drawn before the first blow was struck."

When my friend Judge Douglas came to Chicago on the 9th of July, this speech having been delivered on the 16th of June, he made an harangue there, in which he took hold of this speech of mine, showing that he had carefully read it; and while he paid no attention to *this* matter at all, but complimented me as being a "kind, amiable, and intelligent gentleman," notwithstanding I had said this, he goes on and eliminates, or draws out, from my speech this tendency of mine to set the States at war with one another, to make all the institutions uniform, and set the niggers and white people to marrying together. Then, as the Judge had complimented me with these pleasant titles (I must confess to my weakness), I was a little "taken," for it came from a great man. I was not very much accustomed to flattery, and it came the sweeter to me. I was rather like the Hoosier, with the gingerbread, when he said he reckoned he loved it better than any other man, and got less of it. As the Judge had so flattered me, I could not make up my mind that he meant to deal unfairly with me; so I went to work to show him that he misunderstood the whole scope of my speech, and that I really never intended to set the people at war with one another. As an illustration, the next time I met him, which was at Springfield, I used this expression, that I claimed no right under the Constitution, nor had I any inclination, to enter into the slave States and interfere with the institutions of slavery. He says upon that: Lincoln will not enter into the slave States, but will go to the banks of the Ohio, on this side, and shoot over! He runs on, step by step, in the horse-chestnut style of argument, until in the Springfield speech he says: "Unless he shall be successful in firing his batteries until he shall have extinguished slavery in all the States the Union shall be dissolved." Now, I don't think that was exactly the way to treat "a kind, amiable, intelligent gentleman." I know if I had asked the Judge to show when or where it was I had said that, if I didn't succeed in firing into the slave States until slavery should be extinguished, the Union should be dissolved, he could not have shown it. I understand what he would do. He would say: I don't mean to quote from you, but this was the *result* of what you say. But I have the right to ask, and I do ask now, Did you not put it in such a form that an ordinary reader or listener would take it as an expression *from me?*

In a speech at Springfield, on the night of the 17th, I thought I might as well attend to my own business a little, and I recalled his attention as well as I could to this charge of conspiracy to nationalize slavery. I called his attention to the fact that he had acknowledged in my hearing twice that he had carefully read the speech, and, in the language of the lawyers, as he had twice read the speech, and still had put in no plea or answer, I took a default on him. I insisted that I had a right then to renew that charge of conspiracy. Ten days afterward I met the Judge at Clinton,—that is to say, I was on the ground, but not in the discussion,—and heard him make a speech. Then he comes in with his plea to this charge, for the first time; and his plea when put in, as well as I can recollect it, amounted to this: that he never had any talk with Judge Taney or the President of the United States with regard to the Dred Scott decision before it was made. I (Lincoln) ought to know that the man who makes a charge without knowing it to be true falsifies as much as he who knowingly tells a falsehood; and, lastly, that he would pronounce the whole thing a falsehood; but, he would make no personal application of the charge of falsehood, not because of any regard for the "kind, amiable, intelligent gentleman," but because of his own personal self-respect! I have understood since then (but [turning to Judge Douglas] will not hold the Judge to it if he is not willing) that he has broken through the "self-respect," and has got to saying the thing *out*. The Judge nods to me that it is so. It is fortunate for me that I can keep as good-humored as I do, when the Judge acknowledges that he has been trying to make a question of veracity with me. I know the Judge is a great man, while I am only a small man, but *I feel that I have got him.* I demur to that plea. I waive all objections that it was not filed till after default was taken, and demur to it upon the merits. What if Judge Douglas never did talk with Chief Justice Taney and the President before the Dred Scott decision was made, does it follow that he could not have had as perfect an understanding without talking as with it? I am not disposed to stand upon my legal advantage. I am disposed to take his denial as being like an answer in chancery, that he neither had any knowledge, information, or belief in the existence of such a conspiracy. I am disposed to take his answer as being as broad as though he had put it in these words. And now, I ask, even if he had done so, have not I a right to *prove it on him,* and to offer the evidence of more than two witnesses, by whom to prove it; and if the evidence proves the existence of the conspiracy, does his broader answer denying all knowledge, information, or belief, disturb the fact? It can only show that he was *used* by conspirators, and was not a *leader* of them.

Now, in regard to his reminding me of the moral rule that persons who tell what they do not know to be true falsify as much as those who knowingly tell falsehoods. I remember the rule, and it must be borne in mind that in what I have read to you, I do not say that I *know* such a conspiracy to exist. To that I reply, *I believe it.* If the Judge says that I do *not* believe it, then *he* says what *he* does not know, and falls within his own rule, that he who asserts a thing which he does not know to be true, falsifies as much as he who knowingly tells a falsehood. I want to call your attention to a little discussion on that branch of the case, and the evidence which brought my mind to the conclusion which I expressed as my *belief*. If, in arraying that evidence I had stated anything which was false or erroneous, it needed but that Judge Douglas should point it out, and I would have taken it back, with all the kindness in the world. I do not deal in that way. If I have brought forward anything not a fact, if he will point it out, it will not even ruffle me to take it back. But if he will not point out anything erroneous in the evidence, is it not rather for him to show, by a comparison of the evidence, that I have *reasoned* falsely, than to call the "kind, amiable, intelligent gentleman" a liar? If I have reasoned to a false conclusion, it is the vocation of an able debater to show by argument that I have wandered to an erroneous conclusion. I want to ask your attention to a portion of the Nebraska Bill, which Judge Douglas has quoted: "It being the true intent and meaning of this Act, not to legislate slavery into any Territory or State, nor to exclude it therefrom, but to leave the people thereof perfectly free to form and regulate their domestic institutions in their own way, subject only to the Constitution of the United States." Thereupon Judge Douglas and others began to argue in favor of "popular sovereignty,"—the right of the people to have slaves if they wanted them, and to exclude slavery if they did not want them. "But," said, in substance, a Senator from Ohio (Mr. Chase, I believe), "we more than suspect that you do not mean to allow the people to exclude slavery if they wish to; and if you do mean it, accept an amendment which I propose, expressly authorizing the people to exclude slavery." I believe I have the amendment here before me, which was offered, and under which the people of the Territory, through their representatives, might, if they saw fit, prohibit the existence of slavery therein. And now I state it as a *fact,* to be taken back if there is any mistake about it, that Judge Douglas and those acting with him *voted that amendment down.* I now think that those men who voted it down had a *real reason* for doing so. They know what that reason was. It looks to us, since we have seen the Dred Scott decision pronounced, holding that "under the Constitution" the people cannot exclude slavery,—I say it looks to outsiders, poor, simple, "amiable, intelligent gentlemen," as though the niche was left as a place to put that Dred Scott decision in,—a niche which would have been spoiled by adopting the amendment. And now, I say again, if *this* was not the reason, it will avail the Judge much more to calmly and good-humoredly point out to these people what that *other* reason was for voting the amendment down, than, swelling himself up, to vociferate that he may be provoked to call somebody a liar.

Again: There is in that same quotation from the Nebraska Bill this clause: "It being the true intent and meaning of this bill not to legislate slavery into any Territory or *State*." I have always been puzzled to know what business the word "State" had in that connection. Judge Douglas knows. *He put it there*. He knows what he put it there for. We outsiders cannot say what he put it there for. The law they were passing was not about States, and was not making provisions for States. What was it placed there for? After seeing the Dred Scott decision, which holds that the people cannot exclude slavery from a *Territory*, if another Dred Scott decision shall come, holding that they cannot exclude it from a *State*, we shall discover that when the word was originally put there, it was in view of something which was to come in due time, we shall see that it was the *other half* of something. I now say again, if there is any different reason for putting it there, Judge Douglas, in a good-humored way, without calling anybody a liar, *can tell what the reason was.*

When the Judge spoke at Clinton, he came very near making a charge of falsehood against me. He used, as I found it printed in a newspaper, which, I remember, was very nearly like the real speech, the following language:

"I did not answer the charge [of conspiracy] before, for the reason that I did not suppose there was a man in America with a heart so corrupt as to believe such a charge could be true. I have too much respect for Mr. Lincoln to suppose he is serious in making the charge."

I confess this is rather a curious view, that out of respect for me he should consider I was making what I deemed rather a grave charge in fun. I confess it strikes me rather strangely. But I let it pass. As the Judge did not for a moment believe that there was a man in America whose heart was so "corrupt" as to make such a charge, and as he places me among the "men in America" who have hearts base enough to make such a charge,

I hope he will excuse me if I hunt out another charge very like this; and if it should turn out that in hunting I should find that other, and it should turn out to be Judge Douglas himself who made it, I hope he will reconsider this question of the deep corruption of heart he has thought fit to ascribe to me. In Judge Douglas's speech of March 22, 1858, which I hold in my hand, he says:

"In this connection there is another topic to which I desire to allude. I seldom refer to the course of newspapers, or notice the articles which they publish in regard to myself; but the course of the Washington *Union* has been so extraordinary for the last two or three months, that I think it well enough to make some allusion to it. It has read me out of the Democratic party every other day, at least for two or three months, and keeps reading me out, and, as if it had not succeeded, still continues to read me out, using such terms as 'traitor,' 'renegade,' 'deserter,' and other kind and polite epithets of that nature. Sir, I have no vindication to make of my Democracy against the Washington *Union,* or any other newspapers. I am willing to allow my history and action for the last twenty years to speak for themselves as to my political principles and my fidelity to political obligations. The Washington *Union* has a personal grievance. When its editor was nominated for public printer, I declined to vote for him, and stated that at some time I might give my reasons for doing so. Since I declined to give that vote, this scurrilous abuse, these vindictive and constant attacks have been repeated almost daily on me. Will my friend from Michigan read the article to which I allude?"

This is a part of the speech. You must excuse me from reading the entire article of the Washington *Union,* as Mr. Stuart read it for Mr. Douglas. The Judge goes on and sums up, as I think, correctly:

"Mr. President, you here find several distinct propositions advanced boldly by the Washington *Union* editorially, and apparently *authoritatively;* and any man who questions any of them is denounced as an Abolitionist, a Free-soiler, a fanatic. The propositions are, first, that the primary object of all government at its original institution is the protection of person and property; second, that the Constitution of the United States declares that the citizens of each State shall be entitled to all the privileges and immunities of citizens in the several States;

and that, therefore, thirdly, all State laws, whether organic or otherwise, which prohibit the citizens of one State from settling in another with their slave property, and especially declaring it forfeited, are direct violations of the original intention of the government and Constitution of the United States; and, fourth, that the emancipation of the slaves of the Northern States was a gross outrage of the rights of property, inasmuch as it was involuntarily done on the part of the owner.

"Remember that this article was published in the *Union* on the 17th of November, and on the 18th appeared the first article giving the adhesion of the *Union* to the Lecompton Constitution. It was in these words:

"'KANSAS AND HER CONSTITUTION.—The vexed question is settled. The problem is solved. The dead point of danger is passed. All serious trouble to Kansas affairs is over and gone'—

"And a column nearly of the same sort. Then, when you come to look into the Lecompton Constitution, you find the same doctrine incorporated in it which was put forth editorially in the *Union*. What is it?

"ARTICLE 7, *Section* I. The right of property is before and higher than any constitutional sanction; and the right of the owner of a slave to such slave and its increase is the same and as inviolable as the right of the owner of any property whatever.'

"Then in the schedule is a provision that the Constitution may be amended after 1864 by a two-thirds vote:

"'But no alteration shall be made to affect the right of property in the ownership of slaves.'

"It will be seen by these clauses in the Lecompton Constitution that they are identical in spirit with the *authoritative* article in the Washington *Union* of the day previous to its indorsement of this Constitution."

I pass over some portions of the speech, and I hope that any one who feels interested in this matter will read the entire section of the speech, and see whether I do the Judge injustice. He proceeds:

"When I saw that article in the *Union* of the 17th of November, followed by the glorification of the Lecompton Constitution on the 18th of November, and this clause in the Constitution asserting the doctrine that a State has no right to prohibit slavery within its limits, I saw that

there was a *fatal blow* being struck at the sovereignty of the States of
this Union."

I stop the quotation there, again requesting that it may all be
read. I have read all of the portion I desire to comment upon.
What is this charge that the Judge thinks I must have a very corrupt heart to make? It was a purpose on the part of certain high
functionaries to make it impossible for the people of one State to
prohibit the people of any other State from entering it with their
"property," so called, and making it a slave State. In other words,
it was a charge implying a design to make the institution of slavery national. And now I ask your attention to what Judge Douglas
has himself done here. I know he made that part of the speech
as a reason why he had refused to vote for a certain man for public printer; but when we get at it, the charge itself is the very one
I made against him, that he thinks I am so corrupt for uttering.
Now, whom does he make that charge against? Does he make it
against that newspaper editor merely? No; he says it is identical
in spirit with the Lecompton Constitution, and so the framers of
that Constitution are brought in with the editor of the newspaper in that "fatal blow being struck." He did not call it a "conspiracy." In his language, it is a "fatal blow being struck." And if
the words carry the meaning better when changed from a "conspiracy" into a "fatal blow being struck," I will change *my* expression, and call it "fatal blow being struck." We see the charge
made not merely against the editor of the *Union,* but all the
framers of the Lecompton Constitution; and not only so, but the
article was an *authoritative* article. By whose authority? Is there
any question but he means it was by the authority of the
President and his Cabinet,—the Administration?

Is there any sort of question but he means to make that
charge? Then there are the editors of the *Union,* the framers of
the Lecompton Constitution, the President of the United States
and his Cabinet, and all the supporters of the Lecompton
Constitution, in Congress and out of Congress, who are all
involved in this "fatal blow being struck." I commend to Judge
Douglas's consideration the question of *how corrupt a man's
heart must be to make such a charge!*

Now, my friends, I have but one branch of the subject, in the little time I have left, to which to call your attention; and as I shall come to a close at the end of that branch, it is probable that I shall not occupy quite all the time allotted to me. Although on these questions I would like to talk twice as long as I have, I could not enter upon another head and discuss it properly without running over my time. I ask the attention of the people here assembled and elsewhere to the course that Judge Douglas is pursuing every day as bearing upon this question of making slavery national. Not going back to the records, but taking the speeches he makes, the speeches he made yesterday and day before, and makes constantly all over the country,—I ask your attention to them. In the first place, what is necessary to make the institution national? Not war. There is no danger that the people of Kentucky will shoulder their muskets, and, with a young nigger stuck on every bayonet, march into Illinois and force them upon us. There is no danger of our going over there and making war upon them. Then what is necessary for the nationalization of slavery? It is simply the next Dred Scott decision. It is merely for the Supreme Court to decide that no *State* under the Constitution can exclude it, just as they have already decided that under the Constitution neither Congress nor the Territorial Legislature can do it. When that is decided and acquiesced in, the whole thing is done. This being true, and this being the way, as I think, that slavery is to be made national, let us consider what Judge Douglas is doing every day to that end. In the first place, let us see what influence he is exerting on public sentiment. In this and like communities, public sentiment is everything. With public sentiment, nothing can fail; without it, nothing can succeed. Consequently, he who moulds public sentiment goes deeper than he who enacts statutes or pronounces decisions. He makes statutes and decisions possible or impossible to be executed. This must be borne in mind, as also the additional fact that Judge Douglas is a man of vast influence, so great that it is enough for many men to profess to believe anything when they once find out Judge Douglas professes to believe it. Consider also the attitude he occupies at the head of a large party,—a party which he claims has a majority of all the voters in the country. This man sticks to a decision which forbids the people of a Territory from excluding slavery, and he does so, not because he says it is right in itself,—he does not give any opinion on that,—but because it has been *decided by the court;* and being decided by the court, he is, and you are, bound to take it in your political action as *law,* not that he judges at all of its merits, but because a decision of the court is to him a "Thus saith the Lord." He places it on that ground alone; and you will bear in mind that thus committing himself unreservedly to this decision *commits him to the next one* just as firmly as to this. He did not commit himself on account of the merit or demerit of the decision, but it is a "Thus saith the Lord." The next decision, as much as this, will be a "Thus saith the Lord." There is nothing that can divert or turn him away from this decision. It is nothing that I point out to him that his great prototype, General Jackson, did not believe in the binding force of decisions. It is nothing to him that Jefferson did not so believe. I have said that I have often heard him approve of Jackson's course in disregarding the decision of the Supreme Court pronouncing a National Bank constitutional. He says I did not hear him say so. He denies the accuracy of my recollection. I say he ought to know better than I, but I will make no question about this thing, though it still seems to me that I heard him say it twenty times. I will tell him, though, that he now claims to stand on the Cincinnati platform, which affirms that Congress *cannot* charter a National Bank, in the teeth of that old standing decision that Congress *can* charter a bank. And I remind him of another piece of history on the question of respect for judicial decisions, and it is a piece of Illinois history belonging to a time when the large party to which Judge Douglas belonged were displeased with a decision of the Supreme Court of Illinois, because they had decided that a Governor could not remove a Secretary of State. You will find the whole story in Ford's *History of Illinois,* and I know that Judge Douglas will not deny that he was then in favor of over-slaughing that decision by the mode of adding five new judges, so as to vote down the four old ones. Not only so, but it ended in *the Judge's sitting down on that very bench as one of the five new judges to break down the four old ones.* It was in this way precisely that he got his title of judge. Now, when the Judge tells me that men appointed conditionally to sit as members of a court will have to be catechised beforehand upon some subject, I say, "You know, Judge; you have tried it." When he says a court of this kind will lose the confidence of all men, will be prostituted and disgraced by such a proceeding, I say, "You know best, Judge; you have been through the mill." But I cannot shake Judge Douglas's teeth loose from the Dred Scott decision. Like some obstinate animal (I mean no disrespect) that will hang on when he has once got his teeth fixed, you may cut off a leg, or you may tear away an arm, still he will not relax his hold. And so I may point out to the Judge, and say that he is bespattered all over, from the beginning of his political life to the present time, with attacks upon judicial decisions; I may cut off limb after limb of his public record, and strive to wrench him from a single dictum of the court,—yet I cannot divert him from it. He hangs, to the last, to the Dred Scott decision. These things show there is a purpose *strong as death and eternity* for which he adheres to this decision, and for which he will adhere to *all other decisions* of the same court.

A HIBERNIAN: "Give us something besides Dred Scott."

MR. LINCOLN: Yes; no doubt you want to hear something that don't hurt. Now, having spoken of the Dred Scott decision, one more word, and I am done. Henry Clay, my *beau-ideal* of a statesman, the man for whom I fought all my humble life,— Henry Clay once said of a class of men who would repress all tendencies to liberty and ultimate emancipation that they must, if they would do this, go back to the era of our Independence, and muzzle the cannon which thunders its annual joyous return; they must blow out the moral lights around us; they must penetrate the human soul, and eradicate there the love of liberty; and then, and not till then, could they perpetuate slavery in this country! To my thinking, Judge Douglas is, by his example and vast influence, doing that very thing in this community, when he says that the negro has nothing in the Declaration of Independence. Henry Clay plainly understood the contrary. Judge Douglas is going back to the era of our Revolution, and, to the extent of his ability, muzzling the cannon which thunders its annual joyous return. When he invites any people, willing to have slavery, to establish it, he is blowing out the moral lights around us. When he says he "cares not whether slavery is voted down or up,"—that it is a sacred right of self-government,—he is, in my judgment, penetrating the human soul and eradicating the light of reason and the love of liberty in this American people. And now I will only say that when, by all these means and appliances, Judge Douglas shall succeed in bringing public sentiment to an exact accordance with his own views; when these vast assemblages shall echo back all these sentiments; when they shall come to repeat his views and to avow his principles, and to say all that he says on these mighty questions,— then it needs only the formality of the second Dred Scott decision, which he indorses in advance, to make slavery alike lawful in all the States, old as well as new, North as well as South.

My friends, that ends the chapter. The Judge can take his half-hour.

Mr. Douglas's Reply

FELLOW-CITIZENS: I will now occupy the half-hour allotted to me in replying to Mr. Lincoln. The first point to which I will call your attention is as to what I said about the organization of the Republican party in 1854, and the platform that was formed on the 5th of October of that year, and I will then put the question to Mr. Lincoln, whether or not he approves of each article in that platform, and ask for a specific answer. I did not charge him with being a member of the committee which reported that platform. I charged that that platform was the platform of the Republican party adopted by them. The fact that it was the platform of the Republican party is not denied; but Mr. Lincoln now says that, although his name was on the committee which reported it, that he does not think he was there, but thinks he was in Tazewell, holding court. Now, I want to remind Mr. Lincoln that he was at Springfield when that Convention was held and those resolutions adopted.

The point I am going to remind Mr. Lincoln of is this: that

after I had made my speech in 1854, during the fair, he gave me notice that he was going to reply to me the next day. I was sick at the time, but I stayed over in Springfield to hear his reply and to reply to him. On that day this very Convention, the resolutions adopted by which I have read, was to meet in the Senate chamber. He spoke in the hall of the House; and when he got through his speech—my recollection is distinct, and I shall never forget it—Mr. Codding walked in as I took the stand to reply, and gave notice that the Republican State Convention would meet instantly in the Senate chamber, and called upon the Republicans to retire there and go into this very Convention, instead of remaining and listening to me.

In the first place, Mr. Lincoln was selected by the very men who made the Republican organization, on that day, to reply to me. He spoke for them and for that party, and he was the leader of the party; and on the very day he made his speech in reply to me, preaching up this same doctrine of negro equality under the Declaration of Independence, this Republican party met in Convention. Another evidence that he was acting in concert with them is to be found in the fact that that Convention waited an hour after its time of meeting to hear Lincoln's speech, and Codding, one of their leading men, marched in the moment Lincoln got through, and gave notice that they did not want to hear me, and would proceed with the business of the Convention. Still another fact: I have here a newspaper printed at Springfield, Mr. Lincoln's own town, in October, 1854, a few days afterward, publishing these resolutions, charging Mr. Lincoln with entertaining these sentiments, and trying to prove that they were also the sentiments of Mr. Yates, their candidate for Congress. This has been published on Mr. Lincoln over and over again, and never before has he denied it.

But, my friends, this denial of his that he did not act on the committee is a miserable quibble to avoid the main issue, which is, that this Republican platform declares in favor of the unconditional repeal of the Fugitive Slave law. Has Lincoln answered whether he indorsed that or not? I called his attention to it when I first addressed you, and asked him for an answer, and I then predicted that he would not answer. How does he answer?

Why, that he was not on the committee that wrote the resolutions. I then repeated the next proposition contained in the resolutions, which was to restrict slavery in those States in which it exists, and asked him whether he indorsed it. Does he answer yes, or no? He says in reply, "I was not on the committee at the time; I was up in Tazewell." The next question I put to him was, whether he was in favor of prohibiting the admission of any more slave States into the Union. I put the question to him distinctly, whether, if the people of the Territory, when they had sufficient population to make a State, should form their constitution recognizing slavery, he would vote for or against its admission. He is a candidate for the United States Senate, and it is possible, if he should be elected, that he would have to vote directly on that question. I asked him to answer me and you, whether he would vote to admit a State into the Union, with slavery or without it, as its own people might choose. He did not answer that question. He dodges that question also, under the cover that he was not on the committee at the time, that he was not present when the platform was made. I want to know if he should happen to be in the Senate when a State applied for admission, with a constitution acceptable to her own people, he would vote to admit that State, if slavery was one of its institutions. He avoids the answer.

It is true he gives the Abolitionists to understand by a hint that he would not vote to admit such a State. And why? He goes on to say that the man who would talk about giving each State the right to have slavery or not, as it pleased, was akin to the man who would muzzle the guns which thundered forth the annual joyous return of the day of our Independence. He says that that kind of talk is casting a blight on the glory of this country. What is the meaning of that? That he is not in favor of each State to have the right of doing as it pleases on the slavery question? I will put the question to him again and again, and I intend to force it out of him.

Then, again, this platform, which was made at Springfield by his own party when he was its acknowledged head, provides that Republicans will insist on the abolition of slavery in the District of Columbia, and I asked Lincoln specifically whether he agreed with them in that? ["Did you get an answer?"] He is afraid to answer it. He knows I would trot him down to Egypt. I intend to make him answer there, or I will show the people of Illinois that he does not intend to answer these questions. The Convention to which I have been alluding goes a little further, and pledges itself to exclude slavery from all the Territories over which the General Government has exclusive jurisdiction north of 36 deg. 30 min., as well as south. Now, I want to know whether he approves that provision. I want him to answer, and when he does, I want to know his opinion on another point, which is whether he will redeem the pledge of this platform, and resist the acquirement of any more territory unless slavery therein shall be forever prohibited. I want him to answer this last question. Each of the questions I have put to him are prac-tical questions,—questions based upon the fundamental prin-ciples of the Black Republican party; and I want to know whether he is the first, last, and only choice of a party with whom he does not agree in principle. He does not deny but that that principle was unanimously adopted by the Republican party; he does not deny that the whole Republican party is pledged to it; he does not deny that a man who is not faithful to it is faithless to the Republican party; and now I want to know whether that party is unanimously in favor of a man who does not adopt that creed and agree with them in their principles; I want to know whether the man who does not agree with them, and who is afraid to avow his differences, and who dodges the issue, is the first, last, and only choice of the Republican party.

A Voice: "How about the conspiracy?"

MR. DOUGLAS: Never mind, I will come to that soon enough. But the platform which I have read to you not only lays down these principles, but it adds:

"*Resolved*, That in furtherance of these principles, we will use such constitutional and lawful means as shall seem best adapted to their accomplishment, and that we will support no man for office, under the General or State Government, who is not positively and fully commit-ted to the support of these principles, and whose personal character and conduct is not a guarantee that he is reliable, and who shall not have abjured old party allegiance and ties."

The Black Republican party stands pledged that they will never support Lincoln until he has pledged himself to that platform; but he cannot devise his answer, he has not made up his mind whether he will or not. He talked about everything else he could think of to occupy his hour and a half, and when he could not think of anything more to say, without an excuse for refusing to answer these questions, he sat down long before his time was out.

In relation to Mr. Lincoln's charge of conspiracy against me, I have a word to say. In his speech to-day he quotes a playful part of his speech at Springfield, about Stephen, and James, and Franklin, and Roger, and says that I did not take exception to it. I did not answer it, and he repeats it again. I did not take exception to this figure of his. He has a right to be as playful as he pleases in throwing his arguments together, and I will not object; but I did take objection to his second Springfield speech, in which he stated that he intended his first speech as a charge of corruption or conspiracy against the Supreme Court of the United States, President Pierce, President Buchanan, and myself. That gave the offensive character to the charge. He then said that when he made it he did not know whether it was true or not; but inasmuch as Judge Douglas had not denied it, although he had replied to the other parts of his speech three times, he repeated it as a charge of conspiracy against me, thus charging me with moral turpitude. When he put it in that form, I did say that, inasmuch as he repeated the charge simply because I had not denied it, I would deprive him of the opportunity of ever repeating it again, by declaring that it was, in all its bearings, an infamous lie. He says he will repeat it until I answer his folly and nonsense about Stephen, and Franklin, and Roger, and Bob, and James.

He studied that out, prepared that one sentence with the greatest care, committed it to memory, and put it in his first Springfield speech; and now he carries that speech around, and reads that sentence to show how pretty it is. His vanity is wounded because I will not go into that beautiful figure of his about the building of a house. All I have to say is, that I am not green enough to let him make a charge which he acknowledges he does not know to be true, and then take up my time in answering it, when I know it to be false, and nobody else knows it to be true.

I have not brought a charge of moral turpitude against him. When he, or any other man, brings one against me, instead of disproving it, I will say that it is a lie, and let him prove it if he can.

I have lived twenty-five years in Illinois, I have served you with all the fidelity and ability which I possess, and Mr. Lincoln is at liberty to attack my public action, my votes, and my conduct; but when he dares to attack my moral integrity by a charge of conspiracy between myself, Chief Justice Taney and the Supreme Court, and two Presidents of the United States, I will repel it.

Mr. Lincoln has not character enough for integrity and truth, merely on his own *ipse dixit*, to arraign President Buchanan, President Pierce, and nine Judges of the Supreme Court, not one of whom would be complimented by being put on an equality with him. There is an unpardonable presumption in a man putting himself up before thousands of people, and pretending that his *ipse dixit*, without proof, without fact, and without truth, is enough to bring down and destroy the purest and best of living men.

Fellow-citizens, my time is fast expiring; I must pass on. Mr. Lincoln wants to know why I voted against Mr. Chase's amendment to the Nebraska Bill. I will tell him. In the first place, the bill already conferred all the power which Congress had, by giving the people the whole power over the subject. Chase offered a proviso that they might abolish slavery, which by implication would convey the idea that they could prohibit by not introducing that institution. General Cass asked him to modify his amendment so as to provide that the people might either prohibit or introduce slavery, and thus make it fair and equal. Chase refused to so modify his proviso, and then General Cass and all the rest of us voted it down. Those facts appear on the journals and debates of Congress, where Mr. Lincoln found the charge; and if he had told the whole truth, there would have been no necessity for me to occupy your time in explaining the matter.

Mr. Lincoln wants to know why the word "State," as well as "Territory," was put into the Nebraska Bill. I will tell him. It was put there to meet just such false arguments as he has been adducing. That first, not only the people of the Territories should do as they pleased, but that when they come to be admitted as States, they should come into the Union with or without slavery, as the people determined. I meant to knock in the head this Abolition doctrine of Mr. Lincoln's, that there shall be no more slave States, even if the people want them. And it does not do for him to say, or for any other Black Republican to say, that there is nobody in favor of the doctrine of no more slave States, and that nobody wants to interfere with the right of the people to do as they please. What was the origin of the Missouri difficulty and the Missouri Compromise? The people of Missouri formed a constitution as a slave State, and asked admission into the Union; but the Free-soil party of the North, being in a majority, refused to admit her because she had slavery as one of her institutions. Hence this first slavery agitation arose upon a State, and not upon a Territory; and yet Mr. Lincoln does not know why the word "State" was placed in the Kansas-Nebraska Bill. The whole Abolition agitation arose on that doctrine of prohibiting a State from coming in with slavery or not, as it pleased, and that same doctrine is here in this Republican platform of 1854; it has never been repealed; and every Black Republican stands pledged by that platform never to vote for any man who is not in favor of it. Yet Mr. Lincoln does not know that there is a man in the world who is in favor of preventing a State from coming in as it pleases, notwithstanding. The Springfield platform says that they, the Republican party, will not allow a State to come in under such circumstances. He is an ignorant man.

Now, you see that upon these very points I am as far from bringing Mr. Lincoln up to the line as I ever was before. He does not want to avow his principles. I do want to avow mine, as clear as sunlight in midday. Democracy is founded upon the eternal principle of right. The plainer these principles are avowed before the people, the stronger will be the support which they will receive. I only wish I had the power to make them so clear that they would shine in the heavens for every man, woman, and child to read. The first of those principles that I would proclaim would be in opposition to Mr. Lincoln's doctrine of uniformity between the different States, and I would declare instead the sovereign right of each State to decide the slavery question as well as all other domestic questions for themselves, without interference from any other State or power whatsoever.

When that principle is recognized, you will have peace and harmony and fraternal feeling between all the States of this Union; until you do recognize that doctrine, there will be sectional warfare agitating and distracting the country. What does Mr. Lincoln propose? He says that the Union cannot exist divided into free and slave States. If it cannot endure thus divided, then he must strive to make them all free or all slave, which will inevitably bring about a dissolution of the Union.

Gentlemen, I am told that my time is out, and I am obliged to stop.

Second Joint Debate
FREEPORT, AUGUST 27, 1858

Mr. Lincoln's Speech

LADIES AND GENTLEMEN: On Saturday last, Judge Douglas and myself first met in public discussion. He spoke one hour, I an hour and a half, and he replied for half an hour. The order is now reversed. I am to speak an hour, he an hour and a half, and then I am to reply for half an hour. I propose to devote myself during the first hour to the scope of what was brought within the range of his half-hour speech at Ottawa. Of course there was brought within the scope in that half-hour's speech something of his own opening speech. In the course of that opening argument Judge Douglas proposed to me seven distinct interrogatories. In my speech of an hour and a half, I attended to some other parts of his speech, and incidentally, as I thought, intimated to him that I would answer the rest of his interrogatories on condition only that he should agree to answer as many for me. He made no intimation at the time of the proposition, nor did he in his reply allude at all to that suggestion of mine. I do him no injustice in saying that he occupied at least half of his reply in dealing with me as though I had *refused* to answer his interrogatories. I now propose that I will answer any of the interrogatories, upon condition that he will answer questions from me not exceeding the same number. I give him an opportunity to respond. The Judge remains silent. I now say that I will answer his interrogatories, whether he answers mine or not; and that after I have done so, I shall propound mine to him.

I have supposed myself, since the organization of the Republican party at Bloomington, in May, 1856, bound as a party man by the platforms of the party, then and since. If in any interrogatories which I shall answer I go beyond the scope of what is within these platforms, it will be perceived that no one is responsible but myself.

Having said thus much, I will take up the Judge's interrogatories as I find them printed in the Chicago *Times,* and answer them *seriatim.* In order that there may be no mistake about it, I have copied the interrogatories in writing, and also my answers to them. The first one of these interrogatories is in these words:

Question 1.—"I desire to know whether Lincoln to-day stands, as he did in 1854, in favor of the unconditional repeal of the Fugitive Slave law?"

Answer.—I do not now, nor ever did, stand in favor of the unconditional repeal of the Fugitive Slave law.

Q. 2. "I desire him to answer whether he stands pledged to-day, as he did in 1854, against the admission of any more slave States into the Union, even if the people want them?"

A. I do not now, nor ever did, stand pledged against the admission of any more slave States into the Union.

Q. 3. "I want to know whether he stands pledged against the admission of a new State into the Union with such a constitution as the people of that State may see fit to make?"

A. I do not stand pledged against the admission of a new State into the Union, with such a constitution as the people of that State may see fit to make.

Q. 4. "I want to know whether he stands to-day pledged to the abolition of slavery in the District of Columbia?"

A. I do not stand to-day pledged to the abolition of slavery in the District of Columbia.

Q. 5. "I desire him to answer whether he stands pledged to the prohibition of the slave-trade between the different States?"

A. I do not stand pledged to the prohibition of the slave-trade between the different States.

Q. 6. "I desire to know whether he stands pledged to prohibit slavery in all the Territories of the United States, north as well as south of the Missouri Compromise line?"

A. I am impliedly, if not expressly, pledged to a belief in the *right* and *duty* of Congress to prohibit slavery in all the United States Territories.

Q. 7. "I desire him to answer whether he is opposed to the acquisition of any new territory unless slavery is first prohibited therein?"

A. I am not generally opposed to honest acquisition of territory; and, in any given case, I would or would not oppose such acquisition, accordingly as I might think such acquisition would or would not aggravate the slavery question among ourselves.

Now, my friends, it will be perceived, upon an examination of these questions and answers, that so far I have only answered that I was not *pledged* to this, that, or the other. The Judge has not framed his interrogatories to ask me anything more than this, and I have answered in strict accordance with the interrogatories, and have answered truly, that I am not *pledged* at all upon any of the points to which I have answered. But I am not disposed to hang upon the exact form of his interrogatory. I am rather disposed to take up at least some of these questions, and state what I really think upon them.

As to the first one, in regard to the Fugitive Slave law, I have never hesitated to say, and I do not now hesitate to say, that I think, under the Constitution of the United States, the people of the Southern States are entitled to a Congressional Fugitive Slave law. Having said that, I have had nothing to say in regard to the existing Fugitive Slave law, further than that I think it should have been framed so as to be free from some of the objections that pertain to it, without lessening its efficiency. And inasmuch as we are not now in an agitation in regard to an alteration or modification of that law, I would not be the man to introduce it as a new subject of agitation upon the general question of slavery.

In regard to the other question, of whether I am pledged to the admission of any more slave States into the Union, I state to you very frankly that I would be exceedingly sorry ever to be put in a position of having to pass upon that question. I should be exceedingly glad to know that there would never be another slave State admitted into the Union; but I must add that if slavery shall be kept out of the Territories during the territorial existence of any one given Territory, and then the people shall, having a fair chance and a clear field, when they come to adopt the constitution, do such an extraordinary thing as to adopt a slave constitution, uninfluenced by the actual presence of the institution among them, I see no alternative, if we own the country, but to admit them into the Union.

The third interrogatory is answered by the answer to the second, it being, as I conceive, the same as the second.

The fourth one is in regard to the abolition of slavery in the District of Columbia. In relation to that, I have my mind very distinctly made up. I should be exceedingly glad to see slavery abolished in the District of Columbia. I believe that Congress possesses the constitutional power to abolish it. Yet as a member of Congress, I should not, with my present views, be in favor of *endeavoring* to abolish slavery in the District of Columbia, unless it would be upon these conditions: *First,* that the abolition should be gradual; *second,* that it should be on a vote of the majority of qualified voters in the District; and *third,* that compensation should be made to unwilling owners. With these three conditions, I confess I would be exceedingly glad to see Congress abolish slavery in the District of Columbia, and, in the language of Henry Clay, "sweep from our capital that foul blot upon our nation."

In regard to the fifth interrogatory, I must say here that, as to the question of the abolition of the slave-trade between the different States, I can truly answer, as I have, that I am *pledged* to nothing about it. It is a subject to which I have not given that mature consideration that would make me feel authorized to state a position so as to hold myself entirely bound by it. In other words, that question has never been prominently enough before me to induce me to investigate whether we really have the constitutional power to do it. I could investigate it if I had sufficient time to bring myself to a conclusion upon that subject; but I have not done so, and I say so frankly to you here, and to Judge Douglas. I must say, however, that if I should be of opinion that Congress does possess the constitutional power to abolish the slave-trade among the different States, I should still not be in favor of the exercise of that power, unless upon some conserva-tive principle as I conceive it, akin to what I have said in relation to the abolition of slavery in the District of Columbia.

My answer as to whether I desire that slavery should be pro-hibited in all the Territories of the United States is full and explicit within itself, and cannot be made clearer by any com-ments of mine. So I suppose in regard to the question whether I am opposed to the acquisition of any more territory unless slavery is first prohibited therein, my answer is such that I could add nothing by way of illustration, or making myself better understood, than the answer which I have placed in writing.

Now in all this the Judge has me, and he has me on the record. I suppose he had flattered himself that I was really entertaining one set of opinions for one place, and another set for another place; that I was afraid to say at one place what I uttered at another. What I am saying here I suppose I say to a vast audience as strongly tending to Abolitionism as any audi-ence in the State of Illinois, and I believe I am saying that which, if it would be offensive to any persons and render them enemies to myself, would be offensive to persons in this audience.

I now proceed to propound to the Judge the interrogatories, so far as I have framed them. I will bring forward a new install-ment when I get them ready. I will bring them forward now only reaching to number four.

The first one is:

Question 1.—If the people of Kansas shall, by means entirely unobjectionable in all other respects, adopt a State constitution, and ask admission into the Union under it, *before* they have the requisite number of inhabitants according to the English bill,— some ninety-three thousand,—will you vote to admit them?

Q. 2. Can the people of a United States Territory, in any law-ful way, against the wish of any citizen of the United States, exclude slavery from its limits prior to the formation of a State constitution?

Q. 3. If the Supreme Court of the United States shall decide that States cannot exclude slavery from their limits, are you in favor of acquiescing in, adopting, and following such decision as a rule of political action?

Q. 4. Are you in favor of acquiring additional territory, in disregard of how such acquisition may affect the nation on the slavery question?

As introductory to these interrogatories which Judge Douglas propounded to me at Ottawa, he read a set of resolutions which he said Judge Trumbull and myself had participated in adopting, in the first Republican State Convention, held at Springfield in October, 1854. He insisted that I and Judge Trumbull, and perhaps the entire Republican party, were responsible for the doctrines contained in the set of resolutions which he read, and I understand that it was from that set of resolutions that he deduced the interrogatories which he propounded to me, using these resolutions as a sort of authority for propounding those questions to me. Now, I say here to-day that I do not answer his interrogatories because of their springing at all from that set of resolutions which he read. I answered them because Judge Douglas thought fit to ask them. I do not now, nor ever did, recognize any responsibility upon myself in that set of resolutions. When I replied to him on that occasion, I assured him that I never had anything to do with them. I repeat here to-day that I never in any possible form had anything to do with that set of resolutions. It turns out, I believe, that those resolutions were never passed in any convention held in Springfield. It turns out that they were never passed at any convention or any public meeting that I had any part in. I believe it turns out, in addition to all this, that there was not, in the fall of 1854, any convention holding a session in Springfield, calling itself a Republican State Convention; yet it is true there was a convention, or assemblage of men calling themselves a convention, at Springfield, that did pass *some* resolutions. But so little did I really know of the proceedings of that convention, or what set of resolutions they had passed, though having a general knowledge that there had been such an assemblage of men there, that when Judge Douglas read the resolutions, I really did not know but they had been the resolutions passed then and there. I did not question that they were the resolutions adopted. For I could not bring myself to suppose that Judge Douglas could say what he did upon this subject without *knowing* that it was true. I contented myself, on that occasion, with denying, as I truly could, all connection with them, not denying or affirming whether they were passed at Springfield. Now, it turns out that he had got hold of some resolutions passed at some convention or public meeting in Kane County. I wish to say here, that I don't conceive that in any fair and just mind this discovery relieves me at all. I had just as much to do with the convention in Kane County as that at Springfield. I am as much responsible for the resolutions at Kane County as those at Springfield,—the amount of the responsibility being exactly nothing in either case; no more than there would be in regard to a set of resolutions passed in the moon.

I allude to this extraordinary matter in this canvass for some further purpose than anything yet advanced. Judge Douglas did not make his statement upon that occasion as matters that he believed to be true, but he stated them roundly as *being true,* in such form as to pledge his veracity for their truth. When the whole matter turns out as it does, and when we consider who Judge Douglas is,—that he is a distinguished Senator of the United States; that he has served nearly twelve years as such; that his character is not at all limited as an ordinary Senator of the United States, but that his name has become of world-wide renown,—it is *most extraordinary* that he should so far forget all the suggestions of justice to an adversary, or of prudence to himself, as to venture upon the assertion of that which the slightest investigation would have shown him to be wholly false. I can only account for his having done so upon the supposition that that evil genius which has attended him through his life, giving to him an apparent astonishing prosperity, such as to lead very many good men to doubt there being any advantage in virtue over vice,—I say I can only account for it on the supposition that that evil genius has as last made up its mind to forsake him.

And I may add that another extraordinary feature of the Judge's conduct in this canvass—made more extraordinary by this incident—is, that he is in the habit, in almost all the speeches he makes, of charging falsehood upon his adversaries, myself and others. I now ask whether he is able to find in anything that Judge Trumbull, for instance, has said, or in anything that I have said, a justification at all compared with what we have, in this instance, for that sort of vulgarity.

I have been in the habit of charging as a matter of belief on my part that, in the introduction of the Nebraska Bill into Congress, there was a conspiracy to make slavery perpetual and national. I have arranged from time to time the evidence which establishes and proves the truth of this charge. I recurred to this charge at Ottawa. I shall not now have time to dwell upon it at very great length; but inasmuch as Judge Douglas, in his reply of half an hour, made some points upon me in relation to it, I propose noticing a few of them.

The Judge insists that, in the first speech I made, in which I very distinctly made that charge, he thought for a good while I was in fun! that I was playful; that I was not sincere about it; and that he only grew angry and somewhat excited when he found that I insisted upon it as a matter of earnestness. He says he characterized it as a falsehood so far as I implicated his *moral character* in that transaction. Well, I did not know, till he presented that view, that I had implicated his moral character. He is very much in the habit, when he argues me up into a position I never thought of occupying, of very cosily saying he has no doubt Lincoln is "conscientious" in saying so. He should remember that I did not know but what *he* was ALTOGETHER "CONSCIENTIOUS" in that matter. I can conceive it possible for men to conspire to do a good thing, and I really find nothing in Judge Douglas's course of arguments that is contrary to or inconsistent with his belief of a conspiracy to nationalize and spread slavery as being a good and blessed thing; and so I hope he will understand that I do not at all question but that in all this matter he is entirely "conscientious."

But to draw your attention to one of the points I made in this case, beginning at the beginning: When the Nebraska Bill was introduced, or a short time afterward, by an amendment, I believe, it was provided that it must be considered "the true intent and meaning of this Act not to legislate slavery into any State or Territory, or to exclude it therefrom, but to leave the people thereof perfectly free to form and regulate their own domestic institutions in their own way, subject only to the

Constitution of the United States." I have called his attention to
the fact that when he and some others began arguing that they
were giving an increased degree of liberty to the people in the
Territories over and above what they formerly had on the question of slavery, a question was raised whether the law was enacted to give such unconditional liberty to the people; and to
test the sincerity of this mode of argument, Mr. Chase, of Ohio,
introduced an amendment, in which he made the law—if the
amendment were adopted—expressly declare that the people of
the Territory should have the power to exclude slavery if they
saw fit. I have asked attention also to the fact that Judge Douglas
and those who acted with him voted that amendment down,
notwithstanding it expressed exactly the thing they said was the
true intent and meaning of the law. I have called attention to the
fact that in subsequent times a decision of the Supreme Court
has been made, in which it has been declared that a Territorial
Legislature has no constitutional right to exclude slavery. And I
have argued and said that for men who did intend that the
people of the Territory should have the right to exclude slavery
absolutely and unconditionally, the voting down of Chase's
amendment is wholly inexplicable. It is a puzzle, a riddle. But I
have said, that with men who did look forward to such a decision, or who had it in contemplation that such a decision of the
Supreme Court would or might be made, the voting down of
that amendment would be perfectly rational and intelligible. It
would keep Congress from coming in collision with the decision
when it was made. Anybody can conceive that if there was an
intention or expectation that such a decision was to follow, it
would not be a very desirable party attitude to get into for the
Supreme Court—all or nearly all its members belonging to the
same party—to decide one way, when the party in Congress had
decided the other way. Hence it would be very rational for men
expecting such a decision to keep the niche in that law clear for
it. After pointing this out, I tell Judge Douglas that it looks to me
as though here was the reason why Chase's amendment was
voted down. I tell him that, as he did it, and knows why he did
it, if it was done for a reason different from this, *he knows what
that reason was and can tell us what it was.* I tell him, also, it

will be vastly more satisfactory to the country for him to give some other plausible, intelligible reason *why* it was voted down than to stand upon his dignity and call people liars. Well, on Saturday he did make his answer; and what do you think it was? He says if I had only taken upon myself to tell the whole truth about that amendment of Chase's, no explanation would have been necessary on his part—or words to that effect. Now, I say here that I am quite unconscious of having suppressed anything material to the case, and I am very frank to admit if there is any sound reason other than that which appeared to me material, it is quite fair for him to present it. What reason does he propose? That when Chase came forward with his amendment expressly authorizing the people to exclude slavery from the limits of every Territory, General Cass proposed to Chase, if he (Chase) would add to his amendment that the people should have the power to *introduce* or exclude, they would let it go. This is substantially all of his reply. And because Chase would not do that, they voted his amendment down. Well, it turns out, I believe, upon examination, that General Cass took some part in the little running debate upon that amendment, and then ran away *and did not vote on it at all.* Is not that the fact? So confident, as I think, was General Cass that there was a snake somewhere about, he chose to run away from the whole thing. This is an inference I draw from the fact that, though he took part in the debate, his name does not appear in the ayes and noes. But does Judge Douglas's reply amount to a satisfactory answer? [Cries of "Yes," "Yes," and "No," "No."] There is some little difference of opinion here. But I ask attention to a few more views bearing on the question of whether it amounts to a satisfactory answer. The men who were determined that that amendment should not get into the bill, and spoil the place where the Dred Scott decision was to come in, sought an excuse to get rid of it somewhere. One of these ways—one of these excuses—was to ask Chase to add to his proposed amendment a provision that the people might *introduce* slavery if they wanted to. They very well knew Chase would do no such thing, that Mr. Chase was one of the men differing from them on the broad principle of his insisting that freedom was *better* than slavery,—a man who would not consent to enact a law, penned with his own hand, by which he was made to recognize slavery on the one hand, and liberty on the other, as *precisely equal;* and when they insisted on his doing this, they very well knew they insisted on that which he would not for a moment think of doing, and that they were only bluffing him. I believe (I have not, since he made his answer, had a chance to examine the journals or *Congressional Globe* and therefore speak from memory)—I believe the state of the bill at that time, according to parliamentary rules, was such that no member could propose an additional amendment to Chase's amendment. I rather think this is the truth,—the Judge shakes his head. Very well. I would like to know, then, *if they wanted Chase's amendment fixed over, why somebody else could not have offered to do it?* If they wanted it amended, why did they not offer the amendment? Why did they not *put it in themselves?* But to put it on the other ground: suppose that there was such an amendment offered, and Chase's was an amendment to an amendment; until one is disposed of by parliamentary law, you cannot pile another on. Then all these gentlemen had to do was to vote Chase's on, and then, in the amended form in which the whole stood, add their own amendment to it, if they wanted to put it in that shape. This was all they were obliged to do, and the ayes and noes show that there were thirty-six who voted it down, against ten who voted in favor of it. The thirty-six held entire sway and control. They could in some form or other have put that bill in the exact shape they wanted. If there was a rule preventing their amending it at the time, they could pass that, and then, Chase's amendment being merged, put it in the shape they wanted. They did not choose to do so, but they went into a quibble with Chase to get him to add what they knew he would not add, and because he would not, they stand upon the flimsy pretext for voting down what they argued was the meaning and intent of their own bill. They left room thereby for this Dred Scott decision, which goes very far to make slavery national throughout the United States.

I pass one or two points I have, because my time will very soon expire; but I must be allowed to say that Judge Douglas recurs again, as he did upon one or two other occasions, to the enormity of Lincoln,—an insignificant individual like Lincoln,—upon his *ipse dixit* charging a conspiracy upon a large number of members of Congress, the Supreme Court, and two Presidents, to nationalize slavery. I want to say that, in the first place, I have made no charge of this sort upon my *ipse dixit*. I have only arrayed the evidence tending to prove it, and presented it to the understanding of others, saying what I think it proves, but giving you the means of judging whether it proves it or not. This is precisely what I have done. I have not placed it upon my *ipse dixit* at all. On this occasion, I wish to recall his attention to a piece of evidence which I brought forward at Ottawa on Saturday, showing that he had made substantially the *same charge* against substantially the *same persons,* excluding his dear self from the category. I ask him to give some attention to the evidence which I brought forward that he himself had discovered a "fatal blow being struck" against the right of the people to exclude slavery from their limits, which fatal blow he assumed as in evidence in an article in the Washington *Union,* published "by authority." I ask by whose authority? He discovers a similar or identical provision in the Lecompton Constitution. Made by whom? The framers of that Constitution. Advocated by whom? By all the members of the party in the nation, who advocated the introduction of Kansas into the Union under the Lecompton Constitution.

I have asked his attention to the evidence that he arrayed to prove that such a fatal blow was being struck, and to the facts which he brought forward in support of that charge,—being identical with the one which he thinks so villainous in me. He pointed it, not at a newspaper editor merely, but at the President and his Cabinet and the members of Congress advocating the Lecompton Constitution and those framing that instrument. I must again be permitted to remind him that although my *ipse dixit* may not be as great as his, yet it somewhat reduces the force of his calling my attention to the *enormity* of my making a like charge against him.

Go on, Judge Douglas.

Mr. Douglas's Speech

LADIES AND GENTLEMEN: The silence with which you have listened to Mr. Lincoln during his hour is creditable to this vast audience, composed of men of various political parties. Nothing is more honorable to any large mass of people assembled for the purpose of a fair discussion than that kind and respectful attention that is yielded, not only to your political friends, but to those who are opposed to you in politics.

I am glad that at last I have brought Mr. Lincoln to the conclusion that he had better define his position on certain political questions to which I called his attention at Ottawa. He there showed no disposition, no inclination, to answer them. I did not present idle questions for him to answer, merely for my gratification. I laid the foundation for those interrogatories by showing that they constituted the platform of the party whose nominee he is for the Senate. I did not presume that I had the right to catechise him as I saw proper, unless I showed that his party, or a majority of it, stood upon the platform and were in favor of the propositions upon which my questions were based. I desired simply to know, inasmuch as he had been nominated as the first, last, and only choice of his party, whether he concurred in the platform which that party had adopted for its government. In a few minutes I will proceed to review the answers which he has given to these interrogatories; but, in order to relieve his anxiety, I will first respond to these which he has presented to me. Mark you, he has not presented interrogatories which have ever received the sanction of the party with which I am acting, and hence he has no other foundation for them than his own curiosity.

First, he desires to know if the people of Kansas shall form a constitution by means entirely proper and unobjectionable, and ask admission into the Union as a State, before they have the requisite population for a member of Congress, whether I will vote for that admission. Well, now, I regret exceedingly that he did not answer that interrogatory himself before he put it to me, in order that we might understand, and not be left to infer, on which side he is. Mr. Trumbull, during the last session of

Congress, voted from the beginning to the end against the admission of Oregon, although a free State, because she had not the requisite population for a member of Congress. Mr. Trumbull would not consent, under any circumstances, to let a State, free or slave, come into the Union until it had the requisite population. As Mr. Trumbull is in the field, fighting for Mr. Lincoln, I would like to have Mr. Lincoln answer his own question, and tell me whether he is fighting Trumbull on that issue or not. But I will answer his question. In reference to Kansas, it is my opinion that as she has population enough to constitute a slave State, she has people enough for a free State. I will not make Kansas an exceptional case to the other States of the Union. I hold it to be a sound rule, of universal application, to require a Territory to contain the requisite population for a member of Congress before it is admitted as a State into the Union. I made that proposition in the Senate in 1856, and I renewed it during the last session, in a bill providing that no Territory of the United States should form a constitution and apply for admission until it had the requisite population. On another occasion I proposed that neither Kansas nor any other Territory should be admitted until it had the requisite population. Congress did not adopt any of my propositions containing this general rule, but did make an exception of Kansas. I will stand by that exception. Either Kansas must come in as a free State, with whatever population she may have, or the rule must be applied to all the other Territories alike. I therefore answer at once, that, it having been decided that Kansas has people enough for a slave State, I hold that she has enough for a free State. I hope Mr. Lincoln is satisfied with my answer; and now I would like to get his answer to his own interrogatory,—whether or not he will vote to admit Kansas before she has the requisite population. I want to know whether he will vote to admit Oregon before that Territory has the requisite population. Mr. Trumbull will not, and the same reason that commits Mr. Trumbull against the admission of Oregon commits him against Kansas, even if she should apply for admission as a free State. If there is any sincerity, any truth, in the argument of Mr. Trumbull in the Senate, against the admission of Oregon because she had not 93,420 people, although the population was larger than that of Kansas, he stands pledged against the admission of both Oregon and Kansas until they have 93,420 inhabitants. I would like Mr. Lincoln to answer this question. I would like him to take his own medicine. If he differs with Mr. Trumbull, let him answer his argument against the admission of Oregon, instead of poking questions at me.

The next question propounded to me by Mr. Lincoln is, Can the people of a Territory in any lawful way, against the wishes of any citizen of the United States, exclude slavery from their limits prior to the formation of a State constitution? I answer emphatically, as Mr. Lincoln has heard me answer a hundred times from every stump in Illinois, that in my opinion the people of a Territory can, by lawful means, exclude slavery from their limits prior to the formation of a State constitution. Mr. Lincoln knew that I had answered that question over and over again. He heard me argue the Nebraska Bill on that principle all over the State in 1854, in 1855, and in 1856, and he has no excuse for pretending to be in doubt as to my position on that question. It matters not what way the Supreme Court may hereafter decide as to the abstract question whether slavery may or may not go into a Territory under the Constitution, the people have the lawful means to introduce it or exclude it as they please, for the reason that slavery cannot exist a day or an hour anywhere, unless it is supported by local police regulations. Those police regulations can only be established by the local legislature; and if the people are opposed to slavery, they will elect representatives to that body who will by unfriendly legislation effectually prevent the introduction of it into their midst. If, on the contrary, they are for it, their legislation will favor its extension. Hence, no matter what the decision of the Supreme Court may be on that abstract question, still the right of the people to make a slave Territory or a free Territory is perfect and complete under the Nebraska Bill. I hope Mr. Lincoln deems my answer satisfactory on that point.

In this connection, I will notice the charge which he has introduced in relation to Mr. Chase's amendment. I thought that I had chased that amendment out of Mr. Lincoln's brain at

Ottawa; but it seems that it still haunts his imagination, and he is not yet satisfied. I had supposed that he would be ashamed to press that question further. He is a lawyer, and has been a member of Congress, and has occupied his time and amused you by telling you about parliamentary proceedings. He ought to have known better than to try to palm off his miserable impositions upon this intelligent audience. The Nebraska Bill provided that the legislative power and authority of the said Territory should extend to all rightful subjects of legislation consistent with the organic act and the Constitution of the United States. I did not make any exception as to slavery, but gave all the power that it was possible for Congress to give, without violating the Constitution, to the Territorial Legislature, with no exception or limitation on the subject of slavery at all. The language of that bill which I have quoted gave the full power and the full authority over the subject of slavery, affirmatively and negatively, to introduce it or exclude it, so far as the Constitution of the United States would permit. What more could Mr. Chase give by his amendment? Nothing. He offered his amendment for the identical purpose for which Mr. Lincoln is using it,—to enable demagogues in the country to try and deceive the people.

His amendment was to this effect: it provided that the Legislature should have the power to exclude slavery; and General Cass suggested, "Why not give the power to introduce as well as exclude?" The answer was, "They have the power already in the bill to do both." Chase was afraid his amendment would be adopted if he put the alternative proposition, and so made it fair both ways, but would not yield. He offered it for the purpose of having it rejected. He offered it, as he has himself avowed over and over again, simply to make capital out of it for the stump. He expected that it would be capital for small politicians in the country, and that they would make an effort to deceive the people with it; and he was not mistaken, for Lincoln is carrying out the plan admirably. Lincoln knows that the Nebraska Bill, without Chase's amendment, gave all the power which the Constitution would permit. Could Congress confer any more? Could Congress go beyond the Constitution of the country? We gave all a full grant, with no exception in regard to slavery one way or the other. We left that question as we left all others, to be decided by the people for themselves, just as they please. I will not occupy my time on this question. I have argued it before, all over Illinois. I have argued it in this beautiful city of Freeport; I have argued it in the North, the South, the East, and the West, avowing the same sentiments and the same principles. I have not been afraid to avow my sentiments up here for fear I would be trotted down into Egypt.

The third question which Mr. Lincoln presented is, if the Supreme Court of the United States shall decide that a State of this Union cannot exclude slavery from its own limits, will I submit to it? I am amazed that Lincoln should ask such a question. ["A schoolboy knows better."] Yes, a schoolboy does know better. Mr. Lincoln's object is to cast an imputation upon the Supreme Court. He knows that there never was but one man in America, claiming any degree of intelligence or decency, who ever for a moment pretended such a thing. It is true that the Washington *Union*, in an article published on the 17th of last December, did put forth that doctrine, and I denounced the article on the floor of the Senate, in a speech which Mr. Lincoln now pretends was against the President. The *Union* had claimed that slavery had a right to go into the free States, and that any provisions in the constitution or laws of the free States to the contrary were null and void. I denounced it in the Senate, as I said before, and I was the first man who did. Lincoln's friends, Trumbull, and Seward, and Hale, and Wilson, and the whole Black Republican side of the Senate, were silent. They left it to me to denounce it. And what was the reply made to me on that occasion? Mr. Toombs, of Georgia, got up and undertook to lecture me on the ground that I ought not to have deemed the article worthy of notice, and ought not to have replied to it; that there was not one man, woman, or child south of the Potomac, in any slave State, who did not repudiate any such pretension. Mr. Lincoln knows that that reply was made on the spot, and yet now he asks this question. He might as well ask me, suppose Mr. Lincoln should steal a horse, would I sanction it; and it would be as genteel in me to ask him, in the event he stole a horse, what ought to be done with him. He casts an imputation upon the

Supreme Court of the United States, by supposing that they would violate the Constitution of the United States. I tell him that such a thing is not possible. It would be an act of moral treason that no man on the bench could ever descend to. Mr. Lincoln himself would never in his partisan feelings so far forget what was right as to be guilty of such an act.

The fourth question of Mr. Lincoln is, Are you in favor of acquiring additional territory, in disregard as to how such acquisition may affect the Union on the slavery question? This question is very ingeniously and cunningly put.

The Black Republican creed lays it down expressly that under no circumstances shall we acquire any more territory, unless slavery is first prohibited in the country. I ask Mr. Lincoln whether he is in favor of that proposition. Are you [addressing Mr. Lincoln] opposed to the acquisition of any more territory, under any circumstances, unless slavery is prohibited in it? That he does not like to answer. When I ask him whether he stands up to that article in the platform of his party, he turns, Yankee-fashion, and without answering it, asks me whether I am in favor of acquiring territory without regard to how it may affect the Union on the slavery question. I answer that whenever it becomes necessary, in our growth and progress, to acquire more territory, that I am in favor of it, without reference to the question of slavery; and when we have acquired it, I will leave the people free to do as they please, either to make it slave or free territory, as they prefer. It is idle to tell me or you that we have territory enough. Our fathers supposed that we had enough when our territory extended to the Mississippi River; but a few years' growth and expansion satisfied them that we needed more, and the Louisiana territory, from the west bank of the Mississippi to the British possessions, was acquired. Then we acquired Oregon, then California and New Mexico. We have enough now for the present; but this is a young and growing nation. It swarms as often as a hive of bees; and as new swarms are turned out each year, there must be hives in which they can gather and make their honey. In less than fifteen years, if the same progress that has distinguished this country for the last fifteen years continues, every foot of vacant land between this and the Pacific Ocean, owned by the United States, will be occupied. Will you not continue to increase at the end of fifteen years as well as now? I tell you, increase, and multiply, and expand, is the law of this nation's existence. You cannot limit this great Republic by mere boundary lines, saying, "Thus far shalt thou go, and no farther." Any one of you gentlemen might as well say to a son twelve years old that he is big enough, and must not grow any larger; and in order to prevent his growth, put a hoop around him to keep him to his present size. What would be the result? Either the hoop must burst and be rent asunder, or the child must die. So it would be with this great nation. With our natural increase, growing with a rapidity unknown in any part of the globe, with the tide of emigration that is fleeing from despotism in the Old World to seek refuge in our own, there is a constant torrent pouring into this country that requires more land, more territory upon which to settle; and just as fast as our interests and our destiny require additional territory in the North, in the South, or on the islands of the ocean, I am for it; and when we acquire it, will leave the people, according to the Nebraska Bill, free to do as they please on the subject of slavery and every other question.

I trust now that Mr. Lincoln will deem himself answered on his four points. He racked his brain so much in devising these four questions that he exhausted himself, and had not strength enough to invent the others. As soon as he is able to hold a council with his advisers, Lovejoy, Farnsworth, and Fred Douglass, he will frame and propound others. ["Good, good."] You Black Republicans who say "good" I have no doubt think that they are all good men. I have reason to recollect that some people in this country think that Fred Douglass is a very good man. The last time I came here to make a speech, while talking from the stand to you, people of Freeport, as I am doing to-day, I saw a carriage—and a magnificent one it was—drive up and take a position on the outside of the crowd; a beautiful young lady was sitting on the box-seat, whilst Fred Douglass and her mother reclined inside, and the owner of the carriage acted as driver. I saw this in your own town. ["What of it?"] All I have to say of it is this, that if you, Black Republicans, think that the negro ought

to be on a social equality with your wives and daughters, and
ride in a carriage with your wife, whilst you drive the team, you
have perfect right to do so. I am told that one of Fred Douglass's
kinsmen, another rich black negro, is now travelling in this part
of the State, making speeches for his friend Lincoln as the
champion of black men. ["What have you to say against it?"] All
I have to say on that subject is, that those of you who believe
that the negro is your equal and ought to be on an equality with
you socially, politically, and legally, have a right to entertain
those opinions, and of course will vote for Mr. Lincoln.

I have a word to say on Mr. Lincoln's answers to the interrogatories contained in my speech at Ottawa, and which he has
pretended to reply to here to-day. Mr. Lincoln makes a great
parade of the fact that I quoted a platform as having been
adopted by the Black Republican party at Springfield in 1854,
which, it turns out, was adopted at another place. Mr. Lincoln
loses sight of the thing itself in his ecstasies over the mistake I
made in stating the place where it was done. He thinks that that
platform was not adopted on the right "spot."

When I put the direct questions to Mr. Lincoln to ascertain
whether he now stands pledged to that creed,—to the unconditional repeal of the Fugitive Slave law, a refusal to admit any
more slave States into the Union, even if the people want them,
a determination to apply the Wilmot Proviso, not only to all the
territory we now have, but all that we may hereafter acquire,—
he refused to answer; and his followers say, in excuse, that the
resolutions upon which I based my interrogatories were not
adopted at the *"right spot."* Lincoln and his political friends are
great on *"spots."* In Congress, as a representative of this State,
he declared the Mexican war to be unjust and infamous, and
would not support it, or acknowledge his own country to be
right in the contest, because he said that American blood was
not shed on American soil in the *"right spot."* And now he cannot answer the question I put to him at Ottawa because the resolutions I read were not adopted at the *"right spot."* It may be
possible that I was led into an error as to the *spot* on which the
resolutions I then read were proclaimed, but I was not, and am
not, in error as to the fact of their forming the basis of the creed

of the Republican party when that party was first organized. I will state to you the evidence I had, and upon which I relied for my statement that the resolutions in question were adopted at Springfield on the 5th of October, 1854. Although I was aware that such resolutions had been passed in this district, and nearly all the Northern Congressional districts and county conventions, I had not noticed whether or not they had been adopted by any State convention. In 1856, a debate arose in Congress between Major Thomas L. Harris, of the Springfield District, and Mr. Norton, of the Joliet District, on political matters connected with our State, in the course of which Major Harris quoted those resolutions as having been passed by the first Republican State Convention that ever assembled in Illinois. I knew that Major Harris was remarkable for his accuracy, that he was a very conscientious and sincere man, and I also noticed that Norton did not question the accuracy of this statement. I therefore took it for granted that it was so; and the other day when I concluded to use the resolutions at Ottawa I wrote to Charles H. Lanphier, editor of the *State Register,* at Springfield, calling his attention to them, telling him that I had been informed that Major Harris was lying sick at Springfield, and desiring him to call upon him and ascertain all the facts concerning the resolutions, the time and the place where they were adopted. In reply, Mr. Lanphier sent me two copies of his paper, which I have here. The first is a copy of the *State Register,* published at Springfield, Mr. Lincoln's own town, on the 16th of October, 1854, only eleven days after the adjournment of the Convention, from which I desire to read the following:

"During the late discussions in this city, Lincoln made a speech, to which Judge Douglas replied. In Lincoln's speech he took the broad ground that, according to the Declaration of Independence, the whites and blacks are equal. From this he drew the conclusion, which he several times repeated, that the white man had no right to pass laws for the government of the black man without the nigger's consent. This speech of Lincoln's was heard and applauded by all the Abolitionists assembled in Springfield. So soon as Mr. Lincoln was done speaking, Mr. Codding arose, and requested all the delegates to the Black Republican Convention to withdraw into the Senate chamber. They did so; and after long deliberation, they laid down the following Abolition platform as the platform on which they stood. We call the particular attention of all our readers to it."

Then follows the identical platform, word for word, which I read at Ottawa. Now, that was published in Mr. Lincoln's own town, eleven days after the Convention was held, and it has remained on record up to this day never contradicted.

When I quoted the resolutions at Ottawa and questioned Mr. Lincoln in relation to them, he said that his name was on the committee that reported them, but he did not serve, nor did he think he served, because he was, or thought he was, in Tazewell County at the time the Convention was in session. He did not deny that the resolutions were passed by the Springfield Convention. He did not know better, and evidently thought that they were; but afterward his friends declared that they had discovered that they varied in some respects from the resolutions passed by that Convention. I have shown you that I had good evidence for believing that the resolutions had been passed at Springfield. Mr. Lincoln ought to have known better; but not a word is said about his ignorance on the subject, whilst I, notwithstanding the circumstances, am accused of forgery.

Now, I will show you that if I have made a mistake as to the place where these resolutions were adopted,—and when I get down to Springfield I will investigate the matter, and see whether or not I have,—that the principles they enunciate were adopted as the Black Republican platform ["white, white"], in the various countries and Congressional districts throughout the north end of the State in 1854. This platform was adopted in nearly every county that gave a Black Republican majority for the Legislature in that year, and here is a man [pointing to Mr. Denio, who sat on the stand near Deacon Bross] who knows as well as any living man that it was the creed of the Black Republican party at that time. I would be willing to call Denio as a witness, or any other honest man belonging to that party. I will now read the resolutions adopted at the Rockford Convention on the 30th of August, 1854, which nominated

Washburne for Congress. You elected him on the following platform:

"*Resolved,* That the continued and increasing aggressions of slavery in our country are destructive of the best rights of a free people, and that such aggressions cannot be successfully resisted without the united political action of all good men.

"*Resolved,* That the citizens of the United States hold in their hands a peaceful, constitutional, and efficient remedy against the encroachments of the slave power,—the ballot box; and if that remedy is boldly and wisely applied, the principles of liberty and eternal justice will be established.

"*Resolved,* That we accept this issue forced upon us by the slave power, and, in defence of freedom, will co-operate and be known as Republicans, pledged to the accomplishment of the following purposes:

"To bring the Administration of the Government back to the control of first principles; to restore Kansas and Nebraska to the position of Free Territories; to repeal and entirely abrogate the Fugitive Slave law; to restrict slavery to those States in which it exists; to prohibit the admission of any more slave States into the Union; to exclude slavery from all the Territories over which the General Government has exclusive jurisdiction; and to resist the acquisition of any more Territories, unless the introduction of slavery therein forever shall have been prohibited.

"*Resolved,* That in furtherance of these principles we will use such constitutional and lawful means as shall seem best adapted to their accomplishment, and that we will support no man for office under the General or State Government who is not positively committed to the support of these principles, and whose personal character and conduct is not a guarantee that he is reliable, and shall abjure all party allegiance and ties.

"*Resolved,* That we cordially invite persons of all former political parties whatever, in favor of the object expressed in the above resolutions, to unite with us in carrying them into effect."

Well, you think that is a very good platform, do you not? If you do, if you approve it now, and think it is all right, you will not join with those men who say I libel you by calling these your principles, will you? Now, Mr. Lincoln complains; Mr. Lincoln charges that I did you and him injustice by saying that this was the platform of your party. I am told that Washburne made a speech in Galena last night, in which he abused me awfully for bringing to light this platform, on which he was elected to Congress. He thought that you had forgotten it, as he, and Mr. Lincoln desires to. He did not deny but that you had adopted it, and that he had subscribed to and was pledged by it, but he did not think it was fair to call it up and remind the people that it was their platform.

But I am glad to find that you are more honest in your Abolitionism than your leaders, by avowing that it is your platform, and right in your opinion.

In the adoption of that platform, you not only declared that you would resist the admission of any more slave States, and work for the repeal of the Fugitive Slave law, but you pledged yourselves not to vote for any man for State or Federal offices who was not committed to these principles. You were thus committed. Similar resolutions to those were adopted in your county convention here, and now, with your admissions that they are your platform and embody your sentiments now as they did then, what do you think of Mr. Lincoln, your candidate for the United States Senate, who is attempting to dodge the responsibility of this platform, because it was not adopted in the right spot. I thought that it was adopted in Springfield; but it turns out it was not, that it was adopted at Rockford, and in the various counties which comprise this Congressional district. When I get into the next district I will show that the same platform was adopted there, and so on through the State, until I nail the responsibility of it upon the Black Republican party throughout the State.

A Voice: "Couldn't you modify, and call it brown?"

MR. DOUGLAS: Not a bit. I thought that you were becoming a little brown when your members in Congress voted for the Crittenden-Montgomery bill; but since you have backed out from that position and gone back to Abolitionism you are black, and not brown.

Gentlemen, I have shown you what your platform was in 1854. You still adhere to it. The same platform was adopted by nearly all the counties where the Black Republican party had a majority in 1854. I wish now to call your attention to the action of your representatives in the Legislature when they assembled together at Springfield. In the first place, you must remember that this was the organization of a new party. It is so declared in the resolutions themselves, which say that you are going to dissolve all old party ties and call the new party Republican. The old Whig party was to have its throat cut from ear to ear, and the Democratic party was to be annihilated and blotted out of existence, whilst in lieu of these parties the Black Republican party was to be organized on this Abolition platform. You know who the chief leaders were in breaking up and destroying these two great parties. Lincoln on the one hand, and Trumbull on the other, being disappointed politicians, and having retired or been driven to obscurity by an outraged constituency because of their political sins, formed a scheme to Abolitionize the two parties, and lead the old-line Whigs and old-line Democrats captive, bound hand and foot, into the Abolition camp. Giddings, Chase, Fred Douglass, and Lovejoy were here to christen them whenever they were brought in. Lincoln went to work to dissolve the old-line Whig party. Clay was dead; and although the sod was not yet green on his grave, this man undertook to bring into disrepute those great Compromise measures of 1850, with which Clay and Webster were identified. Up to 1854 the old Whig party and the Democratic party had stood on a common platform so far as this slavery question was concerned. You Whigs and we Democrats differed about the bank, the tariff, distribution, the specie circular, and the sub-treasury, but we agreed on this slavery question, and the true mode of preserving the peace and harmony of the Union. The Compromise measures of 1850 were introduced by Clay, were defended by Webster, and supported by Cass, and were approved by Fillmore, and sanctioned by the national men of both parties. They constituted a common plank upon which both Whigs and Democrats stood. In 1852 the Whig party, in its last National Convention at Baltimore, indorsed and approved these measures of Clay, and so did the National Convention of the Democratic party held that same year. Thus the old-line Whigs and the old-line Democrats stood pledged to the great principle of self-government, which guarantees to the people of each Territory the right to decide the slavery question for themselves. In 1854, after death of Clay and Webster, Mr. Lincoln, on the part of the Whigs, undertook to Abolitionize the Whig party, by dissolving it, transferring the members into the Abolition camp, and making them train under Giddings, Fred Douglass, Lovejoy, Chase, Farnsworth, and other Abolition leaders. Trumbull undertook to dissolve the Democratic party by taking old Democrats into the Abolition camp. Mr. Lincoln was aided in his efforts by many leading Whigs throughout the State, your member of Congress, Mr. Washburne, being one of the most active. Trumbull was aided by many renegades from the Democratic party, among whom were John Wentworth, Tom Turner, and others, with whom you are familiar.

[Mr. TURNER, who was one of the moderators, here interposed, and said that he had drawn the resolutions which Senator Douglas had read.]

MR. DOUGLAS: Yes, and Turner says that he drew these resolutions. ["Hurrah for Turner," "Hurrah for Douglas."] That is right; give Turner cheers for drawing the resolutions if you approve them. If he drew those resolutions, he will not deny that they are the creed of the Black Republican party.

MR. TURNER: They are our creed exactly.

MR. DOUGLAS: And yet Lincoln denies that he stands on them. Mr. Turner says that the creed of the Black Republican party is the admission of no more slave States, and yet Mr. Lincoln declares that he would not like to be placed in a position where he would have to vote for them. All I have to say to friend Lincoln is, that I do not think there is much danger of his being placed in such an embarrassing position as to be obliged to vote on the admission of any more slave States. I propose, out of mere kindness, to relieve him from any such necessity.

When the bargain between Lincoln and Trumbull was completed for Abolitionizing the Whig and Democratic parties, they "spread" over the State, Lincoln still pretending to be an old-line Whig, in order to "rope in" the Whigs, and Trumbull pretending to be as good a Democrat as he ever was, in order to coax the Democrats over into the Abolition ranks. They played the part that "decoy ducks" play down on the Potomac River. In that part of the country they make artificial ducks, and put them on the water in places where the wild ducks are to be found, for the purpose of decoying them. Well, Lincoln and Trumbull played the part of these "decoy ducks," and deceived enough old-line Whigs and old-line Democrats to elect a Black Republican Legislature. When that Legislature met, the first thing it did was to elect as Speaker of the House the very man who is now boasting that he wrote the Abolition platform on which Lincoln will not stand. I want to know of Mr. Turner whether or not, when he was elected, he was a good embodiment of Republican principles?

MR. TURNER: I hope I was then, and am now.

MR. DOUGLAS: He swears that he hopes he was then, and is now. He wrote that Black Republican platform, and is satisfied with it now. I admire and acknowledge Turner's honesty. Every man of you knows that what he says about these resolutions being the platform of the Black Republican party is true, and you also know that each one of these men who are shuffling and trying to deny it are only trying to cheat the people out of their votes for the purpose of deceiving them still more after the election. I propose to trace this thing a little further, in order that you can see what additional evidence there is to fasten this revolutionary platform upon the Black Republican party. When the Legislature assembled, there was a United States Senator to elect in the place of General Shields, and before they proceeded to ballot, Lovejoy insisted on laying down certain principles by which to govern the party. It has been published to the world and satisfactorily proven that there was, at the time the alliance was made between Trumbull and Lincoln to Abolitionize the two parties, an agreement that Lincoln should take Shields's place in the United States Senate, and Trumbull should have mine so soon as they could conveniently get rid of me. When Lincoln was beaten for Shields's place, in a manner I will refer to in a few minutes, he felt very sore and restive; his friends grumbled, and some of them came out and charged that the most infamous treachery had been practiced against him; that the bargain was that Lincoln was to have had Shields's place, and

Trumbull was to have waited for mine, but that Trumbull, having the control of a few Abolitionized Democrats, he prevented them from voting for Lincoln, thus keeping him within a few votes of an election until he succeeded in forcing the party to drop him and elect Trumbull. Well, Trumbull having cheated Lincoln, his friends made a fuss, and in order to keep them and Lincoln quiet, the party were obliged to come forward, in advance, at the last State election, and make a pledge that they would go for Lincoln and nobody else. Lincoln could not be silenced in any other way.

Now, there are a great many Black Republicans of you who do not know this thing was done. ["White, white," and great clamor.] I wish to remind you that while Mr. Lincoln was speaking there was not a Democrat vulgar and blackguard enough to interrupt him. But I know that the shoe is pinching you. I am clinching Lincoln now, and you are scared to death for the result. I have seen this thing before. I have seen men make appointments for joint discussions, and the moment their man has been heard, try to interrupt and prevent a fair hearing of the other side. I have seen your mobs before, and defy your wrath. [Tremendous applause.] My friends, do not cheer, for I need my whole time. The object of the opposition is to occupy my attention in order to prevent me from giving the whole evidence and nailing this double dealing on the Black Republican party. As I have before said, Lovejoy demanded a declaration of principles on the part of the Black Republicans of the Legislature before going into an election for United States Senator. He offered the following preamble and resolutions which I hold in my hand:

"WHEREAS, Human slavery is a violation of the principles of natural and revealed rights; and whereas the fathers of the Revolution, fully imbued with the spirit of these principles, declared freedom to be the inalienable birthright of all men; and whereas the preamble to the Constitution of the United States avers that that instrument was ordained to establish justice, and secure the blessings of liberty to ourselves and our posterity; and whereas, in furtherance of the above principles, slavery was forever prohibited in the old Northwest Territory, and more recently in all that Territory lying west and north of the State of Missouri, by the act of the Federal Government; and whereas the repeal of the prohibition last referred to was contrary to the wishes of the people of Illinois, a violation of an implied compact long deemed sacred by the citizens of the United States, and a wide departure from the uniform action of the General Government in relation to the extension of slavery; therefore,

"*Resolved, by the House of Representatives, the Senate concurring therein,* That our Senators in Congress be instructed, and our Representatives requested, to introduce, if not otherwise introduced, and to vote for a bill to restore such prohibition to the aforesaid Territories, and also to extend a similar prohibition to all territory which now belongs to the United States, or which may hereafter come under their jurisdiction.

"*Resolved,* That our Senators in Congress be instructed, and our Representatives requested, to vote against the admission of any State into the Union, the Constitution of which does not prohibit slavery, whether the territory out of which such State may have been formed shall have been acquired by conquest, treaty, purchase, or from original territory of the United States.

"*Resolved,* That our Senators in Congress be instructed, and our Representatives requested, to introduce and vote for a bill to repeal an Act entitled 'An Act respecting fugitives from justice and persons escaping from the service of their masters'; and, failing in that, for such a modification of it as shall secure the right of *habeas corpus* and trial by jury before the regularly constituted authorities of the State, to all persons claimed as owing service or labor."

Those resolutions were introduced by Mr. Lovejoy immediately preceding the election of Senator. They declared, first, that the Wilmot Proviso must be applied to all territory north of 36 deg., 30 min. Secondly, that it must be applied to all territory south of 36 deg., 30 min. Thirdly, that it must be applied to all the territory now owned by the United States; and finally, that it must be applied to all territory hereafter to be acquired by the United States. The next resolution declares that no more slave States shall be admitted into this Union under any circumstances whatever, no matter whether they are formed out of territory now owned by us or that we may hereafter acquire, by treaty, by Congress, or in any manner whatever. The next resolution demands the unconditional repeal of the Fugitive Slave law, although its unconditional repeal would leave no provision for carrying out that clause of the Constitution of the United States which guarantees the surrender of fugitives. If they could not get an unconditional repeal, they demanded that that law should be so modified as to make it as nearly useless as possible. Now, I want to show you who voted for these resolutions. When the vote was taken on the first resolution it was decided in the affirmative,—yeas 41, nays 32. You will find that this is a strict party vote, between the Democrats on the one hand and the Black Republicans on the other. [Cries of "White, white," and clamor.] I know your name, and always call things by their right name. The point I wish to call your attention to is this: that these resolutions were adopted on the 7th day of February, and that on the 8th they went into an election for a United States Senator, and that day every man who voted for these resolutions, with but two exceptions, voted for Lincoln for the United States Senate. ["Give us their names."] I will read the names over to you if you want them, but I believe your object is to occupy my time.

On the next resolution the vote stood—yeas 33, nays 40; and on the third resolution—yeas 35, nays 47. I wish to impress it upon you that every man who voted for those resolutions, with but two exceptions, voted on the next day for Lincoln for United States Senator. Bear in mind that the members who thus voted for Lincoln were elected to the Legislature pledged to vote for no man for office under the State or Federal Government who was not committed to this Black Republican platform. They were all so pledged. Mr. Turner, who stands by me, and who then represented you, and who says that he wrote those resolutions, voted for Lincoln, when he was pledged not to do so unless Lincoln was in favor of those resolutions. I now ask Mr. Turner [turning to Mr. Turner], did you violate your pledge in voting for Mr. Lincoln, or did he commit himself to your platform before you cast your vote for him?

I could go through the whole list of names here, and show you that all the Black Republicans in the Legislature, who voted for Mr. Lincoln, had voted on the day previous for these resolutions. For instance, here are the names of Sargent and Little, of Jo Daviess and Carroll, Thomas J. Turner of Stephenson,

Lawrence of Boone and McHenry, Swan of Lake, Pinckney of Ogle County, and Lyman of Winnebago. Thus you see every member from your Congressional district voted for Mr. Lincoln, and they were pledged not to vote for him unless he was committed to the doctrine of no more slave States, the prohibition of slavery in the Territories, and the repeal of the Fugitive Slave law. Mr. Lincoln tells you to-day that he is not pledged to any such doctrine. Either Mr. Lincoln was then committed to those propositions, or Mr. Turner violated his pledges to you when he voted for him. Either Lincoln was pledged to each one of those propositions, or else every Black Republican Representative from this Congressional district violated his pledge of honor to his constituents by voting for him. I ask you which horn of the dilemma will you take? Will you hold Lincoln up to the platform of his party or will you accuse every Representative you had in the Legislature of violating his pledge of honor to his constituents? There is no escape for you. Either Mr. Lincoln was committed to those propositions or your members violated their faith. Take either horn of the dilemma you choose. There is no dodging the question; I want Lincoln's answer. He says he was not pledged to repeal the Fugitive Slave law, that he does not quite like to do it; he will not introduce a law to repeal it, but thinks there ought to be some law; he does not tell what it ought to be; upon the whole, he is altogether undecided, and don't know what to think or do. That is the substance of his answer upon the repeal of the Fugitive Slave law. I put the question to him distinctly, whether he indorsed that part of the Black Republican platform which calls for the entire abrogation and repeal of the Fugitive Slave law. He answers, No! that he does not indorse that; but he does not tell what he is for, or what he will vote for. His answer is, in fact, no answer at all. Why cannot he speak out, and say what he is for, and what he will do?

In regard to there being no more slave States, he is not pledged to that. He would not like, he says, to be put in a position where he would have to vote one way or another upon that question. I pray you, do not put him in a position that would embarrass him so much. Gentlemen, if he goes to the Senate, he may be put in that position, and then which way will he vote?

A Voice: "How will you vote?"

MR. DOUGLAS: I will vote for the admission of just such a State as by the form of their constitution the people show they want; if they want slavery, they shall have it; if they prohibit slavery, it shall be prohibited. They can form their institutions to please themselves, subject only to the Constitution; and I, for one, stand ready to receive them into the Union. Why cannot your Black Republican candidates talk out as plain as that when they are questioned?

I do not want to cheat any man out of his vote. No man is deceived in regard to my principles if I have the power to express myself in terms explicit enough to convey my ideas.

Mr. Lincoln made a speech when he was nominated for the United States Senate which covers all these Abolition platforms. He there lays down a proposition so broad in its Abolitionism as to cover the whole ground.

"In my opinion it [the slavery agitation] will not cease until a crisis shall have been reached and passed. 'A house divided against itself cannot stand.' I believe this government cannot endure permanently half slave and half free. I do not expect the house to fall, but I do expect it will cease to be divided. It will become all one thing or all the other. Either the opponents of slavery will arrest the further spread of it, and place it where the public mind shall rest in the belief that it is in the course of ultimate extinction, or its advocates will push it forward till it shall become alike lawful in all the States,—old as well as new, North as well as South."

There you find that Mr. Lincoln lays down the doctrine that this Union cannot endure divided as our fathers made it, with free and slave States. He says they must all become one thing, or all the other; that they must all be free or all slave, or else the Union cannot continue to exist; it being his opinion that to admit any more slave States, to continue to divide the Union into free and slave States, will dissolve it. I want to know of Mr. Lincoln whether he will vote for the admission of another slave State.

He tells you the Union cannot exist unless the States are all free or all slave; he tells you that he is opposed to making them all slave, and hence he is for making them all free, in order that the Union may exist; and yet he will not say that he will not vote against another slave State, knowing that the Union must be dissolved if he votes for it. I ask you if that is fair dealing? The true intent and inevitable conclusion to be drawn from his first Springfield speech is, that he is opposed to the admission of any more slave States under any circumstances. If he is so opposed, why not say so? If he believes this Union cannot endure divided into free and slave States, that they must all become free in order to save the Union, he is bound as an honest man to vote against any more slave States. If he believes it, he is bound to do it. Show me that it is my duty, in order to save the Union, to do a particular act, and I will do it if the Constitution does not prohibit it. I am not for the dissolution of the Union under any circumstances. I will pursue no course of conduct that will give just cause for the dissolution of the Union. The hope of the friends of freedom throughout the world rests upon the perpetuity of this Union. The downtrodden and oppressed people who are suffering under European despotism all look with hope and anxiety to the American Union as the only resting place and permanent home of freedom and self-government.

Mr. Lincoln says that he believes that this Union cannot continue to endure with slave States in it, and yet he will not tell you distinctly whether he will vote for or against the admission of any more slave States, but says he would not like to be put to the test. I do not think he will be put to the test. I do not think that the people of Illinois desire a man to represent them who would not like to be put to the test on the performance of a high constitutional duty. I will retire in shame from the Senate of the United States when I am not willing to be put to the test in the performance of my duty. I have been put to severe tests. I have stood by my principles in fair weather and in foul, in the sunshine and in the rain. I have defended the great principle of self-government here among you when Northern sentiment ran in a torrent against me, and I have defended that same great principle when Southern sentiment came down like an avalanche upon me. I was not afraid of any test they put to me. I knew I was right; I knew my principles were sound; I knew that the people would see in the end that I had done right, and I knew that the God of heaven would smile upon me if I was faithful in the performance of my duty.

Mr. Lincoln makes a charge of corruption against the Supreme Court of the United States, and two presidents of the United States, and attempts to bolster it up by saying that I did the same against the Washington *Union*. Suppose I did make that charge of corruption against the Washington *Union,* when it was true, does that justify him in making a false charge against me and others? That is the question I would put. He says that at the time the Nebraska Bill was introduced, and before it was passed, there was a conspiracy between the judges of the Supreme Court, President Pierce, President Buchanan, and myself, by that bill and the decision of the court to break down the barrier and establish slavery all over the Union. Does he not know that that charge is historically false as against President Buchanan? He knows that Mr. Buchanan was at that time in England, representing this country with distinguished ability at the Court of St. James, that he was there for a long time before and did not return for a year or more after. He knows that to be true, and that fact proves his charge to be false as against Mr. Buchanan. Then, again, I wish to call his attention to the fact that at the time the Nebraska Bill was passed the Dred Scott case was not before the Supreme Court at all; it was not upon the docket of the Supreme Court; it had not been brought there; and the judges in all probability knew nothing of it. Thus the history of the country proves the charge to be false as against them. As to President Pierce, his high character as a man of integrity and honor is enough to vindicate him from such a charge; and as to myself, I pronounce the charge an infamous lie, whenever and wherever made and by whomsoever made. I am willing that Mr. Lincoln should go and rake up every public act of mine, every measure I have introduced, report I have made, speech delivered, and criticise them; but when he charges upon me a corrupt conspiracy for the purpose of perverting the institutions of the country, I brand it as it deserves. I say the history of the country proves it to be false, and that it could not have been possible at the time. But now he tries to protect himself in this charge, because I made a charge against the Washington *Union*. My speech in the Senate against the Washington *Union* was made because it advocated a revolutionary doctrine, by declaring that the free States had not the right to prohibit slavery within their own limits. Because I made that charge against the Washington *Union*, Mr. Lincoln says it was a charge against Mr. Buchanan. Suppose it was: is Mr. Lincoln the peculiar defender of Mr. Buchanan? Is he so interested in the Federal Administration, and so bound to it, that he must jump to the rescue and defend it from every attack that I may make against it? I understand the whole thing. The Washington *Union*, under that most corrupt of all men, Cornelius Wendell, is advocating Mr. Lincoln's claim to the Senate. Wendell was the printer of the last Black Republican House of Representatives; he was a candidate before the present Democratic House, but was ignominiously kicked out; and then he took the money which he had made out of the public printing by means of the Black Republicans, bought the Washington *Union*, and is now publishing it in the name of the Democratic party, and advocating Mr. Lincoln's election to the Senate. Mr. Lincoln therefore considers an attack upon Wendell and his corrupt gang as a personal attack upon him. This only proves what I have charged,— that there is an alliance between Lincoln and his supporters and the Federal office-holders of this State, and the Presidential aspirants out of it, to break me down at home.

Mr. Lincoln feels bound to come in to the rescue of the Washington *Union*. In that speech which I delivered in answer to the Washington *Union*, I made it distinctly against the *Union*, and against the *Union* alone. I did not choose to go beyond that. If I have reason to attack the President's conduct, I will do it in language that will not be misunderstood. When I differed with the President, I spoke out so that you all heard me. That question passed away; it resulted in the triumph of my principle, by allowing the people to do as they please; and there is an end of the controversy, whenever the great principle of self-government,—the right of the people to make their own Constitution, and come into the Union with slavery or without it, as they see proper,—shall again arise, you will find me standing firm in defence of that principle, and fighting whoever fights it. If Mr. Buchanan stands, as I doubt not he will, by the recommendation contained in his message, that hereafter all State constitutions ought to be submitted to the people before the admission of the State into the Union, he will find me standing by him firmly, shoulder to shoulder, in carrying it out. I know Mr. Lincoln's object: he wants to divide the Democratic party, in order that he may defeat me and get to the Senate.

[Mr. DOUGLAS's time here expired, and he stopped on the moment.]

Mr. Lincoln's Rejoinder

MY FRIENDS: It will readily occur to you that I cannot, in half an hour, notice all the things that so able a man as Judge Douglas can say in an hour and a half; and I hope, therefore, if there be anything that he has said upon which you would like to hear something from me, but which I omit to comment upon, you will bear in mind that it would be expecting an impossibility for me to go over his whole ground. I can but take up some of the points that he has dwelt upon, and employ my half-hour specially on them.

The first thing I have to say to you is a word in regard to Judge Douglas's declaration about the "vulgarity and blackguardism" in the audience,—that no such thing, as he says, was shown by any Democrat while I was speaking. Now, I only wish, by way of reply on this subject, to say that while I was speaking, I used no "vulgarity or blackguardism" toward any Democrat.

Now, my friends, I come to all this long portion of the Judge's speech,—perhaps half of it,—which he has devoted to the various resolutions and platforms that have been adopted in the different counties in the different Congressional districts, and in the Illinois Legislature, which he supposes are at variance with the positions I have assumed before you to-day. It is true that many of these resolutions are at variance with the positions I have here assumed. All I have to ask is that we talk reasonably and rationally about it. I happen to know, the Judge's opinion to the contrary notwithstanding, that I have never tried to conceal my opinions, nor tried to deceive any one in reference to them. He may go and examine all the members who voted for me for United States Senator in 1855, after the election of 1854. They were pledged to certain things here at home, and were determined to have pledges from me; and if he will find any of these persons who will tell him anything inconsistent with what I say now, I will resign, or rather retire from the race, and give him no more trouble. The plain truth is this: At the introduction of the Nebraska policy, we believed there was a new era being introduced in the history of the Republic, which tended to the spread and perpetuation of slavery. But in our opposition to that measure we did not agree with one another in everything. The people in the north end of the State were for stronger measures of opposition than we of the central and southern portions of the State, but we were all opposed to the Nebraska doctrine. We had that one feeling and that one sentiment in common. You at the north end met in your conventions and passed your resolutions. We in the middle of the State and farther south did not hold such conventions and pass the same resolutions, although we had in general a common view and a common sentiment. So that these meetings which the Judge has alluded to, and the resolutions he has read from, were local, and did not spread over the whole State. We at last met together in 1856, from all parts of the State, and we agreed upon a common platform. You, who held more extreme notions, either yielded those notions, or, if not wholly yielding them, agreed to yield them practically, for the sake of embodying the opposition to the measures which the opposite party were pushing forward at that time. We met you then, and if there was anything yielded, it was for practical purposes. We agreed then upon a platform for the party throughout the entire State of Illinois, and now we are all bound, as a party, *to that platform.* And I say here to you, if any one expects of me—in case of my election—that I will do anything not signified by our Republican platform and my answers here to-day, I tell you very frankly that person will be deceived. I do not ask for the vote of any one who supposes that I have secret purposes or pledges that I dare not speak out. Cannot the Judge be satisfied? If he fears, in the unfortunate case of my election, that my going to Washington will enable me to advocate sentiments contrary to those which I expressed when you voted for and elected me, I assure him that his fears are wholly needless and groundless. Is the Judge really afraid of any such thing? I'll tell you what he is afraid of. *He is afraid we'll all pull together.* This is what alarms him more than anything else. For my part, I do hope that all of us, entertaining a common sentiment in opposition to what appears to us a design to nationalize and perpetuate slavery, will waive minor differences on questions which either belong to the dead past or the distant future, and all pull together in this struggle. What are your sentiments? If it be true that on the ground which I occupy—ground which I occupy as frankly and boldly as Judge Douglas does his,—my views, though partly coinciding with yours, are not as perfectly in accordance with your feelings as his are, I do say to you in all candor, go for him, and not for me. I hope to deal in all things fairly with Judge Douglas, and with the people of the State, in this contest. And if I should never be elected to any office, I trust I may go down with no stain of falsehood upon my reputation, notwithstanding the hard opinions Judge Douglas chooses to entertain of me.

The Judge has again addressed himself to the Abolition tendencies of a speech of mine made at Springfield in June last. I have so often tried to answer what he is always saying on that melancholy theme that I almost turn with disgust from the discussion,—from the repetition of an answer to it. I trust that nearly all of this intelligent audience have read that speech. If you have, I may venture to leave it to you to inspect it closely, and see whether it contains any of those "bugaboos" which frighten Judge Douglas.

The Judge complains that I did not fully answer his questions. If I have the sense to comprehend and answer those questions, I have done so fairly. If it can be pointed out to me how I can more fully and fairly answer him, I aver I have not the sense to see how it is to be done. He says I do not declare I would in any event vote for the admission of a slave State into the Union. If I have been fairly reported, he will see that I did give an explicit answer to his interrogatories; I did not merely say that I would dislike to be put to the test, but I said clearly, if I were put to the test, and a Territory from which slavery had been excluded should present herself with a State constitution sanctioning slavery,—a most extraordinary thing, and wholly unlikely to happen,—I did not see how I could avoid voting for her admission. But he refuses to understand that I said so, and he wants this audience to understand that I did not say so. Yet it will be so reported in the printed speech that he cannot help seeing it.

He says if I should vote for the admission of a slave State I would be voting for a dissolution of the Union, because I hold that the Union cannot permanently exist half slave and half free. I repeat that I do not believe this government *can* endure permanently half slave and half free; yet I do not admit, nor does it at all follow, that the admission of a single slave State will permanently fix the character and establish this as a universal slave nation. The Judge is very happy indeed at working up these quibbles. Before leaving the subject of answering questions, I aver as my confident belief, when you come to see our speeches in print, that you will find every question which he has asked me more fairly and boldly and fully answered than he has answered those which I put to him. Is not that so? The two speeches may be placed side by side, and I will venture to leave it to impartial judges whether his questions have not been more directly and circumstantially answered than mine.

Judge Douglas says he made a charge upon the editor of the Washington *Union, alone,* of entertaining a purpose to rob the States of their power to exclude slavery from their limits. I undertake to say, and I make the direct issue, that he did *not* make his charge against the editor of the *Union* alone. I will undertake to prove by the record here that he made that charge against more and higher dignitaries than the editor of the Washington *Union.* I am quite aware that he was shirking and dodging around the form in which he put it, but I can make it manifest that he levelled his "fatal blow" against more persons than this Washington editor. Will he dodge it now by alleging that I am trying to defend Mr. Buchanan against the charge? Not at all. Am I not making the same charge myself? I am trying to show that you, Judge Douglas, are a witness on my side. I am not defending Buchanan, and I will tell Judge Douglas that in my opinion, when he made that charge, he had an eye farther north than he has to-day. He was then fighting against people who called *him* a Black Republican and an Abolitionist. It is mixed all through his speech, and it is tolerably manifest that his eye was a great deal farther north than it is to-day. The Judge says that though he made this charge, Toombs got up and declared there was not a man in the United States, except the editor of the *Union,* who was in favor of the doctrines put forth in that article. And thereupon I understand that the Judge withdrew the charge. Although he had taken extracts from the newspaper, and then from the Lecompton Constitution, to show the existence of a conspiracy to bring about a "fatal blow," by which the States were to be deprived of the right of excluding slavery, it all went to pot as soon as Toombs got up and told him it was not true. It reminds me of the story that John Phoenix, the California railroad surveyor, tells. He says they started out from the Plaza to the Mission of Dolores. They had two ways of determining distances. One was by a chain and pins taken over the ground. The other was by a "go-it-ometer,"—an invention of his own,—a three-legged instrument, with which he computed a series of triangles between the points. At night he turned to the chain-man to ascertain what distance they had come, and found that by some mistake he had merely dragged the chain over the ground, without keeping any record. By the "go-it-ometer," he found he had made ten miles. Being skeptical about this, he asked a drayman who was passing how far it was to the Plaza. The drayman replied it was just half a mile; and the surveyor put it down in his book,—just as Judge Douglas says, after he had made his calculations and computations, he took Toombs's statement. I have no doubt that after Judge Douglas had made his charge, he was as easily satisfied about its truth as the surveyor was of the drayman's statement of the distance to the Plaza. Yet it is a fact that the man who put forth all that matter which Douglas deemed a "fatal blow" at State sovereignty was elected by the Democrats as public printer.

Now, gentlemen, you may take Judge Douglas's speech of March 22, 1858, beginning about the middle of page 21, and reading to the bottom of page 24, and you will find the evidence on which I say that he did not make his charge against the editor of the *Union* alone. I cannot stop to read it, but I will give it to the reporters. Judge Douglas said:

"Mr. President, you here find several distinct propositions advanced boldly by the Washington *Union* editorially, and apparently *authoritatively,* and every man who questions any of them is denounced as an Abolitionist, a Free-soiler, a fanatic. The propositions are, first, that the primary object of all government at its original institution is the protection of persons and property; second, that the Constitution of the United States declares that the citizens of each State shall be entitled to all the privileges and immunities of citizens in the several States; and that, therefore, thirdly, all State laws, whether organic or otherwise, which prohibit the citizens of one State from settling in another with their slave property, and especially declaring it forfeited, are direct violations of the original intention of the Government and Constitution of the United States; and, fourth, that the emancipation of the slaves of the Northern States was a gross outrage on the rights of property, inasmuch as it was involuntarily done on the part of the owner.

"Remember that this article was published in the *Union* on the 17th of November, and on the 18th appeared the first article giving the adhesion of the *Union* to the Lecompton Constitution. It was in these words:

"'Kansas and Her Constitution.—The vexed question is settled. The problem is solved. The dead point of danger is passed. All serious trouble to Kansas affairs is over and gone—'

"And a column, nearly, of the same sort. Then, when you come to look into the Lecompton Constitution, you find the same doctrine incorporated in it which was put forth editorially in the *Union*. What is it?

"'Article 7, *Section* 1. The right of property is before and higher than any constitutional sanction; and the right of the owner of a slave to such slave and its increase is the same and as invariable as the right of the owner of any property whatever.'

"Then in the schedule is a provision that the Constitution may be amended after 1864 by a two-thirds vote.

"'But no alteration shall be made to affect the right of property in the ownership of slaves.'

"It will be seen by these clauses in the Lecompton Constitution that they are identical in spirit with this *authoritative* article in the Washington *Union* of the day previous to its indorsement of this Constitution.

"When I saw that article in the *Union* of the 17th of November, followed by the glorification of the Lecompton Constitution on the 18th of November, and this clause in the Constitution asserting the doctrine that a State has no right to prohibit slavery within its limits, I saw that there was a *fatal blow* being struck at the sovereignty of the States of this Union."

Here he says, "Mr. President, you here find several distinct propositions advanced boldly, and apparently *authoritatively.*" By whose authority, Judge Douglas? Again, he says in another place, "It will be seen by these clauses in the Lecompton Constitution that they are identical in spirit with this *authoritative* article." *By whose authority?* Who do you mean to say authorized the publication of these articles? He knows that the Washington *Union* is considered the organ of the Administration. *I* demand of Judge Douglas *by whose authority* he meant to say those articles were published, if not by the authority of the President of the United States and his Cabinet? I defy him to show whom he referred to, if not to these high functionaries in the Federal Government. More than this, he says the articles in that paper and the provisions of the Lecompton Constitution are "identical," and, being identical, he argues that the authors are co-operating and conspiring together. He does not use the word "conspiring," but what other construction can you put upon it? He winds up with this:

"When I saw that article in the *Union* of the 17th of November, followed by the glorification of the Lecompton Constitution on the 18th of November, and this clause in the Constitution asserting the doctrine that a State has no right to prohibit slavery within its limits, I saw that there was a *fatal blow* being struck at the sovereignty of the States of the Union."

I ask him if all this fuss was made over the editor of this newspaper. It would be a terribly "*fatal blow*" indeed which a single man could strike, when no President, no Cabinet officer, no member of Congress, was giving strength and efficiency to the movement. Out of respect to Judge Douglas's good sense I must believe he didn't manufacture his idea of the "fatal" character of that blow out of such a miserable scapegrace as he represents that editor to be. But the Judge's eye is farther south now. Then, it was very peculiarly and decidedly north. His hope rested on the idea of visiting the great "Black Republican" party, and making it the tail of his new kite. He knows he was then expecting from day to day to turn Republican, and place himself at the head of our organization. He has found that these despised "Black Republicans" estimate him by a standard which he has taught them none too well. Hence he is crawling back into his old camp, and you will find him eventually installed in full fellowship among those whom he was then battling, and with whom he now pretends to be at such fearful variance. [Loud applause, and cries of "Go on, go on."] I cannot, gentlemen; my time has expired.

Third Joint Debate
JONESBORO, SEPTEMBER 15, 1858

Mr. Douglas's Speech

LADIES AND GENTLEMEN: I appear before you to-day in pursuance of a previous notice, and have made arrangements with Mr. Lincoln to divide time, and discuss with him the leading political topics that now agitate the country.

Prior to 1854 this country was divided into two great political parties known as Whig and Democratic. These parties differed from each other on certain questions which were then deemed to be important to the best interests of the Republic. Whigs and Democrats differed about a bank, the tariff, distribution, the specie circular and the sub-treasury. On those issues we went before the country and discussed the principles, objects, and measures of the two great parties. Each of the parties could proclaim its principles in Louisiana as well as in Massachusetts, in Kentucky as well as in Illinois. Since that period, a great revolution has taken place in the formation of parties, by which they now seem to be divided by a geographical line, a large party in the North being arrayed under the Abolition or Republican banner, in hostility to the Southern States, Southern people, and Southern institutions. It becomes important for us to inquire how this transformation of parties has occurred, made from those of national principles to geographical factions. You remember that in 1850 this country was agitated from its centre to its circumference about this slavery question. It became necessary for the leaders of the great Whig party and the leaders of the great Democratic party to postpone, for the time being, their particular disputes, and unite first to save the Union before they should quarrel as to the mode in which it was to be governed. During the Congress of 1849–'50, Henry Clay was the leader of the Union men, supported by Cass and Webster, and the leaders of the Democracy and the leaders of the Whigs, in opposition to Northern Abolitionists or Southern Disunionists. That great contest of 1850 resulted in the establishment of the Compromise measures of that year, which measures rested on the great principles that the people of each State and each Territory of this Union ought to be permitted to regulate their own domestic institutions in their own way, subject to no other limitation than that which the Federal Constitution imposes.

I now wish to ask you whether that principle was right or wrong which guaranteed to every State and every community the right to form and regulate their domestic institutions to suit themselves. These measures were adopted, as I have previously said, by the joint action of the Union Whigs and Union Democrats in opposition to Northern Abolitionists and Southern Disunionists. In 1858, when the Whig party assembled, at Baltimore, in National Convention for the last time, they adopted the principle of the Compromise measures of 1850 as their rule of party action in the future. One month thereafter the Democrats assembled at the same place to nominate a candidate for the presidency, and declared the same great principle as the rule of action by which the Democracy would be governed. The Presidential election of 1852 was fought on that basis. It is true that the Whigs claimed special merit for the adoption of those measures, because they asserted that their great Clay originated them, their godlike Webster defended them, and their Fillmore signed the bill making them the law of the land; but, on the other hand, the Democrats claimed special credit for the Democracy, upon the ground that we gave twice as many votes in both Houses of Congress for the passage of these measures as the Whig party.

Thus you see that in the Presidential election of 1852 the Whigs were pledged by their platform and their candidate to the principle of the Compromise measures of 1850, and the

Democracy were likewise pledged by our principles, our platform, and our candidate to the same line of policy, to preserve
peace and quiet between the different sections of this Union.
Since that period the Whig party has been transformed into a
sectional party, under the name of the Republican party, whilst
the Democratic party continues the same national party it was
at that day. All sectional men, all men of Abolition sentiments
and principles, no matter whether they were old Abolitionists or
had been Whigs or Democrats, rally under the sectional
Republican banner, and consequently all national men, all
Union-loving men, whether Whigs, Democrats, or by whatever
name they have been known, ought to rally under the Stars and
Stripes in defence of the Constitution as our fathers made it,
and of the Union as it has existed under the Constitution.

How has this departure from the faith of the Democracy and
the faith of the Whig party been accomplished? In 1854, certain
restless, ambitious, and disappointed politicians throughout the
land took advantage of the temporary excitement created by the
Nebraska Bill to try and dissolve the old Whig party and the old
Democratic party, to Abolitionize their members, and lead
them, bound hand and foot, captives into the Abolition camp. In
the State of New York a convention was held by some of these
men, and a platform adopted, every plank of which was as black
as night, each one relating to the negro, and not one referring to
the interests of the white man. That example was followed
throughout the Northern States, the effort being made to combine all the free States in hostile array against the slave States.
The men who thus thought that they could build up a great sectional party, and through its organization control the political
destinies of this country, based all their hopes on the single fact
that the North was the stronger division of the nation, and
hence, if the North could be combined against the South, a sure
victory awaited their efforts. I am doing no more than justice to
the truth of history when I say that in this State, Abraham
Lincoln, on behalf of the Whigs, and Lyman Trumbull, on
behalf of the Democrats, were the leaders who undertook to
perform this grand scheme of Abolitionizing the two parties to
which they belonged. They had a private arrangement as to

what should be the political destiny of each of the contracting parties before they went into the operation. The arrangement was that Mr. Lincoln was to take the old-line Whigs with him, claiming that he was still as good a Whig as ever, over to the Abolitionists, and Mr. Trumbull was to run for Congress in the Belleville District, and, claiming to be a good Democrat, coax the old Democrats into the Abolition camp; and when, by the joint efforts of the Abolitionized Whigs, the Abolitionized Democrats, and the old-line Abolition and Free-soil party of this State, they should secure a majority in the Legislature, Lincoln was then to be made United States Senator in Shields's place, Trumbull remaining in Congress until I should be accommodating enough to die or resign, and give him a chance to follow Lincoln. That was a very nice little bargain so far as Lincoln and Trumbull were concerned, if it had been carried out in good faith and friend Lincoln had attained to senatorial dignity according to the contract. They went into the contest in every part of the State, calling upon all disappointed politicians to join in the crusade against the Democracy, and appealed to the prevailing sentiments and prejudices in all the northern counties of the State. In three Congressional districts in the north end of the State they adopted, as the platform of this new party thus formed by Lincoln and Trumbull in connection with the Abolitionists, all of those principles which aimed at a warfare on the part of the North against the South. They declared in that platform that the Wilmot Proviso was to be applied to all the Territories of the United States, north as well as south of 36 deg. 30 min., and not only to all the territory we then had, but all that we might hereafter acquire; that hereafter no more slave States should be admitted into this Union, even if the people of such State desired slavery; that the Fugitive Slave law should be absolutely and unconditionally repealed; that slavery should be abolished in the District of Columbia; that the slave trade should be abolished between the different States; and, in fact, every article in their creed related to this slavery question, and pointed to a Northern geographical party in hostility to the Southern States of this Union. Such were their principles in northern Illinois. A little farther south they became bleached, and grew paler just in proportion as public sentiment moderated and changed in this direction. They were Republicans or Abolitionists in the north, anti-Nebraska men down about Springfield, and in this neighborhood they contented themselves with talking about the inexpediency of the repeal of the Missouri Compromise. In the extreme northern counties they brought out men to canvass the State whose complexion suited their political creed; and hence Fred Douglass, the negro, was to be found there, following General Cass, and attempting to speak on behalf of Lincoln, Trumbull, and Abolitionism, against that illustrious senator. Why, they brought Fred Douglass to Freeport, when I was addressing a meeting there, in a carriage driven by the white owner, the negro sitting inside with the white lady and her daughter. When I got through canvassing the northern counties that year, and progressed as far south as Springfield, I was met and opposed in discussion by Lincoln, Lovejoy, Trumbull, and Sidney Breese, who were on one side. Father Giddings, the high-priest of Abolitionism, had just been there, and Chase came about the time I left. ["Why didn't you shoot him?"] I did take a running shot at them; but as I was single-handed against the white, black, and mixed drove, I had to use a shotgun and fire into the crowd, instead of taking them off singly with a rifle. Trumbull had for his lieutenants, in aiding him to Abolitionize the Democracy, such men as John Wentworth of Chicago, Governor Reynolds of Belleville, Sidney Breese of Carlisle, and John Dougherty of Union, each of whom modified his opinions to suit the locality he was in. Dougherty, for instance, would not go much further than to talk about the inexpediency of the Nebraska Bill, whilst his allies at Chicago advocated negro citizenship and negro equality, putting the white man and the negro on the same basis under the law. Now, these men, four years ago, were engaged in a conspiracy to break down the Democracy; to-day they are again acting together for the same purpose! They do not hoist the same flag, they do not own the same principles or profess the same faith, but conceal their union for the sake of policy. In the northern counties, you find that all the conventions are called in the name of the Black Republican party; at Springfield, they dare not call a Republican convention, but invite all the enemies of the Democracy to unite; and when they get down into Egypt, Trumbull issues notices calling upon the *"Free Democracy"* to assemble and hear him speak. I have one of the handbills calling a Trumbull meeting at Waterloo the other day, which I received there, which is in the following language:

"A meeting of the Free Democracy will take place in Waterloo, on Monday, Sept. 13th inst., whereat Hon. Lyman Trumbull, Hon. John Baker and others will address the people upon the different political topics of the day. Members of all parties are cordially invited to be present, and hear and determine for themselves.
"THE MONROE FREE DEMOCRACY."

What is that name of "Free Democrats" put forth for, unless to deceive the people, and make them believe that Trumbull and his followers are not the same party as that which raises the black flag of Abolitionism in the northern part of this State and makes war upon the Democratic party throughout the State? When I put that question to them at Waterloo on Saturday last, one of them rose and stated that they had changed their name for political effect, in order to get votes. There was a candid admission. Their object in changing their party organization and principles in different localities was avowed to be an attempt to cheat and deceive some portion of the people until after the election. Why cannot a political party that is conscious of the rectitude of its purposes and the soundness of its principles declare them everywhere alike? I would disdain to hold any political principles that I could not avow in the same terms in Kentucky that I declared in Illinois, in Charleston as well as in Chicago, in New Orleans as well as in New York. So long as we live under a Constitution common to all the States, our political faith ought to be as broad, as liberal, and just as that Constitution itself, and should be proclaimed alike in every portion of the Union.

But it is apparent that our opponents find it necessary, for partisan effect, to change their colors in different counties in order to catch the popular breeze, and hope with these discordant materials combined together to secure a majority in the

Legislature for the purpose of putting down the Democratic party. This combination did succeed in 1854 so far as to elect a majority of their confederates to the Legislature, and the first important act which they performed was to elect a Senator in the place of the eminent and gallant Senator Shields. His term expired in the United States Senate at that time, and he had to be crushed by the Abolition coalition for the simple reason that he would not join in their conspiracy to wage war against one half of the Union. That was the only objection to General Shields. He had served the people of his State with ability in the Legislature, he had served you with fidelity and ability as Auditor, he had performed his duties to the satisfaction of the whole country at the head of the Land Department at Washington, he had covered the State and the Union with immortal glory on the bloody fields of Mexico in defence of the honor of our flag, and yet he had to be stricken down by this unholy combination. And for what cause? Merely because he would not join a combination of one half of the States to make war upon the other half, after having poured out his heart's blood for all the States of the Union. Trumbull was put in his place by Abolitionism. How did Trumbull get there? Before the Abolitionists would consent to go into an election for United States Senator they required all the members of this new combination to show their hands upon this question of Abolitionism. Lovejoy, one of their high-priests, brought in resolutions defining the Abolition creed, and required them to commit themselves on it by their votes,—yea or nay. In that creed, as laid down by Lovejoy, they declared, first, that the Wilmot Proviso must be put on all the Territories of the United States, north as well as south of 36 deg. 30 min., and that no more territory should ever be acquired unless slavery was at first prohibited therein; second, that no more States should ever be received into the Union unless slavery was first prohibited, by constitutional provision, in such States; third, that the Fugitive Slave law must be immediately repealed, or, failing in that, then such amendments were to be made to it as would render it useless and inefficient for the objects for which it was passed, etc. The next day after these resolutions were offered they were voted upon, part of them carried, and the others defeated, the same men who voted for them, with only two exceptions, voting soon after for Abraham Lincoln as their candidate for the United States Senate. He came within one or two votes of being elected, but he could not quite get the number required, for the simple reason that his friend Trumbull, who was a party to the bargain by which Lincoln was to take Shields's place, controlled a few Abolitionized Democrats in the Legislature, and would not allow them all to vote for him, thus wronging Lincoln by permitting him on each ballot to be almost elected, but not quite, until he forced them to drop Lincoln and elect him (Trumbull), in order to unite the party. Thus you find that although the Legislature was carried that year by the bargain between Trumbull, Lincoln, and the Abolitionists, and the union of these discordant elements in one harmonious party, yet Trumbull violated his pledge, and played a Yankee trick on Lincoln when they came to divide the spoils. Perhaps you would like a little evidence on this point. If you would, I will call Colonel James H. Matheny, of Springfield, to the stand, Mr. Lincoln's especial confidential friend for the last twenty years, and see what he will say upon the subject of this bargain. Matheny is now the Black Republican, or Abolition, candidate for Congress in the Springfield District against the gallant Colonel Harris, and is making speeches all over that part of the State against me and in favor of Lincoln, in concert with Trumbull. He ought to be a good witness, and I will read an extract from a speech which he made in 1856, when he was mad because his friend Lincoln had been cheated. It is one of numerous speeches of the same tenor that were made about that time, exposing this bargain between Lincoln, Trumbull, and the Abolitionists. Matheny then said:

"The Whigs, Abolitionists, Know-Nothings, and renegade Democrats made a solemn compact for the purpose of carrying this State against the Democracy, on this plan: 1st. That they would all combine and elect Mr. Trumbull to Congress, and thereby carry his district for the Legislature, in order to throw all the strength that could be obtained into that body against the Democrats. 2d. That when the Legislature should meet, the officers of that body, such as Speaker, clerks, door-keepers, etc., would be given to the Abolitionists; and 3d. That the Whigs were to have the United States Senator. That, accordingly, in good faith, Trumbull was elected to Congress, and his district carried for the Legislature, and, when it convened, the Abolitionists got all the officers of that body; and, thus far, the 'bond' was fairly executed. The Whigs, on their part, demanded the election of Abraham Lincoln to the United States Senate, that the bond might be fulfilled, the other parties to the contract having already secured to themselves all that was called for. But, in the most perfidious manner, they refused to elect Mr. Lincoln, and the mean, low-lived, sneaking Trumbull succeeded, by pledging all that was required by any party, in thrusting Lincoln aside, and foisting himself, an excrescence from the rotten bowels of the Democracy, into the United States Senate: and thus it has ever been, that an *honest* man makes a bad bargain when he conspires or contracts with rogues."

Matheny thought that his friend Lincoln made a bad bargain when he conspired and contracted with such rogues as Trumbull and his Abolition associates in that campaign. Lincoln was shoved off the track, and he and his friends all at once began to mope, became sour and mad, and disposed to tell, but dare not; and thus they stood for a long time, until the Abolitionists coaxed and flattered him back by their assurances that he should certainly be a Senator in Douglas's place. In that way the Abolitionists have been enabled to hold Lincoln to the alliance up to this time, and now they have brought him into a fight against me, and he is to see if he is again to be cheated by them. Lincoln, this time, though, required more of them than a promise, and holds their bond, if not security, that Lovejoy shall not cheat him as Trumbull did.

When the Republican Convention assembled at Springfield, in June last, for the purpose of nominating State officers only, the Abolitionists could not get Lincoln and his friends into it until they would pledge themselves that Lincoln should be their candidate for the Senate; and you will find, in proof of this, that that Convention passed a resolution unanimously declaring that Abraham Lincoln was the "first, last, and only choice" of the Republicans for United States Senator. He was not willing to have it understood that he was merely their first choice, or their last choice, but their *only* choice. The Black Republican party had nobody else. Browning was nowhere; Governor Bissell was of no account; Archie Williams was not to be taken into consideration; John Wentworth was not worth mentioning; John M. Palmer was degraded; and their party presented the extraordinary spectacle of having but one,—the first, the last, and only— choice for the Senate. Suppose that Lincoln should die, what a horrible condition the Republican party would be in! They would have nobody left. They have no other choice, and it was necessary for them to put themselves before the world in this ludicrous, ridiculous attitude of having no other choice, in order to quiet Lincoln's suspicions, and assure him that he was not to be cheated by Lovejoy, and the trickery by which Trumbull outgeneralled him. Well, gentlemen, I think they will have a nice time of it before they get through. I do not intend to give them any chance to cheat Lincoln at all this time. I intend to relieve him of all anxiety upon that subject, and spare them the mortification of more exposures of contracts violated, and the pledged honor of rogues forfeited.

But I wish to invite your attention to the chief points at issue between Mr. Lincoln and myself in this discussion. Mr. Lincoln, knowing that he was to be the candidate of his party, on account of the arrangement of which I have already spoken, knowing that he was to receive the nomination of the Convention for the United States Senate, had his speech, accepting that nomination, all written and committed to memory ready to be delivered the moment the nomination was announced. Accordingly, when it was made, he was in readiness, and delivered his speech, a portion of which I will read in order that I may state his political principles fairly, by repeating them in his own language:

"We are now far into the fifth year since a policy was instituted for the avowed object, and with the confident promise, of putting an end to slavery agitation; under the operation of that policy, that agitation has not only not ceased, but has constantly augmented. I believe it will not cease until a crisis shall have been reached and passed. 'A house divided against itself cannot stand.' I believe this government cannot endure permanently, half slave and half free. I do not expect the Union to be dissolved, I do not expect the house to fall; but I do expect it will cease to be divided. It will become all one thing or all the other. Either the opponents of slavery will arrest the spread of it, and place it where the public mind shall rest in the belief that it is in the course of ultimate extinction, or its advocates will push it forward until it shall become alike lawful in all the States, North as well as South."

There you have Mr. Lincoln's first and main proposition, upon which he bases his claims, stated in his own language. He tells you that this Republic cannot endure permanently divided into slave and free States, as our fathers made it. He says that they must all become free or all become slave, that they must all be one thing or all be the other, or this government cannot last. Why can it not last, if we will execute the government in the same spirit and upon the same principles upon which it is founded? Lincoln, by his proposition, says to the South: "If you desire to maintain your institutions as they are now, you must not be satisfied with minding your own business, but you must invade Illinois and all the other Northern States, establish slavery in them, and make it universal"; and in the same language he says to the North: "You must not be content with regulating your own affairs and minding your own business, but if you desire to maintain your freedom, you must invade the Southern States, abolish slavery there and everywhere, in order to have the States all one thing or all the other." I say that this is the inevitable and irresistible result of Mr. Lincoln's argument, inviting a warfare between the North and the South, to be carried on with ruthless vengeance until the one section or the other shall be driven to the wall, and become the victim of the rapacity of the other. What good would follow such a system of warfare? Suppose the North should succeed in conquering the South, how much would she be the gainer? or suppose the South should conquer the North, could the Union be preserved in that way? Is this sectional warfare to be waged between the Northern States and Southern States until they all shall become uniform in their local and domestic institutions, merely because Mr. Lincoln says that a house divided against itself cannot stand, and pretends that this Scriptural quotation, this language of our Lord and Master, is applicable to the American Union and the

American Constitution? Washington and his compeers, in the convention that framed the Constitution, made this government divided into free and slave States. It was composed then of thirteen sovereign and independent States, each having sovereign authority over its local and domestic institutions, and all bound together by the Federal Constitution. Mr. Lincoln likens that bond of the Federal Constitution, joining free and slave States together, to a house divided against itself, and says that it is contrary to the law of God, and cannot stand. When did he learn, and by what authority does he proclaim, that this Government is contrary to the law of God and cannot stand? It has stood thus divided into free and slave States from its organization up to this day. During that period we have increased from four millions to thirty millions of people; we have extended our territory from the Mississippi to the Pacific Ocean; we have acquired the Floridas and Texas, and other territory sufficient to double our geographical extent; we have increased in population, in wealth, and in power beyond any example on earth; we have risen from a weak and feeble power to become the terror and admiration of the civilized world; and all this has been done under a Constitution which Mr. Lincoln, in substance, says is in violation of the law of God, and under a Union divided into free and slave States, which Mr. Lincoln thinks, because of such division, cannot stand. Surely Mr. Lincoln is a wiser man than those who framed the Government. Washington did not believe, nor did his compatriots, that the local laws and domestic institutions that were well adapted to the Green Mountains of Vermont were suited to the rice plantations of South Carolina; they did not believe at that day that in a republic so broad and expanded as this, containing such a variety of climate, soil, and interest, that uniformity in the local laws and domestic institutions was either desirable or possible. They believed then, as our experience has proved to us now, that each locality, having different interests, a different climate, and different surroundings, required different local laws, local policy, and local institutions, adapted to the wants of that locality. Thus our government was formed on the principle of diversity in the local institutions and laws, and not on that of uniformity.

As my time flies, I can only glance at these points, and not present them as fully as I would wish, because I desire to bring all the points in controversy between the two parties before you, in order to have Mr. Lincoln's reply. He makes war on the decision of the Supreme Court in the case known as the Dred Scott case. I wish to say to you, fellow-citizens, that I have no war to make on that decision, or any other ever rendered by the Supreme Court. I am content to take that decision as it stands delivered by the highest judicial tribunal on earth,—a tribunal established by the Constitution of the United States for that purpose; and hence that decision becomes the law of the land, binding on you, on me, and on every other good citizen, whether we like it or not. Hence I do not choose to go into an argument to prove before this audience whether or not Chief Justice Taney understood the law better than Abraham Lincoln.

Mr. Lincoln objects to that decision, first and mainly, because it deprives the negro of the rights of citizenship. I am as much opposed to his reason for that objection as I am to the objection itself. I hold that a negro is not and never ought to be a citizen of the United States. I hold that this government was made on the white basis, by white men, for the benefit of white men and their posterity forever, and should be administered by white men and none others. I do not believe that the Almighty made the negro capable of self-government. I am aware that all the Abolition lecturers that you find travelling about through the country are in the habit of reading the Declaration of Independence to prove that all men were created equal, and endowed by their Creator with certain inalienable rights, among which are life, liberty, and the pursuit of happiness. Mr. Lincoln is very much in the habit of following in the track of Lovejoy in this particular, by reading that part of the Declaration of Independence to prove that the negro was endowed by the Almighty with the inalienable right of equality with white men. Now, I say to you, my fellow-citizens, that in my opinion the signers of the Declaration had no reference to the negro whatever when they declared all men to be created equal. They desired to express by that phrase white men, men of European birth and European descent, and had no reference either to the negro, the savage Indians, the Fejee, the Malay, or any other inferior and degraded race, when they spoke of the equality of men. One great evidence that such was their understanding is to be found in the fact that at that time every one of the thirteen colonies was a slaveholding colony, every signer of the Declaration represented a slaveholding constituency, and we know that not one of them emancipated his slaves, much less offered citizenship to them, when they signed the Declaration; and yet, if they intended to declare that the negro was the equal of the white man, and entitled by divine right to an equality with him, they were bound, as honest men, that day and hour to have put their negroes on an equality with themselves. Instead of doing so, with uplifted eyes to heaven they implored the divine blessing upon them, during the seven years' bloody war they had to fight to maintain that Declaration, never dreaming that they were violating divine law by still holding the negroes in bondage and depriving them of equality.

My friends, I am in favor of preserving this government as our fathers made it. It does not follow by any means that because a negro is not your equal or mine, that hence he must necessarily be a slave. On the contrary, it does follow that we ought to extend to the negro every right, every privilege, every immunity, which he is capable of enjoying, consistent with the good of society. When you ask me what these rights are, what their nature and extent is, I tell you that that is a question which each State of this Union must decide for itself. Illinois has already decided the question. We have decided that the negro must not be a slave within our limits; but we have also decided that the negro shall not be citizen within our limits; that he shall not vote, hold office, or exercise any political rights. I maintain that Illinois, as a sovereign State, has a right thus to fix her policy with reference to the relation between the white man and the negro; but while we had that right to decide the question for ourselves, we must recognize the same right in Kentucky and in every other State to make the same decision, or a different one. Having decided our own policy with reference to the black race, we must leave Kentucky and Missouri and every other State perfectly free to make just such a decision as they see proper on that question.

Kentucky has decided that question for herself. She has said that within her limits a negro shall not exercise any political rights, and she also said that a portion of the negroes under the laws of that State shall be slaves. She had as much right to adopt that as her policy as we had to adopt the contrary for our policy. New York has decided that in that State a negro may vote if he has $250 worth of property, and if he owns that much he may vote upon an equality with the white man. I, for one, am utterly opposed to negro suffrage anywhere and under any circumstances; yet, inasmuch as the Supreme Court have decided in the celebrated Dred Scott case that a State has a right to confer the privilege of voting upon free negroes, I am not going to make war upon New York because she has adopted a policy repugnant to my feelings. But New York must mind her own business, and keep her negro suffrage to herself, and not attempt to force it upon us.

In the State of Maine they have decided that a negro may vote and hold office on an equality with a white man. I had occasion to say to the senators from Maine, in a discussion, last session, that if they thought that the white people within the limits of their State were no better than negroes, I would not quarrel with them for it, but they must not say that my white constituents of Illinois were no better than negroes, or we would be sure to quarrel.

The Dred Scott decision covers the whole question, and declares that each State has the right to settle this question of suffrage for itself, and all questions as to the relations between the white man and the negro. Judge Taney expressly lays down the doctrine. I receive it as law, and I say that while those States are adopting regulations on that subject disgusting and abhorrent, according to my views, I will not make war on them if they will mind their own business and let us alone.

I now come back to the question, Why cannot this Union exist forever, divided into free and slave States, as our fathers made it? It can thus exist if each State will carry out the principles upon which our institutions were founded; to wit, the right of each State to do as it pleases, without meddling with its neighbors. Just act upon that great principle, and this Union will not only live forever, but it will extend and expand until it covers the whole continent, and makes this confederacy one grand, ocean-bound Republic. We must bear in mind that we are yet a young nation, growing with a rapidity unequalled in the history of the world, that our natural increase is great, and that the emigration from the Old World is increasing, requiring us to expand and acquire new territory from time to time, in order to give our people land to live upon. If we live upon the principle of State rights and State sovereignty, each State regulating its own affairs and minding its own business, we can go on and extend indefinitely, just as fast and as far as we need the territory. The time may come, indeed has now come, when our interests would be advanced by the acquisition of the island of Cuba. When we get Cuba we must take it as we find it, leaving the people to decide the question of slavery for themselves, without interference on the part of the Federal Government or of any State of this Union. So, when it becomes necessary to acquire any portion of Mexico or Canada, or of this continent or the adjoining islands, we must take them as we find them, leaving the people free to do as they please,—to have slavery or not, as they choose. I never have inquired and never will inquire whether a new State applying for admission has slavery or not for one of her institutions. If the constitution that is presented be the act and deed of the people, and embodies their will, and they have the requisite population, I will admit them, with slavery or without it, just as that people shall determine. My objection to the Lecompton Constitution did not consist in the fact that it made Kansas a slave State. I would have been as much opposed to its admission under such a constitution as a free State as I was opposed to its admission under it as a slave State. I hold that that was a question which the people had a right to decide for themselves, and that no power on earth ought to have interfered with that decision. In my opinion, the Lecompton Constitution was not the act and deed of the people of Kansas, and did not embody their will; and the recent election in that Territory, at which it was voted down by nearly ten to one, shows conclusively that I was right in saying, when the Constitution was presented, that it was not the act and deed of the people, and did not embody their will.

If we wish to preserve our institutions in their purity, and transmit them unimpaired to our latest posterity, we must preserve with religious good faith that great principle of self-government which guarantees to each and every State, old and new, the right to make just such constitutions as they desire, and come into the Union with their own constitution, and not one palmed upon them. Whenever you sanction the doctrine that Congress may crowd a constitution down the throats of an unwilling people, against their consent, you will subvert the great fundamental principle upon which all our free institutions rest. In the future I have no fear that the attempt will ever be made. President Buchanan declared in his annual message that hereafter the rule adopted in the Minnesota case, requiring a constitution to be submitted to the people, should be followed in all future cases; and if he stands by that recommendation, there will be no division in the Democratic party on that principle in the future. Hence, the great mission of the Democracy is to unite the fraternal feeling of the whole country, restore peace and quiet, by teaching each State to mind its own business, and regulate its own domestic affairs, and all to unite in carrying out the constitution as our fathers made it, and thus to preserve the Union and render it perpetual in all time to come. Why should we not act as our fathers who made the government? There was no sectional strife in Washington's army. They were all brethren of a common confederacy; they fought under a common flag that they might bestow upon their posterity a common destiny; and to this end they poured out their blood in common streams, and shared, in some instances, a common grave.

Mr. Lincoln's Reply

LADIES AND GENTLEMEN: There is very much in the principles that Judge Douglas has here enunciated that I most cordially approve, and over which I shall have no controversy with him. In so far as he has insisted that all the States have the right to do exactly as they please about all their domestic relations, including that of slavery, I agree entirely with him. He places me wrong in spite of all I can tell him, though I repeat it again and again, insisting that I have no difference with him upon this subject. I have made a great many speeches, some of which have been printed, and it will be utterly impossible for him to find anything that I have ever put in print contrary to what I now say upon this subject. I hold myself under constitutional obligations to allow the people in all the States, without interference, direct or indirect, to do exactly as they please; and I deny that I have any inclination to interfere with them, even if there were no such constitutional obligation. I can only say again that I am placed improperly—altogether improperly, in spite of all I can say—when it is insisted that I entertain any other view or purposes in regard to that matter.

While I am upon this subject, I will make some answers briefly to certain propositions that Judge Douglas has put. He says, "Why can't this Union endure permanently half slave and half free?" I have said that I supposed it could not, and I will try, before this new audience, to give briefly some of the reasons for entertaining that opinion. Another form of his question is, "Why can't we let it stand as our fathers placed it?" That is the exact difficulty between us. I say that Judge Douglas and his friends have changed it from the position in which our fathers originally placed it. I say, in the way our father's originally left the slavery question, the institution was in the course of ultimate extinction, and the public mind rested in the belief that it *was* in the course of ultimate extinction. I say when this government was first established it was the policy of its founders to prohibit the spread of slavery into the new Territories of the United States, where it had not existed. But Judge Douglas and his friends have broken up that policy, and placed it upon a new basis, by which it is to become national and perpetual. All I have asked or desired anywhere is that it should be placed back again upon the basis that the fathers of our government originally placed it upon. I have no doubt that it *would* become extinct, for all time to come, if we but readopted the policy of the fathers, by restricting it to the limits it has already covered,—restricting it from the new Territories.

I do not wish to dwell at great length on this branch of the subject at this time, but allow me to repeat one thing that I have stated before. Brooks—the man who assaulted Senator Sumner on the floor of the Senate, and who was complimented with dinners, and silver pitchers, and gold-headed canes, and a good many other things for that feat—in one of his speeches declared that when this government was originally established, nobody expected that the institution of slavery would last until this day. That was but the opinion of one man, but it was such an opinion as we can never get from Judge Douglas or anybody in favor of slavery, in the North, at all. You *can* sometimes get it from a Southern man. He said at the same time that the framers of our government did not have the knowledge that experience has taught us; that experience and the invention of the cotton-gin have taught us that the perpetuation of slavery is a necessity. He insisted, therefore, upon its being changed from the basis upon which the fathers of the government left it to the basis of its perpetuation and nationalization.

I insist that this is the difference between Judge Douglas and myself,—that Judge Douglas is helping that change along. I insist upon this government being placed where our fathers originally placed it.

I remember Judge Douglas once said that he saw the evidences on the statute books of Congress of a policy in the origin of government to divide slavery and freedom by a geographical line; that he saw an indisposition to maintain that policy, and therefore he set about studying up a way to settle the institution on the right basis,—the basis which he thought it ought to have been placed upon at first; and in that speech he confesses that he seeks to place it, not upon the basis that the fathers placed it upon, but upon one gotten up on "original principles." When he asks me why we cannot get along with it in the attitude where our fathers placed it, he had better clear up the evidences that he has himself changed it from that basis, that he has himself been chiefly instrumental in changing the policy of the fathers. Any one who will read his speech of the 22d of last March will see that he there makes an open confession, showing that he set about fixing the institution upon an altogether different set of principles. I think I have fully answered him when he asks me why we cannot let it alone upon the basis where our fathers left it, by showing that he has himself changed the whole policy of the government in that regard.

Now, fellow-citizens, in regard to this matter about a contract that was made between Judge Trumbull and myself, and all that long portion of Judge Douglas's speech on this subject,—I wish simply to say what I have said to him before, that he cannot know whether it is true or not, and I *do know* that there is not a word of truth in it. And I have told him so before. I don't want any harsh language indulged in, but I do not know how to deal with this persistent insisting on a story that I know to be utterly without truth. It used to be a fashion amongst men that when a charge was made, some sort of proof was brought forward to establish it, and if no proof was found to exist, the charge was dropped. I don't know how to meet this kind of an argument. I don't want to have a fight with Judge Douglas, and I have no way of making an argument up into the consistency of a corn-cob and stopping his mouth with it. All I can do is, good-humoredly to say that, from the beginning to the end of all that story about a bargain between Judge Trumbull and myself, *there is not a word of truth in it*. I can only ask him to show some sort of evidence of the truth of his story. He brings forward here and reads from what he contends is a speech by James H. Matheny, charging such a bargain between Trumbull and myself. My own opinion is that Matheny did do some such immoral thing as to tell a story that he knew nothing about. I believe he did. I contradicted it instantly, and it has been contradicted by Judge Trumbull, while nobody has produced any proof, because there is none. Now, whether the speech which the Judge brings forward here is really the one Matheny made, I do not know, and I hope the Judge will pardon me for doubting the genuineness of this document, since his production of those Springfield resolutions at Ottawa. I do not wish to dwell at any great length upon this matter. I can say nothing when a long story like this is told, except it is not true, and demand that he who insists upon it shall produce some proof. That is all any man can do, and I leave it in that way, for I know of no other way of dealing with it.

The Judge has gone over a long account of the old Whig and Democratic parties, and it connects itself with this charge against Trumbull and myself. He says that they agreed upon a compromise in regard to the slavery question in 1850; that in a National Democratic Convention resolutions were passed to abide by that compromise as a finality upon the slavery question. He also says that the Whig party in National Convention agreed to abide by and regard as a finality the Compromise of 1850. I understand the Judge to be altogether right about that; I understand that part of the history of the country as stated by him to be correct. I recollect that I, as a member of that party, acquiesced in that compromise. I recollect in the Presidential election which followed, when we had General Scott up for the presidency, Judge Douglas was around berating us Whigs as Abolitionists, precisely as he does to-day,—not a bit of difference. I have often heard him. We could do nothing when the old Whig party was alive that was not Abolitionism, but it has got an extremely good name since it has passed away.

When that Compromise was made it did not repeal the old Missouri Compromise. It left a region of United States territory half as large as the present territory of the United States, north of the line of 36 degrees 30 minutes, in which slavery was prohibited by Act of Congress. This Compromise did not repeal that one. It did not affect or propose to repeal it. But at last it became Judge Douglas's duty, as he thought (and I find no fault with him), as Chairman of the Committee on Territories, to bring in a bill for the organization of a territorial government,—first of one, then of two Territories north of that line. When he did so, it ended in his inserting a provision substantially repealing the Missouri Compromise. That was because the Compromise of 1850 *had not* repealed it. And now I ask why he could not have let that Compromise alone? We were quiet from the agitation of the slavery question. We were making no fuss about it. All had acquiesced in the Compromise measures of 1850. We never had been seriously disturbed by any Abolition agitation before that period. When he came to form governments for the Territories north of the line of 36 degrees 30 minutes, why could he not have let that matter stand as it was

standing? Was it necessary to the organization of a Territory? Not at all. Iowa lay north of the line, and had been organized as a Territory and come into the Union as a State without disturbing that Compromise. There was no sort of necessity for destroying it to organize these Territories. But, gentlemen, it would take up all my time to meet all the little quibbling arguments of Judge Douglas to show that the Missouri Compromise was repealed by the Compromise of 1850. My own opinion is, that a careful investigation of all the arguments to sustain the position that that Compromise was virtually repealed by the Compromise of 1850 would show that they are the merest fallacies. I have the report that Judge Douglas first brought into Congress at the time of the introduction of the Nebraska Bill, which in its original form *did not* repeal the Missouri Compromise, and he there expressly stated that he had forborne to do so *because it had not been done by the Compromise of* 1850. I close this part of the discussion on my part by asking him the question again, "Why, when we had peace under the Missouri Compromise, could you not have let it alone?"

In complaining of what I said in my speech at Springfield, in which he says I accepted my nomination for the senatorship (where, by the way, he is at fault, for if he will examine it, he will find no acceptance in it), he again quotes that portion in which I said that "a house divided against itself cannot stand." Let me say a word in regard to that matter.

He tries to persuade us that there must be a variety in the different institutions of the States of the Union; that that variety necessarily proceeds from the variety of soil, climate, of the face of the country, and the difference in the natural features of the States. I agree to all that. Have these very matters ever produced any difficulty amongst us? Not at all. Have we ever had any quarrel over the fact that they have laws in Louisiana designed to regulate the commerce that springs from the production of sugar? Or because we have a different class relative to the production of flour in this State? Have they produced any differences? Not at all. They are the very cements of this Union. They don't make the house a house divided against itself. They are the props that hold up the house and sustain the Union.

But has it been so with this element of slavery? Have we not always had quarrels and difficulties over it? And when will we cease to have quarrels over it? Like causes produce like effects. It is worth while to observe that we have generally had comparative peace upon the slavery question, and that there has been no cause for alarm until it was excited by the effort to spread it into new territory. Whenever it has been limited to its present bounds, and there has been no effort to spread it, there has been peace. All the trouble and convulsion has proceeded from efforts to spread it over more territory. It was thus at the date of the Missouri Compromise. It was so again with the annexation of Texas; so with the territory acquired by the Mexican war; and it is so now. Whenever there has been an effort to spread it, there has been agitation and resistance. Now, I appeal to this audience (very few of whom are my political friends), as national men, whether we have reason to expect that the agitation in regard to this subject will cease while the causes that tend to reproduce agitation are actively at work? Will not the same cause that produced agitation in 1820, when the Missouri Compromise was formed, that which produced the agitation upon the annexation of Texas, and at other times, work out the same results always? Do you think that the nature of man will be changed, that the same causes that produced agitation at one time will not have the same effect at another?

This has been the result so far as my observation of the slavery question and my reading in history extends. What right have we then to hope that the trouble will cease,—that the agitation will come to an end,—until it shall either be placed back where it originally stood, and where the fathers originally placed it, or, on the other hand, until it shall entirely master all opposition? This is the view I entertain, and this is the reason why I entertained it, as Judge Douglas has read from my Springfield speech.

Now, my friends, there is one other thing that I feel myself under some sort of obligation to mention. Judge Douglas has here to-day—in a very rambling way, I was about saying—spoken of the platforms for which he seeks to hold me responsible. He says, "Why can't you come out and make an open avowal of principles in all places alike?" and he reads from an advertisement that he says was used to notify the people of a speech to be made by Judge Trumbull at Waterloo. In commenting on it he desires to know whether we cannot speak frankly and manfully, as he and his friends do. How, I ask, do his friends speak out their own sentiments? A Convention of his party in this State met on the 21st of April at Springfield, and passed a set of resolutions which they proclaim to the country as their platform. This does constitute their platform, and it is because Judge Douglas claims it is his platform—that these are his principles and purposes—that he has a right to declare he speaks his sentiments "frankly and manfully." On the 9th of June Colonel John Dougherty, Governor Reynolds, and others, calling themselves National Democrats, met in Springfield and adopted a set of resolutions which are as easily understood, as plain and as definite in stating to the country and to the world what they believed in and would stand upon, as Judge Douglas's platform Now, what is the reason that Judge Douglas is not willing that Colonel Dougherty and Governor Reynolds should stand upon their own written and printed platform as well as he upon his? Why must he look farther than their platform when he claims himself to stand by his platform?

Again, in reference to our platform: On the 16th of June the Republicans had their Convention and published their platform, which is as clear and distinct as Judge Douglas's. In it they spoke their principles as plainly and as definitely to the world. What is the reason that Judge Douglas is not willing I should stand upon that platform? Why must he go around hunting for some one who is supporting me or has supported me at some time in his life, and who has said something at some time contrary to that platform? Does the Judge regard that rule as a good one? If it turn out that the rule is a good one for me—that I am responsible for any and every opinion that any man has expressed who is my friend,—then it is a good rule for him. I ask, is it not as good a rule for him as it is for me? In my opinion, it is not a good rule for either of us. Do you think differently, Judge?

MR. DOUGLAS: I do not.]

MR. LINCOLN: Judge Douglas says he does not think differently. I am glad of it. Then can he tell me why he is looking up resolutions of five or six years ago, and insisting that they were my platform, notwithstanding my protest that they are not, and never were my platform, and my pointing out the platform of the State Convention which he delights to say nominated me for the Senate? I cannot see what he means by parading these resolutions, if it is not to hold me responsible for them in some way. If he says to me here that he does not hold the rule to be good, one way or the other, I do not comprehend how he could answer me more fully if he answered me at greater length. I will therefore put in as my answer to the resolutions that he has hunted up against me, what I, as a lawyer, would call a good plea to a bad declaration. I understand that it is a maxim of law that a poor plea may be a good plea to a bad declaration. I think that the opinions the Judge brings from those who support me, yet differ from me, is a bad declaration against me; but if I can bring the same things against him, I am putting in a good plea to that kind of declaration, and now I propose to try it.

At Freeport, Judge Douglas occupied a large part of his time in producing resolutions and documents of various sorts, as I understood, to make me somehow responsible for them; and I propose now doing a little of the same sort of thing for him. In 1850 a very clever gentleman by the name of Thompson Campbell, a personal friend of Judge Douglas and myself, a political friend of Judge Douglas and opponent of mine, was a candidate for Congress in the Galena District. He was interrogated as to his views on this same slavery question. I have here before me the interrogatories, and Campbell's answers to them. I will read them:

INTERROGATORIES.

"1st. Will you, if elected, vote for and cordially support a bill prohibiting slavery in the Territories of the United States?

"2d. Will you vote for and support a bill abolishing slavery in the District of Columbia?

"3d. Will you oppose the admission of any slave States which may be formed out of Texas or the Territories?

"4th. Will you vote for and advocate the repeal of the Fugitive Slave law passed at the recent session of Congress?

"5th. Will you advocate and vote for the election of a Speaker of the House of Representatives who shall be willing to organize the committees of that House so as to give the free States their just influence in the business of legislation?

"6th. What are your views, not only as to the constitutional right of Congress to prohibit the slave-trade between the States, but also as to the expediency of exercising that right immediately?"

CAMPBELL'S REPLY.

"To the first and second interrogatories, I answer unequivocally in the affirmative.

"To the third interrogatory I reply, that I am opposed to the admission of any more slave States into the Union, that may be formed out of Texas or any other Territory.

"To the fourth and fifth interrogatories I unhesitatingly answer in the affirmative.

"To the sixth interrogatory I reply, that so long as the slave States continue to treat slaves as articles of commerce, the Constitution confers power on Congress to pass laws regulating that peculiar COMMERCE, and that the protection of Human Rights imperatively demands the interposition of every constitutional means to prevent this most inhuman and iniquitous traffic.

"T. CAMPBELL."

I want to say here that Thompson Campbell was elected to Congress on that platform, as the Democratic candidate in the Galena District, against Martin P. Sweet.

JUDGE DOUGLAS: Give me the date of the letter.

MR. LINCOLN: The time Campbell ran was in 1850. I have not the exact date here. It was some time in 1850 that these interrogatories were put and the answer given. Campbell was elected to Congress, and served out his term. I think a second election came up before he served out his term, and he was not re-elected. Whether defeated or not nominated, I do not know. [Mr. Campbell was nominated for re-election by the Democratic party, by acclamation.] At the end of his term his very good friend Judge Douglas got him a high office from President Pierce, and sent him off to California. Is not that the fact? Just at the end of his term in Congress it appears that our mutual friend Judge Douglas got our mutual friend Campbell a good office, and sent him to California upon it. And not only so, but on the 27th of last month, when Judge Douglas and myself spoke at Freeport in joint discussion, there was his same friend Campbell, come all the way from California, to help the Judge beat me; and there was poor Martin P. Sweet standing on the platform, trying to help poor me to be elected. That is true of one of Judge Douglas's friends.

So again, in that same race of 1850, there was a Congressional Convention assembled at Joliet, and it nominated R. S. Molony for Congress, and unanimously adopted the following resolution:

"*Resolved,* That we are uncompromisingly opposed to the extension of slavery; and while we would not make such opposition a ground of interference with the interests of the States where it exists, yet we moderately but firmly insist that it is the duty of Congress to oppose its extension into Territory now free, by all means compatible with the obligations of the Constitution, and with good faith to our sister States; that these principles were recognized by the Ordinance of 1787, which received the sanction of Thomas Jefferson, who is acknowledged by all to be the great oracle and expounder of our faith."

Subsequently the same interrogatories were propounded to Dr. Molony which had been addressed to Campbell as above, with the exception of the 6th, respecting the interstate slave trade, to which Dr. Molony, the Democratic nominee for Congress, replied as follows:

"I received the written interrogatories this day, and, as you will see by the La Salle *Democrat* and Ottawa *Free Trader,* I took at Peru on the 5th, and at Ottawa on the 7th, the affirmative side of interrogatories 1st and 2d; and in relation to the admission of any more slave States from Free Territory, my position taken at these meetings, as correctly reported in said papers, was *emphatically* and *distinctly* opposed to it. In relation to the admission of any more slave States from Texas, whether I shall go against it or not will depend upon the opinion that I may hereafter form of the true meaning and nature of the resolutions of annexation. If, by said resolutions, the honor and good faith of the nation is pledged to admit more slave States from Texas when she (Texas) may apply for the admission of such State, then I should, if in Congress, vote for their admission. But if not so

PLEDGED and bound by sacred contract, then a bill for the admission of more slave States from Texas would *never* receive my vote.

"To your fourth interrogatory I answer *most decidedly* in the affirmative, and for reasons set forth in my reported remarks at Ottawa last Monday.

"To your fifth interrogatory I also reply in the affirmative *most cordially,* and that I will use my utmost exertions to secure the nomination and election of a man who will accomplish the objects of said interrogatories. I most cordially approve of the resolutions adopted at the Union meeting held at Princeton on the 27th September ult.

"Yours, etc.,   R. S. MOLONY."

All I have to say in regard to Dr. Molony is that he was the regularly nominated Democratic candidate for Congress in his district; was elected at that time; at the end of his term was appointed to a land-office at Danville. (I never heard anything of Judge Douglas's instrumentality in this.) He held this office a considerable time, and when we were at Freeport the other day there were handbills scattered about notifying the public that after our debate was over R. S. Molony would make a Democratic speech in favor of Judge Douglas. That is all I know of my own personal knowledge. It is added here to this resolution, and truly I believe, that—

"Among those who participated in the Joliet Convention, and who supported its nominee, with his platform as laid down in the resolution of the Convention and in his reply as above given, we call at random the following names, all of which are recognized at this day as leading Democrats:

"Cook County,—E. B. Williams, Charles McDonell, Arno Voss, Thomas Hoyne, Isaac Cook."

I reckon we ought to except Cook.

"F. C. Sherman.

"Will,—Joel A. Matteson, S. W. Bowen.

"Kane,—B. F. Hall, G. W. Renwick, A. M. Herrington, Elijah Wilcox.

"McHenry,—W. M. Jackson, Enos W. Smith, Neil Donnelly.

"La Salle,—John Hise, William Reddick."

William Reddick! another one of Judge Douglas's friends that stood on the stand with him at Ottawa, at the time the Judge says my knees trembled so that I had to be carried away. The names are all here:

"Du Page,—Nathan Allen.
"De Kalb,—Z. B. Mayo."

Here is another set of resolutions which I think are apposite to the matter in hand.

On the 28th of February of the same year a Democratic District Convention was held at Naperville to nominate a candidate for Circuit Judge. Among the delegates were Bowen and Kelly of Will; Captain Naper, H. H. Cody, Nathan Allen, of Du Page; W. M. Jackson, J. M. Strode, P. W. Platt, and Enos W. Smith of McHenry; J. Horsman and others of Winnebago. Colonel Strode presided over the Convention. The following resolutions were unanimously adopted,—the first on motion of P. W. Platt, the second on motion of William M. Jackson:

"*Resolved,* That this Convention is in favor of the Wilmot Proviso, both in *Principle* and *Practice,* and that we know of no good reason why any *person* should oppose the largest latitude in *Free Soil, Free Territory* and *Free Speech.*

"*Resolved,* That in the opinion of this Convention, the time has arrived when *all men should be free,* whites as well as others."

JUDGE DOUGLAS: What is the date of those resolutions?

MR. LINCOLN: I understand it was in 1850, but I do not *know* it. I do not state a thing and say I know it, when I do not. But I have the highest belief that this is so. I know of no way to arrive at the conclusion that there is an error in it. I mean to put a case no stronger than the truth will allow. But what I was going to comment upon is an extract from a newspaper in De Kalb County; and it strikes me as being rather singular, I confess, under the circumstances. There is a Judge Mayo in that county, who is a candidate for the Legislature, for the purpose, if he secures his election, of helping to re-elect Judge Douglas. He is the editor of a newspaper [De Kalb County *Sentinel*], and in that paper I find the extract I am going to read. It is part of an editorial article in which he was electioneering as fiercely as he could for Judge Douglas and against me. It was a curious thing, I think, to be in such a paper. I will agree to that, and the Judge may make the most of it:

> "Our education has been such that we have been rather *in favor of the equality of the blacks; that is, that they should enjoy all the privileges of the whites where they reside.* We are aware that this is not a very popular doctrine. We have had many a confab with some who are now strong 'Republicans,' we taking the broad ground of equality, and they the opposite ground.
>
> "We were brought up in a State where blacks were voters, and we do not know of any inconvenience resulting from it, though perhaps it would not work as well where the blacks are more numerous. We have no doubt of the right of the whites to guard against such an evil, if it is one. Our opinion is that it would be best for all concerned to have the colored population in a State by themselves [in this I agree with him]; but if within the jurisdiction of the United States, *we say by all means they should have the right to have their Senators and Representatives in Congress, and to vote for President.* With us 'worth makes the man, and want of it the fellow.' We have seen many a 'nigger' that we thought more of than some white men."

That is one of Judge Douglas's friends. Now, I do not want to leave myself in an attitude where I can be misrepresented, so I will say I do not think the Judge is responsible for this article; but he is quite as responsible for it as I would be if one of my friends had said it. I think that is fair enough.

I have here also a set of resolutions passed by a Democratic State Convention in Judge Douglas's own good State of Vermont, that I think ought to be good for him too:

> "*Resolved,* That liberty is a right inherent and inalienable in man, and that herein *all men are equal.*
>
> "*Resolved,* That we claim no authority in the Federal Government to abolish slavery in the several States, but we do claim for it Constitutional power perpetually to prohibit the introduction of slavery into territory now free, and abolish it wherever, under the jurisdiction of Congress, it exists.
>
> "*Resolved,* That this power ought immediately to be exercised in prohibiting the introduction and existence of slavery in New Mexico and California, in abolishing slavery and the slave-trade in the District

of Columbia, on the high seas, and wherever else, under the Constitution, it can be reached.

"*Resolved,* That no more slave States should be admitted into the Federal Union.

"*Resolved,* That the Government ought to return to its ancient policy, not to extend, nationalize, or encourage, but to limit, localize, and discourage slavery."

At Freeport I answered several interrogatories that had been propounded to me by Judge Douglas at the Ottawa meeting. The Judge has not yet seen fit to find any fault with the position that I took in regard to those seven interrogatories, which were certainly broad enough, in all conscience, to cover the entire ground. In my answers, which have been printed, and all have had the opportunity of seeing, I take the ground that those who elect me must expect that I will do nothing which will not be in accordance with those answers. I have some right to assert that Judge Douglas has no fault to find with them. But he chooses to still try to thrust me upon different ground, without paying any attention to my answers, the obtaining of which from me cost him so much trouble and concern. At the same time I propounded four interrogatories to him, claiming it as a right that he should answer as many interrogatories for me as I did for him, and I would reserve myself for a future instalment when I got them ready. The Judge, in answering me upon that occasion, put in what I suppose he intends as answers to all four of my interrogatories. The first one of these interrogatories I have before me, and it is in these words:

"*Question* 1.—If the people of Kansas shall, by means entirely unobjectionable in all other respects, adopt a State constitution, and ask admission into the Union under it, *before* they have the requisite number of inhabitants according to the English bill,"—some ninety-three thousand,—"will you vote to admit them?"

As I read the Judge's answer in the newspaper, and as I remember it as pronounced at the time, he does not give any answer which is equivalent to yes or no,—I will or I won't. He answers at very considerable length, rather quarrelling with me for asking the question, and insisting that Judge Trumbull had done something that I ought to say something about, and finally getting out such statements as induce me to infer that he means to be understood he will, in that supposed case, vote for the admission of Kansas. I only bring this forward now for the purpose of saying that if he chooses to put a different construction upon his answer, he may do it. But if he does not, I shall from this time forward assume that he will vote for the admission of Kansas in disregard of the English bill. He has the right to remove any misunderstanding I may have. I only mention it now, that I may hereafter assume this to be the true construction of his answer, if he does not now choose to correct me.

The second interrogatory that I propounded to him was this:

"*Question 2.*—Can the people of a United States Territory, in any lawful way, against the wish of any citizen of the United States, exclude slavery from its limits prior to the formation of a State Constitution?"

To this Judge Douglas answered that they can lawfully exclude slavery from the Territory prior to the formation of a constitution. He goes on to tell us how it can be done. As I understand him, he holds that it can be done by the Territorial Legislature refusing to make any enactments for the protection of slavery in the Territory, and especially by adopting unfriendly legislation to it. For the sake of clearness, I state it again: that they can exclude slavery from the Territory, 1st, by withholding what he assumes to be an indispensable assistance to it in the way of legislation; and, 2d, by unfriendly legislation. If I rightly understand him, I wish to ask your attention for a while to his position.

In the first place, the Supreme Court of the United States has decided that any Congressional prohibition of slavery in the Territories is unconstitutional; that they have reached this proposition as a conclusion from their former proposition, that the Constitution of the United States expressly recognizes property in slaves, and from that other Constitutional provision, that no person shall be deprived of property without due process of law. Hence they reach the conclusion that as the Constitution of the United States expressly recognizes property in slaves, and prohibits any person from being deprived of property without due process of law, to pass an Act of Congress by which a man who owned a slave on one side of a line would be deprived of him if he took him on the other side, is depriving him of that property without due process of law. That I understand to be the decision of the Supreme Court. I understand also that Judge Douglas adheres most firmly to that decision; and the difficulty is, how is it possible for any power to exclude slavery from the Territory, unless in violation of that decision? That is the difficulty.

In the Senate of the United States, in 1850, Judge Trumbull, in a speech substantially, if not directly, put the same interrogatory to Judge Douglas, as to whether the people of a Territory had the lawful power to exclude slavery prior to the formation of a constitution. Judge Douglas then answered at considerable length, and his answer will be found in the *Congressional Globe*, under date of June 9th, 1856. The Judge said that whether the people could exclude slavery prior to the formation of a constitution or not *was a question to be decided by the Supreme Court*. He put that proposition, as will be seen by the *Congressional Globe*, in a variety of forms, all running to the same thing in substance,—that it was a question for the Supreme Court. I maintain that when he says, after the Supreme Court have decided the question, that the people may yet exclude slavery by any means whatever, he does virtually say that it is *not* a question for the Supreme Court. He shifts his ground. I appeal to you whether he did not say it was a question for the Supreme Court? Has not the Supreme Court decided that question? When he now says the people *may* exclude slavery, does he not make it a question for the people? Does he not virtually shift his ground and say that it is *not* a question for the court, but for the people? This is a very simple proposition,—a very plain and naked one. It seems to me that there is no difficulty in deciding it. In a variety of ways he said that it was a question for the Supreme Court. He did not stop then to tell us that, whatever the Supreme Court decides, the people can by withholding necessary "police regulations" keep slavery out. He did not make any such answer. I submit to you now whether the new state of the case has not induced the Judge to sheer away from his original ground. Would not this be the impression of every fair-minded man?

I hold that the proposition that slavery cannot enter a new country without police regulations is historically false. It is not true at all. I hold that the history of this country shows that the institution of slavery was originally planted upon this continent *without* these "police regulations," which the Judge now thinks necessary for the actual establishment of it. Not only so, but is there not another fact: how came this Dred Scott decision to be made? It was made upon the case of a negro being taken and actually held in slavery in Minnesota Territory, claiming his freedom because the Act of Congress prohibited his being so held there. *Will the Judge pretend that Dred Scott was not held there without police regulations?* There is at least one matter of record as to his having been held in slavery in the Territory, not only without police regulations, but in the teeth of Congressional legislation supposed to be valid at the time. This shows that there is vigor enough in slavery to plant itself in a new country even against unfriendly legislation. It takes not only law, but the *enforcement* of law to keep it out. That is the history of this country upon the subject.

I wish to ask one other question. It being understood that the Constitution of the United States guarantees property in slaves in the Territories, if there is any infringement of the right of that property, would not the United States courts, organized for the government of the Territory, apply such remedy as might be necessary in that case? It is a maxim held by the courts that there is no wrong without its remedy; and the courts have a remedy for whatever is acknowledged and treated as a wrong.

Again: I will ask you, my friends, if you were elected members of the Legislature, what would be the first thing you would have to do before entering upon your duties? *Swear to support the Constitution of the United States.* Suppose you believe, as Judge Douglas does, that the Constitution of the United States guarantees to your neighbor the right to hold slaves in that Territory; that they are his property: how can you clear your oaths unless you give him such legislation as is necessary to enable him to enjoy that property? What do you understand by supporting the

Constitution of a State, or of the United States? Is it not to give such constitutional helps to the rights established by that Constitution as may be practically needed? Can you, if you swear to support the Constitution, and believe that the Constitution establishes a right, clear your oath, without giving it support? Do you support the Constitution if, knowing or believing there is a right established under it which needs specific legislation, you withhold that legislation? Do you not violate and disregard your oath? I can conceive of nothing plainer in the world. There can be nothing in the words "support the Constitution," if you may run counter to it by refusing support to any right established under the Constitution. And what I say here will hold with still more force against the Judge's doctrine of "unfriendly legislation." How could you, having sworn to support the Constitution, and believing it guaranteed the right to hold slaves in the Territories, assist in legislation *intended to defeat that right?* That would be violating your own view of the Constitution. Not only so, but if you were to do so, how long would it take the courts to hold your votes unconstitutional and void? Not a moment.

Lastly, I would ask: Is not Congress itself under obligation to give legislative support to any right that is established under the United States Constitution? I repeat the question: Is not Congress itself bound to give legislative support to any right that is established in the United States Constitution? A member of Congress swears to support the Constitution of the United States: and if he sees a right established by that Constitution which needs specific legislative protection, can he clear his oath without giving that protection? Let me ask you why many of us who are opposed to slavery upon principle give our acquiescence to a Fugitive Slave law? Why do we hold ourselves under obligations to pass such a law, and abide by it when it is passed? Because the Constitution makes provision that the owners of slaves shall have the right to reclaim them. It gives the right to reclaim slaves; and that right is, as Judge Douglas says, a barren right, unless there is legislation that will enforce it.

The mere declaration, "No person held to service or labor in one State under the laws thereof, escaping into another, shall in consequence of any law or regulation therein be discharged from such service or labor, but shall be delivered up on claim of the party to whom such service or labor may be due, "is powerless without specific legislation to enforce it." Now, on what ground would a member of Congress, who is opposed to slavery in the abstract, vote for a Fugitive law, as I would deem it my duty to do? Because there is a constitutional right which needs legislation to enforce it. And although it is distasteful to me, I have sworn to support the Constitution; and having so sworn, I cannot conceive that I do support it if I withhold from that right any necessary legislation to make it practical. And if that is true in regard to a Fugitive Slave law, is the right to have fugitive slaves reclaimed any better fixed in the Constitution than the right to hold slaves in the Territories? For this decision is a just exposition of the Constitution, as Judge Douglas thinks. Is the one right any better than the other? Is there any man who, while a member of Congress, would give support to the one any more than the other? If I wished to refuse to give legislative support to slave property in the Territories, if a member of Congress, I could not do it, holding the view that the Constitution establishes that right. If I did it at all, it would be because I deny that this decision properly construes the Constitution. But if I acknowledge, with Judge Douglas, that this decision properly construes the Constitution, I cannot conceive that I would be less than a perjured man if I should refuse in Congress to give such protection to that property as in its nature it needed.

At the end of what I have said here I propose to give the Judge my fifth interrogatory, which he may take and answer at his leisure. My fifth interrogatory is this:

If the slaveholding citizens of a United States Territory should need and demand Congressional legislation for the protection of their slave property in such Territory, would you, as a member of Congress, vote for or against such legislation?

JUDGE DOUGLAS: Will you repeat that? I want to answer that question.

MR. LINCOLN: If the slaveholding citizens of a United States Territory should need and demand Congressional legislation for the protection of their slave property in such Territory, would you, as a member of Congress, vote for or against such legislation?

I am aware that in some of the speeches Judge Douglas has made, he has spoken as if he did not know or think that the Supreme Court had decided that a Territorial Legislature cannot exclude slavery. Precisely what the Judge would say upon the subject—whether he would say definitely that he does not understand they have so decided, or whether he would say he does understand that the court have so decided,—I do not know; but I know that in his speech at Springfield he spoke of it as a thing they had not decided yet; and in his answer to me at Freeport, he spoke of it, so far, again, as I can comprehend it, as a thing that had not yet been decided. Now, I hold that if the Judge does entertain that view, I think that he is not mistaken in so far as it can be said that the court has not decided anything save the mere question of jurisdiction. I know the legal arguments that can be made,—that after a court has decided that it cannot take jurisdiction in a case, it then has decided all that is before it, and that is the end of it. A plausible argument can be made in favor of that proposition; but I know that Judge Douglas has said in one of his speeches that the court went forward, *like honest men as they were,* and decided all the points in the case. If any points are really extra-judicially decided, because not necessarily before them, then this one as to the power of the Territorial Legislature, to exclude slavery is one of them, as also the one that the Missouri Compromise was null and void. They are both extra-judicial, or neither is, according as the court held that they had no jurisdiction in the case between the parties, because of want of capacity of one party to maintain a suit in that court. I want, if I have sufficient time, to show that the court did *pass its opinion;* but that is the only thing actually done in the case. If they did not decide, they showed what they were ready to decide whenever the matter was before them. What is that opinion? After having argued that Congress had no power to pass a law excluding slavery from a United States Territory, they then used language to this effect: That inasmuch as Congress itself could not exercise such a power, it followed as a matter of course that it could not authorize a Territorial government to exercise it; for the Territorial Legislature can do no more than Congress could do. Thus it expressed its opinion emphatically against the power of a Territorial Legislature to exclude slavery, leaving us in just as little doubt on that point as upon any other point they really decided.

Now, my fellow-citizens, I will detain you only a little while longer; my time is nearly out. I find a report of a speech made by Judge Douglas at Joliet, since we last met at Freeport,—published, I believe, in the *Missouri Republican,*—on the 9th of this month, in which Judge Douglas says:

"You know at Ottawa I read this platform, and asked him if he concurred in each and all of the principles set forth in it. He would not answer these questions. At last I said frankly, I wish you to answer them, because when I get them up here where the color of your principles are a little darker than in Egypt, I intend to trot you down to Jonesboro. The very notice that I was going to take him down to Egypt made him tremble in his knees so that he had to be carried from the platform. He laid up seven days, and in the meantime held a consultation with his political physicians; they had Lovejoy and Farnsworth and all the leaders of the Abolition party, they consulted it all over, and at last Lincoln came to the conclusion that he would answer, so he came up to Freeport last Friday."

Now, that statement altogether furnishes a subject for philosophical contemplation. I have been treating it in that way, and I have really come to the conclusion that I can explain it in no other way than by believing the Judge is crazy. If he was in his right mind I cannot conceive how he would have risked disgusting the four or five thousand of his own friends who stood there and knew, as to my having been carried from the platform, that there was not a word of truth in it.

JUDGE DOUGLAS: Didn't they carry you off?

MR. LINCOLN: There! that question illustrates the character of this man Douglas exactly. He smiles now, and says, "Didn't they carry you off?" but he said then "*he had to be carried off*"; and he said it to convince the country that he had so completely broken me down by his speech that I had to be carried away. Now he seeks to dodge it, and asks, "Didn't they carry you off?"

Yes, they did. *"But, Judge Douglas, why didn't you tell the truth?"* I would like to know why you didn't tell the truth about it. And then again "He laid up seven days." He put this in print for the people of the country to read as a serious document. I think if he had been in his sober senses he would not have risked that barefacedness in the presence of thousands of his own friends who knew that I made speeches within six of the seven days at Henry, Marshall County, Augusta, Hancock County, and Macomb, McDonough County, including all the necessary travel to meet him again at Freeport at the end of the six days. Now I say there is no charitable way to look at that statement, except to conclude that he is actually crazy. There is another thing in that statement that alarmed me very greatly as he states it, that he was going to "trot me down to Egypt." Thereby he would have you infer that I would not come to Egypt unless he forced me—that I could not be got here unless he, giant-like, had hauled me down here. That statement he makes, too, in the teeth of the knowledge that I had made the stipulation to come down here *and that he himself had been very reluctant to enter into the stipulation.* More than all this: Judge Douglas, when he made that statement, must have been crazy and wholly out of his sober senses, or else he would have known that when he got me down here, that promise—that windy promise—of his powers to annihilate me, wouldn't amount to anything. Now, how little do I look like being carried away trembling? Let the Judge go on; and after he is done with his half-hour, I want you all, if I can't go home myself, to let me stay and rot here; and if anything happens to the Judge, if I cannot carry him to the hotel and put him to bed, let me stay here and rot. I say, then, here is something *extraordinary* in this statement. I ask you if you know any other living man who would make such a statement? I will ask my friend Casey, over there, if he would do such a thing? Would he send that out and have his men take it as the truth? Did the Judge talk of trotting me down to Egypt to scare me to death? Why, I know this people better than he does. I was raised just a little east of here. I am a part of this people. But the Judge was raised farther north, and perhaps he has some horrid idea of what this people might be induced to do. But really I have talked about this matter perhaps longer than I ought, for it is no great thing; and yet the smallest are often the most difficult things to deal with. The Judge has set about seriously trying to make the impression that when we meet at different places I am literally in his clutches—that I am a poor, helpless, decrepit mouse, and that I can do nothing at all. This is one of the ways he has taken to create that impression. I don't know any other way to meet it except this. I don't want to quarrel with him—to call him a liar; but when I come square up to him I don't know what else to call him if I must tell the truth out. I want to be at peace, and reserve all my fighting powers for necessary occasions. My time now is very nearly out, and I give up the trifle that is left to the Judge, to let him set my knees trembling again, if he can.

Mr. Douglas's Reply

MY FRIENDS: While I am very grateful to you for the enthusiasm which you show for me, I will say in all candor that your quietness will be much more agreeable than your applause, inasmuch as you deprive me of some part of my time whenever you cheer.

I will commence where Mr. Lincoln left off, and make a remark upon this serious complaint of his about my speech at Joliet. I did say there in a playful manner that when I put these questions to Mr. Lincoln at Ottawa he failed to answer, and that he trembled and had to be carried off the stand and required seven days to get up his reply. That he did not walk off from that stand he will not deny. That when the crowd went away from the stand with me, a few persons carried him home on their shoulders and laid him down, he will admit, I wish to say to you that whenever I degrade my friends and myself by allowing them to carry me on their backs along through the public streets, when I am able to walk, I am willing to be deemed crazy. I did not say whether I beat him or he beat me in the argument. It is true I put these questions to him, and I put them not as mere idle questions, but showed that I based them upon the creed of the Black Republican party as declared by their conventions in that

portion of the State which he depends upon to elect him, and
desired to know whether he indorsed that creed. He would not
answer. When I reminded him that I intended bringing him into
Egypt and renewing my questions if he refused to answer, he
then consulted and did get up his answers one week after,—
answers which I may refer to in a few minutes and show you
how equivocal they are. My object was to make him avow
whether or not he stood by the platform of his party; the resolutions I then read and upon which I based my questions had
been adopted by his party in the Galena Congressional District
and the Chicago and Bloomington Congressional Districts,
composing a large majority of the counties in this State that give
Republican or Abolition majorities. Mr. Lincoln cannot and will
not deny that the doctrines laid down in these resolutions were
in substance put forth in Lovejoy's resolutions, which were
voted for by a majority of his party, some of them, if not all,
receiving the support of every man of his party. Hence I laid a
foundation for my questions to him before I asked him whether
that was or was not the platform of his party. He says that he
answered my questions. One of them was whether he would
vote to admit any more slave States into the Union. The creed
of the Republican party as set forth in the resolutions of their
various conventions was that they would under no circumstances vote to admit another slave State. It was put forth in the
Lovejoy resolutions in the Legislature; it was put forth and
passed in a majority of all the counties of this State which give
Abolition or Republican majorities, or elect members to the
Legislature of that school of politics. I had a right to know
whether he would vote for or against the admission of another
slave State in the event the people wanted it. He first answered
that he was not pledged on the subject and then said:

"In regard to the other question, of whether I am pledged to the
admission of any more slave States into the Union, I state to you very
frankly that I would be exceedingly sorry ever to be put in the position
of having to pass on that question. I should be exceedingly glad to
know that there would never be another slave State admitted into the
Union; but I must add that if slavery shall be kept out of the Territories
during the Territorial existence of any one given Territory, and then

the people, having a fair chance and clean field, when they come to adopt a constitution, do such an extraordinary thing as adopt a slave constitution, uninfluenced by the actual presence of the institution among them, I see no alternative, if we own the country, but to admit them into the Union."

Now analyze that answer. In the first place, he says he would be exceedingly sorry to be put in a position where he would have to vote on the question of the admission of a slave State. Why is he a candidate for the Senate if he would be sorry to be put in that position? I trust the people of Illinois will not put him in a position which he would be so sorry to occupy. The next position he takes is that he would be glad to know that there would never be another slave State, yet, in certain contingencies, he might have to vote for one. What is that contingency? If Congress keeps slavery out by law while it is a Territory, and then the people should have a fair chance and should adopt slavery, unin-fluenced by the presence of the institution, he supposed he would have to admit the State. Suppose Congress should not keep slavery out during their Territorial existence, then how would he vote when the people applied for admission into the Union with a slave constitution? That he does not answer; and that is the condition of every Territory we have now got. Slavery is not kept out of Kansas by Act of Congress; and when I put the question to Mr. Lincoln, whether he will vote for the admission with or without slavery, as her people may desire, he will not answer, and you have not an answer from him. In Nebraska, slavery is not prohibited by Act of Congress, but the people are allowed, under the Nebraska Bill, to do as they please on the subject; and when I ask him whether he will vote to admit Nebraska with a slave constitution if her people desire it, he will not answer. So with New Mexico, Washington Territory, Arizona, and the four new States to be admitted from Texas. You cannot get an answer from him to these questions. His answer only applies to a given case, to a condition,—things which he knows do not exist in any one Territory in the Union. He tries to give you to understand that he would allow the people to do as they please, and yet he dodges the question as to every Territory in the Union. I now ask why cannot Mr. Lincoln answer to each of these Territories? He has not done it, and he will not do it. The Abolitionists up north understand that this answer is made with a view of not committing himself on any one Territory now in existence. It is so understood there, and you cannot expect an answer from him on a case that applies to any one Territory, or applies to the new States which by compact we are pledged to admit out of Texas, when they have the requisite population and desire admission. I submit to you whether he has made a frank answer, so that you can tell how he would vote in any one of these cases. "He would be sorry to be put in the position." Why would he be sorry to be put in this position if his duty required him to give the vote? If the people of a Territory ought to be permitted to come into the Union as a State, with slavery or without it, as they pleased, why not give the vote admitting them cheerfully? If in his opinion they ought not to come in with slavery, even if they wanted to, why not say that he would cheerfully vote against their admission? His intimation is that conscience would not let him vote "No," and he would be sorry to do that which his conscience would compel him to do as an honest man.

In regard to the contrast, or bargain, between Trumbull, the Abolitionists, and him, which he denies, I wish to say that the charge can be proved by notorious historical facts. Trumbull, Lovejoy, Giddings, Fred Douglass, Hale and Banks were travelling the State at that time making speeches on the same side and in the same cause with him. He contents himself with the simple denial that any such thing occurred. Does he deny that he, and Trumbull, and Breese, and Giddings, and Chase, and Fred Douglass, and Lovejoy, and all those Abolitionists and deserters from the Democratic party did make speeches all over this State in the same common cause? Does he deny that Jim Matheny was then, and is now, his confidential friend, and does he deny that Matheny made the charge of the bargain and fraud in his own language, as I have read it from his printed speech? Matheny spoke of his own personal knowledge of that bargain existing between Lincoln, Trumbull, and the Abolitionists. He still remains Lincoln's confidential friend, and is now a candidate for Congress, and is canvassing the Springfield District for

Lincoln. I assert that I can prove the charge to be true in detail if I can ever get it where I can summon and compel the attendance of witnesses. I have the statement of another man to the same effect as that made by Matheny, which I am not permitted to use yet; but Jim Matheny is a good witness on that point, and the history of the country is conclusive upon it. That Lincoln up to that time had been a Whig, and then undertook to Abolitionize the Whigs and bring them into the Abolition camp, is beyond denial; that Trumbull up to that time had been a Democrat, and deserted, and undertook to Abolitionize the Democracy, and take them into the Abolition camp, is beyond denial; that they are both now active, leading, distinguished members of this Abolition Republican party, in full communion, is a fact that cannot be questioned or denied.

But Lincoln is not willing to be responsible for the creed of his party. He complains because I hold him responsible; and in order to avoid the issue, he attempts to show that individuals in the Democratic party, many years ago, expressed Abolition sentiments. It is true that Tom Campbell, when a candidate for Congress in 1850, published the letter which Lincoln read. When I asked Lincoln for the date of that letter, he could not give it. The date of the letter has been suppressed by other speakers who have used it, though I take it for granted that Lincoln did not know the date. If he will take the trouble to examine, he will find that the letter was published only two days before the election, and was never seen until after it, except in one county. Tom Campbell would have been beat to death by the Democratic party if that letter had been made public in his district. As to Molony, it is true he uttered sentiments of the kind referred to by Mr. Lincoln, and the best Democrats would not vote for him for that reason. I returned from Washington after the passage of the Compromise measures in 1850, and when I found Molony running under Wentworth's tutelage and on his platform, I denounced him, and declared that he was no Democrat. In my speech at Chicago, just before the election that year, I went before the infuriated people of that city and vindicated the Compromise measures of 1850. Remember the city council had passed resolutions nullifying Acts of Congress and instructing the police to withhold their assistance from the execution of the laws; and as I was the only man in the city of Chicago who was responsible for the passage of the Compromise measures, I went before the crowd, justified each and every one of those measures; and let it be said, to the eternal honor of the people of Chicago, that when they were convinced by my exposition of those measures that they were right, and they had done wrong in opposing them, they repealed their nullifying resolutions, and declared that they would acquiesce in and support the laws of the land. These facts are well known, and Mr. Lincoln can only get up individual instances, dating back to 1849–'50, which are contradicted by the whole tenor of the Democratic creed.

But Mr. Lincoln does not want to be held responsible for the Black Republican doctrine of no more slave States. Farnsworth is the candidate of his party to-day in the Chicago District, and he made a speech in the last Congress in which he called upon God to palsy his right arm if he ever voted for the admission of another slave State, whether the people wanted it or not. Lovejoy is making speeches all over the State for Lincoln now, and taking ground against any more slave States. Washburne, the Black Republican candidate for Congress in the Galena District, is making speeches in favor of this same Abolition platform, declaring no more slave States. Why are men running for Congress in the northern districts, and taking that Abolition platform for their guide, when Mr. Lincoln does not want to be held to it down here in Egypt and in the centre of the State, and objects to it so as to get votes here? Let me tell Mr. Lincoln that his party in the northern part of the State hold to that Abolition platform, and that if they do not in the south and in the centre, they present the extraordinary spectacle of a "house divided against itself," and hence "cannot stand." I now bring down upon him the vengeance of his own Scriptural quotation, and give it a more appropriate application than he did, when I say to him that his party, Abolition in one end of the State, and opposed to it in the other, is a house divided against itself, and cannot stand, and ought not to stand, for it attempts to cheat the American people out of their votes by disguising its sentiments.

Mr. Lincoln attempts to cover up and get over his Abolitionism by telling you that he was raised a little east of you, beyond the Wabash in Indiana, and he thinks that makes a mighty sound and good man of him on all these questions. I do not know that the place where a man is born or raised has much to do with his political principles. The worst Abolitionists I have ever known in Illinois have been men who have sold their slaves in Alabama and Kentucky, and have come here and turned Abolitionists whilst spending the money got for the negroes they sold; and I do not know that an Abolitionist from Indiana or Kentucky ought to have any more credit because he was born and raised among slaveholders. I do not know that a native of Kentucky is more excusable because, raised among slaves, his father and mother having owned slaves, he comes to Illinois, turns Abolitionist, and slanders the graves of his father and mother, and breathes curses upon the institutions under which he was born, and his father and mother bred. True, I was not born out west here. I was born away down in Yankee land, I was born in a valley in Vermont, with the high mountains around me. I love the old green mountains and valleys of Vermont, where I was born, and where I played in my childhood. I went up to visit them some seven or eight years ago, for the first time for twenty odd years. When I got there they treated me very kindly. They invited me to the Commencement of their college, placed me on the seats with their distinguished guests, and conferred upon me the degree of LL.D., in Latin (Doctor of Laws),—the same as they did Old Hickory, at Cambridge, many years ago; and I give you my word and honor I understood just as much of the Latin as he did. When they got through conferring the honorary degree they called upon me for a speech; and I got up, with my heart full and swelling with gratitude for their kindness, and I said to them: "My friends, Vermont is the most glorious spot on the face of this globe for a man to be born in, *provided* he emigrates when he is very young."

I emigrated when I was very young. I came out here when I was a boy, and I found my mind liberalized, and my opinions enlarged, when I got on these broad prairies, with only the heavens to bound my vision, instead of having them circumscribed by the little narrow ridges that surrounded the valley where I was born. But I discard all flings of the land where a man was born; I wish to be judged by my principles, by those great public measures and constitutional principles upon which the peace, the happiness and the perpetuity of this Republic now rest.

Mr. Lincoln has framed another question, propounded it to me, and desired my answer. As I have said before, I did not put a question to him that I did not first lay a foundation for by showing that it was a part of the platform of the party whose votes he is now seeking, adopted in a majority of the counties where he now hopes to get a majority, and supported by the candidates of his party now running in those counties. But I will answer his question. It is as follows: "If the slaveholding citizens of a United States Territory should need and demand Congressional legislation for the protection of their slave property in such Territory, would you, as a member of Congress, vote for or against such legislation?" I answer him that it is a fundamental article in the Democratic creed that there should be non-interference and non-intervention by Congress with slavery in the States or Territories. Mr. Lincoln could have found an answer to his question in the Cincinnati platform, if he had desired it. The Democratic party have always stood by that great principle of non-interference and non-intervention by Congress with slavery in the States and Territories alike, and I stand on that platform now.

Now, I desire to call your attention to the fact that Lincoln did not define his own position in his own question. How does he stand on that question? He put the question to me at Freeport whether or not I would vote to admit Kansas into the Union before she had 93,420 inhabitants. I answered him at once that, it having been decided that Kansas had now population enough for a slave State, she had population enough for a free State.

I answered the question unequivocally; and then I asked him whether he would vote for or against the admission of Kansas before she had 93,420 inhabitants and he would not answer me.

To-day he has called attention to the fact that in his opinion my answer on that question was not quite plain enough, and yet he has not answered it himself. He now puts a question in relation to Congressional interference in the Territories to me. I answer him direct, and yet he has not answered the question himself. I ask you whether a man has any right in common decency to put questions in these public discussions to his opponent which he will not answer himself when they are pressed home to him. I have asked him three times whether he would vote to admit Kansas whenever the people applied with a constitution of their own making and their own adoption under circumstances that were fair, just, and unexceptionable; but I cannot get an answer from him. Nor will he answer the question which he put to me, and which I have just answered, in relation to Congressional interference in the Territories by making a slave code there.

It is true that he goes on to answer the question by arguing that under the decision of the Supreme Court it is the duty of a man to vote for a slave code in the Territories. He says that it is his duty, under the decision that the court has made; and if he believes in that decision he would be a perjured man if he did not give the vote. I want to know whether he is not bound to a decision which is contrary to his opinions just as much as to one in accordance with his opinions. If the decision of the Supreme Court, the tribunal created by the Constitution to decide the question, is final and binding, is he not bound by it just as strongly as if he was for it instead of against it originally? Is every man in this land allowed to resist decisions he does not like, and only support those that meet his approval? What are important courts worth, unless their decisions are binding on all good citizens? It is the fundamental principle of the judiciary that its decisions are final. It is created for that purpose; so that when you cannot agree among yourselves on a disputed point, you appeal to the judicial tribunal, which steps in and decides for you; and that decision is then binding on every good citizen. It is the law of the land just as much with Mr. Lincoln against it as for it. And yet he says if that decision is binding he is a perjured man if he does not vote for a slave code in the different

Territories of this Union. Well, if you [turning to Mr. Lincoln] are not going to resist the decision, if you obey it and do not intend to array mob law against the constituted authorities, then, according to your own statement, you will be a perjured man if you do not vote to establish slavery in these Territories. My doctrine is that, even taking Mr. Lincoln's view, that the decision recognizes the right of a man to carry his slaves into the Territories of the United States if he pleases, yet after he gets there he needs affirmative law to make that right of any value. The same doctrine not only applies to slave property, but all other kinds of property. Chief Justice Taney places it upon the ground that slave property is on an equal footing with other property. Suppose one of your merchants should move to Kansas and open a liquor store: he has a right to take groceries and liquors there; but the mode of selling them, and the circumstances under which they shall be sold, and all the remedies, must be prescribed by local legislation; and if that is unfriendly, it will drive him out just as effectually as if there was a constitutional provision against the sale of liquor. So the absence of local legislation to encourage and support slave property in a Territory excludes it practically just as effectually as if there was a positive constitutional provision against it. Hence I assert that under the Dred Scott decision you cannot maintain slavery a day in a Territory where there is an unwilling people and unfriendly legislation. If the people are opposed to it, our right is a barren, worthless, useless right; and if they are for it, they will support and encourage it. We come right back, therefore, to the practical question,—if the people of a Territory want slavery, they will have it; and if they do not want it, you cannot force it on them. And this is the practical question, the great principle, upon which our institutions rest. I am willing to take the decision of the Supreme Court as it was pronounced by that august tribunal, without stopping to inquire whether I would have decided that way or not. I have had many a decision made against me on questions of law which I did not like, but I was bound by them just as much as if I had had a hand in making them and approved them. Did you ever see a lawyer or a client lose his case that he approved the decision of the court? They always think the decision unjust when it is given against them. In a government of laws, like ours, we must sustain the Constitution as our fathers made it, and maintain the rights of the States as they are guaranteed under the Constitution; and then we will have peace and harmony between the different States and sections of this glorious Union.

Fourth Joint Debate
CHARLESTON, SEPTEMBER 18, 1858

Mr. Lincoln's Speech

LADIES AND GENTLEMEN: It will be very difficult for an audience so large as this to hear distinctly what a speaker says, and consequently it is important that as profound silence be preserved as possible.

While I was at the hotel to-day, an elderly gentleman called upon me to know whether I was really in favor of producing a perfect equality between the negroes and white people. While I had not proposed to myself on this occasion to say much on that subject, yet as the question was asked me I thought I would occupy perhaps five minutes in saying something in regard to it. I will say, then, that I am not, nor ever have been, in favor of bringing about in any way the social and political equality of the white and black races; that I am not, nor ever have been, in favor of making voters or jurors of negroes, nor of qualifying them to hold office, nor to intermarry with white people; and I will say, in addition to this, that there is a physical difference between the white and black races which I believe will forever forbid the two races living together on terms of social and political equality. And inasmuch as they cannot so live, while they do remain together there must be the position of superior and inferior, and I as much as any other man am in favor of having the superior position assigned to the white race. I say upon this occasion I do not perceive that because the white man is to have the superior position the negro should be denied everything. I do not under-

stand that because I do not want a negro woman for a slave I
must necessarily want her for a wife. My understanding is that I
can just let her alone. I am now in my fiftieth year, and I certainly never have had a black woman for either a slave or a wife.
So it seems to me quite possible for us to get along without making either slaves or wives of negroes. I will add to this that I have
never seen, to my knowledge, a man, woman, or child who was
in favor of producing a perfect equality, social and political,
between negroes and white men. I recollect of but one distinguished instance that I ever heard of so frequently as to be
entirely satisfied of its correctness, and that is the case of Judge
Douglas's old friend Colonel Richard M. Johnson. I will also add
to the remarks I have made (for I am not going to enter at large
upon this subject), that I have never had the least apprehension
that I or my friends would marry negroes if there was no law to
keep them from it; but as Judge Douglas and his friends seem
to be in great apprehension that they might, if there were no law
to keep them from it, I give him the most solemn pledge that I
will to the very last stand by the law of this State which forbids
the marrying of white people with negroes. I will add one further word, which is this: that I do not understand that there is
any place where an alteration of the social and political relations
of the negro and the white man can be made, except in the State
Legislature,—not in the Congress of the United States; and as I
do not really apprehend the approach of any such thing myself,
and as Judge Douglas seems to be in constant horror that some
such danger is rapidly approaching, I propose as the best means
to prevent it that the Judge be kept at home, and placed in the
State Legislature to fight the measure. I do not propose
dwelling longer at this time on this subject.

When Judge Trumbull, our other Senator in Congress,
returned to Illinois in the month of August, he made a speech at
Chicago, in which he made what may be called a *charge* against
Judge Douglas, which I understand proved to be very offensive
to him. The Judge was at that time out upon one of his speaking
tours through the country, and when the news of it reached him,
as I am informed, he denounced Judge Trumbull in rather harsh
terms for having said what he did in regard to that matter. I was

travelling at that time, and speaking at the same places with Judge Douglas on subsequent days, and when I heard of what Judge Trumbull had said of Douglas, and what Douglas had said back again, I felt that I was in a position where I could not remain entirely silent in regard to the matter. Consequently, upon two or three occasions I alluded to it, and alluded to it in no other wise than to say that in regard to the charge brought by Trumbull against Douglas, I *personally* knew nothing, and sought to say nothing about it; that I did personally know Judge Trumbull; that I believed him to be a man of veracity; that I believed him to be a man of capacity sufficient to know very well whether an assertion he was making, as a conclusion drawn from a set of facts, was true or false; and as a conclusion of my own from that, I stated it as my belief if Trumbull should ever be called upon, he would prove everything he had said. I said this upon two or three occasions. Upon a subsequent occasion, Judge Trumbull spoke again before an audience at Alton, and upon that occasion not only repeated his charge against Douglas, but arrayed the evidence he relied upon to substantiate it. This speech was published at length; and subsequently at Jacksonville Judge Douglas alluded to the matter. In the course of his speech, and near the close of it, he stated in regard to myself what I will now read: "Judge Douglas proceeded to remark that he should not hereafter occupy his time in refuting such charges made by Trumbull, but that, Lincoln having indorsed the character of Trumbull for veracity, he should hold him (Lincoln) responsible for the slanders." I have done simply what I have told you, to subject me to this invitation to notice the charge. I now wish to say that it had not originally been my purpose to discuss that matter at all But inasmuch as it seems to be the wish of Judge Douglas to hold me responsible for it, then for once in my life I will play General Jackson, and to the just extent I take the responsibility.

I wish to say at the beginning that I will hand to the reporters that portion of Judge Trumbull's Alton speech which was devoted to this matter, and also that portion of Judge Douglas's speech made at Jacksonville in answer to it. I shall thereby furnish the readers of this debate with the complete discussion between Trumbull and Douglas. I cannot now read them, for the reason that it would take half of my first hour to do so. I can only make some comments upon them. Trumbull's charge is in the following words: "Now, the charge is, that there was a plot entered into to have a constitution formed for Kansas, and put in force, without giving the people an opportunity to vote upon it, and that Mr. Douglas was in the plot." I will state, without quoting further, for all will have an opportunity of reading it hereafter, that Judge Trumbull brings forward what he regards as sufficient evidence to substantiate this charge.

It will be perceived Judge Trumbull shows that Senator Bigler, upon the floor of the Senate, had declared there had been a conference among the senators, in which conference it was determined to have an enabling act passed for the people of Kansas to form a constitution under, and in this conference it was agreed among them that it was best not to have a provision for submitting the constitution to a vote of the people after it should be formed. He then brings forward to show, and showing, as he deemed, that Judge Douglas reported the bill back to the Senate with that clause stricken out. He then shows that there was a new clause inserted into the bill, which would in its nature *prevent* a reference of the constitution back for a vote of the people,—if, indeed, upon a mere silence in the law, it could be assumed that they had the right to vote upon it. These are the general statements that he has made.

I propose to examine the points in Judge Douglas's speech in which he attempts to answer that speech of Judge Trumbull's. When you come to examine Judge Douglas's speech, you will find that the first point he makes is: "Suppose it were true that there was such a change in the bill, and that I struck it out,—is that a proof of a plot to force a constitution upon them against their will?" His striking out such a provision, if there was such a one in the bill, he argues, does not establish the proof that it was stricken out for the purpose of robbing the people of that right. I would say, in the first place, that that would be a *most manifest* reason for it. It is true, as Judge Douglas states, that many Territorial bills have passed without having such a provision in them. I believe it is true, though I am not certain, that in some instances constitutions framed under such bills have been submitted to a vote of the people with the law silent upon the subject; but it does not appear that they once had their enabling acts framed with an express provision *for* submitting the constitution to be framed to a vote of the people, and then that they were stricken out when Congress did not mean to alter the effect of the law. That there have been bills which never had the provision in, I do not question; but when was that provision taken out of one that it was in? More especially does this evidence tend to prove the proposition that Trumbull advanced, when we remember that the provision was stricken out of the bill almost simultaneously with the time that Bigler says there was a conference among certain senators, and in which it was agreed that a bill should be passed leaving that out. Judge Douglas, in answering Trumbull, omits to attend to the testimony of Bigler, that there was a meeting in which it was agreed they should so frame the bill that there should be no submission of the constitution to a vote of the people. The Judge does not notice this part of it. If you take this as one piece of evidence, and then ascertain that simultaneously Judge Douglas struck out a provision that did require it to be submitted, and put the two together, I think it will make a pretty fair show of proof that Judge Douglas did, as Trumbull says, enter into a plot to put in force a constitution for Kansas, without giving the people any opportunity of voting upon it.

But I must hurry on. The next proposition that Judge Douglas puts is this: "But upon examination it turns out that the Toombs bill never did contain a clause requiring the constitution to be submitted." This is a mere question of fact, and can be determined by evidence. I only want to ask this question: Why did not Judge Douglas say that these words were not stricken out of the Toombs bill, or this bill from which it is alleged the provision was stricken out,—a bill which goes by the name of Toombs, because he originally brought it forward? I ask why, if the Judge wanted to make a direct issue with Trumbull, did he not take the exact proposition Trumbull made in his speech, and say it was not stricken out? Trumbull has given the exact words that he says were in the Toombs bill, and he alleges that when the bill came back, they were stricken out. Judge Douglas does not say that the words which Trumbull says were stricken out were not so stricken out, but he says there was no provision in the Toombs bill to submit the constitution to a vote of the people. We see at once that he is merely making an issue upon the meaning of the words. He has not undertaken to say that Trumbull tells a lie about these words being stricken out, but he is really, when pushed up to it, only taking an issue upon the meaning of the words. Now, then, if there be any issue upon the meaning of the words, or if there be upon the question of fact as to whether these words were stricken out, I have before me what I suppose to be a genuine copy of the Toomb's bill, in which it can be shown that the words Trumbull says were in it were, in fact, originally there. If there be any dispute upon the fact, I have got the documents here to show they were there. If there be any controversy upon the sense of the words,— whether these words which were stricken out really constituted a provision for submitting the matter to a vote of the people,— as that is a matter of argument, I think I may as well use Trumbull's own argument. He says that the proposition is in these words:

"That the following propositions be and the same are hereby offered to the said Convention of the people of Kansas when formed, for their free acceptance or rejection; which, if accepted by the Convention *and ratified by the people at the election for the adoption of the constitution,* shall be obligatory upon the United States and the said State of Kansas."

Now, Trumbull alleges that these last words were stricken out of the bill when it came back, and he says this was a provision for submitting the constitution to a vote of the people; and his argument is this: "Would it have been possible to ratify the land propositions at the election for the adoption of the constitution, unless such an election was to be held?" This is Trumbull's argument. Now, Judge Douglas does not meet the charge at all, but he stands up and says there was no such proposition in that bill for submitting the constitution to be framed to a vote of the people. Trumbull admits that the language is not a direct provision for submitting it, but it is a provision necessarily implied from another provision. He asks you how it is possible to ratify the land proposition at the election for the adoption of the constitution, if there was no election to be held for the adoption of the constitution. And he goes on to show that it is not any less a law because the provision is put in that indirect shape than it would be if it were put directly. But I presume I have said enough to draw attention to this point, and I pass it by also.

Another one of the points that Judge Douglas makes upon Trumbull, and at very great length, is, that Trumbull, while the bill was pending, said in a speech in the Senate that he supposed the constitution to be made would have to be submitted to the people. He asks, if Trumbull thought so then, what ground is there for anybody thinking otherwise now? Fellow-citizens, this much may be said in reply: That bill had been in the hands of a party to which Trumbull did not belong. It had been in the hands of the committee at the head of which Judge Douglas stood. Trumbull perhaps had a printed copy of the original Toombs bill. I have not the evidence on that point except a sort of inference I draw from the general course of business there. What alterations, or what provisions in the way of altering, were going on in committee, Trumbull had no means of knowing, until the altered bill was reported back. Soon afterwards, when it was reported back, there was a discussion over it, and perhaps Trumbull in reading it hastily in the altered form did not perceive all the bearings of the alterations. He was hastily borne into the debate, and it does not follow that because there was something in it Trumbull did not perceive, that something did not exist. More than this, is it true that what Trumbull did can have any effect on what Douglas did? Suppose Trumbull had been in the plot with these other men, would that let Douglas out of it? Would it exonerate Douglas that Trumbull didn't then perceive he was in the plot? He also asks the question: Why didn't Trumbull propose to amend the bill, if he thought it needed any amendment? Why, I believe that everything Judge Trumbull had proposed, particularly in connection with this question of Kansas and Nebraska, since he had been on the floor of the Senate, had been promptly voted down by Judge Douglas and his friends. He had no promise that an amendment offered by him to anything on this subject would receive the slightest consideration. Judge Trumbull did bring to the notice of the Senate at that time the fact that there was no provision for submitting the constitution about to be made for the people of Kansas to a vote of the people. I believe I may venture to say that Judge Douglas made some reply to this speech of Judge Trumbull's, *but he never noticed that part of it at all.* And so the thing passed by. I think, then, the fact that Judge Trumbull offered no amendment does not throw much blame upon him; and if it did, it does not reach the question of fact *as to what Judge Douglas was doing.* I repeat, that if Trumbull had himself been in the plot, it would not at all relieve the others who were in it from blame. If I should be indicted for murder, and upon the trial it should be discovered that I had been implicated in that murder, but that the prosecuting witness was guilty too, that would not at all touch the question of my crime. It would be no relief to my neck that they discovered this other man who charged the crime upon me to be guilty too.

Another one of the points Judge Douglas makes upon Judge Trumbull is, that when he spoke in Chicago he made his charge to rest upon the fact that the bill had the provision in it for submitting the constitution to a vote of the people when it went into his (Judge Douglas's) hands, that it was missing when he reported it to the Senate, and that in a public speech he had subsequently said the alterations in the bill were made while it was in committee, and that they were made in consultation between him (Judge Douglas) and Toombs. And Judge Douglas goes on to comment upon the fact of Trumbull's adducing in his Alton speech the proposition that the bill not only came back with that proposition stricken out, but with another clause and another provision in it, saying that "until the complete execution of this Act there shall be no election in said Territory,"—which, Trumbull argued, was not only taking the provision for submitting to a vote of the people out of the bill, but was adding an affirmative one, in that it prevented the people from exercising the right under a bill that was merely silent on the question. Now, in regard to what he says, that Trumbull shifts the issue, that he shifts his ground,—and I believe he uses the term that, "it being proven false, he has changed ground,"—I call upon all of you, when you come to examine that portion of Trumbull's speech (for it will make a part of mine), to examine whether Trumbull has shifted his ground or not. I say he did not shift his ground, but that he brought forward his original charge and the evidence to sustain it yet more fully, but precisely as he originally made it. Then, in addition thereto, he brought in a new piece of evidence. He shifted no ground. He brought no new piece of evidence inconsistent with his former testimony; but he brought a new piece, tending, as he thought, and as I think, to prove his proposition. To illustrate: A man brings an accusation against another, and on trial the man making the charge introduces A and B to prove the accusation. At a second trial he introduces the same witnesses, who tell the same story as before, and a third witness, who tells the same thing, and in addition gives further testimony corroborative of the charge. So with Trumbull. There was no shifting of ground, nor inconsistency of testimony between the new piece of evidence and what he originally introduced.

But Judge Douglas says that he himself moved to strike out that last provision of the bill, and that on his motion it was stricken out and a substitute inserted. That I presume is the truth. I presume it is true that that last proposition was stricken out by Judge Douglas. Trumbull has not said it was not; Trumbull has himself said that it was so stricken out. He says: "I am now speaking of the bill as Judge Douglas reported it back. It was amended somewhat in the Senate before it passed, but I am speaking of it as he brought it back." Now, when Judge Douglas parades the fact that the provision was stricken out of the bill when it came back, he asserts nothing contrary to what Trumbull alleges. Trumbull has only said that he originally put it in,—not that he did not strike it out. Trumbull says it was not in the bill when it went to the committee. When it came back it was in, and Judge Douglas said the alterations were made by him in consultation with Toombs. Trumbull alleges, therefore,

as his conclusion, that Judge Douglas put it in. Then, if Douglas
wants to contradict Trumbull and call him a liar, let him say he
did not put it in, and not that he didn't take it out again. It is said
that a bear is sometimes hard enough pushed to drop a cub; and
so I presume it was in this case. I presume the truth is that
Douglas put it in, and afterward took it out. That, I take it, is the
truth about it. Judge Trumbull says one thing, Douglas says
another thing, and the two don't contradict one another at all.
The question is, what did he put it in for? In the first place, what
did he take the other provision out of the bill for,—the provision
which Trumbull argued was necessary for submitting the constitution to a vote of the people? What did he take that out for;
and, having taken it out, what did he put this in for? I say that in
the run of things it is not unlikely forces conspire to render it
vastly expedient for Judge Douglas to take that latter clause out
again. The question that Trumbull has made is that Judge
Douglas put it in; and he don't meet Trumbull at all unless he
denies that.

In the clause of Judge Douglas's speech upon this subject he
uses this language toward Judge Trumbull. He says: "He forges
his evidence from beginning to end; and by falsifying the record,
he endeavors to bolster up his false charge." Well, that is a pretty
serious statement—Trumbull forges his evidence from beginning to end. Now, upon my own authority I say that it is not true.
What is a forgery? Consider the evidence that Trumbull has
brought forward. When you come to read the speech, as you will
be able to, examine whether the evidence is a forgery from
beginning to end. He had the bill or document in his hand like
that [holding up a paper]. He says that is a copy of the Toombs
bill,—the amendment offered by Toombs. He says that is a copy
of the bill as it was introduced and went into Judge Douglas's
hands. Now, does Judge Douglas say that is a forgery? That is one
thing Trumbull brought forward. Judge Douglas says he forged it
from beginning to end! That is the "beginning," we will say. Does
Douglas say that is a forgery? Let him say it to-day, and we will
have a subsequent examination upon this subject. Trumbull then
holds up another document like this, and says that is an exact
copy of the bill as it came back in the amended form out of Judge

Douglas's hands. Does Judge Douglas say that is a forgery? Does he say it in his general sweeping charge? Does he say so now? If he does not, then take this Toombs bill and the bill in the amended form, and it only needs to compare them to see that the provision is in the one and not in the other; it leaves the inference inevitable that it was taken out.

But, while I am dealing with this question, let us see what Trumbull's other evidence is. One other piece of evidence I will read. Trumbull says there are in this original Toombs bill these words:

"That the following propositions be and the same are hereby offered to the said Convention of the people of Kansas, when formed, for their free acceptance or rejection; which, if accepted by the Convention and ratified by the people at the election for the adoption of the constitution, shall be obligatory upon the United States and the said State of Kansas."

Now, if it is said that this is a forgery, we will open the paper here and see whether it is or not. Again, Trumbull says, as he goes along, that Mr. Bigler made the following statement in his place in the Senate, December 9, 1857:

"I was present when that subject was discussed by senators before the bill was introduced, and the question was raised and discussed, whether the constitution, when formed, should be submitted to a vote of the people. It was held by those most intelligent on the subject that, in view of all the difficulties surrounding that Territory, the danger of any experiment at that time of a popular vote, it would be better there should be no such provision in the Toombs bill; and it was my understanding, in all the intercourse I had, that the Convention would make a constitution, and send it here, without submitting it to the popular vote."

Then Trumbull follows on:

"In speaking of this meeting again on the 21st December, 1857 [*Congressional Globe*, same vol., page 113], Senator Bigler said:

"'Nothing was further from my mind than to allude to any social or confidential interview. The meeting was not of that character. Indeed, it was semi-official, and called to promote the public good. My recollection was clear that I left the conference under the impression that it had been deemed best to adopt measures to admit Kansas as a State through the agency of one popular election, and that for delegates to this Convention. This impression was stronger because I thought the spirit of the bill infringed upon the doctrine of non-intervention, to which I had great aversion; but with the hope of accomplishing a great good, and as no movement had been made in that direction in the Territory, I waived this objection, and concluded to support the measure. I have a few items of testimony as to the correctness of these impressions, and with their submission I shall be content. I have before me the bill reported by the senator from Illinois on the 7th of March, 1856, providing for the admission of Kansas as a State, the third section of which reads as follows:

"" 'That the following propositions be, and the same are hereby offered to the said Convention of the people of Kansas, when formed, for their free acceptance or rejection; which, if accepted by the Convention and ratified by the people at the election for the adoption of the constitution, shall be obligatory upon the United States and the said State of Kansas."

" 'The bill read in his place by the senator from Georgia on the 25th of June, and referred to the Committee on Territories, contained the same section word for word. Both these bills were under consideration at the conference referred to; but, sir, when the senator from Illinois reported the Toombs bill to the Senate with amendments, the next morning, it did not contain that portion of the third section which indicated to the Convention that the constitution should be approved by the people. The words *and ratified by the people at the election for the adoption of the constitution*" had been stricken out.' "

Now, these things Trumbull says were stated by Bigler upon the floor of the Senate on certain days, and that they are recorded in the *Congressional Globe* on certain pages. Does Judge Douglas say this is a forgery? Does he say there is no such thing in the *Congressional Globe?* What does he mean when he says Judge Trumbull forges his evidence from beginning to end? So again he says in another place that Judge Douglas, in his speech, December 9, 1857 (*Congressional Globe,* part I., page 15), stated:

"That during the last session of Congress, I [Mr. Douglas] reported a bill from the Committee on Territories, to authorize the people of Kansas to assemble and form a constitution for themselves.

Subsequently the senator from Georgia [Mr. Toombs] brought forward a substitute for my bill, which, *after having been modified by him and myself in consultation,* was passed by the Senate."

Now, Trumbull says this is a quotation from a speech of Douglas, and is recorded in the *Congressional Globe.* Is *it* a forgery? Is it there or not? It may not be there, but I want the Judge to take these pieces of evidence, and distinctly say they are forgeries if he dare do it.

A Voice: "He will."

MR. LINCOLN: Well, sir, you had better not commit him. He gives other quotations,—another from Judge Douglas. He says:

"I will ask the senator to show me an intimation, from any one member of the Senate, in the whole debate on the Toombs bill, and in the Union, from any quarter, that the constitution was not to be submitted to the people. I will venture to say that on all sides of the chamber it was so understood at the time. If the opponents of the bill had understood it was not, they would have made the point on it; and if they had made it, we should certainly have yielded to it, and put in the clause. That is a discovery made since the President found out that it was not safe to take it for granted that that would be done, which ought in fairness to have been done."

Judge Trumbull says Douglas made that speech, and it is recorded. Does Judge Douglas say it is a forgery, and was not true? Trumbull says somewhere, and I propose to skip it, but it will be found by any one who will read this debate, that he did distinctly bring it to the notice of those who were engineering the bill, that it lacked that provision; and then he goes on to give another quotation from Judge Douglas, where Judge Trumbull uses this language:

"Judge Douglas, however, on the same day and in the same debate, probably recollecting or being reminded of the fact that I had objected to the Toombs bill when pending that it did not provide for a submission of the constitution to the people, made another statement, which is to be found in the same volume of the *Globe,* page 22, in which he says:

"'That the bill was silent on this subject was true, and my attention was called to that about the time it was passed; and I took the fair construction to be, that powers not delegated were reserved, and that of course the constitution would be submitted to the people.'

"Whether this statement is consistent with the statement just before made, that had the point been made it would have been yielded to, or that it was a new discovery, you will determine."

So I say. I do not know whether Judge Douglas will dispute this, and yet maintain his position that Trumbull's evidence "was forged from beginning to end." I will remark that I have not got these *Congressional Globes* with me. They are large books, and difficult to carry about, and if Judge Douglas shall say that on these points where Trumbull has quoted from them there are no such passages there, I shall not be able to prove they are there upon this occasion, but I will have another chance. Whenever he points out the forgery and says, "I declare that this particular thing which Trumbull has uttered is not to be found where he says it is," then my attention will be drawn to that, and I will arm myself for the contest,—stating now that I have not the slightest doubt on earth that I will find every quotation just where Trumbull says it is. Then the question is, How can Douglas call that a forgery? How can he make out that it is a forgery? What is a forgery? It is the bringing forward something in writing or in print purporting to be of certain effect when it is altogether untrue. If you come forward with my note for one hundred dollars when I have never given such a note, there is a forgery. If you come forward with a letter purporting to be written by me which I never wrote, there is another forgery. If you produce anything in writing or in print saying it is so and so, the document not being genuine, a forgery has been committed. How do you make this a forgery when every piece of the evidence is genuine? If Judge Douglas does say these documents and quotations are false and forged, he has a full right to do so; but until he does it specifically, we don't know how to get at him. If he does say they are false and forged, I will then look further into it, and I presume I can procure the certificates of the proper officers that they are genuine copies. I have no doubt each of these extracts will be found exactly where Trumbull says it is. Then I leave it to you if Judge Douglas, in making his sweeping charge that Judge Trumbull's evidence is forged from beginning to end, at all meets the case,—if that is the way to get at the facts. I repeat again, if he will point out which one is a forgery, I will carefully examine it, and if it proves that any one of them is really a forgery, it will not be me who will hold to it any longer. I have always wanted to deal with everyone I meet candidly and honestly. If I have made any assertion not warranted by facts, and it is pointed out to me, I will withdraw it cheerfully. But I do not choose to see Judge Trumbull calumniated, and the evidence he has brought forward branded in general terms "a forgery from beginning to end." This is not the legal way of meeting a charge, and I submit to all intelligent persons, both friends of Judge Douglas and of myself, whether it is.

The point upon Judge Douglas is this: The bill that went into his hands had the provision in it for a submission of the constitution to the people; and I say its language amounts to an express provision for a submission, and that he took the provision out. He says it was known that the bill was silent in this particular; *but I say, Judge Douglas, it was not silent when you got it.* It was vocal with the declaration, when you got it, for a submission of the constitution to the people. And now, my direct question to Judge Douglas is, to answer why, if he deemed the bill silent on this point, he found it necessary to strike out those particular harmless words. If he had found the bill silent and without this provision, he might say what he does now. If he supposes it was implied that the constitution would be submitted to a vote of the people, how could these two lines so encumber the statute as to make it necessary to strike them out? How could he infer that a submission was still implied, after its express provision had been stricken from the bill? I find the bill vocal with the provision, while he silenced it. He took it out, and although he took out the other provision preventing a submission to a vote of the people, I ask, *Why did you first put it in?* I ask him whether he took the original provision out, which Trumbull alleges was in the bill. If he admits that he did take it, *I ask him what he did it for.* It looks to us as if he had altered the bill. If it looks differently to him,—if he has a different reason for his action from the one we assign him—he can tell it. I insist upon knowing why he made the bill silent upon that point when it was vocal before he put his hands upon it.

I was told, before my last paragraph, that my time was within three minutes of being out. I presume it is expired now; I therefore close.

Senator Douglas's Speech

LADIES AND GENTLEMEN: I had supposed that we assembled here to-day for the purpose of a joint discussion between Mr. Lincoln and myself upon the political questions that now agitate the whole country. The rule of such discussions is, that the opening speaker shall touch upon all the points he intends to discuss, in order that his opponent, in reply, shall have the opportunity of answering them. Let me ask you what questions of public policy, relating to the welfare of this State or the Union, has Mr. Lincoln discussed before you? Mr. Lincoln simply contented himself at the outset by saying that he was not in favor of social and political equality between the white man and the negro, and did not desire the law so changed as to make the latter voters or eligible to office. I am glad that I have at last succeeded in getting an answer out of him upon this question of negro citizenship and eligibility to office, for I have been trying to bring him to the point on it ever since this canvass commenced.

I will now call your attention to the question which Mr. Lincoln has occupied his entire time in discussing. He spent his whole hour in retailing a charge made by Senator Trumbull against me. The circumstances out of which that charge was manufactured occurred prior to the last Presidential election, over two years ago. If the charge was true, why did not Trumbull made it in 1856, when I was discussing the questions of that day all over this State with Lincoln and him, and when it was pertinent to the then issue? He was then as silent as the grave on the subject. If that charge was true, the time to have brought it forward was the canvass of 1856, the year when the Toombs bill passed the Senate. When the facts were fresh in the public mind, when the Kansas question was the paramount question of the day, and when such a charge would have had a material bearing on the election, why did he and Lincoln remain silent then, knowing that such a charge could be made and proven if true? Were they not false to you and false to the country in going through that entire campaign concealing their knowledge of this enormous conspiracy which, Mr. Trumbull says, he then knew and would not tell? Mr. Lincoln intimates, in his speech, a good reason why Mr. Trumbull would not tell, for he says that it might be true, as I proved that it was at Jacksonville, that Trumbull was also in the plot, yet that the fact of Trumbull's being in the plot would not in any way relieve me. He illustrates this argument by supposing himself on trial for murder, and says that it would be no extenuating circumstance if, on his trial another man was found to be a party to his crime. Well, if Trumbull was in the plot, and concealed it in order to escape the odium which would have fallen upon himself, I ask you whether you can believe him now when he turns State's evidence, and avows his own infamy in order to implicate me. I am amazed that Mr. Lincoln should now come forward and indorse that charge, occupying his whole hour in reading Mr. Trumbull's speech in support of it. Why, I ask, does not Mr. Lincoln make a speech of his own instead of taking up his time reading Trumbull's speech at Alton? I supposed that Mr. Lincoln was capable of making a public speech on his own account, or I should not have accepted the banter from him for a joint discussion. ["How about the charges?"] Do not trouble yourselves. I am going to make my speech in my own way, and I trust, as the Democrats listened patiently and respectfully to Mr. Lincoln, that his friends will not interrupt me when I am answering him. When Mr. Trumbull returned from the East, the first thing he did when he landed in Chicago was to make a speech wholly devoted to assaults upon my public character and public action. Up to that time I had never alluded to his course in Congress, or to him directly or indirectly, and hence his assaults upon me were entirely without provocation and without excuse. Since then he has been travelling from one end of the State to the other, repeating his vile charge. I propose now to read it in his own language:

"Now, fellow-citizens, I make the distinct charge that there was a preconcerted arrangement and plot entered into by the very men who now claim credit for opposing a constitution formed and put in force without giving the people any opportunity to pass upon it. This, my friends, is a serious charge, but I charge it to-night that the very men who traverse the country under banners proclaiming popular sovereignty, by design concocted a bill on purpose to force a constitution upon that people."

In answer to some one in the crowd who asked him a question, Trumbull said:

"And you want to satisfy yourself that he was in the plot to force a constitution upon that people? I will satisfy you. I will cram the truth down any honest man's throat until he cannot deny it. And to the man who does deny it, I will cram the lie down his throat till he shall cry 'Enough!'

"It is preposterous; it is the most damnable effrontery that man ever put on, to conceal a scheme to defraud and cheat the people out of their rights, and then claim credit for it."

That is the polite language Senator Trumbull applied to me, his colleague, when I was two hundred miles off. Why did he not speak out as boldly in the Senate of the United States, and cram the lie down my throat when I denied the charge, first made by Bigler, and made him take it back? You all recollect how Bigler assaulted me when I was engaged in a hand-to-hand fight, resisting a scheme to force a constitution on the people of Kansas against their will. He then attacked me with this charge; but I proved its utter falsity, nailed the slander to the counter, and made him take the back track. There is not an honest man in America who read that debate who will pretend that the charge is true. Trumbull was then present in the Senate, face to face with me; and why did he not then rise and repeat the charge, and say he would cram the lie down my throat? I tell you that Trumbull then knew it was a lie. He knew that Toombs denied that there ever was a clause in the bill he brought forward calling for and requiring a submission of the Kansas Constitution to the people. I will tell you what the facts of the case were: I introduced a bill to authorize the people of Kansas

to form a constitution, and come into the Union as a State whenever they should have the requisite population for a member of
Congress, and Mr. Toombs proposed a substitute, authorizing
the people of Kansas, with their then population of only 25,000,
to form a constitution, and come in at once. The question at
issue was, whether we would admit Kansas with a population of
25,000 or make her wait until she had the ratio entitling her to
a representative in Congress, which was 93,420. That was the
point of dispute in the Committee on Territories, to which both
my bill and Mr. Toombs's substitute had been referred. I was
overruled by a majority of the committee, my proposition rejected, and Mr. Toombs's proposition to admit Kansas then, with
her population of 25,000, adopted. Accordingly a bill to carry
out his idea of immediate admission was reported as a substitute
for mine; the only points at issue being, as I have already said,
the question of population, and the adoption of safeguards
against frauds at the election. Trumbull knew this,—the whole
Senate knew it,—and hence he was silent at that time. He
waited until I became engaged in this canvass, and finding that
I was showing up Lincoln's Abolitionism and negro equality doctrines, that I was driving Lincoln to the wall, and white men
would not support his rank Abolitionism, he came back from the
East and trumped up a system of charges against me, hoping
that I would be compelled to occupy my entire time in defending myself, so that I would not be able to show up the enormity
of the principles of the Abolitionists. Now, the only reason, and
the true reason, why Mr. Lincoln has occupied the whole of his
first hour in this issue between Trumbull and myself, is, to conceal from this vast audience the real questions which divide the
two great parties.

I am not going to allow them to waste much of my time with
these personal matters. I have lived in this State twenty-five
years, most of that time have been in public life, and my record
is open to you all. If that record is not enough to vindicate me
from these petty, malicious assaults, I despise ever to be elected
to office by slandering my opponents and traducing other men.
Mr. Lincoln asks you to elect him to the United States Senate
to-day solely because he and Trumbull can slander me. Has he

given any other reason? Has he avowed what he was desirous to do in Congress on any one question? He desires to ride into office not upon his own merits, not upon the merits and soundness of his principles, but upon his success in fastening a stale old slander upon me.

I wish you to bear in mind that up to the time of the introduction of the Toombs bill, and after its introduction, there had never been an Act of Congress for the admission of a new State which contained a clause requiring its constitution to be submitted to the people. The general rule made the law silent on the subject, taking it for granted that the people would demand and compel a popular vote on the ratification of their constitution. Such was the general rule under Washington, Jefferson, Madison, Jackson, and Polk, under the Whig Presidents and the Democratic Presidents, from the beginning of the government down, and nobody dreamed that an effort would ever be made to abuse the power thus confided to the people of a Territory. For this reason our attention was not called to the fact of whether there was or was not a clause in the Toombs bill compelling submission, but it was taken for granted that the constitution would be submitted to the people whether the law compelled it or not.

Now, I will read from the report by me as chairman of the Committee on Territories at the time I reported back the Toombs substitute to the Senate. It contained several things which I had voted against in committee, but had been overruled by a majority of the members, and it was my duty as chairman of the Committee to report the bill back as it was agreed upon by them. The main point upon which I had been overruled was the question of population. In my report accompanying the Toombs bill, I said:

"In the opinion of your Committee, whenever a constitution shall be formed in any Territory, preparatory to its admission into the Union as a State, justice, the genius of our institutions, the whole theory of our republican system, imperatively demand that the voice of the people shall be fairly expressed, and their will embodied in that fundamental law, without fraud, or violence, or intimidation, or any other improper or unlawful influence, and subject to no other restrictions than those imposed by the Constitution of the United States."

There you find that we took it for granted that the constitution was to be submitted to the people, whether the bill was silent on the subject or not. Suppose I had reported it so, following the example of Washington, Adams, Jefferson, Madison, Monroe, Adams, Jackson, Van Buren, Harrison, Tyler, Polk, Taylor, Fillmore, and Pierce, would that fact have been evidence of a conspiracy to force a constitution upon the whole people of Kansas against their will? If the charge which Mr. Lincoln makes be true against me, it is true against Zachary Taylor, Millard Fillmore, and every Whig President, as well as every Democratic President, and against Henry Clay, who, in the Senate or House, for forty years advocated bills similar to the one I reported, no one of them containing a clause compelling the submission of the constitution to the people. Are Mr. Lincoln and Mr. Trumbull prepared to charge upon all those eminent men, from the beginning of the government down to the present day, that the absence of a provision compelling submission, in the various bills passed by them, authorizing the people of Territories to form State constitutions, is evidence of a corrupt design on their part to force a constitution upon an unwilling people?

I ask you to reflect on these things, for I tell you that there is a conspiracy to carry this election for the Black Republicans by slander, and not by fair means. Mr. Lincoln's speech this day is conclusive evidence of the fact. He has devoted his entire time to an issue between Mr. Trumbull and myself, and has not uttered a word about the politics of the day. Are you going to elect Mr. Trumbull's colleague upon an issue between Mr. Trumbull and me? I thought I was running against Abraham Lincoln, that he claimed to be my opponent, had challenged me to a discussion of the public questions of the day with him, and was discussing these questions with me; but it turns out that his only hope is to ride into office on Trumbull's back, who will carry him by falsehood.

Permit me to pursue this subject a little further. An examination of the record proves that Trumbull's charge—that the Toombs bill originally contained a clause requiring the constitution to be submitted to the people—*is false*. The printed copy of the bill which Mr. Lincoln held up before you, and which he pretends contains such a clause, merely contains a clause requiring a submission of the land grant, and *there is no clause in it requiring a submission of the constitution*. Mr. Lincoln cannot find such a clause in it. My report shows that we took it for granted that the people would require a submission of the constitution, and secure it for themselves. There never was a clause in the Toombs bill requiring the constitution to be submitted; Trumbull knew it at the time, and his speech made on the night of its passage discloses the fact that he knew it was silent on the subject. Lincoln pretends, and tells you, that Trumbull has not changed his evidence in support of his charge since he made his speech in Chicago. Let us see. The Chicago *Times* took up Trumbull's Chicago speech, compared it with the official records of Congress, and proved that speech to be false in its charge that the original Toombs bill required a submission of the constitution to the people. Trumbull then saw that he was caught, and his falsehood exposed, and he went to Alton, and, under the very walls of the penitentiary, made a new speech, in which he predicated his assault upon me in the allegation that I had caused to be voted into the Toombs bill a clause which prohibited the Convention from submitting the constitution to the people, and quoted what he pretended was the clause. Now, has not Mr. Trumbull entirely changed the evidence on which he bases his charge? The clause which he quoted in his Alton speech (which he has published and circulated broadcast over the State) as having been put into the Toombs bill by me, is in the following words: "And until the complete execution of this Act, no other election shall be held in said Territory."

Trumbull says that the object of that amendment was to prevent the Convention from submitting the constitution to a vote of the people.

Now, I will show you that when Trumbull made that statement at Alton he knew it to be untrue. I read from Trumbull's speech in the Senate on the Toombs bill on the night of its passage. He then said:

"There is nothing said in this bill, so far as I have discovered, about submitting the constitution, which is to be formed, to the people for their sanction or rejection. Perhaps the Convention will have the right to submit it, if it should think proper, but it is certainly not compelled to do so, according to the provisions of the bill."

Thus you see that Trumbull, when the bill was on its passage in the Senate, said that it was silent on the subject of submission, and that there was nothing in the bill one way or the other on it. In his Alton speech he says there was a clause in the bill preventing its submission to the people, and that I had it voted in as an amendment. Thus I convict him of falsehood and slander by quoting from him, on the passage of the Toombs bill in the Senate of the United States, his own speech, made on the night of July 2, 1856, and reported in the *Congressional Globe* for the first session of the thirty-fourth Congress, vol. 33. What will you think of a man who makes a false charge, and falsifies the records to prove it? I will now show you that the clause which Trumbull says was put in the bill on my motion was never put in at all by me, but was stricken out on my motion, and another substituted in its place. I call your attention to the same volume of the *Congressional Globe* to which I have already referred, page 795, where you will find the following report of the proceedings of the Senate:

"MR. DOUGLAS: I have an amendment to offer from the Committee on Territories. On page 8, section 11, strike out the words 'until the complete execution of this Act, no other election shall be held in said Territory,' and insert the amendment which I hold in my hand."

You see from this that I moved to strike out the very words that Trumbull says I put in. The Committee on Territories overruled me in committee, and put the clause in; but as soon as I got the bill back into the Senate, I moved to strike it out, and put another clause in its place. On the same page you will find that my amendment was agreed to *unanimously*. I then offered another amendment, recognizing the right of the people of

Kansas, under the Toombs bill, to order just such elections as they saw proper. You can find it on page 796 of the same volume. I will read it:

"MR. DOUGLAS: I have another amendment to offer from the Committee, to follow the amendment which has been adopted. The bill reads now: 'And until the complete execution of this Act, no other election shall be held in said Territory.' It has been suggested that it should be modified in this way, 'And to avoid conflict in the complete execution of this Act, all other elections in said Territory are hereby postponed until such time as said Convention shall appoint,' so that they can appoint the day in the event that there should be a failure to come into the Union."

The amendment was *unanimously* agreed to,—clearly and distinctly recognizing the right of the convention to order just as many elections as they saw proper in the execution of the act. Trumbull concealed in his Alton speech the fact that the clause he quoted had been stricken out in my motion, and the other fact that this other clause was put in the bill on my motion, and made the false charge that I incorporated into the bill a clause preventing submission, in the face of the fact, that, on my motion, the bill was so amended before it passed as to recognize in express words the right and duty of submission.

On this record that I have produced before you, I repeat my charge that Trumbull did falsify the public records of the country, in order to make his charge against me, and I tell Mr. Abraham Lincoln that if he will examine these records, he will then know that what I state is true. Mr. Lincoln has this day indorsed Mr. Trumbull's veracity after he had my word for it that that veracity was proved to be violated and forfeited by the public records. It will not do for Mr. Lincoln, in parading his calumnies against me, to put Mr. Trumbull between him and the odium and responsibility which justly attaches to such calumnies. I tell him that I am as ready to prosecute the indorser as the maker of a forged note. I regret the necessity of occupying my time with these petty personal matters. It is unbecoming the dignity of a canvass for an office of the character for which we are candidates. When I commenced the canvass at Chicago, I spoke of Mr. Lincoln in terms of kindness as an old friend; I said that he was a good citizen, of unblemished character, against whom I had nothing to say. I repeated these complimentary remarks about him in my successive speeches, until he became the indorser for these and other slanders against me. If there is anything personally disagreeable, uncourteous, or disreputable in these personalities, the sole responsibility rests on Mr. Lincoln, Mr. Trumbull, and their backers.

I will show you another charge made by Mr. Lincoln against me, as an offset to his declaration of willingness to take back anything that is incorrect, and to correct any false statement he may have made. He has several times charged that the Supreme Court, President Pierce, President Buchanan, and myself, at the time I introduced the Nebraska Bill in January, 1854, at Washington, entered into a conspiracy to establish slavery all over this country. I branded this charge as a falsehood, and then he repeated it, asked me to analyze its truth and answer it. I told him: "Mr. Lincoln, I know what you are after—you want to occupy my time in personal matters, to prevent me from showing up the revolutionary principles which the Abolition party— whose candidate you are—have proclaimed to the world." But he asked me to analyze his proof, and I did so. I called his attention to the fact that at the time the Nebraska Bill was introduced, there was no such case as the Dred Scott case pending in the Supreme Court, nor was it brought there for years afterwards, and hence that it was impossible there could have been any conspiracy between the judges of the Supreme Court and the other parties involved. I proved by the record that the charge was false, and what did he answer? Did he take it back like an honest man and say that he had been mistaken? No; he repeated the charge, and said that, although there was no such case pending that year, there was an understanding between the Democratic owners of Dred Scott and the judges of the Supreme Court and other parties involved, that the case should be brought up. I then demanded to know who these Democratic owners of Dred Scott were. He could not or would not tell; he did not know. In truth, there were no Democratic owners of Dred Scott on the face of the land. Dred Scott was owned at that time by the Rev. Dr. Chaffee, an Abolition member of Congress from Springfield, Massachusetts, and his wife; and Mr. Lincoln ought to have known that Dred Scott was so owned, for the reason that as soon as the decision was announced by the court Dr. Chaffee and his wife executed a deed emancipating him, and put that deed on record. It was a matter of public record, therefore, that at the time the case was taken to the Supreme Court Dred Scott was owned by an Abolition member of Congress, a friend of Lincoln's and a leading man of his party, while the defence was conducted by Abolition lawyers,—and thus the Abolitionists managed both sides of the case. I have exposed these facts to Mr. Lincoln, and yet he will not withdraw his charge of conspiracy. I now submit to you whether you can place any confidence in a man who continues to make a charge when its utter falsity is proven by the public records. I will state another fact to show how utterly reckless and unscrupulous this charge against the Supreme Court, President Pierce, President Buchanan, and myself is. Lincoln says that President Buchanan was in the conspiracy at Washington in the winter of 1854, when the Nebraska Bill was introduced. The history of this country shows that James Buchanan was at that time representing this country at the Court of St. James, Great Britain, with distinguished ability and usefulness, that he had not been in the United States for nearly a year previous, and that he did not return until about three years after. Yet Mr. Lincoln keeps repeating this charge of conspiracy against Mr. Buchanan when the public records prove it to be untrue. Having proved it to be false as far as the Supreme Court and President Buchanan are concerned, I drop it, leaving the public to say whether I, by myself, without their concurrence, could have gone into a conspiracy with them. My friends, you see that the object clearly is to conduct the canvass on personal matters, and hunt me down with charges that are proven to be false by the public records of the country. I am willing to throw open my whole public and private life to the inspection of any man or all men who desire to investigate it. Having resided among you twenty-five years, during nearly the whole of which time a public man, exposed to more assaults, perhaps more abuse, than any man living of my age, or who ever did live, and having survived it all and still commanded your confidence, I am willing to trust to your knowledge of me and my public conduct without making any more defence against these assaults.

Fellow-citizens, I came here for the purpose of discussing the leading political topics which now agitate the country. I have no charges to make against Mr. Lincoln, none against Mr. Trumbull, and none against any man who is a candidate, except in repelling their assaults upon me. If Mr. Lincoln is a man of bad character, I leave you to find it out; if his votes in the past are not satisfactory, I leave others to ascertain the fact; if his course on the Mexican war was not in accordance with your notions of patriotism and fidelity to our own country as against a public enemy, I leave you to ascertain the fact. I have no assaults to make upon him, except to trace his course on the questions that now divide the country and engross so much of the people's attention.

You know that prior to 1854 this country was divided into two great political parties, one the Whig, the other the Democratic. I, as a Democrat for twenty years prior to that time, had been in public discussions in this State as an advocate of Democratic principles, and I can appeal with confidence to every old-line Whig within the hearing of my voice to bear testimony that during all that period I fought you Whigs like a man on every question that separated the two parties. I had the highest respect for Henry Clay as a gallant party leader, as an eminent statesman, and as one of the bright ornaments of this country; but I conscientiously believed that the Democratic party was right on the questions which separated the Democrats from the Whigs. The man does not live who can say that I ever personally assailed Henry Clay or Daniel Webster, or any one of the leaders of that great party, whilst I combated with all my energy the measures they advocated. What did we differ about in those days? Did Whigs and Democrats differ about this slavery question? On the contrary, did we not, in 1850, unite to a man in favor of that system of Compromise measures which Mr. Clay introduced, Webster defended, Cass supported, and Fillmore approved and made the law of the land by his signature? While we agreed on those Compromise measures, we differed about a bank, the tariff, distribution, the specie circular, the sub-treasury, and other questions of that description. Now, let me ask you which one of those questions on which Whigs and Democrats then differed now remains to divide the two great parties? Every one of those questions which divided Whigs and Democrats has passed away, the country has outgrown them, they have passed into history. Hence it is immaterial whether you were right or I was right on the bank, the sub-treasury, and other questions, because they no longer continue living issues. What, then, has taken the place of those questions about which we once differed? The slavery question has now become the leading and controlling issue; that question on which you and I agreed, on which the Whigs and Democrats united, has now become the leading issue between the national Democracy on the one side and the Republican, or Abolition, party on the other.

Just recollect for a moment the memorable contest of 1850, when this country was agitated from its centre to its circumference by the slavery agitation. All eyes in this nation were then turned to the three great lights that survived the days of the Revolution. They looked to Clay, then in retirement at Ashland, and to Webster and Cass, in the United States Senate. Clay had retired to Ashland, having, as he supposed, performed his mission on earth, and was preparing himself for a better sphere of existence in another world. In that retirement he heard the discordant, harsh, and grating sounds of sectional strife and disunion, and he aroused and came forth and resumed his seat in the Senate, that great theatre of his great deeds. From the moment that Clay arrived among us he became the leader of all the Union men, whether Whigs or Democrats. For nine months we each assembled, each day, in the council-chamber, Clay in the chair, with Cass upon his right hand, and Webster upon his left, and the Democrats and Whigs gathered around, forgetting differences, and only animated by one common, patriotic sentiment, to devise means and measures by which we could defeat the mad and revolutionary scheme of the Northern Abolitionists and Southern Disunionists. We did devise those means, Clay brought them forward, Cass advocated them, the Union

Democrats and Union Whigs voted for them, Fillmore signed them, and they gave peace and quiet to the country. Those Compromise measures of 1850 were founded upon the great fundamental principle that the people of each State and each Territory ought to be left free to form and regulate their own domestic institutions in their own way, subject only to the Federal Constitution. I will ask every old-line Democrat and every old-line Whig within the hearing of my voice if I have not truly stated the issues as they then presented themselves to the country. You recollect that the Abolitionists raised a howl of indignation, and cried for vengeance and the destruction of Democrats and Whigs both, who supported those Compromise measures of 1850. When I returned home to Chicago, I found the citizens inflamed and infuriated against the authors of those great measures. Being the only man in that city who was held responsible for affirmative votes on all those measures, I came forward and addressed the assembled inhabitants, defended each and every one of Clay's Compromise measures as they passed the Senate and the House and were approved by President Fillmore. Previous to that time, the city council had passed resolutions nullifying the Act of Congress, and instructing the police to withhold all assistance from its execution; but the people of Chicago listened to my defence, and, like candid, frank, conscientious men, when they became convinced that they had done an injustice to Clay, Webster, Cass, and all of us who had supported those measures, they repealed their nullifying resolutions, and declared that the laws should be executed and the supremacy of the Constitution maintained. Let it always be recorded in history to the immortal honor of the people of Chicago that they returned to their duty when they found that they were wrong, and did justice to those whom they had blamed and abused unjustly. When the Legislature of this State assembled that year, they proceeded to pass resolutions approving the Compromise measures of 1850. When the Whig party assembled in 1852 at Baltimore in National Convention for the last time, to nominate Scott for the presidency, they adopted as a part of their platform the Compromise measures of 1850, as the cardinal plank upon which every Whig would stand, and by which he would regulate his future conduct. When the Democratic party assembled at the same place one month after, to nominate General Pierce, we adopted the same platform so far as those Compromise measures were concerned, agreeing that we would stand by those glorious measures as a cardinal article in the Democratic faith. Thus you see that in 1852 all the old Whigs and all the old Democrats stood on a common plank so far as this slavery question was concerned, differing on other questions.

Now, let me ask, how is it that since that time so many of you Whigs have wandered from the true path marked out by Clay, and carried out broad and wide by the great Webster? How is it that so many old-line Democrats have abandoned the old faith of their party, and joined with Abolitionism and Free-soilism to overturn the platform of the old Democrats, and the platform of the old Whigs? You cannot deny that since 1854 there has been a great revolution on this one question. How has it been brought about? I answer, that no sooner was the sod grown green over the grave of the immortal Clay, no sooner was the rose planted on the tomb of the godlike Webster, than many of the leaders of the Whig party, such as Seward of New York, and his followers, led off and attempted to Abolitionize the Whig party, and transfer all your old Whigs, bound hand and foot, into the Abolition camp. Seizing hold of the temporary excitement produced in this country by the introduction of the Nebraska Bill, the disappointed politicians in the Democratic party united with the disappointed politicians in the Whig party, and endeavored to form a new party, composed of all the Abolitionists, or Abolitionized Democrats and Abolitionized Whigs, banded together in an Abolition platform.

And who led that crusade against national principles in this State? I answer, Abraham Lincoln on behalf of the Whigs, and Lyman Trumbull on behalf of the Democrats, formed a scheme by which they would Abolitionize the two great parties in this State, on condition that Lincoln should be sent to the United States Senate in place of General Shields, and that Trumbull should go to Congress from the Belleville District until I would be accommodating enough either to die or resign for his benefit, and then he was to go to the Senate in my place. You all remember that during the year 1854 these two worthy gentlemen, Mr. Lincoln and Mr. Trumbull, one an old-line Whig and the other an old-line Democrat, were hunting in partnership to elect a Legislature against the Democratic party. I canvassed the State that year from the time I returned home until the election came off, and spoke in every county that I could reach during that period. In the northern part of the State I found Lincoln's ally in the person of FRED DOUGLASS, THE NEGRO, preaching Abolition doctrines, while Lincoln was discussing the same principles down here, and Trumbull, a little farther down, was advocating the election of members to the Legislature who would act in concert with Lincoln's and Fred Douglass's friends. I witnessed an effort made at Chicago by Lincoln's then associates, and now supporters, to put Fred Douglass, the negro, on the stand, at a Democratic meeting, to reply to the illustrious General Cass when he was addressing the people there. They had the same negro hunting me down, and they now have a negro traversing the northern counties of the State and speaking in behalf of Lincoln. Lincoln knows that when we were at Freeport in joint discussion there was a distinguished colored friend of his there then who was on the stump for him, and who made a speech there the night before we spoke, and another the night after, a short distance from Freeport, in favor of Lincoln; and in order to show how much interest the colored brethren felt in the success of their brother Abe, I have with me here, and would read it if it would not occupy too much of my time, a speech made by Fred Douglass in Poughkeepsie, N.Y., a short time since, to a large convention in which he conjures all the friends of negro equality and negro citizenship to rally as one man around Abraham Lincoln, the perfect embodiment of their principles, and by all means to defeat Stephen A. Douglas. Thus you find that this Republican party in the northern part of the State had colored gentlemen for their advocates in 1854, in company with Lincoln and Trumbull, as they have now. When, in October, 1854, I went down to Springfield to attend the State Fair, I found the leaders of this party all assembled together under the title of an anti-Nebraska meeting. It was Black

Republicans up north and anti-Nebraska at Springfield. I found Lovejoy, a high-priest of Abolitionism, and Lincoln, one of the leaders who was towing the old-line Whigs into the Abolition camp, and Trumbull, Sidney Breese, and Governor Reynolds, all making speeches against the Democratic party and myself, at the same place and in the same cause. The same men who are now fighting the Democratic party and the regular Democratic nominees in this State were fighting us then. They did not then acknowledge that they had become Abolitionists, and many of them deny it now. Breeze, Dougherty, and Reynolds were then fighting the Democracy under the title of anti-Nebraska men, and now they are fighting the Democracy under the pretence that they are *Simon pure* Democrats, saying that they are authorized to have every office-holder in Illinois beheaded who prefers the election of Douglas to that of Lincoln or the success of the Democratic ticket in preference to the Abolition ticket for members of Congress, State officers, members of the Legislature, or any office in the State. They canvassed the State against us in 1854, as they are doing now, owning different names and different principles in different localities, but having a common object in view, viz.: the defeat of all men holding national principles in opposition to this sectional Abolition party. They carried the Legislature in 1854, and when it assembled in Springfield they proceeded to elect a United States Senator, all voting for Lincoln, with one or two exceptions, which exceptions prevented them from quite electing him. And why should they not elect him? Had not Trumbull agreed that Lincoln should have Shields's place? Had not the Abolitionists agreed to it? Was it not the solemn compact, the condition on which Lincoln agreed to Abolitionize the old Whigs, that he should be Senator? Still, Trumbull, having control of a few Abolitionized Democrats, would not allow them all to vote for Lincoln on any one ballot, and thus kept him for some time within one or two votes of an election, until he worried out Lincoln's friends, and compelled them to drop him and elect Trumbull, in violation of the bargain. I desire to read you a piece of testimony in confirmation of the notoriously public facts which I have stated to you. Colonel James H. Matheny, of Springfield, is, and for twenty years has been, the confidential personal and political friend and manager of Mr. Lincoln. Matheny is this very day the candidate of the Republican or Abolition party for Congress against the gallant Major Thos. L. Harris, in the Springfield District, and is making speeches for Lincoln and against me. I will read you the testimony of Matheny about this bargain between Lincoln and Trumbull when they undertook to Abolitionize Whigs and Democrats only four years ago. Matheny, being mad at Trumbull for having played a Yankee trick on Lincoln, exposed the bargain in a public speech two years ago, and I will read the published report of that speech, the correctness of which Mr. Lincoln will not deny:

"The Whigs, Abolitionists, Know-Nothings, and renegade Democrats made a solemn compact for the purpose of carrying this State against the Democracy, on this plan: 1st, that they would all combine and elect Mr. Trumbull to Congress, and thereby carry his district for the Legislature, in order to throw all the strength that could be obtained into that body against the Democrats; 2d, that when the Legislature should meet, the officers of that body, such as Speaker, clerks, door-keepers, etc. would be given to the Abolitionists; and, 3d, that the Whigs were to have the United States Senator. That accordingly, in good faith, Trumbull was elected to Congress, and his district carried for the Legislature; and when it convened, the Abolitionists got all the officers of that body, and thus far the 'bond' was fairly executed. The Whigs, on their part, demanded the election of Abraham Lincoln to the United States Senate, that the bond might be fulfilled, the other parties to the contract having already secured to themselves all that was called for. But, in the most perfidious manner, they refused to elect Mr. Lincoln; and the mean, low-lived, sneaking Trumbull succeeded, by pleading all that was required by any party, in thrusting Lincoln aside, and foisting himself, an excrescence from the rotten bowels of the Democracy, into the United States Senate; and thus it has ever been, that an *honest* man makes a bad bargain when he conspires or contracts with rogues."

Lincoln's confidential friend Matheny thought that Lincoln made a bad bargain when he conspired with such rogues as Trumbull and the Abolitionists. I would like to know whether Lincoln had as high opinion of Trumbull's veracity when the latter agreed to support him for the Senate and then cheated him as he does now, when Trumbull comes forward and makes charges against me. You could not then prove Trumbull an honest man either by Lincoln, by Matheny, or by any of Lincoln's friends. They charged everywhere that Trumbull had cheated them out of the bargain, and Lincoln found sure enough that it was a *bad bargain* to contract and conspire with rogues.

And now I will explain to you what has been a mystery all over the State and Union—the reason why Lincoln was nominated for the United States Senate by the Black Republican Convention. You know it has never been usual for any party or any convention to nominate a candidate for United States Senator. Probably this was the first time that such a thing was ever done. The Black Republican Convention had not been called for that purpose, but to nominate a State ticket, and every man was surprised and many disgusted when Lincoln was nominated. Archie Williams thought he was entitled to it, Browning knew that he deserved it, Wentworth was certain that he would get it, Peck had hopes, Judd felt sure that he was the man, and Palmer had claims and had made arrangements to secure it; but to their utter amazement, Lincoln was nominated by the Convention, and not only that, but he received the nomination unanimously, by a resolution declaring that Abraham Lincoln was "the first, last, and only choice" of the Republican party. How did this occur? Why, because they could not get Lincoln's friends to make another bargain with "rogues," unless the whole party would come up as one man and pledge their honor that they would stand by Lincoln first, last, and all the time, and that he should not be cheated by Lovejoy this time, as he was by Trumbull before. Thus, by passing this resolution, the Abolitionists are all for him, Lovejoy and Farnsworth are canvassing for him, Giddings is ready to come here in his behalf, and the negro speakers are already on the stump for him, and he is sure not to be cheated this time. He would not go into the arrangement until he got their bond for it, and Trumbull is compelled now to take the stump, get up false charges against me, and travel all over the State to try and elect Lincoln, in order to keep Lincoln's friends quiet about the bargain in which Trumbull cheated them four years ago. You see, now, why it is that Lincoln and Trumbull are so mighty fond of each other. They have entered into a conspiracy to break me down by these assaults upon my public character, in order to draw my attention from a fair exposure of the mode in which they attempted to Abolitionize the old Whig and the old Democratic parties and lead them captive into the Abolition camp. Do you not all remember that Lincoln went around here four years ago making speeches to you, and telling that you should all go for the Abolition ticket, and swearing that he was as good a Whig as he ever was? and that Trumbull went all over the State making pledges to the old Democrats, and trying to coax them into the Abolition camp, swearing by his Maker, with the uplifted hand, that he was still a Democrat, always intended to be, and that never would he desert the Democratic party? He got your votes to elect an Abolition Legislature, which passed Abolition resolutions, attempted to pass Abolition laws, and sustained Abolitionists for office, State and National. Now the same game is attempted to be played over again. Then Lincoln and Trumbull made captives of the old Whigs and old Democrats and carried them into the Abolition camp, where Father Giddings, the high-priest of Abolitionism, received and christened them in the dark cause just as fast as they were brought in. Giddings found the converts so numerous that he had to have assistance, and he sent. for John P. Hale, N. P. Banks, Chase, and other Abolitionists, and they came on, and with Lovejoy and Fred Douglass, the negro, helped to baptize these new converts as Lincoln, Trumbull, Breese, Reynolds, and Dougherty could capture them and bring them within the Abolition clutch. Gentlemen, they are now around, making the same kind of speeches. Trumbull was down in Monroe County the other day, assailing me, and making a speech in favor of Lincoln; and I will show you under what notice his meeting was called. You see these people are Black Republicans or Abolitionists up north, while at Springfield to-day they dare not call their Convention "Republican," but are obliged to say "a Convention of all men opposed to the Democratic party";

and in Monroe County and lower Egypt Trumbull advertises their meetings as follows:

"A meeting of the Free Democracy will take place at Waterloo on Monday, September 21st inst., whereat Hon. Lyman Trumbull, Hon. John Baker, and others will address the people upon the different political topics of the day. Members of all parties are cordially invited to be present, and hear and determine for themselves.

"THE FREE DEMOCRACY.

"September 9, 1858."

Did you ever before hear of this new party, called the "Free Democracy"?

What object have these Black Republicans in changing their name in every county? They have one name in the north, another in the centre, and another in the south. When I used to practise law before my distinguished judicial friend whom I recognize in the crowd before me, if a man was charged with horse-stealing, and the proof showed that he went by one name in Stephenson County, another in Sangamon, a third in Monroe, and a fourth in Randolph, we thought that the fact of his changing his name so often to avoid detection was pretty strong evidence of his guilt. I would like to know why it is that this great Free-soil Abolition party is not willing to avow the same name in all parts of the State? If this party believes that its course is just, why does it not avow the same principles in the North and in the South, in the East and in the West, wherever the American flag waves over American soil?

A Voice: "The party does not call itself Black Republican in the North."

MR. DOUGLAS: Sir, if you will get a copy of the paper published at Waukegan, fifty miles from Chicago, which advocates the election of Mr. Lincoln, and has his name flying at its masthead, you will find that it declares that "this paper is devoted to the cause" of *Black Republicanism.* I had a copy of it, and intended to bring it down here into Egypt to let you see what name the party rallied under up in the northern part of the State, and to convince you that their principles are as different in the two sections of the State as is their name. I am sorry that

I have mislaid it and have not got it here. Their principles in the north are jet-black, in the centre they are in color a decent mulatto, and in lower Egypt they ar almost white. Why, I admired many of the white sentiments contained in Lincoln's speech at Jonesboro, and could not help but contrast them with the speeches of the same distinguished orator made in the northern part of the State. Down here he denies that the Black Republican party is opposed to the admission of any more slave States, under any circumstances, and says that they are willing to allow the people of each State, when it wants to come into the Union, to do just as it pleases on the question of slavery. In the north, you find Lovejoy, their candidate for Congress in the Bloomington District, Farnsworth, their candidate in the Chicago District, and Washburne, their candidate in the Galena District, all declaring that never will they consent, under any circumstances, to admit another slave State, even if the people want it. Thus, while they avow one set of principles up there, they avow another and entirely different set down here. And here let me recall to Mr. Lincoln the Scriptural quotation which he has applied to the Federal Government, that a house divided against itself cannot stand, and ask him how does he expect this Abolition party to stand when in one half of the State it advocates a set of principles which it has repudiated in the other half.

I am told that I have but eight minutes more. I would like to talk to you an hour and a half longer, but I will make the best use I can of the remaining eight minutes. Mr. Lincoln said in his first remarks that he was not in favor of the social and political equality of the negro with the white man. Everywhere up north he has declared that he was not in favor of the social and political equality of the negro, but he would not say whether or not he was opposed to negroes voting and negro citizenship. I want to know whether he is for or against negro citizenship. He declared his utter opposition to the Dred Scott decision, and advanced as a reason that the court had decided that it was not possible for a negro to be a citizen under the Constitution of the United States. If he is opposed to the Dred Scott decision for that reason, he must be in favor of conferring the right and privilege of citizenship upon the negro. I have been trying to get an answer from him on that point, but have never yet obtained one, and I will show you why. In every speech he made in the north he quoted the Declaration of Independence to prove that all men were created equal, and insisted that the phrase "all men" included the negro as well as the white man, and that the equality rested upon divine law. Here is what he said on that point:

"I should like to know if, taking this old Declaration of Independence, which declares that all men are equal upon principle, and making exceptions to it, where will it stop? If one man says it does not mean a negro, why may not another say it does not mean some other man? If that Declaration is not the truth, let us get the statute book in which we find it and tear it out."

Lincoln maintains there that the Declaration of Independence asserts that the negro is equal to the white man, and that under divine law; and if he believes so it was rational for him to advocate negro citizenship, which when allowed puts the negro on an equality under the law. I say to you in all frankness, gentlemen, that in my opinion a negro is not a citizen, cannot be, and ought not to be under the Constitution of the United States. I will not even qualify my opinion to meet the declaration of one of the judges of the Supreme Court in the Dred Scott case, that "a negro descended from African parents, who was imported into this country as a slave, is not a citizen, and cannot be." I say that this government was established on the white basis. It was made by white men for the benefit of white men and their posterity forever, and never should be administered by any except white men. I declare that a negro ought not to be a citizen, whether his parents were imported into this country as slaves or not, or whether or not he was born here. It does not depend upon the place a negro's parents were born, or whether they were slaves or not, but upon the fact that he is a negro, belonging to a race incapable of self-government, and for that reason ought not to be on an equality with white men.

My friends, I am sorry that I have not time to pursue this argument further, as I might have done but for the fact that Mr. Lincoln compelled me to occupy a portion of my time in repelling those gross slanders and falsehoods that Trumbull has invented against me and put in circulation. In conclusion, let me ask you why should this government be divided by a geographical line—arraying all men North in one great hostile party against all men South? Mr. Lincoln tells you in his speech at Springfield that a house divided against itself cannot stand; that this government divided into free and slave States cannot endure permanently; that they must either be all free or all slave; all one thing or all the other. Why cannot this government endure divided into free and slave States, as our fathers made it? When this government was established by Washington, Jefferson, Madison, Jay, Hamilton, Franklin, and the other sages and patriots of that day, it was composed of free States and slave States, bound together by one common Constitution. We have existed and prospered from that day to this thus divided, and have increased with a rapidity never before equalled, in wealth, the extension of territory, and all the elements of power and greatness, until we have become the first nation on the face of the globe. Why can we not thus continue to prosper? We can if we will live up to and execute the government upon those principles upon which our fathers established it. During the whole period of our existence Divine Providence has smiled upon us, and showered upon our nation richer and more abundant blessings than have ever been conferred upon any other.

Mr. Lincoln's Rejoinder

FELLOW-CITIZENS: It follows as a matter of course that a half-hour answer to a speech of an hour and a half can be but a very hurried one. I shall only be able to touch upon a few of the points suggested by Judge Douglas, and give them a brief attention, while I shall have to totally omit others for the want of time.

Judge Douglas has said to you that he has not been able to get from me an answer to the question whether I am in favor of negro citizenship. So far as I know the Judge never asked me the question before. He shall have no occasion to ever ask it again,

for I tell him very frankly that I am not in favor of negro citizenship. This furnishes me an occasion for saying a few words
upon the subject. I mentioned in a certain speech of mine,
which has been printed, that the Supreme Court had decided
that a negro could not possibly be made a citizen; and without
saying what was my ground of complaint in regard to that, or
whether I had any ground of complaint, Judge Douglas has from
that thing manufactured nearly everything that he ever says
about my disposition to produce an equality between the
negroes and the white people. If any one will read my speech,
he will find I mentioned that as one of the points decided in the
course of the Supreme Court opinions, but I did not state what
objection I had to it. But Judge Douglas tells the people what
my objection was when I did not tell them myself. Now, my
opinion is that the different States have the power to make a
negro a citizen under the Constitution of the United States if
they choose. The Dred Scott decision decides that they have not
that power. If the State of Illinois had that power, I should be
opposed to the exercise of it. That is all I have to say about it.

Judge Douglas has told me that he heard my speeches north
and my speeches south; that he had heard me at Ottawa and at
Freeport in the north and recently at Jonesboro in the south,
and there was a very different cast of sentiment in the speeches
made at the different points. I will not charge upon Judge
Douglas that he wilfully misrepresents me, but I call upon every
fair-minded man to take these speeches and read them, *and I
dare him to point out any difference between my speeches north
and south*. While I am here perhaps I ought to say a word, if I
have the time, in regard to the latter portion of the Judge's
speech, which was a sort of declamation in reference to my having said I entertained the belief that this government would not
endure half slave and half free. I have said so, and I did not say
it without what seemed to me to be good reasons. It perhaps
would require more time than I have now to set forth these reasons in detail; but let me ask you a few questions. Have we ever
had any peace on this slavery question? When are we to have
peace upon it, if it is kept in the position it now occupies? How
are we ever to have peace upon it? That is an important ques-

tion. To be sure, if we will all stop, and allow Judge Douglas and his friends to march on in their present career until they plant the institution all over the nation, here and wherever else our flag waves, and we acquiesce in it, there will be peace. But let me ask Judge Douglas how he is going to get the people to do that? They have been wrangling over this question for at least forty years. This was the cause of the agitation resulting in the Missouri Compromise; this produced the troubles at the annexation of Texas, in the acquisition of the territory acquired in the Mexican War. Again, this was the trouble which was quieted by the Compromise of 1850, when it was settled *"forever"* as both the great political parties declared in their National Conventions. That "forever" turned out to be just four years, *when Judge Douglas himself reopened it.* When is it likely to come to an end? He introduced the Nebraska Bill in 1854 to put *another end* to the slavery agitation. He promised that it would finish it all up immediately, and he has never made a speech since, until he got into a quarrel with the President about the Lecompton Constitution, in which he has not declared that we are *just at the end* of the slavery agitation. But in one speech, I think last winter, he did say that he didn't quite see when the end of the slavery agitation would come. Now he tells us again that it is all over and the people of Kansas have voted down the Lecompton Constitution. How is it over? That was only one of the attempts at putting an end to the slavery agitation—one of these "final settlements." Is Kansas in the Union? Has she formed a constitution that she is likely to come in under? Is not the slavery agitation still an open question in that Territory? Has the voting down of that constitution put an end to all the trouble? Is that more likely to settle it than every one of these previous attempts to settle the slavery agitation? Now, at this day in the history of the world we can no more foretell where the end of this slavery agitation will be than we can see the end of the world itself. The Nebraska-Kansas Bill was introduced four years and a half ago, and if the agitation is ever to come to an end we may say we are four years and a half nearer the end. So, too, we can say we are four years and a half nearer the end of the world, and we can just as clearly see the end of the world as we can see the end of this agitation. The Kansas settlement did not conclude it. If Kansas should sink to-day, and leave a great vacant space in the earth's surface, this vexed question would still be among us. I say, then, there is no way of putting an end to the slavery agitation amongst us but to put it back upon the basis where our fathers placed it; no way but to keep it out of our new Territories,—to restrict it forever to the old States where it now exists. Then the public mind *will* rest in the belief that it is in the course of ultimate extinction. That is one way of putting an end to the slavery agitation.

The other way is for us to surrender and let Judge Douglas and his friends have their way and plant slavery over all the States; cease speaking of it as in any way a wrong; regard slavery as one of the common matters of property, and speak of negroes as we do of our horses and cattle. But while it drives on in its state of progress as it is now driving, and as it has driven for the last five years, I have ventured the opinion, and I say to-day, that we will have no end to the slavery agitation until it takes one turn or the other. I do not mean that when it takes a turn toward ultimate extinction it will be in a day, nor in a year, nor in two years. I do not suppose that in the most peaceful way ultimate extinction would occur in less than a hundred years at least; but that it will occur in the best way for both races, in God's own good time, I have no doubt. But, my friends, I have used up more of my time than I intended on this point.

Now, in regard to this matter about Trumbull and myself having made a bargain to sell out the entire Whig and Democratic parties in 1854: Judge Douglas brings forward no evidence to sustain his charge, except the speech Matheny is said to have made in 1856, in which he told a cock-and-bull story of that sort, upon the same moral principles that Judge Douglas tells it here to-day. This is the simple truth. I do not care greatly for the story, but this is the truth of it: and I have twice told Judge Douglas to his face that from beginning to end there is not one word of truth in it. I have called upon him for the proof, and he does not at all meet me as Trumbull met him upon that of which we were just talking, by producing the record. He didn't bring the record because there was no record for him to bring. When he asks if I am ready to indorse Trumbull's veracity after he has broken a bargain with me, I reply that if Trumbull *had* broken a bargain with me I would not be likely to indorse his veracity; but I am ready to indorse his veracity because *neither in that thing, nor in any other, in all the years that I have known Lyman Trumbull, have I known him to fail of his word or tell a falsehood large or small.* It is for that reason that I indorse Lyman Trumbull.

MR. JAMES BROWN (*Douglas postmaster*): What does Ford's History say about him?

MR. LINCOLN: Some gentleman asks me what Ford's History says about him. My own recollection is that Ford speaks of Trumbull in very disrespectful terms in several portions of his book, *and that he talks a great deal worse of Judge Douglas.* I refer you, sir, to the History for examination.

Judge Douglas complains at considerable length about a disposition on the part of Trumbull and myself to attack him personally. I want to attend to that suggestion a moment. I don't want to be unjustly accused of dealing illiberally or unfairly with an adversary, either in court or in a political canvass or anywhere else. I would despise myself if I supposed myself ready to deal less liberally with an adversary than I was willing to be treated myself. Judge Douglas in a general way, without putting it in a direct shape, revives the old charge against me in reference to the Mexican War. He does not take the responsibility of putting it in a very definite form, but makes a general reference to it. That charge is more than ten years old. He complains of Trumbull and myself because he says we bring charges against him one or two years old. He knows, too, that in regard to the Mexican War story the more respectable papers of his own party throughout the State have been compelled to take it back and acknowledge that it was a lie.

[Here MR. LINCOLN turned to the crowd on the platform, and, selecting Hon. ORLANDO B. FICKLIN, led him forward and said:]

I do not mean to do anything with Mr. Ficklin except to present his face and tell you that *he personally knows it to be a lie!* He was a member of Congress at the only time I was in

Congress, and [Ficklin] knows that whenever there was an attempt to procure a vote of mine which would indorse the origin and justice of the war, I refused to give such indorsement and voted against it; but I never voted against the supplies for the army, and he knows, as well as Judge Douglas, that whenever a dollar was asked by way of compensation or otherwise for the benefit of the soldiers *I gave all the votes that Ficklin or Douglas did, and perhaps more.*

MR. FICKLIN: My friends, I wish to say this in reference to the matter: Mr. Lincoln and myself are just as good personal friends as Judge Douglas and myself. In reference to this Mexican War, my recollection is that when Ashmun's resolution [amendment] was offered by Mr. Ashmun of Massachusetts, in which he declared that the Mexican War was unnecessary and unconstitutionally commenced by the President—my recollection is that Mr. Lincoln voted for that resolution.

MR. LINCOLN: That is the truth. Now, you all remember that was a resolution censuring the President for the manner in which the war was *begun.* You know they have charged that I voted against the supplies, by which I starved the soldiers who were out fighting the battles of their country. I say that Ficklin knows it is false. When that charge was brought forward by the Chicago *Times,* the Springfield *Register* [Douglas's organ] reminded the *Times* that the charge really applied to John Henry; and I do know that John Henry *is now making speeches and fiercely battling for Judge Douglas.* If the Judge now says that he offers this as a sort of setoff to what I said to-day in reference to Trumbull's charge, then I remind him that he made this charge before I said a word about Trumbull's. He brought this forward at Ottawa, the first time we met face to face; and in the opening speech that Judge Douglas made he attacked me in regard to a matter ten years old. Isn't he a pretty man to be whining about people making charges against him only *two* years old!

The Judge thinks it is altogether wrong that I should have dwelt upon this charge of Trumbull's at all. I gave the apology for doing so in my opening speech. Perhaps it didn't fix your attention. I said that when Judge Douglas was speaking at places where I spoke on the succeeding day he used very harsh language about this charge. Two or three times afterward I said I had confidence in Judge Trumbull's veracity and intelligence; and my own opinion was, from what I knew of the character of Judge Trumbull, that he would vindicate his position and prove whatever he had stated to be true. This I repeated two or three times; and then I dropped it, without saying anything more on the subject for weeks—perhaps a month. I passed it by without noticing it at all till I found, at Jacksonville, Judge Douglas in the plenitude of his power is not willing to answer Trumbull and let me alone, but he comes out there and uses this language: "He should not hereafter occupy his time in refuting such charges made by Trumbull but that, Lincoln having indorsed the character of Trumbull for veracity, he should hold him [Lincoln] responsible for the slanders." What was Lincoln to do? Did he not do right, when he had the fit opportunity of meeting Judge Douglas here, to tell him he was ready for the responsibility? I ask a candid audience whether in doing thus Judge Douglas was not the assailant rather than I? Here I meet him face to face, and say I am ready to take the responsibility, so far as it rests on me.

Having done so I ask the attention of this audience to the question whether I have succeeded in sustaining the charge, and whether Judge Douglas has at all succeeded in rebutting it? You all heard me call upon him to say *which of these pieces of evidence was a forgery.* Does he say that what I present here as a copy of the original Toombs bill is a forgery? Does he say that what I present as a copy of the bill reported by himself is a forgery, or what is presented as a transcript from the *Globe* of the quotations from Bigler's speech is a forgery? Does he say the quotations from his own speech are forgeries? Does he say this transcript from Trumbull's speech is a forgery? ["He didn't deny one of them."] *I would then like to know how it comes about that when each piece of a story is true the whole story turns out false.* I take it these people have some sense; they see plainly that Judge Douglas is playing cuttle-fish,—a small species of fish that has no mode of defending itself when pursued except by throwing out a black fluid, which makes the water so dark the enemy cannot see it, and thus it escapes. Ain't the Judge playing the cuttle-fish?

Now, I would ask very special attention to the consideration of Judge Douglas's speech at Jacksonville; and when you shall read his speech of to-day, I ask you to watch closely and see which of these pieces of testimony, every one of which he says is a forgery, he has shown to be such. *Not one of them has he shown to be a forgery.* Then I ask the original question, if each of the pieces of testimony is true, *how is it possible that the whole is a falsehood?*

In regard to Trumbull's charge that he [Douglas] inserted a provision into the bill to prevent the constitution being submitted to the people, what was his answer? He comes here and reads from the *Congressional Globe* to show that on his motion that provision was struck out of the bill. Why, Trumbull has not said it was not stricken out, but Trumbull says he [Douglas] put it in; and it is no answer to the charge to say he afterwards took it out. Both are perhaps true. It was in regard to that thing precisely that I told him he had dropped the cub. Trumbull shows you that by his introducing the bill it was his cub. It is no answer to that assertion to call Trumbull a liar merely because he did not specially say that Douglas struck it out. Suppose that were the case, does it answer Trumbull? I assert that you [pointing to an individual] are here to-day, and you undertake to prove me a liar by showing that you were in Mattoon yesterday. I say that you took your hat off your head, and you prove me a liar by putting it on your head. That is the whole force of Douglas's argument.

Now, I want to come back to my original question. Trumbull says that Judge Douglas had a bill with a provision in it for submitting a constitution to be made to a vote of the people of Kansas. Does Judge Douglas deny that fact? Does he deny that the provision which Trumbull reads was put in that bill? Then Trumbull says he struck it out. Does he dare to deny that? He does not, and I have the right to repeat the question,—*Why Judge Douglas took it out?* Bigler has said there was a combination of certain senators, among whom he did not include Judge Douglas, by which it was agreed that the Kansas Bill should have a clause in it not to have the constitution formed under it submitted to a vote of the people. He did not say that Douglas was among them, but we prove by another source that about the same time Douglas comes into the Senate *with that provision stricken out of the bill.* Although Bigler cannot say they were all working in concert, yet it looks very much as if the thing was agreed upon and done with a mutual understanding after the conference; and while we do not know that it was absolutely so, yet it looks so probable that we have a right to call upon the man who knows the true reason why it was done *to tell what the true reason was.* When he will not tell what the true reason was, he stands in the attitude of an accused thief who has stolen goods in his possession, and when called to account refuses to tell where he got them. Not only is this the evidence, but when he comes in with the bill having the provision stricken out, he tells us in a speech, not then but since, that these alterations and modifications in the bill *had been made by* HIM, *in consultation with Toombs, the originator of the bill.* He tells us the same to-day. He says there were certain modifications made in the bill in committee that he did not vote for. I ask you to remember, while certain amendments were made which he disapproved of, but which a majority of the committee voted in, he has himself told us that in this particular *the alterations and modifications were made by him, upon consultation with Toombs.* We have his own word that these alterations were made *by him,* and not by the committee. Now, I ask, what is the reason Judge Douglas is so chary about coming to the exact question? What is the reason he will not tell you anything about HOW it was made, BY WHOM it was made, or that he remembers it being made at all? Why does he stand playing upon the meaning of words and quibbling around the edges of the evidence? If he can explain all this, but leaves it unexplained, I have the right to infer that Judge Douglas understood it was the purpose of his party, in engineering that bill through, to make a constitution, and have Kansas come into the Union with that constitution, *without its being submitted to a vote of the people.* If he will explain his action on this question, by giving a *better reason* for the facts that happened than he has done, it will be satisfactory. But until he does that—until he gives a better or more plausible reason than he has offered against the evidence in the case—*I suggest to him it will not avail him at all that he swells himself up, takes on dignity, and calls people liars*. Why, sir, there is not a word in Trumbull's speech that depends on Trumbull's veracity at all. He has only arrayed the evidence and told you what follows as a matter of reasoning. There is not a statement in the whole speech that depends on Trumbull's word. If you have ever studied geometry, you remember that by a course of reasoning Euclid proves that all the angles in a triangle are equal to two right angles. Euclid has shown you how to work it out. Now, if you undertake to disprove that proposition, and to show that it is erroneous, would you prove it to be false by calling Euclid a liar? They tell me that my time is out, and therefore I close.

Fifth Joint Debate
GALESBURGH, OCTOBER 7, 1858

Mr. Douglas's Speech

LADIES AND GENTLEMEN: Four years ago I appeared before the people of Knox County for the purpose of defending my political action upon the Compromise measures of 1850 and the passage of the Kansas-Nebraska Bill. Those of you before me who were present then will remember that I vindicated myself for supporting those two measures by the fact that they rested upon the great fundamental principle that the people of each State and each Territory of this Union have the right, and ought to be permitted to exercise the right, of regulating their own domestic concerns in their own way, subject to no other limitation or restriction than that which the Constitution of the United States imposes upon them. I then called upon the people of Illinois to decide whether that principle of self-government was right or wrong. If it was and is right, then the Compromise measures of 1850 were right, and consequently, the Kansas and Nebraska Bill, based upon the same principle, must necessarily have been right.

The Kansas and Nebraska Bill declared, in so many words, that it was the true intent and meaning of the act not to legislate slavery into any State or Territory, nor to exclude it therefrom, but to leave the people thereof perfectly free to form and regulate their domestic institutions in their own way, subject only to the Constitution of the United States. For the last four years I have devoted all my energies, in private and public, to commend that principle to the American people. Whatever else may be said in condemnation or support of my political course I apprehend that no honest man will doubt the fidelity with which, under all circumstances, I have stood by it.

During the last year a question arose in the Congress of the United States whether or not that principle would be violated by the admission of Kansas into the Union under the Lecompton Constitution. In my opinion, the attempt to force Kansas in under that constitution was a gross violation of the principle enunciated in the Compromise measures of 1850, and Kansas and Nebraska Bill of 1854, and therefore I led off in the fight against the Lecompton Constitution, and conducted it until the effort to carry that constitution through Congress was abandoned. And I can appeal to all men, friends and foes, Democrats and Republicans, Northern men and Southern men, that during the whole of that fight I carried the banner of popular sovereignty aloft, and never allowed it to trail in the dust, or lowered my flag until victory perched upon our arms. When the Lecompton Constitution was defeated, the question arose in the minds of those who had advocated it what they should next resort to in order to carry out their views. They devised a measure known as the English bill, and granted a general amnesty and political pardon to all men who had fought against the Lecompton Constitution, provided they would support that bill. I for one did not choose to accept the pardon, or to avail myself of the amnesty granted on that condition. The fact that the supporters of Lecompton were willing to forgive all differences of opinion at that time in the event those who opposed it favored the English bill, was an admission they did not think that opposition to Lecompton impaired a man's standing in the Democratic party. Now, the question arises, what was that English bill which certain men are now attempting to make a test of political orthodoxy in this country? It provided, in substance, that the Lecompton Constitution should be sent back to the people of Kansas for their adoption or rejection, at an election which was held in August last, and in case they refused admission under it, that Kansas should be kept out of the Union until she had 93,420 inhabitants. I was in favor of sending the constitution back in order to enable the people to say whether or not it was their act and deed, and embodied their will; but the other proposition, that if they refused to come into the Union under it they should be kept out until they had double or treble the population they then had, I never would sanction by my vote. The reason why I could not sanction it is to be found in the fact that by the English bill, if the people of Kansas had only agreed to become a slaveholding State under the Lecompton Constitution, they could have done so with 35,000 people, but if they insisted on being a free State, as they had a right to do, then they were to be punished by being kept out of the Union until they had nearly three times that population. I then said in my place in the Senate, as I now say to you, that whenever Kansas has population enough for a slave State she has population enough for a free State. I have never yet given a vote, and I never intend to record one, making an odious and unjust distinction between the different States of this Union. I hold it to be a fundamental principle in our republican form of government that all the States of this Union, old and new, free and slave, stand on an exact equality. Equality among the different States is a cardinal principle on which all our institutions rest. Wherever, therefore, you make a discrimination, saving to a slave State that it shall be admitted with 35,000 inhabitants, and a free State that it shall not be admitted until it has 93,000 or 100,000 inhabitants, you are throwing the whole weight of the Federal Government into the scale in favor of one class of States against the other. Nor would I, on the other hand, any sooner sanction the doctrine that a free State could be admitted into the Union with 35,000 people, while a slave State was kept out until it had 93,000. I have always declared in the Senate my willingness, and I am willing now to adopt the rule, that no Territory shall ever become a State until it has the requisite population for a member of Congress, according to the then existing ratio. But while I have always been, and am now, willing to adopt that general rule, I was not willing and would not consent to make an exception of Kansas, as a punishment for her obstinacy in demanding the right to do as she pleased in the formation of her constitution. It is proper that I should remark here, that my opposition to the Lecompton Constitution did not rest upon the peculiar position taken by Kansas on the subject of slavery. I held then, and hold now, that if the people of Kansas want a slave State, it is their right to make one, and be received into the Union under it; if, on the contrary, they want a free State, it is their right to have it, and no man should ever oppose their admission because they ask it under the one or the other. I hold to that great principle of self-government which asserts the right of every people to decide for themselves the nature and character of the domestic institutions and fundamental law under which they are to live.

The effort has been and is now being made in this State by certain postmasters and other Federal office-holders to make a test of faith on the support of the English bill. These men are now making speeches all over the State against me and in favor of Lincoln, either directly or indirectly, because I would not sanction a discrimination between slave and free States by voting for the English bill. But while that bill is made a test in Illinois for the purpose of breaking up the Democratic organization in this State, how is it in the other States? Go to Indiana, and there you find English himself, the author of the English bill, who is a candidate for re-election to Congress, has been forced by public opinion to abandon his own darling project, and to give a promise that he will vote for the admission of Kansas at once, whenever she forms a constitution in pursuance of law and ratifies it by a majority vote of her people. Not only is this the case with English himself, but I am informed that every Democratic candidate for Congress in Indiana takes the same ground. Pass to Ohio, and there you find that Groesbeck, and Pendleton, and Cox, and all the other anti-Lecompton men who stood shoulder to shoulder with me against the Lecompton Constitution, but voted for the English bill, now repudiate it and take the same ground that I do on that question. So it is with the Joneses and others of Pennsylvania, and so it is with every other Lecompton Democrat in the free States. They now abandon even the English bill, and come back to the true platform which I proclaimed at the time in the Senate, and upon which the Democracy of Illinois now stand. And yet, notwithstanding the fact that every Lecompton and anti-Lecompton Democrat in the free States has abandoned the English bill, you are told that it is to be made a test upon me, while the power and patronage of the Government are all exerted to elect men to Congress in the other States who occupy the same position with reference to it that I do. It seems that my political offence consists in the fact that I first did not vote for the English bill, and thus pledge myself to keep Kansas out of the Union until she has a population of 93,420, and then return home, violate that pledge, repudiate the bill, and take the opposite ground. If I had done this, perhaps the Administration would now be advocating my re-election, as it is that of the others who have pursued this course. I did not choose to give that pledge, for the reason that I did not intend to carry out that principle. I never will consent, for the sake of conciliating the frowns of power, to pledge myself to do that which I do not intend to perform. I now submit the question to you, as my constituency, whether I was not right, first, in resisting the adopting of the Lecompton Constitution, and, secondly, in resisting the English bill. I repeat that I opposed the Lecompton Constitution because it was not the act and deed on the people of Kansas, and did not embody their will. I denied the right of any power on earth, under our system of government, to force a constitution on an unwilling people. There was a time when some men could pretend to believe that the Lecompton Constitution embodied the will of the people of Kansas; but that time has passed. The question was referred to the people of Kansas under the English bill last August, and then, at a fair election, they rejected the Lecompton Constitution by a vote of from eight to ten against it to one in its favor. Since it has been voted down by so overwhelming a majority, no man can pretend that it was the act and deed of that people. I submit the question to you whether or not, if it had not been for me, that constitution would have been crammed down the throats of the people of Kansas against their consent. While at least ninety-nine out of every hundred people here present agree that I was right in defeating that project, yet my enemies use the fact that I did defeat it, by doing right, to break me down and put another man in the United States Senate in my place.

The very men who acknowledge that I was right in defeating Lecompton now form an alliance with Federal office-holders, professed Lecompton men, to defeat me, because I did right. My political opponent, Mr. Lincoln, has no hope on earth, and has never dreamed that he had a chance of success, were it not for the aid that he is receiving from Federal office-holders, who are using their influence and the patronage of the government against me in revenge for my having defeated the Lecompton Constitution. What do you Republicans think of a political organization that will try to make an unholy and unnatural combination with its professed foes to beat a man merely because he has done right? You know such is the fact with regard to your own party. You know that the axe of decapitation is suspended over every man in office in Illinois, and the terror of proscription is threatened every Democrat by the present Administration, unless he supports the Republican ticket in preference to my Democratic associates and myself. I could find an instance in the postmaster of the city of Galesburgh, and in every other postmaster in this vicinity, all of whom have been stricken down simply because they discharged the duties of their offices honestly, and supported the regular Democratic ticket in this State in the right. The Republican party is availing itself of unworthy means in the present contest to carry the election, because its leaders know that if they let this chance slip they will never have another, and their hopes of making this a Republican State will be blasted forever.

Now, let me ask you whether the country has any interest in sustaining this organization, known as the Republican party. That party is unlike all other political organizations in this country. All other parties have been national in their character,— have avowed their principles alike in the slave and free States, in Kentucky as well as Illinois, in Louisiana as well as in Massachusetts. Such was the case with the old Whig party, and such was and is the case with the Democratic party. Whigs and Democrats could proclaim their principles boldly and fearlessly in the North and in the South, in the East and in the West, wherever the Constitution ruled, and the American flag waved over American soil.

But now you have a sectional organization, a party which appeals to the Northern section of the Union against the Southern, a party which appeals to Northern passion, Northern pride, Northern ambition, and Northern prejudices, against Southern people, the Southern States, and Southern institutions. The leaders of that party hope that they will be able to unite the Northern States in one great sectional party; and inasmuch as the North is the strongest section, that they will thus be enabled to outvote, conquer, govern and control the South. Hence you find that they now make speeches advocating principles and measures which cannot be defended in any slaveholding State of this Union. Is there a Republican residing in Galesburgh who can travel into Kentucky and carry his principles with him across the Ohio? What Republican from Massachusetts can visit the Old Dominion without leaving his principles behind him when he crosses Mason and Dixon's line? Permit me to say to you in perfect good-humor, but in all sincerity, that no political creed is sound which cannot be proclaimed fearlessly in every State of this Union where the Federal Constitution is the supreme law of the land. Not only is this Republican party unable to proclaim its principles alike in the North and South, in the free States and in the slave States, but it cannot even proclaim them in the same forms and give them the same strength and meaning in all parts of the same State. My friend Lincoln finds it extremely difficult to manage a debate in the centre part of the State, where there is a mixture of men from the North and the South. In the extreme northern part of Illinois he can proclaim as bold and radical Abolitionism as ever Giddings, Lovejoy, or Garrison enunciated; but when he gets down a little farther south he claims that he is an old-line Whig, a disciple of Henry Clay, and declares that he still adheres to the old-line Whig creed, and has nothing whatever to do with Abolitionism, or negro equality, or negro citizenship. I once before hinted this of Mr. Lincoln in a public speech, and at Charleston he defied me to show that there was any difference between his speeches in the North and in the South, and that they were not in strict harmony. I will now call your attention to two of them, and you can then say whether you would be apt to believe that the same man ever uttered both. In a speech in reply to me at Chicago in July last, Mr. Lincoln, in speaking of the equality of the negro with the white man, used the following language:

"I should like to know, if, taking this old Declaration of Independence, which declares that all men are equal upon principle, and making exceptions to it, where will it stop? If one man says it does not mean a negro, why may not another man say it does not mean another man? If the Declaration is not the truth, let us get the statute book in which we find it, and tear it out. Who is so bold as to do it? If it is not true, let us tear it out."

You find that Mr. Lincoln there proposed that if the doctrine of the Declaration of Independence, declaring all men to be born equal, did not include the negro and put him on an equality with the white man, that we should take the statute book and tear it out. He there took the ground that the negro race is included in the Declaration of Independence as the equal of the white race, and that there could be no such thing as a distinction in the races, making one superior and the other inferior. I read now from the same speech:

"My friends [he says], I have detained you about as long as I desire to do, and I have only to say, let us discard all this quibbling about this man and the other man, this race and that race and the other race being inferior, and therefore they must be placed in an inferior position, discarding our standard that we have left us. Let us discard all these things, and unite as one people throughout this land, until we shall once more stand up declaring that all men are created equal."

["That's right," etc.]

Yes, I have no doubt that you think it is right; but the Lincoln men down in Coles, Tazewell, and Sangamon counties *do not* think it is right. In the conclusion of the same speech, talking to the Chicago Abolitionists, he said: "I leave you, hoping that the lamp of liberty will burn in your bosoms until there shall no longer be a doubt that all men are created free and equal." ["Good, good."] Well, you say "Good" to that, and you are going to vote for Lincoln because he holds that doctrine. I will not blame you for supporting him on that ground, but I will show you, in immediate contrast with that doctrine, what Mr. Lincoln said down in Egypt in order to get votes in that locality, where they do not hold to such a doctrine. In a joint discussion between Mr. Lincoln and myself, at Charleston, I think, on the 18th of last month, Mr. Lincoln, referring to this subject, used the following language:

"I will say then, that I am not, nor never have been, in favor of bringing about in any way the social and political equality of the white and black races; that I am not, nor ever have been, in favor of making voters of the free negroes, or jurors, or qualifying them to hold office, or having them to marry with white people. I will say, in addition, that there is a physical difference between the white and black races which, I suppose, will forever forbid the two races living together upon terms of social and political equality; and inasmuch as they cannot so live, that while they do remain together there must be the position of superior and inferior, that I as much as any other man am in favor of the superior position being assigned to the white man."

["Good for Lincoln."]

Fellow-citizens, here you find men hurrahing for Lincoln, and saying that he did right, when in one part of the State he stood up for negro equality, and in another part, for political effect, discarded the doctrine, and declared that there always must be a superior and inferior race. Abolitionists up North are expected and required to vote for Lincoln because he goes for the equality of the races, holding that by the Declaration of Independence the white man and the negro were created equal, and endowed by the divine law with that equality, and down South he tells the old Whigs, the Kentuckians, Virginians, and Tennesseeans, that there is a physical difference in the races, making one superior and the other inferior, and that he is in favor of maintaining the superiority of the white race over the negro. Now, how can you reconcile those two positions of Mr. Lincoln? He is to be voted for in the South as a pro-slavery man, and he is to be voted for in the North as an Abolitionist. Up here he thinks it is all nonsense to talk about a difference between the races, and says that we must "discard all quibbling about this race and that race and the other race being inferior, and therefore they must be placed in an inferior position." Down South he makes this "quibble" about this race and that race and the other race being inferior as the creed of his party, and declares that the negro can never be elevated to the position of the white man. You find that his political meetings are called by different names in different counties in the State. Here they are called Republican meetings; but in old Tazewell, where Lincoln made a speech last Tuesday, he did not address a *Republican* meeting, but "a grand rally of the *Lincoln men.*" There are very few Republicans there, because Tazewell County is filled with old Virginians and Kentuckians, all of whom are Whigs or Democrats; and if Mr. Lincoln had called an Abolition or Republican meeting there, he would not get many votes. Go down into Egypt, and you will find that he and his party are operating under an alias there, which his friend Trumbull has given them, in order that they may cheat the people. When I was down in Monroe County a few weeks ago, addressing the people, I saw handbills posted announcing that Mr. Trumbull was going to speak in behalf of Lincoln; and what do you think the name of his party was there? Why, the *"Free Democracy."* Mr. Trumbull and Mr. Jehu Baker were announced to address the Free Democracy of Monroe County, and the bill was signed, "Many Free Democrats." The reason that Lincoln and his party adopted the name of "Free Democracy" down there was because Monroe County has always been an old-fashioned Democratic county, and hence it was necessary to make the people believe that they were Democrats, sympathized with them, and were fighting for Lincoln as Democrats. Come up to Springfield, where Lincoln now lives, and always has lived, and you find that the Convention of his party which assembled to nominate candidates for Legislature, who are expected to vote for him if elected, dare not adopt the name of Republican, but assembled under the title of "all opposed to the Democracy." Thus you find that Mr. Lincoln's creed cannot travel through even one half of the counties of this State, but that it changes its hues and becomes lighter and lighter as it travels from the extreme north, until it is nearly white when it reaches the extreme south end of the State.

I ask you, my friends, why cannot Republicans avow their principles alike everywhere? I would despise myself if I thought that I was procuring your votes by concealing my opinions, and by avowing one set of principles in one part of the State, and a different set in another part. If I do not truly and honorably represent your feelings and principles, then I ought not to be your Senator; and I will never conceal my opinions, or modify or change them a hair's breadth, in order to get votes. I tell you that this Chicago doctrine of Lincoln's—declaring that the negro and the white man are made equal by the Declaration of Independence and by Divine Providence—is a monstrous heresy. The signers of the Declaration of Independence never dreamed of the negro when they were writing that document. They referred to white men, to men of European birth, and European descent, when they declared the equality of all men. I see a gentleman there in the crowd shaking his head. Let me remind him that when Thomas Jefferson wrote that document, he was the owner, and so continued until his death, of a large number of slaves. Did he intend to say in that Declaration that his negro slaves, which he held and treated as property, were created his equals by divine law, and that he was violating the law of God every day of his life by holding them as slaves? It must be borne in mind that when that Declaration was put forth, every one of the thirteen Colonies were slaveholding Colonies, and every man who signed that instrument represented a slaveholding constituency. Recollect, also, that no one of them emancipated his slaves, much less put them on an equality with himself, after he signed the Declaration. On the contrary, they all continued to hold their negroes as slaves during the Revolutionary War. Now, do you believe—are you willing to have it said—that every man who signed the Declaration of Independence declared the negro his equal, and then was hypocrite enough to continue to hold him as a slave, in violation of what he believed to be the divine law? And yet when you say that the Declaration of Independence includes the negro, you charge the signers of it with hypocrisy.

I say to you, frankly, that in my opinion this government was made by our fathers on the white basis. It was made by white men for the benefit of white men and their posterity forever, and was intended to be administered by white men in all time to come. But while I hold that under our Constitution and political system the negro is not a citizen, cannot be a citizen, and ought not to be a citizen, it does not follow by any means that he should be a slave. On the contrary, it does follow that the negro, as an inferior race, ought to possess every right, every privilege, every immunity, which he can safely exercise, consistent with the safety of the society in which he lives. Humanity requires, and Christianity commands, that you shall extend to every inferior being, and every dependent being, all the privileges, immunities, and advantages which can be granted to them, consistent with the safety of society. If you ask me the nature and extent of these privileges, I answer that that is a question which the people of each State must decide for themselves. Illinois has decided that question for herself. We have said that in this State the negro shall not be a slave, nor shall he be a citizen. Kentucky holds a different doctrine. New York holds one different from either, and Maine one different from all. Virginia, in her policy on this question, differs in many respects from the others, and so on, until there are hardly two States whose policy is exactly alike in regard to the relation of the white man and the negro. Nor can you reconcile them and make them alike. Each State must do as it pleases. Illinois had as much right to adopt the policy which we have on that subject as Kentucky had to adopt a different policy. The great principle of this government is, that each State has the right to do as it pleases on all these questions, and no other State or power on earth has the right to interfere with us, or complain of us merely because our system differs from theirs. In the Compromise measures of 1850, Mr. Clay declared that this great principle ought to exist in the Territories as well as in the States, and I reasserted his doctrine in the Kansas and Nebraska Bill of 1854.

But Mr. Lincoln cannot be made to understand, and those who are determined to vote for him, no matter whether he is a pro-slavery man in the South and a negro equality advocate in the North, cannot be made to understand how it is that in a Territory the people can do as they please on the slavery question under the Dred Scott decision. Let us see whether I cannot explain it to the satisfaction of all impartial men. Chief Justice Taney has said, in his opinion in the Dred Scott case, that a negro slave, being property, stands on an equal footing with other property, and that the owner may carry them into United States territory the same as he does other property. Suppose any two of you, neighbors, should conclude to go to Kansas, one carrying $100,000 worth of negro slaves, and the other $100,000 worth of mixed merchandise, including quantities of liquors. You both agree that under that decision you may carry your property to Kansas; but when you get it there, the merchant who is possessed of the liquors is met by the Maine liquor law, which prohibits the sale or use of his property, and the owner of the slaves is met by equally unfriendly legislation, which makes his property worthless after he gets it there. What is the right to carry your property into the Territory worth to either, when unfriendly legislation in the Territory renders it worthless after you get it there? The slaveholder when he gets his slaves there finds that there is no local law to protect him in holding them, no slave code, no police regulation maintaining and supporting him in his right, and he discovers at once that the absence of such friendly legislation excludes his property from the Territory just as irresistibly as if there was a positive constitutional prohibition excluding it. Thus you find it is with any kind of property in a Territory: it depends for its protection on the local and municipal law. If the people of a Territory want slavery, they make friendly legislation to introduce it; but if they do not want it, they withhold all protection from it, and then it cannot exist there. Such was the view taken on the subject by different Southern men when the Nebraska Bill passed. See the speech of Mr. Orr, of South Carolina, the present Speaker of the House of Representatives of Congress, made at that time; and there you will find this whole doctrine argued out at full length. Read the speeches of other Southern Congressmen, Senators and Representatives, made in 1854, and you will find that they took the same view of the subject as Mr. Orr,—that slavery could never be forced on a people who did not want it. I hold that in this country there is no power on the face of the globe that can force any institution on an unwilling people. The great fundamental principle of our government is that the people of each State and each Territory shall be left perfectly free to decide for themselves what shall be the nature and character of their institutions. When this government was made, it was based on that principle. At the time of its formation there were twelve slaveholding States and one free State in this Union. Suppose this doctrine of Mr. Lincoln and the Republicans, of uniformity of laws of all the States on the subject of slavery, had prevailed; suppose Mr. Lincoln himself had been a member of the Convention which framed the Constitution, and that he had risen in that august body, and, addressing the father of his country, had said as he did at Springfield: "A house divided against itself cannot stand. I believe this government cannot endure permanently, half slave and half free. I do not expect the Union to be dissolved, I do not expect the house to fall, but I do expect it will cease to be divided. It will become all one thing or all the other." What do you think would have been the result? Suppose he had made that Convention believe that doctrine, and they had acted upon it, what do you think would have been the result? Do you believe that the one free State would have outvoted the twelve slaveholding States, and thus abolish slavery? On the contrary, would not the twelve slaveholding States have outvoted the one free State, and under his doctrine have fastened slavery by an irrevocable constitutional provision upon every inch of the American Republic? Thus you see that the doctrine he now advocates, if proclaimed at the beginning of the government, would have established slavery everywhere throughout the American continent; and are you willing, now that we have the majority section, to exercise a power which we never would have submitted to when we were in the minority? If the Southern States had attempted to control our institutions, and make the States all slave, when they had the power, I ask would you have submitted to it? If you would not, are you willing, now that we have become the strongest, under that great principle of self-government that allows each State to do as it pleases, to attempt to control the Southern institutions? Then, my friends, I say to you that there is but one path of

peace in this Republic, and that is to administer this government as our fathers made it, divided into free and slave States,
allowing each State to decide for itself whether it wants slavery
or not. If Illinois will settle the slavery question for herself, and
mind her own business and let her neighbors alone, we will be
at peace with Kentucky and every other Southern State. If
every other State in the Union will do the same, there will be
peace between the North and the South, and in the whole
Union.

Mr. Lincoln's Reply

MY FELLOW-CITIZENS: A very large portion of the speech which
Judge Douglas has addressed to you has previously been delivered and put in print. I do not mean that for a hit upon the
Judge at all. If I had not been interrupted, I was going to say that
such an answer as I was able to make to a very large portion of
it had already been more than once made and published. There
has been an opportunity afforded to the public to see our
respective views upon the topics discussed in a large portion of
the speech which he has just delivered. I make these remarks
for the purpose of excusing myself for not passing over the
entire ground that the Judge has traversed. I however desire to
take up some of the points that he has attended to, and ask your
attention to them, and I shall follow him backwards upon some
notes which I have taken, reversing the order, by beginning
where he concluded.

The Judge has alluded to the Declaration of Independence,
and insisted that negroes are not included in that Declaration;
and that it is a slander upon the framers of that instrument to
suppose that negroes were meant therein; and he asks you: Is it
possible to believe that Mr. Jefferson, who penned the immortal paper, could have supposed himself applying the language of
that instrument to the negro race, and yet held a portion of that
race in slavery? Would he not at once have freed them? I only
have to remark upon this part of the Judge's speech (and that,
too, very briefly, for I shall not detain myself, or you, upon that

point for any great length of time), that I believe the entire records of the world, from the date of the Declaration of Independence up to within three years ago, may be searched in vain for one single affirmation, from one single man, that the negro was not included in the Declaration of Independence; I think I may defy Judge Douglas to show that he ever said so, that Washington ever said so, that any President ever said so, that any member of Congress ever said so, or that any living man upon the whole earth ever said so, until the necessities of the present policy of the Democratic party, in regard to slavery, had to invent that affirmation. And I will remind Judge Douglas and this audience that while Mr. Jefferson was the owner of slaves, as undoubtedly he was, in speaking upon this very subject he used the strong language that "he trembled for his country when he remembered that God was just"; and I will offer the highest premium in my power to Judge Douglas if he will show that he, in all his life, ever uttered a sentiment at all akin to that of Jefferson.

The next thing to which I will ask your attention is the Judge's comments upon the fact, as he assumes it to be, that we cannot call our public meetings as Republican meetings; and he instances Tazewell County as one of the places where the friends of Lincoln have called a public meeting and have not dared to name it a Republican meeting. He instances Monroe County as another, where Judge Trumbull and Jehu Baker addressed the persons whom the Judge assumes to be the friends of Lincoln calling them the "Free Democracy." I have the honor to inform Judge Douglas that he spoke in that very county of Tazewell last Saturday, and I was there on Tuesday last; and when he spoke there, he spoke under a call not venturing to use the word "Democrat." [Turning to Judge Douglas.] What think you of this?

So, again, there is another thing to which I would ask the Judge's attention upon this subject. In the contest of 1856 his party delighted to call themselves together as the "National Democracy"; but now, if there should be a notice put up anywhere for a meeting of the "National Democracy," Judge Douglas and his friends would not come. They would not suppose themselves invited. They would understand that it was a call for those hateful postmasters whom he talks about.

Now a few words in regard to these extracts from speeches of mine which Judge Douglas has read to you, and which he supposes are in very great contrast to each other. Those speeches have been before the public for a considerable time, and if they have any inconsistency in them, if there is any conflict in them, the public have been able to detect it. When the Judge says, in speaking on this subject, that I make speeches of one sort for the people of the northern end of the State, and of a different sort for the southern people, he assumes that I do not understand that my speeches will be put in print and read north and south. I knew all the while that the speech that I made at Chicago, and the one I made at Jonesboro and the one at Charleston, would all be put in print, and all the reading and intelligent men in the community would see them and know all about my opinions. And I have not supposed, and do not now suppose, that there is any conflict whatever between them. But the Judge will have it that if we do not confess that there is a sort of inequality between the white and black races which justifies us in making them slaves, we must then insist that there is a degree of equality that requires us to make them our wives. Now, I have all the while taken a broad distinction in regard to that matter; and that is all there is in these different speeches which he arrays here; and the entire reading of either of the speeches will show that that distinction was made. Perhaps by taking two parts of the same speech he could have got up as much of a conflict as the one he has found. I have all the while maintained that in so far as it should be insisted that there was an equality between the white and black races that should produce a perfect social and political equality, it was an impossibility. This you have seen in my printed speeches, and with it I have said that in their right to "life, liberty, and the pursuit of happiness," as proclaimed in that old Declaration, the inferior races are our equals. And these declarations I have constantly made in reference to the abstract moral question, to contemplate and consider when we are legislating about any new country which is not already cursed with the actual presence of the evil,—slavery. I have never manifested any impatience with the necessities that spring from the actual presence of black people amongst us, and the actual existence of slavery amongst us where it does already exist; but I have insisted that, in legislating for new countries where it does not exist there is no just rule other than that of moral and abstract right! With reference to those new countries, those maxims as to the right of a people to "life, liberty, and the pursuit of happiness" were the just rules to be constantly referred to. There is no misunderstanding this, except by men interested to misunderstand it. I take it that I have to address an intelligent and reading community, who will peruse what I say, weigh it, and then judge whether I advanced improper or unsound views, or whether I advanced hypocritical, and deceptive, and contrary views in different portions of the country. I believe myself to be guilty of no such thing as the latter, though, of course, I cannot claim that I am entirely free from all error in the opinions I advance.

The Judge has also detained us awhile in regard to the distinction between his party and our party. His he assumes to be a national party,—ours a sectional one. He does this in asking the question whether this country has any interest in the maintenance of the Republican party. He assumes that our party is altogether sectional, that the party to which he adheres is national; and the argument is, that no party can be a rightful party—and be based upon rightful principles—unless it can announce its principles everywhere. I presume that Judge Douglas could not go into Russia and announce the doctrine of our national Democracy; he could not denounce the doctrine of kings and emperors and monarchies in Russia; and it may be true of this country that in some places we may not be able to proclaim a doctrine as clearly true as the truth of democracy, because there is a section so directly opposed to it that they will not tolerate us in doing so. Is it the true test of the soundness of a doctrine that in some places people won't let you proclaim it? Is that the way to test the truth of any doctrine? Why, I understood that at one time the people of Chicago would not let Judge Douglas preach a certain favorite doctrine of his. I commend to his consideration the question whether he takes that as a test of the unsoundness of what he wanted to preach.

There is another thing to which I wish to ask attention for a little while on this occasion. What has always been the evidence brought forward to prove that the Republican party is a sectional party? The main one was that in the Southern portion of the Union the people did not let the Republicans proclaim their doctrines amongst them. That has been the main evidence brought forward,—that they had no supporters, or substantially none, in the slave States. The South have not taken hold of our principles as we announce them; nor does Judge Douglas now grapple with those principles. We have a Republican State Platform, laid down in Springfield in June last, stating our position all the way through the questions before the country. We are now far advanced in this canvass. Judge Douglas and I have made perhaps forty speeches apiece, and we have now for the fifth time met face to face in debate, and up to this day I have not found either Judge Douglas or any friend of his taking hold of the Republican platform, or laying his finger upon anything in it that is wrong. I ask you all to recollect that. Judge Douglas turns away from the platform of principles to the fact that he can find people somewhere who will not allow us to announce those principles. If he had great confidence that our principles were wrong, he would take hold of them and demonstrate them to be wrong. But he does not do so. The only evidence he has of their being wrong is in the fact that there are people who won't allow us to preach them. I ask again, is that the way to test the soundness of a doctrine?

I ask his attention also to the fact that by the rule of nationality he is himself fast becoming sectional. I ask his attention to the fact that his speeches would not go as current now south of the Ohio River as they have formerly gone there. I ask his attention to the fact that he felicitates himself to-day that all the Democrats of the free States are agreeing with him, while he omits to tell us that the Democrats of any slave State agree with him. If he has not thought of this, I commend to his consideration the evidence in his own declaration, on this day, of his becoming sectional too. I see it rapidly approaching. Whatever may be the result of this ephemeral contest between Judge Douglas and myself, I see the day rapidly approaching when his pill of sectionalism, which he has been thrusting down the throats of Republicans for years past, will be crowded down his own throat.

Now, in regard to what Judge Douglas said (in the beginning of his speech) about the Compromise of 1850 containing the principles of the Nebraska Bill, although I have often presented my views upon that subject, yet as I have not done so in this canvass, I will, if you please, detain you a little with them. I have always maintained, so far as I was able, that there was nothing of the principle of the Nebraska Bill in the Compromise of 1850 at all,—nothing whatever. Where can you find the principle of the Nebraska Bill in that Compromise? If anywhere, in the two pieces of the Compromise organizing the Territories of New Mexico and Utah. It was expressly provided in these two acts that when they came to be admitted into the Union they should be admitted with or without slavery, as they should choose, by their own constitutions. Nothing was said in either of those acts as to what was to be done in relation to slavery during the Territorial existence of those Territories, while Henry Clay constantly made the declaration (Judge Douglas recognizing him as a leader) that, in his opinion, the old Mexican laws would control that question during the Territorial existence, and that these old Mexican laws excluded slavery. How can that be used as a principle for declaring that during the Territorial existence as well as at the time of framing the constitution the people, if you please, might have slaves if they wanted them? I am not discussing the question whether it is right or wrong; but how are the New Mexican and Utah laws patterns for the Nebraska Bill? I maintain that the organization of Utah and New Mexico *did not* establish a general principle at all. It had no feature of establishing a general principle. The acts to which I have referred were a part of a general system of Compromises. They did not lay down what was proposed as a regular policy for the Territories, only an agreement in this particular case to do in that way, because other things were done that were to be a compensation for it. They were allowed to come in in that shape, because in another way it was paid for,—considering that as a part of that system of measures called the Compromise of 1850, which finally included half-a-dozen acts. It included the admission of California as a free State, which was kept out of the Union for half a year because it had formed a free constitution. It included the settlement of the boundary of Texas, which had been undefined before, which was in itself a slavery question; for if you pushed the line farther west, you made Texas larger, and made more slave territory; while, if you drew the line toward the east, you narrowed the boundary and diminished the domain of slavery, and by so much increased free territory. It included the abolition of the slave trade in the District of Columbia. It included the passage of a new Fugitive Slave law. All these things were put together, and, though passed in separate acts, were nevertheless, in legislation (as the speeches at the time will show), made to depend upon each other. Each got votes with the understanding that the other measures were to pass, and by this system of compromise, in that series of measures, those two bills—the New Mexico and Utah bills—were passed: and I say for that reason they could not be taken as models, framed upon their own intrinsic principle, for all future Territories. And I have the evidence of this in the fact that Judge Douglas, a year afterward, or more than a year afterward, perhaps, when he first introduced bills for the purpose of framing new Territories, did not attempt to follow these bills of New Mexico and Utah; and even when he introduced this Nebraska Bill, I think you will discover that he did not exactly follow them. But I do not wish to dwell at great length upon this branch of the discussion. My own opinion is, that a thorough investigation will show most plainly that the New Mexico and Utah bills were part of a system of compromise, and not designed as patterns for future Territorial legislation; and that this Nebraska Bill did not follow them as a pattern at all.

The Judge tells, in proceeding, that he is opposed to making any odious distinctions between free and slave States. I am altogether unaware that the Republicans are in favor of making any odious distinctions between the free and slave States. But there is still a difference, I think, between Judge Douglas and the

Republicans in this. I suppose that the real difference between Judge Douglas and his friends, and the Republicans on the contrary, is, that the Judge is not in favor of making any difference between slavery and liberty; that he is in favor of eradicating, of pressing out of view, the questions of preference in this country for free or slave institutions; and consequently every sentiment he utters discards the idea that there is any wrong in slavery. Everything that emanates from him or his coadjutors in their course of policy carefully excludes the thought that there is anything wrong in slavery. All their arguments, if you will consider them, will be seen to exclude the thought that there is anything whatever wrong in slavery. If you will take the Judge's speeches, and select the short and pointed sentences expressed by him,—as his declaration that he "don't care whether slavery is voted up or down,"—you will see at once that this is perfectly logical, if you do not admit that slavery is wrong. If you do admit that it is wrong, Judge Douglas cannot logically say he don't care whether a wrong is voted up or voted down. Judge Douglas declares that if any community wants slavery they have a right to have it. He can say that logically, if he says that there is no wrong in slavery; but if you admit that there is a wrong in it, he cannot logically say that anybody has a right to do wrong. He insists that upon the score of equality the owners of slaves and owners of property—of horses and every other sort of property—should be alike, and hold them alike in a new Territory. That is perfectly logical if the two species of property are alike and are equally founded in right. But if you admit that one of them is wrong, you cannot institute any equality between right and wrong. And from this difference of sentiment,—the belief on the part of one that the institution is wrong, and a policy springing from that belief which looks to the arrest of the enlargement of that wrong, and this other sentiment, that it is no wrong, and a policy sprung from that sentiment, which will tolerate no idea of preventing the wrong from growing larger, and looks to there never being an end to it through all the existence of things,—arises the real difference between Judge Douglas and his friends on the one hand and the Republicans on the other. Now, I confess myself as belonging to that class in the country who contemplate slavery as a moral, social, and political evil, having due regard for its actual existence amongst us and the difficulties of getting rid of it in any satisfactory way, and to all the constitutional obligations which have been thrown about it; but, nevertheless, desire a policy that looks to the prevention of it as a wrong, and looks hopefully to the time when as a wrong it may come to an end.

Judge Douglas has again, for, I believe, the fifth time, if not the seventh, in my presence, reiterated his charge of a conspiracy or combination between the National Democrats and Republicans. What evidence Judge Douglas has upon this subject I know not, inasmuch as he never favors us with any. I have said upon a former occasion, and I do not choose to suppress it now, that I have no objection to the division in the Judge's party. He got it up himself. It was all his and their work. He had, I think, a great deal more to do with the steps that led to the Lecompton Constitution than Mr. Buchanan had; though at last, when they reached it, they quarrelled over it, and their friends divided upon it. I am very free to confess to Judge Douglas that I have no objection to the division; but I defy the Judge to show any evidence that I have in any way promoted that division, unless he insists on being a witness himself in merely saying so. I can give all fair friends of Judge Douglas here to understand exactly the view that Republicans take in regard to that division. Don't you remember how two years ago the opponents of the Democratic party were divided between Fremont and Fillmore? I guess you do. Any Democrat who remembers that division will remember also that he was at the time very glad of it, and then he will be able to see all there is between the National Democrats and the Republicans. What we now think of the two divisions of Democrats, you then thought of the Fremont and Fillmore divisions. That is all there is of it.

But if the Judge continues to put forward the declaration that there is an unholy and unnatural alliance between the Republicans and the National Democrats, I now want to enter my protest against receiving him as an entirely competent witness upon that subject. I want to call to the Judge's attention an attack he made upon me in the first one of these debates, at

Ottawa, on the 21st of August. In order to fix extreme Abolitionism upon me, Judge Douglas read a set of resolutions which he declared had been passed by a Republican State Convention, in October, 1854, at Springfield, Illinois, and he declared I had taken part in that Convention. It turned out that although a few men calling themselves an anti-Nebraska State Convention had sat at Springfield about that time, yet neither did I take any part in it, nor did it pass the resolutions or any such resolutions as Judge Douglas read. So apparent had it become that the resolutions which he read had not been passed at Springfield at all, nor by a State Convention in which I had taken part, that seven days afterward, at Freeport, Judge Douglas declared that he had been misled by Charles H. Lanphier, editor of the *State Register,* and Thomas L. Harris, member of Congress in that district, and he promised in that speech that when he went to Springfield he would investigate the matter. Since then Judge Douglas has been to Springfield, and I presume has made the investigation; but a month has passed since he has been there, and, so far as I know, he has made no report of the result of his investigation. I have waited as I think sufficient time for the report of that investigation, and I have some curiosity to see and hear it. A fraud, an absolute forgery was committed, and the perpetration of it was traced to the three,—Lanphier, Harris, and Douglas. Whether it can be narrowed in any way so as to exonerate any one of them, is what Judge Douglas's report would probably show.

It is true that the set of resolutions read by Judge Douglas were published in the Illinois *State Register* on the 16th of October, 1854, as being the resolutions of an anti-Nebraska Convention which had sat in that same month of October, at Springfield. But it is also true that the publication in the *Register* was a forgery then, and the question is still behind, which of the three, if not all of them, committed that forgery. The idea that it was done by mistake is absurd. The article in the Illinois *State Register* contains part of the real proceedings of that Springfield Convention, showing that the writer of the article had the real proceedings before him, and purposely threw out the genuine resolutions passed by the Convention and fraudulently substituted the others. Lanphier then, as now, was the editor of the *Register*, so that there seems to be but little room for his escape. But then it is to be borne in mind that Lanphier had less interest in the object of that forgery than either of the other two. The main object of that forgery at that time was to beat Yates and elect Harris to Congress, and that object was known to be exceedingly dear to Judge Douglas at that time. Harris and Douglas were both in Springfield when the Convention was in session, and although they both left before the fraud appeared in the *Register*, subsequent events show that they have both had their eyes fixed upon that Convention.

The fraud having been apparently successful upon the occasion, both Harris and Douglas have more than once since then been attempting to put it to new uses. As the fisherman's wife, whose drowned husband was brought home with his body full of eels, said when she was asked what was to be done with him, *"Take the eels out and set him again,"* so Harris and Douglas have shown a disposition to take the eels out of that stale fraud by which they gained Harris's election, and set the fraud again more than once. On the 9th of July, 1856, Douglas attempted a repetition of it upon Trumbull on the floor of the Senate of the United States, as will appear from the appendix of the *Congressional Globe* of that date.

On the 9th of August, Harris attempted it again upon Norton in the House of Representatives, as will appear by the same documents,—the appendix to the *Congressional Globe* of that date. On the 21st of August last, all three—Lanphier, Douglas, and Harris—reattempted it upon me at Ottawa. It has been clung to and played out again and again as an exceedingly high trump by this blessed trio. And now that it has been discovered publicly to be a fraud we find that Judge Douglas manifests no surprise at it at all. He makes no complaint of Lanphier, who must have known it to be a fraud from the beginning. He, Lanphier, and Harris are just as cosey now and just as active in the concoction of new schemes as they were before the general discovery of this fraud. Now, all this is very natural if they are all alike guilty in that fraud, and it is very unnatural if any one of them is innocent. Lanphier perhaps insists that the rule of honor among thieves does not quite require him to take all upon himself, and consequently my friend Judge Douglas finds it difficult to make a satisfactory report upon his investigation. But meanwhile the three are agreed that each is *"a most honorable man."*

Judge Douglas requires an indorsement of his truth and honor by a re-election to the United States Senate, and he makes and reports against me and against Judge Trumbull, day after day, charges which we know to be utterly untrue, without for a moment seeming to think that this one unexplained fraud, which he promised to investigate, will be the least drawback to his claim to belief. Harris ditto. He asks a re-election to the lower House of Congress without seeming to remember at all that he is involved in this dishonorable fraud! The Illinois *State Register,* edited by Lanphier, then, as now, the central organ of both Harris and Douglas, continues to din the public ear with this assertion, without seeming to suspect that these assertions are at all lacking in title to belief.

After all, the question still recurs upon us, How did that fraud originally get into the *State Register?* Lanphier then, as now, was the editor of that paper. Lanphier knows. Lanphier cannot be ignorant of how and by whom it was originally concocted. Can he be induced to tell, or, if he has told, can Judge Douglas be induced to tell how it originally was concocted? It may be true that Lanphier insists that the two men for whose benefit it was originally devised shall at least bear their share of it! How that is, I do not know, and while it remains unexplained I hope to be pardoned if I insist that the mere fact of Judge Douglas making charges against Trumbull and myself is not quite sufficient evidence to establish them!

While we were at Freeport, in one of these joint discussions, I answered certain interrogatories which Judge Douglas had propounded to me, and then in turn propounded some to him, which he in a sort of way answered. The third one of these interrogatories I have with me, and wish now to make some comments upon it. It was in these words: "If the Supreme Court of the United States shall decide that the States cannot exclude slavery from their limits, are you in favor of acquiescing in, adhering to, and following such decision as a rule of political action?"

To this interrogatory Judge Douglas made no answer in any just sense of the word. He contented himself with sneering at the thought that it was possible for the Supreme Court ever to make such a decision. He sneered at me for propounding the interrogatory. I had not propounded it without some reflection, and I wish now to address to this audience some remarks upon it.

In the second clause of the sixth article, I believe it is, of the Constitution of the United States, we find the following language:

"This Constitution and the laws of the United States which shall be made in pursuance thereof, and all treaties made, or which shall be made, under the authority of the United States, shall be the supreme law of the land; and the judges in every State shall be bound thereby, anything in the Constitution or laws of any State to the contrary notwithstanding."

The essence of the Dred Scott case is compressed into the sentence which I will now read: "Now, as we have already said in an earlier part of this opinion, upon a different point, the right of property in a slave is distinctly and expressly affirmed in the Constitution." I repeat it, *"The right of property in a slave is distinctly and expressly affirmed in the Constitution"!* What is it to be *"affirmed"* in the Constitution? Made firm in the Constitution,—so made that it cannot be separated from the Constitution without breaking the Constitution; durable as the Constitution, and part of the Constitution. Now, remembering the provision of the Constitution which I have read—affirming that that instrument is the supreme law of the land; that the judges of every State shall be bound by it, any law or constitution of any State to the contrary notwithstanding; that the right of property in a slave is affirmed in that Constitution, is made, formed into, and cannot be separated from it without breaking it; durable as the instrument; part of the instrument;—what follows as a short and even syllogistic argument from it? I think it follows, and I submit to the consideration of men capable of arguing whether, as I state it, in syllogistic form, the argument has any fault in it:

Nothing in the Constitution or laws of any State can destroy a right distinctly and expressly affirmed in the Constitution of the United States.

The right of property in a slave is distinctly and expressly affirmed in the Constitution of the United States.

Therefore, nothing in the Constitution or laws of any State can destroy the right of property in a slave.

I believe that no fault can be pointed out in that argument; assuming the truth of the premises, the conclusion, so far as I have capacity at all to understand it, follows inevitably. There is a fault in it as I think, but the fault is not in the reasoning; but the falsehood in fact is a fault of the premises. I believe that the right of property in a slave *is not* distinctly and expressly affirmed in the Constitution, and Judge Douglas thinks it *is*. I believe that the Supreme Court and the advocates of that decision may search in vain for the place in the Constitution where the right of property in a slave is distinctly and expressly affirmed. I say, therefore, that I think one of the premises is not true in fact. But it is true with Judge Douglas. It is true with the Supreme Court who pronounced it. They are stopped from denying it, and being stopped from denying it, the conclusion follows that, the Constitution of the United States being the supreme law, no constitution or law can interfere with it. It being affirmed in the decision that the right of property in a slave is distinctly and expressly affirmed in the Constitution, the conclusion inevitably follows that no State law or constitution can destroy that right. I then say to Judge Douglas and to all others that I think it will take a better answer than a sneer to show that those who have said that the right of property in a slave is distinctly and expressly affirmed in the Constitution, are not prepared to show that no constitution or law can destroy that right. I say I believe it will take a far better argument than a mere sneer to show to the minds of intelligent men that whoever has so said is not prepared, whenever public sentiment is so far advanced as to justify it, to say the other. This is but an opinion, and the opinion of one very humble man; but it is my opinion that the Dred Scott decision, as it is, never would have been made in its present form if the party that made it had not been sustained previously by the elections. My own opinion is, that the new Dred Scott decision, deciding against the right of the people of the States to exclude slavery, will never be made if that party is not sustained by the elections. I believe, further, that it is just as sure to be made as to-morrow is to come, if that party shall be sustained. I have said, upon a former occasion, and I repeat it now, that the course of argument that Judge Douglas makes use of upon this subject (I charge not his motives in this), is preparing the public mind for that new Dred Scott decision. I have asked him again to point out to me the reasons for his first adherence to the Dred Scott decision as it is. I have turned his attention to the fact that General Jackson differed with him in regard to the political obligation of a Supreme Court decision. I have asked his attention to the fact that Jefferson differed with him in regard to the political obligation of a Supreme Court decision. Jefferson said that "Judges are as honest as other men, and not more so." And he said, substantially, that whenever a free people should give up in absolute submission to any department of government, retaining for themselves no appeal from it, their liberties were gone. I have asked his attention to the fact that the Cincinnati platform, upon which he says he stands, disregards a time-honored decision of the Supreme Court, in denying the power of Congress to establish a National Bank. I have asked his attention to the fact that he himself was one of the most active instruments at one time in breaking down the Supreme Court of the State of Illinois because it had made a decision distasteful to him,—a struggle ending in the remarkable circumstance of his sitting down as one of the new Judges who were to overslaugh that decision; getting his title of Judge in that very way.

So far in this controversy I can get no answer at all from Judge Douglas upon these subjects. Not one can I get from him, except that he swells himself up and says, "All of us who stand by the decision of the Supreme Court are the friends of the Constitution; all you fellows that dare question it in any way are the enemies of the Constitution." Now, in this very devoted adherence to this decision, in opposition to all the great political leaders whom he has recognized as leaders, in opposition to his former self and history, there is something very marked. And the manner in which he adheres to it,—not as being right upon the merits, as he conceives (because he did not discuss that at all), but as being absolutely obligatory upon every one simply because of the source from whence it comes, as that which no man can gainsay, whatever it may be,—this is another marked feature of his adherence to that decision. It marks it in this respect, that it commits him to the next decision, whenever it comes, as being as obligatory as this one, since he does not investigate it, and won't inquire whether this opinion is right or wrong. So he takes the next one without inquiring whether *it* is right or wrong. He teaches men this doctrine, and in so doing prepares the public mind to take the next decision when it comes, without any inquiry. In this I think I argue fairly (without questioning motives at all) that Judge Douglas is most ingeniously and powerfully preparing the public mind to take that decision when it comes; and not only so, but he is doing it in various other ways. In these general maxims about liberty, in his assertions that he "don't care whether slavery is voted up or voted down"; that "whoever wants slavery has a right to have it"; that "upon principles of equality it should be allowed to go everywhere"; that "there is no inconsistency between free and slave institutions"—in this he is also preparing (whether purposely or not) the way for making the institution of slavery national! I repeat again, for I wish no misunderstanding, that I do not charge that he means it so; but I call upon your minds to inquire, if you were going to get the best instrument you could, and then set it to work in the most ingenious way, to prepare the public mind for this movement, operating in the free States, where there is now an abhorrence of the institution of slavery, could you find an instrument so capable of doing it as Judge Douglas, or one employed in so apt a way to do it?

I have said once before, and I will repeat it now, that Mr. Clay, when he was once answering an objection to the Colonization Society, that it had a tendency to the ultimate emancipation of the slaves, said that:

"those who would repress all tendencies to liberty and ultimate emancipation must do more than put down the benevolent efforts of the Colonization Society: they must go back to the era of our liberty and independence, and muzzle the cannon that thunders its annual joyous return; they must blow out the moral lights around us; they must penetrate the human soul, and eradicate the light of reason and the love of liberty!"

And I do think—I repeat, though I said it on a former occasion—that Judge Douglas and whoever, like him, teaches that the negro has no share, humble though it may be, in the Declaration of Independence, is going back to the era of our liberty and independence, and, so far as in him lies, muzzling the cannon that thunders its annual joyous return; that he is blowing out the moral lights around us, when he contends that whoever wants slaves has a right to hold them; that he is penetrating, so far as lies in his power, the human soul, and eradicating the light of reason and the love of liberty, when he is in every possible way preparing the public mind, by his vast influence, for making the institution of slavery perpetual and national.

There is, my friends, only one other point to which I will call your attention for the remaining time that I have left me, and perhaps I shall not occupy the entire time that I have, as that one point may not take me clear through it.

Among the interrogatories that Judge Douglas propounded to me at Freeport, there was one in about this language: "Are you opposed to the acquisition of any further territory to the United States, unless slavery shall first be prohibited therein?" I answered, as I thought, in this way: that I am not generally opposed to the acquisition of additional territory, and that I would support a proposition for the acquisition of additional territory according as my supporting it was or was not calculated to aggravate this slavery question amongst us. I then proposed to Judge Douglas another interrogatory, which was correlative to that: "Are you in favor of acquiring additional territory, in disregard of how it may affect us upon the slavery question?" Judge Douglas answered,—that is, in his own way he answered it. I believe that, although he took a good many words to answer it, it was a little more fully answered than any other. The substance of his answer was that this country would continue to expand; that it would need additional territory; that it was as absurd to suppose that we could continue upon our present territory, enlarging in population as we are, as it would be to hoop a boy twelve years of age, and expect him to grow to man's size without bursting the hoops. I believe it was something like that. Consequently, he was in favor of the acquisition of further territory as fast as we might need it, in disregard of how it might affect the slavery question. I do not say this as giving his exact language, but he said so substantially; and he would leave the question of slavery, where the territory was acquired, to be settled by the people of the acquired territory. ["That's the doctrine."] May be it is; let us consider that for a while. This will probably, in the run of things, become one of the concrete manifestations of this slavery question. If Judge Douglas's policy upon this question succeeds, and gets fairly settled down, until all opposition is crushed out, the next thing will be a grab for the territory of poor Mexico, an invasion of the rich lands of South America, then the adjoining islands will follow, each one of which promises additional slave-fields. And this question is to be left to the people of those countries for settlement. When we get Mexico, I don't know whether the Judge will be in favor of the Mexican people that we get with it settling that question for themselves and all others; because we know the Judge has a great horror for mongrels, and I understand that the people of Mexico are most decidedly a race of mongrels. I understand that there is not more than one person there out of eight who is pure white, and I suppose from the Judge's previous declaration that when we get Mexico, or any considerable portion of it, that he will be in favor of these mongrels settling the question, which would bring him somewhat into collision with his horror of an inferior race.

It is to be remembered, though, that this power of acquiring additional territory is a power confided to the President and the Senate of the United States. It is a power not under the control of the representatives of the people any further than they, the President and the Senate, can be considered the representatives of the people. Let me illustrate that by a case we have in our history. When we acquired the territory from Mexico in the Mexican War, the House of Representatives, composed of the immediate representatives of the people, all the time insisted that the territory thus to be acquired should be brought in upon condition that slavery should be forever prohibited therein, upon the terms and in the language that slavery had been prohibited from coming into this country. That was insisted upon constantly and never failed to call forth an assurance that any territory thus acquired should have that prohibition in it, so far as the House of Representatives was concerned. But at last the President and Senate acquired the territory without asking the House of Representatives anything about it, and took it without that prohibition. They have the power of acquiring territory without the immediate representatives of the people being called upon to say anything about it, and thus furnishing a very apt and powerful means of bringing new territory into the Union, and, when it is once brought into the country, involving us anew in this slavery agitation. It is therefore, as I think, a very important question for the consideration of the American people, whether the policy of bringing in additional territory, without considering at all how it will operate upon the safety of the Union in reference to this one great disturbing element in our national politics, shall be adopted as the policy of the country. You will bear in mind that it is to be acquired, according to the Judge's view, as fast as it is needed, and the indefinite part of this proposition is that we have only Judge Douglas and his class of men to decide how fast it is needed. We have no clear and certain way of determining or demonstrating how fast territory is needed by the necessities of the country. Whoever wants to go out filibustering, then, thinks that more territory is needed. Whoever wants wider slave-fields feels sure that some additional territory is needed as slave territory. Then it is as easy to show the necessity of additional slave-territory as it is to assert anything that is incapable of absolute demonstration. Whatever motive a man or a set of men may have for making annexation of property or territory, it is very easy to assert, but much less easy to disprove, that it is necessary for the wants of the country.

And now it only remains for me to say that I think it is a very grave question for the people of this Union to consider, whether, in view of the fact that this slavery question has been the only one that has ever endangered our Republican institutions, the only one that has ever threatened or menaced a dissolution of the Union, that has ever disturbed us in such a way as to make us fear for the perpetuity of our liberty,—in view of these facts, I think it is an exceedingly interesting and important question for this people to consider whether we shall engage in the policy of acquiring additional territory, discarding altogether from our consideration, while obtaining new territory, the question how it may affect us in regard to this, the only endangering element to our liberties and national greatness. The Judge's view has been expressed. I, in my answer to his question, have expressed mine. I think it will become an important and practical question. Our views are before the public. I am willing and anxious that they should consider them fully; that they should turn it about and consider the importance of the question, and arrive at a just conclusion as to whether it is or is not wise in the people of this Union, in the acquisition of new territory, to consider whether it will add to the disturbance that is existing amongst us—whether it will add to the one and only danger that has ever threatened the perpetuity of the Union or our own liberties. I think it is extremely important that they shall decide, and rightly decide, that question before entering upon that policy.

And now, my friends, having said the little I wish to say upon this head, whether I have occupied the whole of the remnant of my time or not, I believe I could not enter upon any new topic so as to treat it fully, without transcending my time, which I would not for a moment think of doing. I give way to Judge Douglas.

Mr. Douglas's Reply

GENTLEMEN: The highest compliment you can pay me during the brief half-hour that I have to conclude is by observing a strict silence. I desire to be heard rather than to be applauded.

The first criticism that Mr. Lincoln makes on my speech was that it was in substance what I have said everywhere else in the State where I have addressed the people. I wish I could say the same of his speech. Why, the reason I complain of him is because he makes one speech north, and another south— because he has one set of sentiments for the Abolition counties, and another set for the counties opposed to Abolitionism. My point of complaint against him is that I cannot induce him to hold up the same standard, to carry the same flag, in all parts of the State. He does not pretend, and no other man will, that I have one set of principles for Galesburgh, and another for Charleston. He does not pretend that I hold to one doctrine in Chicago, and an opposite one in Jonesboro. I have proved that he has a different set of principles for each of these localities. All I asked of him was that he should deliver the speech that he has made here to-day in Coles County instead of in old Knox. It would have settled the question between us in that doubtful county. Here I understand him to reaffirm the doctrine of negro equality, and to assert that by the Declaration of Independence the negro is declared equal to the white man. He tells you to-day that the negro was included in the Declaration of Independence when it asserted that all men were created equal. ["We believe it."] Very well.

Mr. Lincoln asserts to-day, as he did at Chicago, that the negro was included in that clause of the Declaration of Independence which says that all men were created equal and endowed by the Creator with certain inalienable rights, among which are life, liberty, and the pursuit of happiness. If the negro was made his equal and mine, if that equality was established by divine law, and was the negro's inalienable right, how came he to say at Charleston to the Kentuckians residing in that section of our State that the negro was physically inferior to the white man, belonged to an inferior race, and he was for keeping him in that inferior condition. There he gave the people to under-stand that there was no moral question involved, because, the inferiority being established, it was only a question of degree, and not a question of right; here, to-day, instead of making it a question of degree, he makes it a moral question; says that it is a great crime to hold the negro in that inferior condition. ["He's right."] Is he right now, or was he right in Charleston? ["Both."] He is right, then, sir, in your estimation, not because he is consistent, but because he can trim his principles any way, in any section, so as to secure votes. All I desire of him is that he will declare the same principles in the south that he does in the north.

But did you notice how he answered my position that a man should hold the same doctrines throughout the length and breadth of this Republic? He said, "Would Judge Douglas go to Russia and proclaim the same principles he does here?" I would remind him that Russia is not under the American Constitution. If Russia was a part of the American Republic, under our Federal Constitution, and I was sworn to support the Constitution, I would maintain the same doctrine in Russia that I do in Illinois. The slaveholding States are governed by the same Federal Constitution as ourselves, and hence a man's principles, in order to be in harmony with the Constitution, must be the same in the South as they are in the North, the same in the free States as they are in the slave States. Whenever a man advocates one set of principles in one section, and another set in another section, his opinions are in violation of the spirit of the Constitution which he has sworn to support. When Mr. Lincoln went to Congress in 1847 and, laying his hand upon the Holy Evangelists, made a solemn vow, in the presence of high Heaven, that he would be faithful to the Constitution, what did he mean,—the Constitution as he expounds it in Galesburgh, or the Constitution as he expounds it in Charleston?

Mr. Lincoln has devoted considerable time to the circumstance that at Ottawa I read a series of resolutions as having been adopted at Springfield, in this State, on the 4th or 5th of October, 1854, which happened not to have been adopted there. He has used hard names; has dared to talk about fraud, about forgery, and has insinuated that there was a conspiracy between Mr. Lanphier, Mr. Harris, and myself to perpetrate a forgery. Now, bear in mind that he does not deny that these resolutions were adopted in a majority of all the Republican counties of this State in that year; he does not deny that they were declared to be the platform of this Republican party in the first Congressional District, in the second, in the third, and in many counties of the fourth, and that they thus became the platform of his party in a majority of the counties upon which he now relies for support; he does not deny the truthfulness of the resolutions, but takes exception to the *spot* on which they were adopted. He takes to himself great merit because he thinks they were not adopted on the right spot for me to use them against him, just as he was very severe in Congress upon the Government of his country when he thought that he had discovered that the Mexican War was not begun in the right *spot*, and was therefore unjust. He tries very hard to make out that there is something very extraordinary in the place where the thing was done, and not in the thing itself. I never believed before that Abraham Lincoln would be guilty of what he has done this day in regard to those resolutions. In the first place, the moment it was intimated to me that they had been adopted at Aurora and Rockford instead of Springfield, I did not wait for him to call my attention to the fact, but led off, and explained in my first meeting after the Ottawa debate what the mistake was, and how it had been made. I supposed that for an honest man, conscious of his own rectitude, that explanation would be sufficient. I did not wait for him, after the mistake was made, to call my attention to it, but frankly explained it at once as an honest man would. I also gave the authority on which I had stated that these resolutions were adopted by the Springfield Republican Convention; that I had seen them quoted by Major Harris in a debate in Congress, as having been adopted by the first Republican State Convention in Illinois, and that I had written to him and asked him for the authority as to the time and place of their adoption; that, Major Harris being extremely ill, Charles H. Lanphier had written to me, for him, that they were adopted at Springfield on the 5th of October, 1854, and had sent me a copy of the Springfield paper containing them. I read them from the newspaper just as Mr. Lincoln reads the proceedings of meetings held years ago from the newspapers. After giving that explanation, I did not think there was an honest man in the State of Illinois who doubted that I had been led into the error, if it was such, innocently, in the way I detailed; and I will now say that I do not now believe that there is an honest man on the face of the globe who will not regard with abhorrence and disgust Mr. Lincoln's insinuations of my complicity in that forgery, if it was a forgery. Does Mr. Lincoln wish to push these things to the point of personal difficulties here? I commenced this contest by treating him courteously and kindly; I always spoke of him in words of respect; and in return he has sought and is now seeking to divert public attention from the enormity of his revolutionary principles by impeaching men's sincerity and integrity, and inviting personal quarrels.

I desired to conduct this contest with him like a gentleman; but I spurn the insinuation of complicity and fraud made upon the simple circumstance of an editor of a newspaper having made a mistake as to the place where a thing was done, but not as to the thing itself. These resolutions were the platform of this Republican party of Mr. Lincoln's of that year. They were adopted in a majority of the Republican counties in the State; and when I asked him at Ottawa whether they formed the platform upon which he stood, he did not answer, and I could not get an answer out of him. He then thought, as I thought, that those resolutions were adopted at the Springfield Convention, but excused himself by saying that he was not there when they were adopted, but had gone to Tazewell court in order to avoid being present at the Convention. He saw them published as having been adopted at Springfield, and so did I, and he knew that if there was a mistake in regard to them, that I had nothing under heaven to do with it. Besides, you find that in all these northern counties where the Republican candidates are running pledged to him, that the conventions which nominated them adopted that identical platform. One cardinal point in that platform which he shrinks from is this: that there shall be no more slave States admitted into the Union, even if the people want them. Lovejoy stands pledged against the admission of any more slave States. ["Right, so do we."] So do you, you say. Farnsworth stands pledged against the admission of any more slave States. Washburne stands pledged the same way. The candidate for the Legislature who is running on Lincoln's ticket in Henderson and

Warren stands committed by his vote in the Legislature to the same thing; and I am informed, but do not know of the fact, that your candidate here is also so pledged. ["Hurrah for him! Good!"] Now, you Republicans all hurrah for him, and for the doctrine of "no more slave States," and yet Lincoln tells you that his conscience will not permit him to sanction that doctrine, and complains because the resolutions I read at Ottawa made him, as a member of the party, responsible for sanctioning the doctrine of no more slave States. You are one way, you confess, and he is, or pretends to be, the other; and yet you are both governed by *principle* in supporting one another. If it be true, as I have shown it is, that the whole Republican party in the northern part of the State stands committed to the doctrine of no more slave States, and that this same doctrine is repudiated by the Republicans in the other part of the State, I wonder whether Mr. Lincoln and his party do not present the case which he cited from the Scriptures, of a house divided against itself which cannot stand! I desire to know what are Mr. Lincoln's principles and the principles of his party. I hold, and the party with which I am identified hold, that the people of each State, old and new, have the right to decide the slavery question for themselves; and when I used the remark that I did not care whether slavery was voted up or down, I used it in the connection that I was for allowing Kansas to do just as she pleased on the slavery question. I said that I did not care whether they voted slavery up or down, because they had the right to do as they pleased on the question, and therefore my action would not be controlled by any such consideration. Why cannot Abraham Lincoln, and the party with which he acts, speak out their principles so that they may be understood? Why do they claim to be one thing in one part of the State, and another in the other part? Whenever I allude to the Abolition doctrines, which he considers a slander to be charged with being in favor of, you all indorse them, and hurrah for them, not knowing that your candidate is ashamed to acknowledge them.

I have a few words to say upon the Dred Scott decision, which has troubled the brain of Mr. Lincoln so much. He insists that that decision would carry slavery into the free States, notwithstanding that the decision says directly the opposite, and goes into a long argument to make you believe that I am in favor of, and would sanction, the doctrine that would allow slaves to be brought here and held as slaves contrary to our Constitution and laws. Mr. Lincoln knew better when he asserted this; he knew that one newspaper, and, so far as is within my knowledge, but one, ever asserted that doctrine, and that I was the first man in either House of Congress that read that article in debate, and denounced it on the floor of the Senate as revolutionary. When the Washington *Union,* on the 17th of last November, published an article to that effect, I branded it at once, and denounced it; and hence the *Union* has been pursuing me ever since. Mr. Toombs, of Georgia, replied to me, and said that there was not a man in any of the slave States south of the Potomac River that held any such doctrine. Mr. Lincoln knows that there is not a member of the Supreme Court who holds that doctrine; he knows that every one of them, as shown by their opinions, holds the reverse. Why this attempt, then, to bring the Supreme Court into disrepute among the people? It looks as if there was an effort being made to destroy public confidence in the highest judicial tribunal on earth. Suppose he succeeds in destroying public confidence in the court, so that the people will not respect its decisions, but will feel at liberty to disregard them and resist the laws of the land, what will he have gained? He will have changed the government from one of laws into that of a mob, in which the strong arm of violence will be substituted for the decisions of the courts of justice. He complains because I did not go into an argument reviewing Chief Justice Taney's opinion, and the other opinions of the different judges, to determine whether their reasoning is right or wrong on the questions of law. What use would that be? He wants to take an appeal from the Supreme Court to this meeting, to determine whether the questions of law were decided properly. He is going to appeal from the Supreme Court of the United States to every town meeting, in the hope that he can excite a prejudice against that court, and on the wave of that prejudice ride into the Senate of the United States, when he could not get there on his own principles or his own merits. Suppose he should succeed in getting into the Senate of the United States, what then will he have to do with the decision of the Supreme Court in the Dred Scott case? Can he reverse that decision when he gets there? Can he act upon it? Has the Senate any right to reverse it or revise it? He will not pretend that it has. Then why drag the matter into this contest, unless for the purpose of making a false issue, by which he can direct public attention from the real issue.

He has cited General Jackson in justification of the war he is making on the decision of the court. Mr. Lincoln misunderstands the history of the country if he believes there is any parallel in the two cases. It is true that the Supreme Court once decided that if a Bank of the United States was a necessary fiscal agent of the government, it was constitutional, and if not, that it was unconstitutional, and also, that whether or not it was necessary for that purpose was a political question for Congress, and not a judicial one for the courts to determine. Hence the court would not determine the bank unconstitutional. Jackson respected the decision, obeyed the law, executed it, and carried it into effect during its existence; but after the charter of the bank expired, and a proposition was made to create a new bank, General Jackson said, "It is unnecessary and improper, and therefore I am against it on constitutional grounds as well as those of expediency." Is Congress bound to pass every act that is constitutional? Why, there are a thousand things that are constitutional, but yet are inexpedient and unnecessary, and you surely would not vote for them merely because you had the right to? And because General Jackson would not do a thing which he had a right to do, but did not deem expedient or proper, Mr. Lincoln is going to justify himself in doing that which he has no right to do. I ask him whether he is not bound to respect and obey the decisions of the Supreme Court as well as I. The Constitution has created that court to decide all constitutional questions in the last resort; and when such decisions have been made, they become the law of the land, and you, and he, and myself, and every other good citizen, are bound by them. Yet he argues that I am bound by their decisions, and he is not. He says that their decisions are binding on Democrats, but not on

Republicans. Are not Republicans bound by the laws of the land as well as Democrats? And when the court has fixed the construction of the Constitution on the validity of a given law, is not their decision binding upon Republicans as well as upon Democrats? Is it possible that you Republicans have the right to raise your mobs and oppose the laws of the land and the constituted authorities, and yet hold us Democrats bound to obey them? My time is within half a minute of expiring, and all I have to say is, that I stand by the laws of the land. I stand by the Constitution as our fathers made it, by the laws as they are enacted, and by the decisions of the court, upon all points within their jurisdiction, as they are pronounced by the highest tribunal on earth; and any man who resists these must resort to mob law and violence to overturn the government of laws.

Sixth Joint Debate
QUINCY, OCTOBER 13, 1858

Mr. Lincoln's Speech

LADIES AND GENTLEMEN: I have had no immediate conference with Judge Douglas, but I will venture to say that he and I will perfectly agree that your entire silence, both when I speak and when he speaks, will be most agreeable to us.

In the month of May, 1856, the elements in the State of Illinois which have since been consolidated into the Republican party assembled together in a State Convention at Bloomington. They adopted at that time what, in political language, is called a platform. In June of the same year the elements of the Republican party in the nation assembled together in a National Convention at Philadelphia. They adopted what is called the National Platform. In June, 1858,—the present year,—the Republicans of Illinois reassembled at Springfield, in State Convention, and adopted again their platform, as I suppose not differing in any essential particular from either of the former ones, but perhaps adding something in relation to the new developments of political progress in the country.

The Convention that assembled in June last did me the honor, if it be one, and I esteem it such, to nominate me as their candidate for the United States Senate. I have supposed that, in entering upon this canvass, I stood generally upon these platforms. We are now met together on the 13th of October of the same year, only four months from the adoption of the last platform, and I am unaware that in this canvass, from the beginning until to-day, any one of our adversaries has taken hold of our platforms, or laid his finger upon anything that he calls wrong in them.

In the very first one of these joint discussions between Senator Douglas and myself, Senator Douglas, without alluding at all to these platforms, or any one of them, of which I have spoken, attempted to hold me responsible for a set of resolutions passed long before the meeting of either one of these conventions of which I have spoken. And as a ground for holding me responsible for these resolutions, he assumed that they had been passed at a State Convention of the Republican party, and that I took part in that Convention. It was discovered afterward that this was erroneous, that the resolutions which he endeavored to hold me responsible for had not been passed by any State Convention anywhere, had not been passed at Springfield, where he supposed they had, or assumed that they had, and that they had been passed in no convention in which I had taken part. The Judge, nevertheless, was not willing to give up the point that he was endeavoring to make upon me, and he therefore thought to still hold me to the point that he was endeavoring to make, by showing that the resolutions that he read had been passed at a local convention in the northern part of the State, although it was not a local convention that embraced my residence at all, nor one that reached, as I suppose, nearer than one hundred and fifty or two hundred miles of where I was when it met, nor one in which I took any part at all. He also introduced other resolutions, passed at other meetings, and by combining the whole, although they were all antecedent to the two State Conventions and the one National Convention I have mentioned, still he insisted, and now insists, as I understand, that I am in some way responsible for them.

At Jonesboro, on our third meeting, I insisted to the Judge that I was in no way rightfully held responsible for the proceedings of this local meeting or convention, in which I had taken no part, and in which I was in no way embraced; but I insisted to him that if he thought I was responsible for every man or every set of men everywhere, who happen to be my friends, the rule ought to work both ways, and he ought to be responsible for the acts and resolutions of all men or sets of men who were or are now his supporters and friends, and gave him a pretty long string of resolutions, passed by men who are now his friends, and announcing doctrines for which he does not desire to be held responsible.

This still does not satisfy Judge Douglas. He still adheres to his proposition, that I am responsible for what some of my friends in different parts of the State have done, but that he is not responsible for what his have done. At least, so I understand him. But in addition to that, the Judge, at our meeting in Galesburgh, last week, undertakes to establish that I am guilty of a species of double dealing with the public; that I make speeches of a certain sort in the north, among the Abolitionists, which I would not make in the south, and that I make speeches of a certain sort in the south which I would not make in the north. I apprehend, in the course I have marked out for myself, that I shall not have to dwell at very great length upon this subject.

As this was done in the Judge's opening speech at Galesburgh, I had an opportunity, as I had the middle speech then, of saying something in answer to it. He brought forward a quotation or two from a speech of mine delivered at Chicago, and then, to contrast with it, he brought forward an extract from a speech of mine at Charleston, in which he insisted that I was greatly inconsistent, and insisted that his conclusion followed, that I was playing a double part, and speaking in one region one way, and in another region another way. I have not time now to dwell on this as long as I would like, and wish only now to requote that portion of my speech at Charleston which the Judge quoted, and then make some comments upon it. This he quotes from me as being delivered at Charleston, and I believe correctly:

"I will say, then, that I am not, nor ever have been, in favor of bringing about in any way the social and political equality of the white and black races; that I am not, nor ever have been, in favor of making voters or jurors of negroes, nor of qualifying them to hold office, nor to intermarry with white people; and I will say, in addition to this, that there is a physical difference between the white and black races which will forever forbid the two races living together on terms of social and political equality. And inasmuch as they cannot so live while they do remain together, there must be the position of superior and inferior. I am as much as any other man in favor of having the superior position assigned to the white race."

This, I believe, is the entire quotation from the Charleston speech, as Judge Douglas made it. His comments are as follows:

"Yes, here you find men who hurrah for Lincoln, and say he is right when he discards all distinction between races, or when he declares that he discards the doctrine that there is such a thing as a superior and inferior race; and Abolitionists are required and expected to vote for Mr. Lincoln because he goes for the equality of races, holding that in the Declaration of Independence the white man and negro were declared equal, and endowed by divine law with equality. And down South, with the old-line Whigs, with the Kentuckians, the Virginians and the Tennesseeans, he tells you that there is a physical difference between the races, making the one superior, the other inferior, and he is in favor of maintaining the superiority of the white race over the negro."

Those are the Judges comments. Now, I wish to show you that a month, or only lacking three days of a month, before I made the speech at Charleston, which the Judge quotes from, he had himself heard me say substantially the same thing It was in our first meeting, at Ottawa—and I will say a word about where it was, and the atmosphere it was in, after a while—but at our first meeting, at Ottawa, I read an extract from an old speech of mine, made nearly four years ago, not merely to show my sentiments, but to show that my sentiments were long entertained and openly expressed; in which extract I expressly declared that my own feelings would not admit a social and political equality between the white and black races, and that even if my own feelings would admit of it, I still knew that the public sentiment of the country would not, and that such a thing was an utter impossibility, or substantially that. That extract from my old speech the reporters by some sort of accident passed over, and it was not reported. I lay no blame upon anybody. I suppose they thought that I would hand it over to them, and dropped reporting while I was reading it, but afterward went away without getting it from me. At the end of that quotation from my old speech, which I read at Ottawa, I made the comments which were reported at that time, and which I will now read, and ask you to notice how very nearly they are the same as Judge Douglas says were delivered by me down in Egypt. After reading, I added these words:

"Now, gentlemen, I don't want to read at any great length; but this is the true complexion of all I have ever said in regard to the institution of slavery or the black race, and this is the whole of it: anything that argues me into his idea of perfect social and political equality with the negro, is but a specious and fantastical arrangement of words by which a man can prove a horse-chestnut to be a chestnut horse. I will say here, while upon this subject, that I have no purpose, directly or indirectly, to interfere with the institution in the States where it exists. I believe I have no right to do so. I have no inclination to do so. I have no purpose to introduce political and social equality between the white and black races. There is a physical difference between the two which, in my judgment, will probably forever forbid their living together on the footing of perfect equality; and inasmuch as it becomes a necessity that there must be a difference, I, as well as Judge Douglas, am in favor of the race to which I belong having the superior position. I have never said anything to the contrary, but I hold that, notwithstanding all this, there is no reason in the world why the negro is not entitled to all the rights enumerated in the Declaration of Independence,—the right of life, liberty, and the pursuit of happiness. I hold that he is as much entitled to these as the white man. I agree with Judge Douglas that he is not my equal in many respects, certainly not in color, perhaps not in intellectual and moral endowments; but in the right to eat the bread, without the leave of anybody else, which his own hand earns, he is my equal and the equal of Judge Douglas, and the equal of every other man."

I have chiefly introduced this for the purpose of meeting the Judge's charge that the quotation he took from my Charleston speech was what I would say down South among the Kentuckians, the Virginians, etc., but would not say in the regions in which was supposed to be more of the Abolition element. I now make this comment: That speech from which I have now read the quotation, and which is there given correctly—perhaps too much so for good taste—was made away up North in the Abolition District of this State *par excellence,* in the Lovejoy District, in the personal presence of Lovejoy, for he was on the stand with us when I made it. It had been made and put in print in that region only three days less than a month before the speech made at Charleston, the like of which Judge Douglas thinks I would not make where there was any Abolition element. I only refer to this matter to say that I am altogether unconscious of having attempted any double-dealing anywhere; that upon one occasion I may say one thing, and leave other things unsaid, and *vice versa,* but that I have said anything on one occasion that is inconsistent with what I have said elsewhere, I deny,—at least I deny it so far as the intention is concerned. I find that I have devoted to this topic a larger portion of my time than I had intended. I wished to show, but I will pass it upon this occasion, that in the sentiment I have occasionally advanced upon the Declaration of Independence I am entirely borne out by the sentiments advanced by our old Whig leader, Henry Clay, and I have the book here to show it from; but because I have already occupied more time than I intended to do on that topic, I pass over it.

At Galesburgh, I tried to show that by the Dred Scott decision, pushed to its legitimate consequences, slavery would be established in all the States as well as in the Territories. I did this because, upon a former occasion, I had asked Judge Douglas whether, if the Supreme Court should make a decision declaring that the States had not the power to exclude slavery from their limits, he would adopt and follow that decision as a rule of political action; and because he had not directly answered that question, but had merely contented himself with sneering at it, I again introduced it, and tried to show that the conclusion that I stated followed inevitably and logically from the proposition already decided by the court. Judge Douglas had the privilege of replying to me at Galesburgh, and again he gave me no direct answer as to whether he would or would not sustain such a decision if made. I give him his third chance to say yes or no. He is not obliged to do either,—probably he will not do either; but I give him the third chance. I tried to show then that this result, this conclusion, inevitably followed from the point already decided by the court. The Judge, in his reply, again sneers at the thought of the court making any such decision, and in the course of his remarks upon this subject uses the language which I will now read. Speaking of me, the Judge says: "He goes on and insists that the Dred Scott decision would carry slavery into the free States, notwithstanding the decision itself says the contrary." And he adds: "Mr. Lincoln knows that there is no member of the Supreme Court that holds that doctrine. He knows that every one of them in their opinions held the reverse."

I especially introduce this subject again for the purpose of saying that I have the Dred Scott decision here, and I will thank Judge Douglas to lay his finger upon the place in the entire opinions of the court where any one of them "says the contrary." It is very hard to affirm a negative with entire confidence. I say, however, that I have examined that decision with a good deal of care, as a lawyer examines a decision, and, so far as I have been able to do so, the court has nowhere in its opinions said that the States have the power to exclude slavery, nor have they used other language saying substantially that. I also say, so far as I can find, not one of the concurring judges has said that the States can exclude slavery, nor said anything that was substantially that. The nearest approach that any one of them has made to it, so far as I can find, was by Judge Nelson, and the approach he made to it was exactly, in substance, the Nebraska Bill,—that the States had the exclusive power over the question of slavery, so far as they are not limited by the Constitution of the United States. I asked the question, therefore, if the non-concurring judges, McLean or Curtis, had asked to get an express declaration that the States could absolutely exclude slavery from their limits, what reason have we to believe that it would not have been voted down by the majority of the judges, just as Chase's amendment was voted down by Judge Douglas and his compeers when it was offered to the Nebraska Bill.

Also, at Galesburgh, I said something in regard to those Springfield resolutions that Judge Douglas had attempted to use upon me at Ottawa, and commented at some length upon the fact that they were, as presented, not genuine. Judge Douglas in his reply to me seemed to be somewhat exasperated. He said he would never have believed that Abraham Lincoln, as he kindly called me, would have attempted such a thing as I had attempted upon that occasion; and among other expressions which he used toward me, was that I dared to say forgery,—that I had *dared* to say forgery [turning to Judge Douglas]. Yes, Judge, I did dare to say forgery. But in this political canvass the Judge ought to remember that I was not the first who *dared* to say forgery. At Jacksonville, Judge Douglas made a speech in answer to something said by Judge Trumbull, and at the close of what he said upon that subject, he *dared* to say that Trumbull had forged his evidence. He said, too, that he should not concern himself with Trumbull any more, but thereafter he should hold Lincoln responsible for the slanders upon him. When I met him at Charleston after that, although I think that I should not have noticed the subject if he had not said he would hold me responsible for it, I spread out before him the statements of the evidence that Judge Trumbull had used, and I asked Judge Douglas, piece by piece, to put his finger upon one piece of all that evidence that he would say was a forgery! When I went through with each and every piece, Judge Douglas did not *dare* then to say that any piece of it was a forgery. So it seems that there are some things that Judge Douglas dares to do, and some that he dares not to do.

A Voice: "It's the same thing with you."

MR. LINCOLN: Yes, sir, it's the same thing with me. I do dare to say forgery when it's true, and don't dare to say forgery when it's false. Now I will say here to this audience and to Judge Douglas I have not dared to say he committed a forgery, and I never shall until I know it; but I did dare to say—just to suggest to the Judge—that a forgery had been committed, which by his own showing had been traced to him and two of his friends. I dared to suggest to him that he had expressly promised in one of his public speeches to investigate that matter, and I dared to suggest to him that there was an implied promise that when he investigated it he would make known the result. I dared to suggest to the Judge that he could not expect to be quite clear of suspicion of that fraud, for since the time that promise was made he had been with those friends, and had not kept his promise in regard to the investigation and the report upon it. I am not a very daring man, but I dared that much, Judge, and I am not much scared about it yet. When the Judge says he wouldn't have believed of Abraham Lincoln that he would have made such an attempt as that he reminds me of the fact that he entered upon this canvass with the purpose to treat me courteously; that touched me somewhat. It sets me to thinking. I was aware, when it was first agreed that Judge Douglas and I were to have these seven joint discussions, that they were the successive acts of a drama, perhaps I should say, to be enacted, not merely in the face of audiences like this, but in the face of the nation, and to some extent, by my relation to him, and not from anything in myself, in the face of the world; and I am anxious that they should be conducted with dignity and in the good temper which would be befitting the vast audiences before which it was conducted. But when Judge Douglas got home from Washington and made his first speech in Chicago, the evening afterward I made some sort of a reply to it. His second speech was made at Bloomington, in which he commented upon my speech at Chicago and said that I had used language ingeniously contrived to conceal my intentions,—or words to that effect. Now, I understand that this is an imputation upon my veracity and my candor. I do not know what the Judge understood by it, but in our first discussion, at Ottawa, he led off by charging a bargain, somewhat corrupt in its character, upon Trumbull and myself,—that we had entered into a bargain, one of the terms of which was that Trumbull was to Abolitionize the old Democratic party, and I (Lincoln) was to Abolitionize the old Whig party; I pretending to be as good an old-line Whig as ever. Judge Douglas may not understand that he implicated my truthfulness and my honor when he said I was doing one thing and pretending another; and I misunderstood him if he thought he was treating me in a dignified way, as a man of honor and truth, as he now claims he was disposed to treat me. Even after that time, at Galesburgh, when he brings forward an extract from a speech made at Chicago and an extract from a speech made at Charleston, to prove that I was trying to play a double part,—

that I was trying to cheat the public, and get votes upon one set of principles at one place, and upon another set of principles at another place,—I do not understand but what he impeaches my honor, my veracity, and my candor; and because *he* does this, I do not understand that I am bound, if I see a truthful ground for it, to keep my hands off of him. As soon as I learned that Judge Douglas was disposed to treat me in this way, I signified in one of my speeches that I should be driven to draw upon whatever of humble resources I might have,—to adopt a new course with him. I was not entirely sure that I should be able to hold my own with him, but I at least had the purpose made to do as well as I could upon him; and now I say that I will not be the first to cry "Hold." I think it originated with the Judge, and when he quits, I probably will. But I shall not ask any favors at all. He asks me, or he asks the audience, if I wish to push this matter to the point of personal difficulty. I tell him, no. He did not make a mistake, in one of his early speeches, when he called me an "amiable" man, though perhaps he did when he called me an "intelligent" man. It really hurts me very much to suppose that I have wronged anybody on earth. I again tell him, no! I very much prefer, when this canvass shall be over, however it may result, that we at least part without any bitter recollections of personal difficulties.

The Judge, in his concluding speech at Galesburgh, says that I was pushing this matter to a personal difficulty, to avoid the responsibility for the enormity of my principles. I say to the Judge and this audience, now, that I will again state our principles, as well as I hastily can, in all their enormity, and if the Judge hereafter chooses to confine himself to a war upon these principles, he will probably not find me departing from the same course.

We have in this nation this element of domestic slavery. It is a matter of absolute certainty that it is a disturbing element. It is the opinion of all the great men who have expressed an opinion upon it, that it is a dangerous element. We keep up a controversy in regard to it. That controversy necessarily springs from difference of opinion; and if we can learn exactly—can reduce to the lowest elements—what that difference of opinion

is, we perhaps shall be better prepared for discussing the different systems of policy that we would propose in regard to that
disturbing element. I suggest that the difference of opinion,
reduced to its lowest of terms, is no other than the difference
between the men who think slavery a wrong and those who do
not think it wrong. The Republican party think it wrong; we
think it is a moral, a social, and a political wrong. We think it as
a wrong not confining itself merely to the persons or the States
where it exists, but that it is a wrong in its tendency, to say the
least, that extends itself to the existence of the whole nation.
Because we think it wrong, we propose a course of policy that
shall deal with it as a wrong. We deal with it as with any other
wrong, in so far as we can prevent its growing any larger, and so
deal with it that in the run of time there may be some promise
of an end to it. We have a due regard to the actual presence of
it amongst us, and the difficulties of getting rid of it in any satisfactory way, and all the constitutional obligations thrown about
it. I suppose that in reference both to its actual existence in the
nation, and to our constitutional obligations, we have no right at
all to disturb it in the States where it exists, and we profess that
we have no more inclination to disturb it than we have the right
to do it. We go further than that: we don't propose to disturb it
where, in one instance, we think the Constitution would permit
us. We think the Constitution would permit us to disturb it in
the District of Columbia. Still, we do not propose to do that,
unless it should be in terms which I don't suppose the nation is
very likely soon to agree to,—the terms of making the emancipation gradual, and compensating the unwilling owners. Where
we suppose we have the constitutional right, we restrain ourselves in reference to the actual existence of the institution and
the difficulties thrown about it. We also oppose it as an evil so
far as it seeks to spread itself. We insist on the policy that shall
restrict it to its present limits. We don't suppose that in doing
this we violate anything due to the actual presence of the institution, or anything due to the constitutional guaranties thrown
around it.

We oppose the Dred Scott decision in a certain way, upon
which I ought perhaps to address you a few words. We do not

propose that when Dred Scott has been decided to be a slave by the court, we, as a mob, will decide him to be free. We do not propose that, when any other one, or one thousand, shall be decided by that court to be slaves, we will in any violent way disturb the rights of property thus settled; but we nevertheless do oppose that decision as a political rule which shall be binding on the voter to vote for nobody who thinks it wrong, which shall be binding on the members of Congress or the President to favor no measure that does not actually concur with the principles of that decision. We do not propose to be bound by it as a political rule in that way, because we think it lays the foundation, not merely of enlarging and spreading out what we consider an evil, but it lays the foundation for spreading that evil into the States themselves. We propose so resisting it as to have it reversed if we can, and a new judicial rule established upon this subject.

I will add this: that if there be any man who does not believe that slavery is wrong in the three aspects which I have mentioned, or in any one of them, that man is misplaced, and ought to leave us; while on the other hand, if there be any man in the Republican party who is impatient over the necessity springing from its actual presence, and is impatient of the constitutional guaranties thrown around it, and would act in disregard of these, he too is misplaced, standing with us. He will find his place somewhere else; for we have a due regard, so far as we are capable of understanding them, for all these things. This, gentlemen, as well as I can give it, is a plain statement of our principles in all their enormity.

I will say now that there is a sentiment in the country contrary to me,—a sentiment which holds that slavery is not wrong, and therefore it goes for the policy that does not propose dealing with it as a wrong. That policy is the Democratic policy, and that sentiment is the Democratic sentiment. If there be a doubt in the mind of any one of this vast audience that this is really the central idea of the Democratic party in relation to this subject, I ask him to bear with me while I state a few things tending, as I think, to prove that proposition. In the first place, the leading man—I think I may do my friend Judge Douglas the honor of calling him such—advocating the present Democratic policy never himself says it is wrong. He has the high distinction, so far as I know, of never having said slavery is either right or wrong. Almost everybody else says one or the other, but the Judge never does. If there be a man in the Democratic party who thinks it is wrong, and yet clings to that party, I suggest to him, in the first place, that his leader don't talk as he does, for he never says that it is wrong. In the second place, I suggest to him that if he will examine the policy proposed to be carried forward, he will find that he carefully excludes the idea that there is anything wrong in it. If you will examine the arguments that are made on it, you will find that every one carefully excludes the idea that there is anything wrong in slavery. Perhaps that Democrat who says he is as much opposed to slavery as I am will tell me that I am wrong about this. I wish him to examine his own course in regard to this matter a moment, and then see if his opinion will not be changed a little. You say it is wrong; but don't you constantly object to anybody else saying so? Do you not constantly argue that this is not the right place to oppose it? You say it must not be opposed in the free States, because slavery is not here; it must not be opposed in the slave States, because it is there; it must not be opposed in politics, because that will make a fuss; it must not be opposed in the pulpit, because it is not religion. Then where is the place to oppose it? There is no suitable place to oppose it. There is no place in the country to oppose this evil overspreading the continent, which you say yourself is coming. Frank Blair and Gratz Brown tried to get up a system of gradual emancipation in Missouri, had an election in August, and got beat, and you, Mr. Democrat, threw up your hat, and hallooed "Hurrah for Democracy!" So I say, again, that in regard to the arguments that are made, when Judge Douglas says he "don't care whether slavery is voted up or voted down," whether he means that as an individual expression of sentiment, or only as a sort of statement of his views on national policy, it is alike true to say that he can thus argue logically if he don't see anything wrong in it; but he cannot say so logically if he admits that slavery is wrong. He cannot say that he would as soon see a wrong voted up as voted down. When Judge Douglas says that whoever or whatever community wants slaves, they have a right to have them, he is perfectly logical, if there is nothing wrong in the institution; but if you admit that it is wrong, he cannot logically say that anybody has a right to do wrong. When he says that slave property and horse and hog property are alike to be allowed to go into the Territories, upon the principles of equality, he is reasoning truly, if there is no difference between them as property; but if the one is property held rightfully, and the other is wrong, then there is no equality between the right and wrong; so that, turn it in any way you can, in all the arguments sustaining the Democratic policy, and in that policy itself, there is a careful, studied exclusion of the idea that there is anything wrong in slavery. Let us understand this. I am not, just here, trying to prove that we are right, and they are wrong. I have been stating where we and they stand, and trying to show what is the real difference between us; and I now say that whenever we can get the question distinctly stated, can get all these men who believe that slavery is in some of these respects wrong to stand and act with us in treating it as a wrong,—then, and not till then, I think we will in some way come to an end of this slavery agitation.

Mr. Douglas's Reply

LADIES AND GENTLEMEN: Permit me to say that unless silence is observed it will be impossible for me to be heard by this immense crowd, and my friends can confer no higher favor upon me than by omitting all expressions of applause or approbation. I desire to be heard rather than to be applauded. I wish to address myself to your reason, your judgment, your sense of justice, and not to your passions.

I regret that Mr. Lincoln should have deemed it proper for him again to indulge in gross personalities and base insinuations in regard to the Springfield resolutions. It has imposed upon me the necessity of using some portion of my time for the purpose of calling your attention to the facts of the case, and it will then be for you to say what you think of a man who can predicate such a charge upon the circumstances as he has in this. I had seen the platform adopted by a Republican Congressional Convention held in Aurora, the Second Congressional District, in September, 1854, published as purporting to be the platform of the Republican party. That platform declared that the Republican party was pledged never to admit another slave State into the Union, and also that it was pledged to prohibit slavery in all the Territories of the United States, not only all that we then had, but all that we should thereafter acquire, and to repeal unconditionally the Fugitive Slave law, abolish slavery in the District of Columbia, and prohibit the slave-trade between the different States. These and other articles against slavery were contained in this platform, and unanimously adopted by the Republican Congressional Convention in that district. I had also seen that the Republican Congressional Conventions at Rockford, in the First District, and at Bloomington, in the Third, had adopted the same platform that year, nearly word for word, and had declared it to be the platform of the Republican party. I had noticed that Major Thomas L. Harris, a member of Congress from the Springfield District, had referred to that platform in a speech in Congress as having been adopted by the first Republican State Convention which assembled in Illinois. When I had occasion to use the fact in this canvass, I wrote to Major Harris to know on what day that Convention was held, and to ask him to send me its proceedings. He being sick, Charles H. Lanphier answered my letter by sending me the published proceedings of the Convention held at Springfield on the 5th of October, 1854, as they appeared in the report of the *State Register.* I read those resolutions from that newspaper the same as any of you would refer back and quote any fact from the files of a newspaper which had published it. Mr. Lincoln pretends that after I had so quoted those resolutions he discovered that they had never been adopted at Springfield. He does not deny their adoption by the Republican party at Aurora, at Bloomington, and at Rockford, and by nearly all the Republican County Conventions in northern Illinois where his party is in a majority, but merely because they were not adopted on the *"spot"* on which I said they were, he chooses to quibble about the place rather than meet and discuss the merits of the resolutions themselves. I stated when I quoted them that I did so from the *State Register*. I gave my authority. Lincoln believed at the time, as he has since admitted, that they had been adopted at Springfield, as published. Does he believe now that I did not tell the truth when I quoted those resolutions? He knows, in his heart, that I quoted them in good faith, believing at the time that they had been adopted at Springfield. I would consider myself an infamous wretch, if, under such circumstances, I could charge any man with being a party to a trick or a fraud. And I will tell him, too, that it will not do to charge a forgery on Charles H. Lanphier or Thomas L. Harris. No man on earth, who knows them, and knows Lincoln, would take his oath against their word. There are not two men in the State of Illinois who have higher characters for truth, for integrity, for moral character and for elevation of tone, as gentlemen, than Mr. Lanphier and Mr. Harris. Any man who attempts to make such charges as Mr. Lincoln has indulged in against them, only proclaims himself a slanderer.

I will now show you that I stated with entire fairness, as soon as it was made known to me, that there was a mistake about the spot where the resolutions had been adopted, although their truthfulness, as a declaration of the principles of the Republican party, had not and could not be questioned. I did not wait for Lincoln to point out the mistake, but the moment I discovered it, I made a speech, and published it to the world, correcting the error. I corrected it myself, as a gentleman and an honest man, and as I always feel proud to do when I have made a mistake. I wish Mr. Lincoln could show that he has acted with equal fairness and truthfulness when I have convinced him that he has been mistaken. I will give you an illustration to show you how he acts in a similar case: In a speech at Springfield, he charged Chief Justice Taney and his associates, President Pierce, President Buchanan, and myself, with having entered into a conspiracy at the time the Nebraska Bill was introduced, by which the Dred Scott decision was to be made by the Supreme Court, in order to carry slavery everywhere under the Constitution. I called his attention to the fact that at the time alluded to, to wit, the introduction of the Nebraska Bill, it was not possible that such a conspiracy could have been entered into, for the reason that the Dred Scott case had never been taken before the Supreme Court, and was not taken before it for a year after; and I asked him to take back that charge. Did he do it? I showed him that it was impossible that the charge could be true; I proved it by the record; and I then called upon him to retract his false charge. What was his answer? Instead of coming out like an honest man and doing so, he reiterated the charge, and said that if the case had not gone up to the Supreme Court from the courts of Missouri at the time he charged that the judges of the Supreme Court entered into the conspiracy, yet, that there was an understanding with the Democratic owners of Dred Scott that they would take it up. I have since asked him who the Democratic owners of Dred Scott were, but he could not tell, and why? Because there were no such Democratic owners in existence. Dred Scott at the time was owned by the Rev. Dr. Chaffee, an Abolition member of Congress, of Springfield, Massachusetts, in right of his wife. He was owned by one of Lincoln's friends, and not by Democrats at all; his case was conducted in court by Abolition lawyers, so that both the prosecution and the defence were in the hands of the Abolition political friends of Mr. Lincoln. Notwithstanding I thus proved by the record that his charge against the Supreme Court was false, instead of taking it back, he resorted to another false charge to sustain the infamy of it. He also charged President Buchanan with having been a party to the conspiracy. I directed his attention to the fact that the charge could not possibly be true, for the reason that at the time specified, Mr. Buchanan was not in America, but was three thousand miles off, representing the United States at the Court of St. James, and had been there for a year previous, and did not return until three years afterward. Yet I never could get Mr. Lincoln to take back his false charge, although I have called upon him over and over again. He refuses to do it, and either remains silent or resorts to other tricks to try and palm his slander off on the country. Therein you will find the difference between Mr. Lincoln and myself. When I make a mistake, as an honest man I correct it without being asked to do so; but when he makes a false charge, he sticks to it, and never corrects it. One word more in regard to these resolutions: I quoted them at Ottawa merely to ask Mr. Lincoln whether he stood on that platform. That was the purpose for which I quoted them. I did not think that I had a right to put idle questions to him, and I first laid a foundation for my questions by showing that the principles which I wished him either to affirm or deny had been adopted by some portion of his friends, at least, as their creed. Hence I read the resolutions and put the questions to him, and he then refused to answer them. Subsequently, one week afterward, he did answer a part of them, but the others he has not answered up to this day.

Now, let me call your attention for a moment to the answers which Mr. Lincoln made at Freeport to the questions which I propounded to him at Ottawa, based upon the platform adopted by a majority of the Abolition counties of the State, which now, as then, supported him. In answer to my question whether he indorsed the Black Republican principle of "no more slave States," he answered that he was not pledged against the admission of any more slave States, but that he would be very sorry if he should ever be placed in a position where he would have to vote on the question; that he would rejoice to know that no more slave States would be admitted into the Union.

"But [he added] if slavery shall be kept out of the Territories during the Territorial existence of any one given Territory, and then the people shall, having a fair chance and a clear field when they come to adopt the constitution, do such an extraordinary thing as to adopt a slave constitution, uninfluenced by the actual presence of the institution among them, I see no alternative, if we own the country, but to admit them into the Union."

The point I wish him to answer is this: Suppose Congress should not prohibit slavery in the Territory, and it applied for admission with a constitution recognizing slavery, then how would he vote? His answer at Freeport does not apply to any territory in America. I ask you [turning to Lincoln], will you vote to admit Kansas into the Union, with just such a constitution as her people want, with slavery or without, as they shall determine? He will not answer. I have put that question to him time and time again, and have not been able to get an answer out of him. I ask you again, Lincoln, will you vote to admit New Mexico, when she has the requisite population, with such a constitution as her people adopt, either recognizing slavery or not, as they shall determine? He will not answer. I put the same question to him in reference to Oregon and the new States to be carved out of Texas, in pursuance of the contract between Texas and the United States, and he will not answer. He will not answer these questions in reference to any Territory now in existence, but says that if Congress should prohibit slavery in a Territory, and when its people asked for admission as a State they should adopt slavery as one of their institutions, that he supposes he would have to let it come in. I submit to you whether that answer of his to my question does not justify me in saying that he has a fertile genius in devising language to conceal his thoughts. I ask you whether there is an intelligent man in America who does not believe that that answer was made for the purpose of concealing what he intended to do. He wished to make the old-line Whigs believe that he would stand by the Compromise measures of 1850, which declared that the States might come into the Union with slavery, or without, as they pleased, while Lovejoy and his Abolition allies up north explained to the Abolitionists that in taking this ground he preached good Abolition doctrine, because his proviso would not apply to any Territory in America, and therefore there was no chance of his being governed by it. It would have been quite easy for him to have said that he would let the people of a State do just as they pleased, if he desired to convey such an idea. Why did he not do it? He would not answer my question directly, because up north the Abolition creed declares that there shall be no more slave States, while down south, in Adams County, in Coles, and in Sangamon, he and his friends are afraid to advance that doctrine. Therefore, he gives an evasive and equivocal answer, to be construed one way in the south and another way in the north, which, when analyzed, it is apparent is not an answer at all with reference to any territory now in existence.

Mr. Lincoln complains that in my speech the other day at

Galesburgh I read an extract from a speech delivered by him at Chicago, and then another from his speech at Charleston, and compared them, thus showing the people that he had one set of principles in one part of the State, and another in the other part. And how does he answer that charge? Why, he quotes from his Charleston speech as I quoted from it, and then quotes another extract from a speech which he made at another place, which he says is the same as the extract from his speech at Charleston; but he does not quote the extract from his Chicago speech, upon which I convicted him of double-dealing. I quoted from his Chicago speech to prove that he held one set of principles up north among the Abolitionists, and from his Charleston speech to prove that he held another set down at Charleston and in southern Illinois. In his answer to this charge, he ignores entirely his Chicago speech, and merely argues that he said the same thing which he said at Charleston at another place. If he did, it follows that he has twice, instead of once, held one creed in one part of the State, and a different creed in another part. Up at Chicago, in the opening of the campaign, he reviewed my reception speech, and undertook to answer my argument attacking his favorite doctrine of negro equality. I had shown that it was a falsification of the Declaration of Independence to pretend that that instrument applied to and included negroes in the clause declaring that all men were created equal. What was Lincoln's reply? I will read from his Chicago speech and the one which he did not quote, and dare not quote, in this part of the State. He said:

"I should like to know if, taking this old Declaration of Independence, which declares that all men are equal upon principle, and making exceptions to it, where will it stop? If one man says it does not mean a negro, why may not another man say it does not mean another man? If that declaration is not the truth, let us get the statute book in which we find it, and tear it out."

There you find that Mr. Lincoln told the Abolitionists of Chicago that if the Declaration of Independence did not declare that the negro was created by the Almighty the equal of the white man, that you ought to take that instrument and tear out the clause which says that all men were created equal. But let me call your attention to another part of the same speech. You know that in his Charleston speech, an extract from which he has read, he declared that the negro belongs to an inferior race, is physically inferior to the white man, and should always be kept in an inferior position. I will now read to you what he said at Chicago on that point. In concluding his speech at that place, he remarked:

"My friends, I have detained you about as long as I desire to do, and I have only to say, let us discard all this quibbling about this man and the other man, this race, and that race, and the other race being inferior, and therefore they must be placed in an inferior position, discarding our standard that we have left us. Let us discard all these things, and unite as one people throughout this land until we shall once more stand up declaring that all men are created equal."

Thus you see that when addressing the Chicago Abolitionists he declared that all distinctions of race must be discarded and blotted out, because the negro stood on an equal footing with the white man; that if one man said the Declaration of Independence did not mean a negro when it declared all men created equal, that another man would say that it did not mean another man; and hence we ought to discard all differences between the negro race and all other races, and declare them all created equal. Did old Giddings, when he came down among you four years ago, preach more radical Abolitionism than this? Did Lovejoy, or Lloyd Garrison, or Wendell Phillips, or Fred Douglass ever take higher Abolition grounds than that? Lincoln told you that I had charged him with getting up these personal attacks to conceal the enormity of his principles, and then commenced talking about something else, omitting to quote this part of his Chicago speech which contained the enormity of his principles to which I alluded. He knew that I alluded to his negro-equality doctrines when I spoke of the enormity of his principles, yet he did not find it convenient to answer on that point. Having shown you what he said in his Chicago speech in reference to negroes being created equal to white men, and about discarding all distinctions between the two races, I will again read to you what he said at Charleston:

"I will say, then, that I am not nor ever have been in favor of bringing about in any way the social and political equality of the white and black races; that I am not nor ever have been in favor of making voters of the free negroes, or jurors, or qualifying them to hold office, or having them to marry with white people. I will say in addition, that there is a physical difference between the white and black races, which, I suppose, will forever forbid the two races living together upon terms of social and political equality, and inasmuch as they cannot so live, that while they do remain together there must be the position of superior and inferior, that I as much as any other man am in favor of the superior position being assigned to the white man."

A voice: "That's the doctrine."

MR. DOUGLAS: Yes, sir, that is good doctrine; but Mr. Lincoln is afraid to advocate it in the latitude of Chicago, where he hopes to get his votes. It is good doctrine in the anti-Abolition counties for him, and his Chicago speech is good doctrine in the Abolition counties. I assert, on the authority of these two speeches of Mr. Lincoln, that he holds one set of principles in the Abolition counties, and a different and contradictory set in the other counties. I do not question that he said at Ottawa what he quoted; but that only convicts him further, by proving that he has twice contradicted himself, instead of once. Let me ask him why he cannot avow his principles the same in the north as in the south,—the same in every county,—if he has a conviction that they are just? But I forgot,—he would not be a Republican if his principles would apply alike to every part of the country. The party to which he belongs is bounded and limited by geographical lines. With their principles, they cannot even cross the Mississippi River on your ferry-boats. They cannot cross over the Ohio into Kentucky. Lincoln himself cannot visit the land of his fathers, the scenes of his childhood, the graves of his ancestors, and carry his Abolition principles, as he declared them at Chicago, with him.

This Republican organization appeals to the North against the South; it appeals to Northern passion, Northern prejudice, and Northern ambition, against Southern people, Southern States, and Southern institutions, and its only hope of success is by that appeal. Mr. Lincoln goes on to justify himself in making a war upon slavery upon the ground that Frank Blair and Gratz Brown did not succeed in their warfare upon the institution in Missouri. Frank Blair was elected to Congress in 1856, from the State of Missouri, as a Buchanan Democrat, and he turned Fremonter after the people elected him, thus belonging to one party before election, and another afterward. What right then had he to expect, after having thus cheated his constituency, that they would support him at another election? Mr. Lincoln thinks it is his duty to preach a crusade in the free States against slavery, because it is a crime, as he believes, and ought to be extinguished, and because the people of the slave States will never abolish it. How is he going to abolish it? Down in the southern part of the State he takes the ground openly that he will not interfere with slavery where it exists, and says that he is not now and never was in favor of interfering with slavery where it exists in the States. Well, if he is not in favor of that, how does he expect to bring slavery in a course of ultimate extinction? How can he extinguish it in Kentucky, in Virginia, in all the slave States by his policy, if he will not pursue a policy which will interfere with it in the States where it exists? In his speech at Springfield before the Abolition, or Republican, Convention, he declared his hostility to any more slave States in this language:

"Under the operation of that policy the agitation has not only not ceased, but has constantly augmented. In my opinion, it will not cease until a crisis shall have been reached and passed. 'A house divided against itself cannot stand.' I believe this government cannot endure permanently half slave and half free. I do not expect the Union to be dissolved, I do not expect the house to fall; but I do expect it will cease to be divided. It will become all one thing, or all the other. Either the opponents of slavery will arrest the further spread of it, and place it where the public mind shall rest in the belief that it is in the course of ultimate extinction, or its advocates will push it forward until it shall become alike lawful in all the States,—old as well as new, North as well as South."

Mr. Lincoln there told his Abolition friends that this government could not endure permanently, divided into free and slave States as our fathers made it, and that it must become all free or all slave; otherwise, that the government could not exist. How then does Lincoln propose to save the Union, unless by compelling all the States to become free, so that the house shall not be divided against itself? He intends making them all free; he will preserve the Union in that way; and yet he is not going to interfere with slavery where it now exists. How is he going to bring it about? Why he will agitate, he will induce the North to agitate, until the South shall be worried out and forced to abolish slavery. Let us examine the policy by which that is to be done. He first tells you that he would prohibit slavery everywhere in the Territories. He would thus confine slavery within its present limits. When he thus gets it confined, and surrounded, so that it cannot spread, the natural laws of increase will go on until the negroes will be so plenty that they cannot live on the soil. He will hem them in until starvation seizes them, and by starving them to death he will put slavery in the course of ultimate extinction. If he is not going to interfere with slavery in the States, but intends to interfere and prohibit it in the Territories, and thus smother slavery out, it naturally follows that he can extinguish it only by extinguishing the negro race; for his policy would drive them to starvation. This is the humane and Christian remedy that he proposes for the great crime of slavery!

He tells you that I will not argue the question whether slavery is right or wrong. I tell you why I will not do it. I hold that, under the Constitution of the United States, each State of this Union has a right to do as it pleases on the subject of slavery. In Illinois we have exercised that sovereign right by prohibiting slavery within our own limits. I approve of that line of policy. We have performed our whole duty in Illinois. We have gone as far as we have a right to go under the Constitution of our common country. It is none of our business whether slavery exists in Missouri or not. Missouri is a sovereign State of this Union, and has the same right to decide the slavery question for herself that Illinois has to decide it for herself. Hence I do not choose to

occupy the time allotted to me in discussing a question that we
have no right to act upon. I thought that you desired to hear us
upon those questions coming within our constitutional power of
action. Lincoln will not discuss these. What one question has he
discussed that comes within the power or calls for the action or
interference of an United States Senator? He is going to discuss
the rightfulness of slavery when Congress cannot act upon it
either way. He wishes to discuss the merits of the Dred Scott
decision when, under the Constitution, a senator has no right to
interfere with the decision of judicial tribunals. He wants your
exclusive attention to two questions that he has no power to act
upon; to two questions that he could not vote upon if he was in
Congress; to two questions that are not practical,—in order to
conceal from your attention other questions which he might be
required to vote upon should he ever become a member of
Congress. He tells you that he does not like the Dred Scott decision. Suppose he does not, how is he going to help himself? He
says that he will reverse it. How will he reverse it? I know of but
one mode of reversing judicial decisions, and that is by appealing from the inferior to the superior court. But I have never yet
learned how or where an appeal could be taken from the
Supreme Court of the United States! The Dred Scott decision
was pronounced by the highest tribunal on earth. From that
decision there is no appeal, this side of heaven. Yet, Mr. Lincoln
says he is going to reverse that decision. By what tribunal will he
reverse it? Will he appeal to a mob? Does he intend to appeal to
violence, to Lynch law? Will he stir up strife and rebellion in the
land, and overthrow the court by violence? He does not deign to
tell you how he will reverse the Dred Scott decision, but keeps
appealing each day from the Supreme Court of the United
States to political meetings in the country. He wants me to argue
with you the merits of each point of that decision before this
political meeting. I say to you, with all due respect, that I choose
to abide by the decisions of the Supreme Court as they are pronounced. It is not for me to inquire, after a decision is made,
whether I like it in all the points or not. When I used to practise
law with Lincoln, I never knew him to be beat in a case that he
did not get mad at the judge, and talk about appealing; and

when I got beat, I generally thought the court was wrong, but I never dreamed of going out of the courthouse and making a stump speech to the people against the judge, merely because I had found out that I did not know the law as well as he did. If the decision did not suit me, I appealed until I got to the Supreme Court; and then if that court, the highest tribunal in the world, decided against me, I was satisfied, because it is the duty of every law-abiding man to obey the constitutions, the laws, and the constituted authorities. He who attempts to stir up odium and rebellion in the country against the constituted authorities is stimulating the passions of men to resort to violence and to mobs instead of to the law. Hence, I tell you that I take the decisions of the Supreme Court as the law of the land, and I intend to obey them as such.

But Mr. Lincoln says that I will not answer his question as to what I would do in the event of the court making so ridiculous a decision as he imagines they would by deciding that the free State of Illinois could not prohibit slavery within her own limits. I told him at Freeport why I would not answer such a question. I told him that there was not a man possessing any brains in America, lawyer or not, who ever dreamed that such a thing could be done. I told him then, as I do now, that by all the principles set forth in the Dred Scott decision, it is impossible. I told him then, as I do now, that it is an insult to men's understanding, and a gross calumny on the court, to presume in advance that it was going to degrade itself so low as to make a decision known to be in direct violation of the Constitution.

A Voice: "The same thing was said about the Dred Scott decision before it passed."

MR. DOUGLAS: Perhaps you think that the court did the same thing in reference to the Dred Scott decision: I have heard a man talk that way before. The principles contained in the Dred Scott decision had been affirmed previously in various other decisions. What court or judge ever held that a negro was a citizen? The State courts had decided that question over and over again, and the Dred Scott decision on that point only affirmed what every court in the land knew to be the law.

But I will not be drawn off into an argument upon the merits of the Dred Scott decision. It is enough for me to know that the Constitution of the United States created the Supreme Court for the purpose of deciding all disputed questions touching the true construction of that instrument, and when such decisions are pronounced, they are the law of the land, binding on every good citizen. Mr. Lincoln has a very convenient mode of arguing upon the subject. He holds that because he is a Republican that he is not bound by the decisions of the court, but that I, being a Democrat, am so bound. It may be that Republicans do not hold themselves bound by the laws of the land and the Constitution of the country as expounded by the courts; it may be an article in the Republican creed that men who do not like a decision have a right to rebel against it: but when Mr. Lincoln preaches that doctrine, I think he will find some honest Republican—some law-abiding man in that party—who will repudiate such a monstrous doctrine. The decision in the Dred Scott case is binding on every American citizen alike; and yet Mr. Lincoln argues that the Republicans are not bound by it because they are opposed to it, whilst Democrats are bound by it, because we will not resist it. A Democrat cannot resist the constituted authorities of this country; a Democrat is a law-abiding man; a Democrat stands by the Constitution and the laws, and relies upon liberty as protected by law, and not upon mob or political violence.

I have never yet been able to make Mr. Lincoln understand, nor can I make any man who is determined to support him, right or wrong, understand how it is that under the Dred Scott decision the people of a Territory, as well as a State, can have slavery or not, just as they please. I believe that I can explain that proposition to all constitution-loving, law-abiding men in a way that they cannot fail to understand it. Chief Justice Taney, in his opinion in the Dred Scott case, said that, slaves being property, the owner of them has a right to take them into a Territory the same as he would any other property; in other words, that slave property, so far as the right to enter a Territory is concerned, stands on the same footing with other property. Suppose we grant that proposition. Then any man has a right to go to Kansas and take his property with him; but when he gets there, he must rely upon the local law to protect his property, whatever it may be. In order to illustrate this, imagine that three of you conclude to go to Kansas. One takes $10,000 worth of slaves, another $10,000 worth of liquors, and the third $10,000 worth of dry-goods. When the man who owns the dry-goods arrives out there and commences selling them, he finds that he is stopped and prohibited from selling until he gets a license, to pay for which will destroy all the profits he can make on his goods. When the man with the liquors gets there and tries to sell, he finds a Maine liquor law in force which prevents him. Now, of what use is his right to go there with his property unless he is protected in the enjoyment of that right after he gets there? The man who gets there with his slaves finds that there is no law to protect him when he arrives there. He has no remedy if his slaves run away to another country; there is no slave code or police regulations; and the absence of them excludes his slaves from the Territory just as effectually and as positively as a constitutional prohibition could.

Such was the understanding when the Kansas and Nebraska Bill was pending in Congress. Read the speech of Speaker Orr, of South Carolina, in the House of Representatives, in 1856, on the Kansas question, and you will find that he takes the ground that while the owner of a slave has a right to go into a Territory and carry his slaves with him, that he cannot hold them one day or hour unless there is a slave code to protect him. He tells you that slavery would not exist a day in South Carolina, or any other State, unless there was a friendly people and friendly legislation. Read the speeches of that giant in intellect, Alexander H. Stephens, of Georgia, and you will find them to the same effect. Read the speeches of Sam Smith, of Tennessee, and of all Southern men, and you will find that they all understood this doctrine then as we understand it now. Mr. Lincoln cannot be made to understand it, however. Down at Jonesboro, he went on to argue that if it be the law that a man has a right to take his slaves into territory of the United States under the Constitution, that then a member of Congress was perjured if he did not vote for a slave code. I ask him whether the decision of the Supreme Court is not binding upon him as well as on me? If so, and he holds that he would be perjured if he did not vote for a slave code under it, I ask him whether, if elected to Congress, he will so vote. I have a right to his answer, and I will tell you why. He put that question to me down in Egypt, and did it with an air of triumph. This was about the form of it: In the event that a slave-holding citizen of one of the Territories should need and demand a slave code to protect his slaves, will you vote for it? I answered him that a fundamental article in the Democratic creed, as put forth in the Nebraska Bill and the Cincinnati platform, was non-intervention by Congress with slavery in the States and Territories, and hence that I would not vote in Congress for any code of laws either for or against slavery in any Territory. I will leave the people perfectly free to decide that question for themselves.

Mr. Lincoln and the Washington *Union* both think this a monstrous bad doctrine. Neither Mr. Lincoln nor the Washington *Union* like my Freeport speech on that subject. The *Union*, in a late number, has been reading me out of the Democratic party because I hold that the people of a Territory, like those of a State, have the right to have slavery or not, as they please. It has devoted three and a half columns to prove certain propositions, one of which I will read. It says:

"We propose to show that Judge Douglas's action in 1850 and 1854 was taken with especial reference to the announcement of doctrine and programme which was made at Freeport. The declaration at Freeport was that 'in his opinion the people can, by lawful means, exclude slavery from a Territory before it comes in as a State'; and he declared that his competitor had 'heard him argue the Nebraska Bill on that principle all over Illinois in 1854, 1855, and 1856, and had no excuse to pretend to have any doubt upon that subject.'"

The Washington *Union* there charges me with the monstrous crime of now proclaiming on the stump the same doctrine that I carried out in 1850, by supporting Clay's Compromise measures. The *Union* also charges that I am now proclaiming the same doctrine that I did in 1854 in support of the Kansas and Nebraska Bill. It is shocked that I should now stand where I stood in 1850, when I was supported by Clay, Webster, Cass, and the great men of that day, and where I stood in 1854 and in 1856, when Mr. Buchanan was elected President. It goes on to prove, and succeeds in proving, from my speeches in Congress on Clay's Compromise measures, that I held the same doctrines at that time that I do now, and then proves that by the Kansas and Nebraska Bill I advanced the same doctrine that I now advance. It remarks:

"So much for the course taken by Judge Douglas on the Compromises of 1850. The record shows, beyond the possibility of cavil or dispute, that he expressly intended in those bills to give the Territorial Legislatures power to exclude slavery. How stands his record in the memorable session of 1854, with reference to the Kansas-Nebraska Bill itself? We shall not overhaul the votes that were given on that notable measure; our space will not afford it. We have his own words, however, delivered in his speech closing the great debate on that bill on the night of March 3, 1854, to show that *he meant* to do in 1854 precisely what *he had meant* to do in 1858. The Kansas-Nebraska Bill being upon its passage, he said":

It then quotes my remarks upon the passage of the bill as follows:

"The principle which we propose to carry into effect by this bill is this: That Congress shall neither legislate slavery into any Territory or State, nor out of the same; but the people shall be left free to regulate their domestic concerns in their own way, subject only to the Constitution of the United States. In order to carry this principle into practical operation, it becomes necessary to remove whatever legal obstacles might be found in the way of its free exercise. It is only for the purpose of carrying out this great fundamental principle of self-government that the bill renders the eighth section of the Missouri Act inoperative and void.

"Now, let me ask, will those senators who have arraigned me, or any one of them, have the assurance to rise in his place and declare that this great principle was never thought of or advocated as applicable to Territorial bills, in 1850; that, from that session until the present, nobody ever thought of incorporating this principle in all new Territorial organizations, etc., etc.? I will begin with the Compromises of 1850. Any senator who will take the trouble to examine our journals will find that on the 25th of March of that year I reported from the

Committee on Territories two bills, including the following measures: the admission of California, a Territorial government for Utah, a Territorial government for New Mexico, and the adjustment of the Texas boundary. These bills proposed to leave the people of Utah and New Mexico free to decide the slavery question for themselves, *in the precise language of the Nebraska Bill* now under discussion. A few weeks afterward the committee of thirteen took those bills and put a wafer between them, and reported them back to the Senate as one bill, with some slight amendments. *One of these amendments was, that the Territorial Legislatures should not legislate upon the subject of African slavery. I objected to this provision,* upon the ground that it subverted the great principle of self-government, *upon which the bill had been originally framed by the Territorial Committee.* On the first trial the Senate refused to strike it out, but subsequently did so, upon full debate, in order to establish that principle as the rule of action in Territorial organizations."

The *Union* comments thus upon my speech on that occasion:

"Thus it is seen that, in framing the Nebraska-Kansas Bill, Judge Douglas framed it in the terms and upon the model of those of Utah and New Mexico, and that in the debate he took pains expressly to revive the recollection of the voting which had taken place upon amendments affecting the powers of the Territorial Legislatures over the subject of slavery in the bills of 1850, in order to give the same meaning, force, and effect to the Nebraska-Kansas Bill on this subject as had been given to those of Utah and New Mexico."

The *Union* proves the following propositions: First, that I sustained Clay's Compromise measures on the ground that they established the principle of self-government in the Territories. Secondly, that I brought in the Kansas and Nebraska Bill, founded upon the same principles as Clay's Compromise measures of 1850; and, thirdly, that my Freeport speech is in exact accordance with those principles. And what do you think is the imputation that the *Union* casts upon me for all this? It says that my Freeport speech is not Democratic, and that I was not a Democrat in 1854 or in 1850! Now is not that funny? Think that the author of the Kansas and Nebraska Bill was not a Democrat when he introduced it! The *Union* says I was not a sound Democrat in 1850, nor in 1854, nor in 1856, nor am I in 1858, because I have always taken and now occupy the ground that the people of a Territory, like those of a State, have the right to decide for themselves whether slavery shall or shall not exist in a Territory! I wish to cite, for the benefit of the Washington *Union* and the followers of that sheet, one authority on that point, and I hope the authority will be deemed satisfactory to that class of politicians. I will read from Mr. Buchanan's letter accepting the nomination of the Democratic Convention, for the Presidency. You know that Mr. Buchanan, after he was nominated, declared to the Keystone Club, in a public speech, that he was no longer James Buchanan but the embodiment of the Democratic platform. In his letter to the committee which informed him of his nomination, accepting it, he defined the meaning of the Kansas and Nebraska Bill and the Cincinnati platform in these words:

"The recent legislation of Congress respecting domestic slavery, derived as it has been from the original and pure fountain of legitimate political power, the will of the majority, promises ere long to allay the dangerous excitement. This legislation is founded upon principles as ancient as free government itself, and, in accordance with them, has simply declared that the people of a Territory, like those of a State, shall decide for themselves whether slavery shall or shall not exist within their limits."

Thus you see that James Buchanan accepted the nomination at Cincinnati on the condition that the people of a Territory, like those of a State, should be left to decide for themselves whether slavery should or should not exist within their limits. I sustained James Buchanan for the Presidency on that platform as adopted at Cincinnati, and expounded by himself. He was elected President on that platform, and now we are told by the Washington *Union* that no man is a true Democrat who stands on the platform on which Mr. Buchanan was nominated, and which he has explained and expounded himself. We are told that a man is not a Democrat who stands by Clay, Webster, and Cass, and the Compromise measures of 1850, and the Kansas and Nebraska Bill of 1854. Whether a man be a Democrat or not on that platform, I intend to stand there as

long as I have life. I intend to cling firmly to that principle
which declares the right of each State and each Territory to
settle the question of slavery, and every other domestic question, for themselves. I hold that if they want a slave State they
have a right under the Constitution of the United States to
make it so, and if they want a free State, it is their right to have
it. But the *Union*, in advocating the claims of Lincoln over me
to the Senate, lays down two unpardonable heresies which it
says I advocate. The first is the right of the people of a
Territory, the same as a State, to decide for themselves the
question whether slavery shall exist within their limits, in the
language of Mr. Buchanan; and the second is, that a constitution shall be submitted to the people of a Territory for its
adoption or rejection before their admission as a State under
it. It so happens that Mr. Buchanan is pledged to both these
heresies, for supporting which the Washington *Union* has read
me out of the Democratic church. In his annual message he
said he trusted that the example of the Minnesota case would
be followed in all future cases, requiring a submission of the
constitution; and in his letter of acceptance, he said that the
people of a Territory, the same as a State, had the right to
decide for themselves whether slavery should exist within their
limits. Thus you find that this little corrupt gang who control
the *Union* and wish to elect Lincoln in preference to me,—
because, as they say, of these two heresies which I support,—
denounce President Buchanan when they denounce me, if he
stands now by the principles on which he was elected. Will
they pretend that he does not now stand by the principles on
which he was elected? Do they hold that he has abandoned the
Kansas-Nebraska Bill, the Cincinnati platform, and his own
letter accepting his nomination, all of which declare the right
of the people of a Territory, the same as a State, to decide the
slavery question for themselves? I will not believe that he has
betrayed or intends to betray the platform which elected him,
but if he does I will not follow him. I will stand by that great
principle no matter who may desert it. I intend to stand by it,
for the purpose of preserving peace between the North and
the South, the free and the slave States. If each State will only

agree to mind its own business and let its neighbors alone, there will be peace forever between us.

We in Illinois tried slavery when a Territory, and found it was not good for us in this climate, and with our surroundings, and hence we abolished it. We then adopted a free State constitution, as we had a right to do. In this State we have declared that a negro shall not be a citizen, and we have also declared that he shall not be a slave. We had a right to adopt that policy. Missouri has just as good a right to adopt the other policy. I am now speaking of rights under the Constitution, and not of moral or religious rights. I do not discuss the morals of the people of Missouri, but let them settle that matter for themselves. I hold that the people of the slave-holding States are civilized men as well as ourselves, that they bear consciences as well as we, and that they are accountable to God and their posterity, and not to us. It is for them to decide, therefore, the moral and religious right of the slavery question for themselves, within their own limits. I assert that they had as much right under the Constitution to adopt the system of policy which they have as we had to adopt ours. So it is with every other State in this Union. Let each State stand firmly by that great constitutional right, let each State mind its own business and let its neighbors alone, and there will be no trouble on this question. If we will stand by that principle, then Mr. Lincoln will find that this Republic can exist forever divided into free and slave States, as our fathers made it and the people of each State have decided. Stand by that great principle, and we can go on as we have been, increasing in wealth, in population, in power, and in all the elements of greatness, until we shall be the admiration and terror of the world. We can go on and enlarge as our population increases and requires more room, until we make this continent one ocean-bound republic. Under that principle the United States can perform that great mission, that destiny, which Providence has marked out for us. Under that principle we can receive with entire safety that stream of intelligence which is constantly flowing from the Old World to the New, filling up our prairies, clearing our wildernesses, and building cities, towns, railroads, and other internal improvements, and thus make this the asylum of the oppressed of the whole earth. We have this great mission to perform, and it can only be performed by adhering faithfully to that principle of self-government on which our institutions were all established. I repeat that the principle is the right of each State, each Territory, to decide this slavery question for itself, to have slavery or not, as it chooses; and it does not become Mr. Lincoln, or anybody else, to tell the people of Kentucky that they have no consciences, that they are living in a state of iniquity, and that they are cherishing an institution to their bosoms in violation of the law of God. Better for him to adopt the doctrine of "Judge not, lest ye shall be judged." Let him perform his own duty at home, and he will have a better fate in the future. I think there are objects of charity enough in the free States to excite the sympathies and open the pockets of all the benevolence we have amongst us, without going abroad in search of negroes, of whose condition we know nothing. We have enough objects of charity at home, and it is our duty to take care of our own poor and our own suffering, before we go abroad to intermeddle with other people's business.

My friends, I am told that my time is within two minutes of expiring. I have omitted many topics that I would like to have discussed before you at length. There were many points touched by Mr. Lincoln that I have not been able to take up for the want of time. I have hurried over each subject that I have discussed as rapidly as possible, so as to omit but few; but one hour and a half is not time sufficient for a man to discuss at length one half of the great questions which are now dividing the public mind.

In conclusion, I desire to return to you my grateful acknowledgments for the kindness and the courtesy with which you have listened to me. It is something remarkable that in an audience as vast as this, composed of men of opposite politics and views, with their passions highly excited, there should be so much courtesy, kindness, and respect exhibited, not only toward one another, but toward the speakers; and I feel that it is due to you that I should thus express my gratitude for the kindness with which you have treated me.

Mr. Lincoln's Rejoinder

MY FRIENDS: Since Judge Douglas has said to you in his conclusion that he had not time in an hour and a half to answer all
I had said in an hour, it follows of course that I will not be able
to answer in half an hour all that he said in an hour and a half.

I wish to return to Judge Douglas my profound thanks for his
public annunciation here to-day, to be put on record, that his
system of policy in regard to the institution of slavery *contemplates that it shall last forever*. We are getting a little nearer the
true issue of this controversy, and I am profoundly grateful for
this one sentence. Judge Douglas asks you, Why cannot the
institution of slavery, or rather, why cannot the nation, part slave
and part free, continue as our fathers made it, *forever?* In the
first place, I insist that our fathers *did not* make this nation half
slave and half free, or part slave and part free. I insist that they
found the institution of slavery existing here. They did not make
it so but they left it so because they knew of no way to get rid of
it at that time. When Judge Douglas undertakes to say that, as a
matter of choice, the fathers of the government made this
nation part slave and part free, *he assumes what is historically a
falsehood*. More than that: when the fathers of the government
cut off the source of slavery by the abolition of the slave-trade,
and adopted a system of restricting it from the new Territories
where it had not existed, I maintain that they placed it where
they understood, and all sensible men understood, it was in the
course of ultimate extinction; and when Judge Douglas asks me
why it cannot continue as our fathers made it, I ask him why he
and his friends could not let it remain as our fathers made it?

It is precisely all I ask of him in relation to the institution of
slavery, that it shall be placed upon the basis that our fathers
placed it upon. Mr. Brooks, of South Carolina, once said, and
truly said, that when this government was established, no one
expected the institution of slavery to last until this day, and that
the men who formed this government were wiser and better
than the men of these days; but the men of these days had experience which the fathers had not, and that experience had
taught them the invention of the cotton-gin, and this had made

the perpetuation of the institution of slavery a necessity in this country. Judge Douglas could not let it stand upon the basis which our fathers placed it, but removed it, and *put it upon the cotton-gin basis*. It is a question, therefore, for him and his friends to answer, why they could not let it remain where the fathers of the government originally placed it.

I hope nobody has understood me as trying to sustain the doctrine that we have a right to quarrel with Kentucky, or Virginia, or any of the slave States, about the institution of slavery,—thus giving the Judge an opportunity to be eloquent and valiant against us in fighting for their rights. I expressly declared in my opening speech that I had neither the inclination to exercise, nor the belief in the existence of, the right to interfere with the States of Kentucky or Virginia in doing as they pleased with slavery or any other existing institution. Then what becomes of all his eloquence in behalf of the rights of States, which are assailed by no living man?

But I have to hurry on, for I have but a half hour. The Judge has informed me, or informed this audience, that the Washington *Union* is laboring for my election to the United States Senate. This is news to me,—not very ungrateful news either. [Turning to Mr. W. H. Carlin, who was on the stand]—I hope that Carlin will be elected to the State Senate, and will vote for me. [Mr. Carlin shook his head.] Carlin don't fall in, I perceive, and I suppose he will not do much for me; but I am glad of all the support I can get, anywhere, if I can get it without practicing any deception to obtain it. In respect to this large portion of Judge Douglas's speech in which he tries to show that in the controversy between himself and the Administration party he is in the right, I do not feel myself at all competent or inclined to answer him. I say to him, "Give it to them,—give it to them just all you can!" and, on the other hand, I say to Carlin, and Jake Davis, and to this man Wogley up here in Hancock, "Give it to Douglas,—just pour it into him!"

Now, in regard to this matter of the Dred Scott decision, I wish to say a word or two. After all, the Judge will not say whether, if a decision is made holding that the people of the *States* cannot exclude slavery, he will support it or not. He obstinately refuses to say what he will do in that case. The judges of the Supreme Court as obstinately refused to say what they would do on this subject. Before this I reminded him that at Galesburgh he said the judges had expressly declared the contrary, and you remember that in my opening speech I told him I had the book containing that decision here, and I would thank him to lay his finger on the place where any such thing was said. He has occupied his hour and a half, and he has not ventured to try to sustain his assertion. *He never will.* But he is desirous of knowing how we are going to reverse that Dred Scott decision. Judge Douglas ought to know how. Did not he and his political friends find a way to reverse the decision of that same court in favor of the constitutionality of the National Bank? Didn't they find a way to do it so effectually that they have reversed it as completely as any decision ever was reversed, so far as its practical operation is concerned? And let me ask you, didn't Judge Douglas find a way to reverse the decision of our Supreme Court when it decided that Carlin's father—old Governor Carlin had not the constitutional power to remove a Secretary of State? Did he not appeal to the "MOBS," as he calls them? Did he not make speeches in the lobby to show how villainous that decision was, and how it ought to be overthrown? Did he not succeed, too, in getting an act passed by the Legislature to have it overthrown? And didn't he himself sit down on that bench as one of the five added judges, who were to overslaugh the four old ones,—getting his name of "Judge" in that way, and no other? If there is a villainy in using disrespect or making opposition to Supreme Court decisions, I commend it to Judge Douglas's earnest consideration. I know of no man in the State of Illinois who ought to know so well about *how much* villainy it takes to oppose a decision of the Supreme Court as our honorable friend Stephen A. Douglas.

Judge Douglas also makes the declaration that I say the Democrats are bound by the Dred Scott decision, while the Republicans are not. In the sense in which he argues, I never said it; but I will tell you what I have said and what I do not hesitate to repeat to-day. I have said that as the Democrats believe that decision to be correct, and that the extension of slavery is affirmed in the National Constitution, they are bound to support it as such; and I will tell you here that General Jackson once said each man was bound to support the Constitution "as he understood it." Now, Judge Douglas understands the Constitution according to the Dred Scott decision, and he is bound to support it as he understands it. I understand it another way, and therefore I am bound to support it in the way in which I understand it. And as Judge Douglas believes that decision to be correct, I will remake that argument if I have time to do so. Let me talk to some gentleman down there among you who looks me in the face. We will say you are a member of the Territorial Legislature, and, like Judge Douglas, you believe that the right to take and hold slaves there is a constitutional right The first thing you do is to *swear you will support the Constitution,* and all rights guaranteed therein; that you will, whenever your neighbor needs your legislation to support his constitutional rights, not withhold that legislation. If you withhold that necessary legislation for the support of the Constitution and constitutional rights, do you not commit perjury? I ask every sensible man if that is not so? That is undoubtedly just so, say what you please. Now, that is precisely what Judge Douglas says, that this is a constitutional right. Does the Judge mean to say that the Territorial Legislature in legislating may, by withholding necessary laws, or by passing unfriendly laws, *nullify that constitutional right?* Does he mean to say that? Does he mean to ignore the proposition so long and well established in law, that what you cannot do directly, you cannot do indirectly? Does he mean that? The truth about the matter is this: Judge Douglas has sung pæans to his "Popular Sovereignty" doctrine until his Supreme Court, co-operating with him, has *squatted* his Squatter Sovereignty out. But he will keep up this species of humbuggery about Squatter Sovereignty. He has at last invented this sort of *do-nothing sovereignty,*—that the people may exclude slavery by a sort of "sovereignty" that is exercised by doing nothing at all. Is not that running his Popular Sovereignty down awfully? Has it not got down as thin as the homeopathic soup that was made by boiling the shadow of a pigeon that had starved to death? But at last, when it is brought to the test of close reasoning, there is not even that thin decoction of it left. It is a presumption impossible in the domain of thought. It is precisely no other than the putting of that most unphilosophical proposition, that two bodies can occupy the same space at the same time. The Dred Scott decision covers the whole ground, and while it occupies it, there is no room even for the shadow of a starved pigeon to occupy the same ground.

Judge Douglas, in reply to what I have said about having upon a previous occasion made the speech at Ottawa as the one he took an extract from at Charleston, says it only shows that I practised the deception twice. Now, my friends, are any of you obtuse enough to swallow that? Judge Douglas had said I had made a speech at Charleston that I would not make up north, and I turned around and answered him by showing I *had* made that same speech up north,—had made it at Ottawa; made it in his hearing; made it in *the* Abolition District,—in Lovejoy's District,—in the personal presence of Lovejoy himself,—in the same atmosphere exactly in which I had made my Chicago speech, of which he complains so much.

Now, in relation to my not having said anything about the quotation from the Chicago speech: he thinks that is a terrible subject for me to handle. Why, gentlemen, I can show you that the substance of the Chicago speech I delivered two years ago in "Egypt," as he calls it. It was down at Springfield. That speech is here in this book, and I could turn to it and read it to you but for the lack of time. I have not now the time to read it. ["Read it, read it."] No, gentlemen, I am obliged to use discretion in disposing most advantageously of my brief time. The Judge has taken great exception to my adopting the heretical statement in the Declaration of Independence, that "all men are created equal," and he has a great deal to say about negro equality. I want to say that in sometimes alluding to the Declaration of Independence, I have only uttered the sentiments that Henry Clay used to hold. Allow me to occupy your time a moment with what he said. Mr. Clay was at one time called upon in Indiana, and in a way that I suppose was very insulting, to liberate his slaves; and he made a written reply to that application, and one portion of it is in these words:

"What is the *foundation* of this appeal to me in Indiana to liberate the slaves under my care in Kentucky? It is a general declaration in the act announcing to the world the independence of the thirteen American colonies, that *'men are created equal.'* Now, as an abstract principle, *there is no doubt of the truth of that declaration,* and it is desirable in the *original construction* of society, and in organized societies, to keep it in view as a great fundamental principle."

When I sometimes, in relation to the organization of new societies in new countries, where the soil is clean and clear, insisted that we should keep that principle in view, Judge Douglas will have it that I want a negro wife. He never can be brought to understand that there is any middle ground on this subject. I have lived until my fiftieth year, and have never had a negro woman either for a slave or a wife, and I think I can live fifty centuries, for that matter, without having had one for either. I maintain that you may take Judge Douglas's quotations from my Chicago speech, and from my Charleston speech, and the Galesburgh speech,—in his speech of to-day,—and compare them over, and I am willing to trust them with you upon his proposition that they show rascality or double-dealing. I deny that they do.

The Judge does not seem at all disposed to have peace, but I find he is disposed to have a personal warfare with me. He says that my oath would not be taken against the bare word of Charles H. Lanphier or Thomas L. Harris. Well, that is altogether a matter of opinion. It is certainly not for me to vaunt my word against oaths of these gentlemen, but I will tell Judge Douglas again the facts upon which I *"dared"* to say they proved a forgery. I pointed out at Galesburgh that the publication of these resolutions in the Illinois *State Register* could not have been the result of accident, as the proceedings of that meeting bore unmistakable evidence of being done by a man who *knew* it was a forgery; that it was a publication partly taken from the real proceedings of the Convention, and partly from the proceedings of a convention at another place,—which showed that he had the real proceedings before him, and taking one part of the resolutions, he threw out another part, and substituted false and fraudulent ones in their stead. I pointed that out to him, and also that his friend Lanphier, who was editor of the *Register* at that time and now is, must have known how it was done. Now, whether *he* did it, or got some friend to do it for him, I could not tell, but he certainly knew all about it. I pointed out to Judge Douglas that in his Freeport speech he had promised to *investigate* that matter. Does he now say that he did not make that promise? I have a right to ask *why he did not keep it*. I call upon him to tell here to-day why he did not keep that promise. That fraud has been traced up so that it lies between him, Harris, and Lanphier. There is little room for escape for Lanphier. Lanphier is doing the Judge good service, and Douglas desires his word to be taken for the truth. He desires Lanphier to be taken as authority in what he states in his newspaper. He desires Harris to be taken as a man of vast credibility; and when this thing lies among them, they will not press it to show where the guilt really belongs. Now, as he has said that he would investigate it, and implied that he would tell us the result of his investigation, I demand of him to tell why he did not investigate it, if he did not; and if he did, *why he won't tell the result*. I call upon him for that.

This is the third time that Judge Douglas has assumed that he learned about these resolutions by Harris's attempting to use them against Norton on the floor of Congress. I tell Judge Douglas the public records of the country show that *he* himself attempted it upon Trumbull a month before Harris tried them on Norton; that Harris had the opportunity of *learning it from him*, rather than he from Harris. I now ask his attention to that part of the record on the case. My friends, I am not disposed to detain you longer in regard to that matter.

I am told that I still have five minutes left. There is another matter I wish to call attention to. He says, when he discovered there was a mistake in that case, he came forward magnanimously, without my calling his attention to it, and explained it. I will tell you how he became so magnanimous. When the newspapers of our side had discovered and published it, and put it beyond his power to deny it, then he came forward and made a virtue of necessity by acknowledging it. Now he argues that all the point there was in those resolutions, although never passed at Springfield, is retained by their being passed at other localities. Is that true? He said I had a hand in passing them, in his opening speech,—that I was in the convention and helped to pass them. Do the resolutions touch me at all? It strikes me there is some difference between holding a man responsible for an act which he *has not* done and holding him responsible for an act that he *has* done. You will judge whether there is any difference in the "*spots.*" And he has taken credit for great magnanimity in coming forward and acknowledging what is proved on him beyond even the capacity of Judge Douglas to deny; and he has more capacity in that way than any other living man.

Then he wants to know why I won't withdraw the charge in regard to a conspiracy to make slavery national, as he has withdrawn the one he made. May it please his worship, I will withdraw it *when it is proven false on me as that was proven false on him.* I will add a little more than that. I will withdraw it whenever a reasonable man shall be brought to believe that the charge is not true. I have asked Judge Douglas's attention to certain matters of fact tending to prove the charge of a conspiracy to nationalize slavery, and he says he convinces me that this is all untrue because Buchanan was not in the country at that time, and because the Dred Scott case had not then got into the Supreme Court; and he says that I say the *Democratic* owners of Dred Scott got up the case. I never did say that. I defy Judge Douglas to show that I ever said so, *for I never uttered it.* [One of Mr. Douglas's reporters gesticulated affirmatively at Mr. Lincoln.] I don't care if your hireling does say I did, I tell you myself that *I never said the "Democratic" owners of Dred Scott got up the case.* I have never pretended to know whether Dred Scott's owners were Democrats, or Abolitionists, or Freesoilers or Border Ruffians. I have said that there is evidence about the case tending to show that it was a made-up case, for the purpose of getting that decision. I have said that that evidence was very strong in the fact that when Dred Scott was declared to be a slave, the owner of him made him free, showing that he had had the case tried and the question settled for such use as could be made of that decision; he cared nothing about the property thus declared to be his by that decision. But my time is out, and I can say no more.

Seventh Joint Debate
ALTON, OCTOBER 15, 1858

Senator Douglas's Speech

LADIES AND GENTLEMEN: It is now nearly four months since the canvass between Mr. Lincoln and myself commenced. On the 16th of June the Republican Convention assembled at Springfield and nominated Mr. Lincoln as their candidate for the United States Senate, and he, on that occasion, delivered a speech in which he laid down what he understood to be the Republican creed, and the platform on which he proposed to stand during the contest. The principal points in that speech of Mr. Lincoln's were: First, that this government could not endure permanently divided into free and slave States, as our fathers made it; that they must all become free or all become slave; all become one thing, or all become the other,—otherwise this Union could not continue to exist. I give you his opinions almost in the identical language he used. His second proposition was a crusade against the Supreme Court of the United States because of the Dred Scott decision, urging as an especial reason for his opposition to that decision that it deprived the negroes of the rights and benefits of that clause in the Constitution of the United States which guarantees to the citizens of each State all the rights, privileges, and immunities of the citizens of the several States. On the 10th of July I returned home, and delivered a speech to the people of Chicago, in which I announced it to be my purpose to appeal to the people of Illinois to sustain the course I had pursued in Congress. In that speech I joined issue with Mr. Lincoln on the points which he had presented. Thus there was an issue clear and distinct made up between us on these two propositions laid down in the speech of Mr. Lincoln at Springfield, and controverted by me in my reply to him at Chicago. On the next day, the 11th of July, Mr. Lincoln replied to me at Chicago, explaining at some length and reaffirming the positions which he had taken in his Springfield speech. In that Chicago speech he even went further than he had before, and uttered sentiments in regard to the negro being on an equality with the white man. He adopted in support of this position the argument which Lovejoy and Codding and other Abolition lecturers had made familiar in the northern and central portions of the State: to wit, that the Declaration of Independence having declared all men free and equal, by divine law, also that negro equality was an inalienable right, of which they could not be deprived. He insisted, in that speech, that the Declaration of Independence included the negro in the clause asserting that all men were created equal, and went so far as to say that if one man was allowed to take the position that it did not include the negro, others might take the position that it did not include other men. He said that all these distinctions between this man and that man, this race and the other race, must be discarded, and we must all stand by the Declaration of Independence, declaring that all men were created equal.

The issue thus being made up between Mr. Lincoln and myself on three points, we went before the people of the State. During the following seven weeks, between the Chicago speeches and our first meeting at Ottawa, he and I addressed large assemblages of the people in many of the central counties. In my speeches I confined myself closely to those three positions which he had taken, controverting his proposition that this Union could not exist as our fathers made it, divided into free and slave States, controverting his proposition of a crusade against the Supreme Court because of the Dred Scott decision, and controverting his proposition that the Declaration of Independence included and meant the negroes as well as the white men, when it declared all men to be created equal. I supposed at that time that these propositions constituted a distinct issue between us, and that the opposite positions we had taken upon them we would be willing to be held to in every part of the State. I never intended to waver one hair's breadth from that issue either in the north or the south, or wherever I should address the people of Illinois. I hold that when the time arrives that I cannot proclaim my political creed in the same terms, not only in the northern, but the southern part of Illinois, not only in the Northern, but the Southern States, and wherever the American flag waves over American soil, that then there must be something wrong in that creed; so long as we live under a common Constitution, so long as we live in a confederacy of sovereign and equal States, joined together as one for certain purposes, that any political creed is radically wrong which cannot be proclaimed in every State and every section of that Union, alike. I took up Mr. Lincoln's three propositions in my several speeches, analyzed them, and pointed out what I believed to be the radical errors contained in them. First, in regard to his doctrine that this government was in violation of the law of God, which says that a house divided against itself cannot stand, I repudiated it as a slander upon the immortal framers of our Constitution. I then said, I have often repeated, and now again assert, that in my opinion our government can endure forever, divided into free and slave States as our fathers made it,—each State having the right to prohibit, abolish, or sustain slavery, just as it pleases. This government was made upon the great basis of the sovereignty of the States, the right of each State to regulate its own domestic institutions to suit itself; and that right was conferred with the understanding and expectation that, inasmuch as each locality had separate interests, each locality must have different and distinct local and domestic institutions, corresponding to its wants and interests. Our fathers knew when they made the government that the laws and institutions which were well adapted to the Green Mountains of Vermont were unsuited to the rice plantations of South Carolina. They knew then, as well as we know now, that the laws and institutions which would be well adapted to the beautiful prairies of Illinois would not be suited to the mining regions of California. They knew that in a republic as broad as this, having such a variety of soil, climate, and interest, there must necessarily be a corresponding variety of local laws,—the policy and institutions of each State adapted to its condition and wants. For this reason this Union was established on the right of each State to do as it pleased on the question of slavery, and every other question; and the various States were not allowed to complain of, much less interfere with, the policy of their neighbors.

Suppose the doctrine advocated by Mr. Lincoln and the Abolitionists of this day had prevailed when the Constitution was made, what would have been the result? Imagine for a moment that Mr. Lincoln had been a member of the Convention that framed the Constitution of the United States, and that when its members were about to sign that wonderful document, he had arisen in that Convention as he did at Springfield this summer, and, addressing himself to the President, had said: "A house divided against itself cannot stand; this government divided into free and slave States cannot endure, they must all be free or all be slave; they must all be one thing, or all the other, otherwise, it is a violation of the law of God, and cannot continue to exist";—suppose Mr. Lincoln had convinced that body of sages that that doctrine was sound, what would have been the result? Remember that the Union was then composed of thirteen States, twelve of which were slaveholding, and one free. Do you think that the one free State would have outvoted the twelve slaveholding States, and thus have secured the abolition of slavery? On the other hand, would not the twelve slaveholding States have outvoted the one free State, and thus have fastened slavery, by a constitutional provision, on every foot of the American Republic forever? You see that if this Abolition doctrine of Mr. Lincoln had prevailed when the government was made, it would have established slavery as a permanent institution in all the States, whether they wanted it or not; and the question for us to determine in Illinois now, as one of the free States, is whether or not we are willing, having become the majority section, to enforce a doctrine on the minority which we would have resisted with our heart's blood had it been attempted on us when we were in a minority. How has the South lost her power as the majority sec-

tion in this Union, and how have the free States gained it,
except under the operation of that principle which declares the
right of the people of each State and each Territory to form and
regulate their domestic institutions in their own way? It was
under that principle that slavery was abolished in New
Hampshire, Rhode Island, Connecticut, New York, New
Jersey, and Pennsylvania; it was under that principle that one
half of the slaveholding States became free; it was under that
principle that the number of free States increased until, from
being one out of twelve States, we have grown to be the majority of States of the whole Union, with the power to control the
House of Representatives and Senate, and the power, consequently, to elect a President by Northern votes, without the aid
of a Southern State. Having obtained this power under the
operation of that great principle, are you now prepared to
abandon the principle and declare that merely because we have
the power you will wage a war against the Southern States and
their institutions until you force them to abolish slavery everywhere?

After having pressed these arguments home on Mr. Lincoln
for seven weeks, publishing a number of my speeches, we met
at Ottawa in joint discussion, and he then began to crawfish a
little, and let himself down. I there propounded certain questions to him. Amongst others, I asked him whether he would
vote for the admission of any more slave States, in the event the
people wanted them. He would not answer. I then told him that
if he did not answer the question there, I would renew it at
Freeport, and would then trot him down into Egypt, and again
put it to him. Well, at Freeport, knowing that the next joint discussion took place in Egypt, and being in dread of it, he did
answer my question in regard to no more slave States in a mode
which he hoped would be satisfactory to me, and accomplish the
object he had in view. I will show you what his answer was. After
saying that he was not pledged to the Republican doctrine of
"no more slave States," he declared:

"I state to you freely, frankly, that I should be exceedingly sorry to
ever be put in the position of having to pass upon that question. I

should be exceedingly glad to know that there never would be another slave State admitted into this Union."

Here permit me to remark, that I do not think the people will ever force him into a position against his will. He went on to say:

"But I must add, in regard to this, that if slavery shall be kept out of the Territory during the Territorial existence of any one given Territory, and then the people should, having a fair chance and a clear field, when they come to adopt a constitution, if they should do the extraordinary thing of adopting a slave constitution uninfluenced by the actual presence of the institution among them, I see no alternative, if we own the country, but we must admit it into the Union."

That answer Mr. Lincoln supposed would satisfy the old-line Whigs, composed of Kentuckians and Virginians, down in the southern part of the State. Now, what does it amount to? I desired to know whether he would vote to allow Kansas to come into the Union with slavery or not, as her people desired. He would not answer, but in a roundabout way said that if slavery should be kept out of a Territory during the whole of its Territorial existence, and then the people, when they adopted a State Constitution, asked admission as a slave State, he supposed he would have to let the State come in. The case I put to him was an entirely different one. I desired to know whether he would vote to admit a State if Congress had not prohibited slavery in it during its Territorial existence, as Congress never pretended to do under Clay's Compromise measures of 1850. He would not answer, and I have not yet been able to get an answer from him. I have asked him whether he would vote to admit Nebraska if her people asked to come in as a State with a constitution recognizing slavery, and he refused to answer. I have put the question to him with reference to New Mexico, and he has not uttered a word in answer. I have enumerated the Territories, one after another, putting the same question to him with reference to each, and he has not said, and will not say, whether, if elected to Congress, he will vote to admit any Territory now in existence with such a constitution as her people may adopt. He invents a case which does not exist, and cannot exist under this government, and answers it; but he will not answer the question I put to him in connection with any of the Territories now in existence. The contract we entered into with Texas when she entered the Union obliges us to allow four States to be formed out of the old State, and admitted with or without slavery, as the respective inhabitants of each may determine. I have asked Mr. Lincoln three times in our joint discussions whether he would vote to redeem that pledge, and he has never yet answered. He is as silent as the grave on the subject. He would rather answer as to a state of the case which will never arise than commit himself by telling what he would do in a case which would come up for his action soon after his election to Congress. Why can he not say whether he is willing to allow the people of each State to have slavery or not as they please, and to come into the Union, when they have the requisite population, as a slave or a free State as they decide? I have no trouble in answering the question. I have said everywhere, and now repeat it to you, that if the people of Kansas want a slave State they have a right, under the Constitution of the United States, to form such a State, and I will let them come into the Union with slavery or without, as they determine. If the people of any other Territory desire slavery, let them have it. If they do not want it, let them prohibit it. It is their business, not mine. It is none of our business in Illinois whether Kansas is a free State or a slave State. It is none of your business in Missouri whether Kansas shall adopt slavery or reject it. It is the business of her people, and none of yours. The people of Kansas have as much right to decide that question for themselves as you have in Missouri to decide it for yourselves, or we in Illinois to decide it for ourselves.

And here I may repeat what I have said in every speech I have made in Illinois, that I fought the Lecompton Constitution to its death not because of the slavery clause in it, but because it was not the act and deed of the people of Kansas. I said then in Congress, and I say now, that if the people of Kansas want a slave State, they have a right to have it. If they wanted the Lecompton Constitution, they had a right to have it. I was opposed to that constitution because I did not believe that it was the act and deed of the people, but, on the contrary, the act of a small, pitiful minority acting in the name of the majority. When at last it was determined to send that constitution back to the people, and, accordingly, in August last, the question of admission under it was submitted to a popular vote, the citizens rejected it by nearly ten to one, thus showing conclusively that I was right when I said that the Lecompton Constitution was not the act and deed of the people of Kansas, and did not embody their will.

I hold that there is no power on earth, under our system of government, which has the right to force a constitution upon an unwilling people. Suppose that there had been a majority of ten to one in favor of slavery in Kansas, and suppose there had been an Abolition President and an Abolition Administration, and by some means the Abolitionists succeeded in forcing an Abolition constitution upon those slaveholding people, would the people of the South have submitted to that act for an instant? Well, if you of the South would not have submitted to it a day, how can you, as fair, honorable, and honest men, insist on putting a slave constitution on a people who desire a free State? Your safety and ours depend upon both of us acting in good faith, and living up to that great principle which asserts the right of every people to form and regulate their domestic institutions to suit themselves, subject only to the Constitution of the United States.

Most of the men who denounced my course on the Lecompton question objected to it, not because I was not right, but because they thought it expedient at that time, for the sake of keeping the party together, to do wrong. I never knew the Democratic party to violate any one of its principles, out of policy or expediency, that it did not pay the debt with sorrow. There is no safety or success for our party unless we always do right, and trust the consequences to God and the people. I chose not to depart from principle for the sake of expediency on the Lecompton question, and I never intend to do it on that or any other question.

But I am told that I would have been all right if I had only voted for the English bill after Lecompton was killed. You know a general pardon was granted to all political offenders on the Lecompton question, provided they would only vote for the

English bill. I did not accept the benefits of that pardon, for the reason that I had been right in the course I had pursued, and hence did not require any forgiveness. Let us see how the result has been worked out. English brought in his bill referring the Lecompton Constitution back to the people, with the provision that if it was rejected, Kansas should be kept out of the Union until she had the full ratio of population required for a member of Congress,—thus in effect declaring that if the people of Kansas would only consent to come into the Union under the Lecompton Constitution, and have a slave State when they did not want it, they should be admitted with a population of 35,000; but that if they were so obstinate as to insist upon having just such a constitution as they thought best, and to desire admission as a free State, then they should be kept out until they had 93,420 inhabitants. I then said, and I now repeat to you, that whenever Kansas has people enough for a slave State she has people enough for a free State. I was and am willing to adopt the rule that no State shall ever come into the Union until she has the full ratio of population for a member of Congress, provided that rule is made uniform. I made that proposition in the Senate last winter, but a majority of the senators would not agree to it; and I then said to them, If you will not adopt the general rule, I will not consent to make an exception of Kansas.

I hold that it is a violation of the fundamental principles of this government to throw the weight of Federal power into the scale, either in favor of the free or the slave States. Equality among all the States of this Union is a fundamental principle in our political system. We have no more right to throw the weight of the Federal Government into the scale in favor of the slave-holding than the free States, and least of all should our friends in the South consent for a moment that Congress should with-hold its powers either way when they know that there is a major-ity against them in both Houses of Congress.

Fellow-citizens, how have the supporters of the English bill stood up to their pledges not to admit Kansas until she obtained a population of 93,420 in the event she rejected the Lecompton Constitution? How? The newspapers inform us that English himself, whilst conducting his canvass for re-election, and in order to secure it, pledged himself to his constituents that if returned he would disregard his own bill and vote to admit Kansas into the Union with such population as she might have when she made application. We are informed that every Democratic candidate for Congress in all the States where elections have recently been held was pledged against the English bill, with perhaps one or two exceptions. Now, if I had only done as these anti-Lecompton men who voted for the English bill in Congress, pledging themselves to refuse to admit Kansas if she refused to become a slave State until she had a population of 93,420, and then returned to their people, forfeited their pledge, and made a new pledge to admit Kansas at any time she applied, without regard to population, I would have had no trouble. You saw the whole power and patronage of the Federal Government wielded in Indiana, Ohio, and Pennsylvania to re-elect anti-Lecompton men to Congress who voted against Lecompton, then voted for the English bill, and then denounced the English bill, and pledged themselves to their people to disregard it. My sin consists in not having given a pledge, and then in not having afterward forfeited it. For that reason, in this State, every postmaster, every route agent, every collector of the ports, and every Federal office-holder forfeits his head the moment he expresses a preference for the Democratic candidates against Lincoln and his Abolition associates. A Democratic Administration which we helped to bring into power deems it consistent with its fidelity to principle and its regard to duty to wield its power in this State in behalf of the Republican Abolition candidates in every county and every Congressional District against the Democratic party. All I have to say in reference to the matter is, that if that Administration have not regard enough for principle, if they are not sufficiently attached to the creed of the Democratic party, to bury forever their personal hostilities in order to succeed in carrying out our glorious principles, I have. I have no personal difficulty with Mr. Buchanan or his Cabinet. He chose to make certain recommendations to Congress, as he had a right to do, on the Lecompton question. I could not vote in favor of them. I had as much right to judge for myself how I should vote as he had how he should recommend. He undertook to say to me, "If you do not vote as I tell you I will take off the heads of your friends." I replied to him, "You did not elect me. I represent Illinois, and I am accountable to Illinois, as my constituency, and to God; but not to the President or to any other power on earth."

And now this warfare is made on me because I would not surrender my convictions of duty, because I would not abandon my constituency, and receive the orders of the executive authorities how I should vote in the Senate of the United States. I hold that an attempt to control the Senate on the part of the Executive is subversive of the principles of our Constitution. The Executive Department is independent of the Senate, and the Senate is independent of the President. In matters of legislation the President has a veto on the action of the Senate, and in appointments and treaties the Senate has a veto on the President. He has no more right to tell me how I shall vote on his appointments than I have to tell him whether he shall veto or approve a bill that the Senate has passed. Whenever you recognize the right of the Executive to say to a senator, "Do this, or I will take off the heads of your friends," you convert this government from a republic into a despotism. Whenever you recognize the right of a President to say to a member of Congress, "Vote as I tell you, or I will bring a power to bear against you at home which will crush you," you destroy the independence of the representative, and convert him into a tool of Executive power. I resisted this invasion of the constitutional rights of a senator, and I intend to resist it as long as I have a voice to speak or a vote to give. Yet Mr. Buchanan cannot provoke me to abandon one iota of Democratic principles out of revenge or hostility to his course. I stand by the platform of the Democratic party, and by its organization, and support its nominees. If there are any who choose to bolt, the fact only shows that they are not as good Democrats as I am.

My friends, there never was a time when it was as important for the Democratic party, for all national men, to rally and stand together, as it is to-day. We find all sectional men giving up past differences and continuing the one question of slavery; and when we find sectional men thus uniting, we should unite to resist them and their treasonable designs. Such was the case in 1850, when Clay left the quiet and peace of his home, and again entered upon public life to quell agitation and restore peace to a distracted Union. Then we Democrats, with Cass at our head, welcomed Henry Clay, whom the whole national regarded as having been preserved by God for the times. He became our leader in that great fight, and we rallied around him the same as the Whigs rallied around old Hickory in 1832 to put down nullification. Thus you see that whilst Whigs and Democrats fought fearlessly in old times about banks, the tariff, distribution, the specie circular, and the sub-treasury, all united as a band of brothers when the peace, harmony, or integrity of the Union was imperiled. It was so in 1850, when Abolitionism had even so far divided this country, North and South, as to endanger the peace of the Union; Whigs and Democrats united in establishing the Compromise measures of that year and restoring tranquillity and good feeling. These measures passed on the joint action of the two parties. They rested on the great principle that the people of each State and each Territory should be left perfectly free to form and regulate their domestic institutions to suit themselves. You Whigs and we Democrats justified them in that principle. In 1854, when it became necessary to organize the Territories of Kansas and Nebraska, I brought forward the bill on the same principle. In the Kansas-Nebraska Bill you find it declared to be the true intent and meaning of the act not to legislate slavery into any State or Territory, nor to exclude it therefrom, but to leave the people thereof perfectly free to form and regulate their domestic institutions in their own way. I stand on that same platform in 1858 that I did in 1850, 1854, and 1856. The Washington *Union*, pretending to be the organ of the Administration, in the number of the 5th of this month devotes three columns and a half to establish these propositions: first, that Douglas, in his Freeport speech, held the same doctrine that he did in his Nebraska Bill in 1854; second, that in 1854 Douglas justified the Nebraska Bill upon the ground that it was based upon the same principle as Clay's Compromise measures of 1850. The *Union* thus proved that Douglas was the same in 1858 that he was in 1856, 1854, and 1850, and consequently argued that he was never a Democrat. Is it not funny that I was never a Democrat? There is no pretence that I have changed a hair's breadth. The *Union* proves by my speeches that I explained the Compromise measures of 1850 just as I do now, and that I explained the Kansas and Nebraska Bill in 1854 just as I did in my Freeport speech, and yet says that I am not a Democrat, and cannot be trusted, because I have not changed during the whole of that time. It has occurred to me that in 1854 the author of the Kansas and Nebraska Bill was considered a pretty good Democrat. It has occurred to me that in 1856, when I was exerting every nerve and every energy for James Buchanan, standing on the same platform then that I do now, that I was a pretty good Democrat. They now tell me that I am not a Democrat, because I assert that the people of a Territory, as well as those of a State, have the right to decide for themselves whether slavery can or cannot exist in such Territory. Let me read what James Buchanan said on that point when he accepted the Democratic nomination for the presidency in 1856. In his letter of acceptance, he used the following language:

"The recent legislation of Congress respecting domestic slavery, derived as it has been from the original and pure fountain of legitimate political power, the will of the majority, promises ere long to allay the dangerous excitement. This legislation is founded upon principles as ancient as free government itself, and, in accordance with them, has simply declared that the people of a Territory, like those of a State, shall decide for themselves whether slavery shall or shall not exist within their limits."

Dr. Hope will there find my answer to the question he propounded to me before I commenced speaking. Of course, no man will consider it an answer who is outside of the Democratic organization, bolts Democratic nominations, and indirectly aids to put Abolitionists into power over Democrats. But whether Dr. Hope considers it an answer or not, every fair-minded man will see that James Buchanan has answered the question, and has asserted that the people of a Territory, like those of a State, shall decide for themselves whether slavery shall or shall not exist within their limits. I answer specifically if you want a further answer, and say that while, under the decision of the Supreme Court, as recorded in the opinion of Chief Justice Taney, slaves are property like all other property, and can be carried into any Territory of the United States the same as any other description of property, yet when you get them there they are subject to the local law of the Territory just like all other property. You will find in a recent speech delivered by that able and eloquent statesman Hon. Jefferson Davis, at Bangor, Maine, that he took the same view of this subject that I did in my Freeport speech. He there said:

"If the inhabitants of any Territory should refuse to enact such laws and police regulations as would give security to their property or to his, it would be rendered more or less valueless in proportion to the difficulties of holding it without such protection. In the case of property in the labor of man, or what is usually called slave property, the insecurity would be so great that the owner could not ordinarily retain it. Therefore, though the right would remain, the remedy being withheld, it would follow that the owner would be practically debarred, by the circumstances of the case, from taking slave property into a Territory where the sense of the inhabitants was opposed to its introduction. So much for the oft-repeated fallacy of forcing slavery upon any community."

You will also find that the distinguished Speaker of the present House of Representatives, Hon. Jas. L. Orr, construed the Kansas and Nebraska Bill in this same way in 1856, and also that great intellect of the South, Alex. H. Stephens, put the same construction upon it in Congress that I did in my Freeport speech. The whole South are rallying to the support of the doctrine that if the people of a Territory want slavery, they have a right to have it, and if they do not want it, that no power on earth can force it upon them. I hold that there is no principle on earth more sacred to all the friends of freedom than that which says that no institution, no law, no constitution, should be forced on an unwilling people contrary to their wishes; and I assert that the Kansas and Nebraska Bill contains that principle. It is the great principle contained in that bill. It is the principle on which

James Buchanan was made President. Without that principle, he never would have been made President of the United States. I will never violate or abandon that doctrine, if I have to stand alone. I have resisted the blandishments and threats of power on the one side, and seduction on the other, and have stood immovably for that principle, fighting for it when assailed by Northern mobs, or threatened by Southern hostility. I have defended it against the North and the South, and I will defend it against whoever assails it, and I will follow it wherever its logical conclusions lead me. I say to you that there is but one hope, one safety for this country, and that is to stand immovably by that principle which declares the right of each State and each Territory to decide these questions for themselves. This government was founded on that principle, and must be administered in the same sense in which it was founded.

But the Abolition party really think that under the Declaration of Independence the negro is equal to the white man, and that negro equality is an inalienable right conferred by the Almighty, and hence that all human laws in violation of it are null and void. With such men it is no use for me to argue. I hold that the signers of the Declaration of Independence had no reference to negroes at all when they declared all men to be created equal. They did not mean negroes, nor the savage Indians, nor the Feejee Islanders, nor any other barbarous race. They were speaking of white men. They alluded to men of European birth and European descent,—to white men, and to none others,—when they declared that doctrine. I hold that this government was established on the white basis. It was established by white men for the benefit of white men and their posterity forever, and should be administered by white men, and none others. But it does not follow by any means, that merely because the negro is not a citizen, and merely because he is not our equal, that, therefore, he should be a slave. On the contrary, it does follow that we ought to extend to the negro race, and to all other dependent races, all the rights, all the privileges, and all the immunities which they can exercise consistently with the safety of society. Humanity requires that we should give them all these privileges; Christianity commands that we should extend those privileges to them. The question then arises, What are those privileges, and what is the nature and extent of them? My answer is, that that is a question which each State must answer for itself. We in Illinois have decided it for ourselves. We tried slavery, kept it up for twelve years, and, finding that it was not profitable, we abolished it for that reason, and became a free State. We adopted in its stead the policy that a negro in this State shall not be a slave and shall not be a citizen. We have a right to adopt that policy. For my part, I think it is a wise and sound policy for us. You in Missouri must judge for yourselves whether it is a wise policy for you. If you choose to follow our example, very good; if you reject it, still well,—it is your business, not ours. So with Kentucky. Let Kentucky adopt a policy to suit herself. If we do not like it we will keep away from it; and if she does not like ours, let her stay at home, mind her own business, and let us alone. If the people of all the States will act on that great principle, and each State mind its own business, attend to its own affairs, take care of its own negroes, and not meddle with its neighbors, then there will be peace between the North and the South, the East and the West, throughout the whole Union.

Why can we not thus have peace? Why should we thus allow a sectional party to agitate this country, to array the North against the South, and convert us into enemies instead of friends, merely that a few ambitious men may ride into power on a sectional hobby? How long is it since these ambitious Northern men wished for a sectional organization? Did any one of them dream of a sectional party as long as the North was the weaker section and the South the stronger? Then all were opposed to sectional parties; but the moment the North obtained the majority in the House and Senate by the admission of California, and could elect a President without the aid of Southern votes, that moment ambitious Northern men formed a scheme to excite the North against the South, and make the people be governed in their votes by geographical lines, thinking that the North, being the stronger section, would outvote the South, and consequently they, the leaders, would ride into office on a sectional hobby. I am told that my hour is out. It was very short.

Mr. Lincoln's Reply

LADIES AND GENTLEMEN: I have been somewhat, in my own mind, complimented by a large portion of Judge Douglas's speech,—I mean that portion which he devotes to the controversy between himself and the present Administration. This is the seventh time Judge Douglas and myself have met in these joint discussions, and he has been gradually improving in regard to his war with the Administration. At Quincy, day before yesterday, he was a little more severe upon the Administration than I had heard him upon any occasion, and I took pains to compliment him for it. I then told him to give it to them with all the power he had; and as some of them were present, I told them I would be very much obliged if they would *give it to him* in about the same way. I take it he has now vastly improved upon the attack he made then upon the Administration. I flatter myself he has really taken my advice on this subject. All I can say now is to re-commend to him and to them what I then commended,—to prosecute the war against one another in the most vigorous manner. I say to them again: "Go it, husband!—Go it, bear!"

There is one other thing I will mention before I leave this branch of the discussion,—although I do not consider it much of my business, anyway. I refer to that part of the Judge's remarks where he undertakes to involve Mr. Buchanan in an inconsistency. He reads something from Mr. Buchanan, from which he undertakes to involve him in an inconsistency; and he gets something of a cheer for having done so. I would only remind the Judge that while he is very valiantly fighting for the Nebraska Bill and the repeal of the Missouri Compromise, it has been but a little while since he was the *valiant advocate* of the Missouri Compromise. I want to know if Buchanan has not as much right to be inconsistent as Douglas has. Has Douglas the *exclusive right*, in this country, of being *on all sides of all ques-*

tions? Is nobody allowed that high privilege but himself? Is he to have an entire *monopoly* on that subject?

So far as Judge Douglas addressed his speech to me, or so far as it was about me, it is my business to pay some attention to it. I have heard the Judge state two or three times what he has stated to-day, that in a speech which I made at Springfield, Illinois, I had in a very especial manner complained that the Supreme Court in the Dred Scott case had decided that a negro could never be a citizen of the United States. I have omitted by some accident heretofore to analyze this statement, and it is required of me to notice it now. In point of fact it is *untrue.* I never have complained *especially* of the Dred Scott decision because it held that a negro could not be a citizen, and the Judge is always wrong when he says I ever did so complain of it. I have the speech here, and I will thank him or any of his friends to show where I said that a negro should be a citizen, and complained especially of the Dred Scott decision because it declared he could not be one. I have done no such thing; and Judge Douglas, so persistently insisting that I have done so, has strongly impressed me with the belief of a predetermination on his part to misrepresent me. He could not get his foundation for insisting that I was in favor of this negro equality anywhere else as well as he could by assuming that untrue proposition. Let me tell this audience what is true in regard to that matter; and the means by which they may correct me if I do not tell them truly is by a recurrence to the speech itself. I spoke of the Dred Scott decision in my Springfield speech, and I was then endeavoring to prove that the Dred Scott decision was a portion of a system or scheme to make slavery national in this country. I pointed out what things had been decided by the court. I mentioned as a fact that they had decided that a negro could not be a citizen; that they had done so, as I supposed, to deprive the negro, under all circumstances, of the remotest possibility of ever becoming a citizen and claiming the rights of a citizen of the United States under a certain clause of the Constitution. I stated that, without making any complaint of it at all. I then went on and stated the other points decided in the case; name-ly, that the bringing of a negro into the State of Illinois and holding him in slavery for two years here was a matter in regard to which they would not decide whether it would make him free or not; that they decided the further point that taking him into a United States Territory where slavery was prohibited by Act of Congress did not make him free, because that Act of Congress, as they held, was unconstitutional. I mentioned these three things as making up the points decided in that case. I mentioned them in a lump, taken in connection with the introduction of the Nebraska Bill, and the amendment of Chase, offered at the time, declaratory of the right of the people of the Territories to *exclude slavery*, which was voted down by the friends of the bill. I mentioned all these things together, as evidence tending to prove a combination and conspiracy to make the institution of slavery national. In that connection and in that way I mentioned the decision on the point that a negro could not be a citizen, and in no other connection.

Out of this Judge Douglas builds up his beautiful fabrication of my purpose to introduce a perfect social and political equality between the white and black races. His assertion that I made an "especial objection" (that is his exact language) to the decision on this account is untrue in point of fact.

Now, while I am upon this subject, and as Henry Clay has been alluded to, I desire to place myself, in connection with Mr. Clay, as nearly right before this people as may be. I am quite aware what the Judge's object is here by all these allusions. He knows that we are before an audience having strong sympathies southward, by relationship, place of birth, and so on. He desires to place me in an extremely Abolition attitude. He read upon a former occasion, and alludes, without reading, to-day to a portion of a speech which I delivered in Chicago. In his quotations from that speech, as he has made them upon former occasions, the extracts were taken in such a way as, I suppose, brings them within the definition of what is called *garbling*,—taking portions of a speech which, when taken by themselves, do not present the entire sense of the speaker as expressed at the time. I propose, therefore, out of that same speech, to show how one portion of it which he skipped over (taking an extract before and an extract after) will give a different idea, and the true idea I intended to convey. It will take me some little time to read it, but I believe I will occupy the time that way.

You have heard him frequently allude to my controversy with him in regard to the Declaration of Independence. I confess that I have had a struggle with Judge Douglas on that matter, and I will try briefly to place myself right in regard to it on this occasion. I said—and it is between the extracts Judge Douglas has taken from this speech, and put in his published speeches:

> "It may be argued that there are certain conditions that make necessities and impose them upon us, and to the extent that a necessity is imposed upon a man he must submit to it. I think that was the condition in which we found ourselves when we established this government. We had slaves among us, we could not get our Constitution unless we permitted them to remain in slavery, we could not secure the good we did secure if we grasped for more; and having by necessity submitted to that much, it does not destroy the principle that is the charter of our liberties. Let the charter remain as our standard."

Now, I have upon all occasions declared as strongly as Judge Douglas against the disposition to interfere with the existing institution of slavery. You hear me read it from the same speech from which he takes garbled extracts for the purpose of proving upon me a disposition to interfere with the institution of slavery, and establish a perfect social and political equality between negroes and white people.

Allow me while upon this subject briefly to present one other extract from a speech of mine, more than a year ago, at Springfield, in discussing this very same question, soon after Judge Douglas took his ground that negroes were not included in the Declaration of Independence:

> "I think the authors of that notable instrument intended to include *all* men, but they did not mean to declare all men equal *in all respects.* They did not mean to say all men were equal in color, size, intellect, moral development, or social capacity. They defined with tolerable distinctness in what they did consider all men created equal,—equal in certain inalienable rights, among which are life, liberty, and the pursuit of happiness. This they said, and this they meant. They did not mean to assert the obvious untruth that all were then actually enjoying

that equality, or yet that they were about to confer it immediately upon them. In fact they had no power to confer such a boon. They meant simply to declare the *right,* so that the *enforcement* of it might follow as fast as circumstances should permit.

"They meant to set up a standard maxim for free society which should be familiar to all,—constantly looked to, constantly labored for, and even, though never perfectly attained, constantly approximated, and thereby constantly spreading and deepening its influence, and augmenting the happiness and value of life to all people, of all colors, everywhere."

There again are the sentiments I have expressed in regard to the Declaration of Independence upon a former occasion,—sentiments which have been put in print and read wherever anybody cared to know what so humble an individual as myself chose to say in regard to it.

At Galesburgh, the other day, I said, in answer to Judge Douglas, that three years ago there never had been a man, so far as I knew or believed, in the whole world, who had said that the Declaration of Independence did not include negroes in the term "all men." I reassert it to-day. I assert that Judge Douglas and all his friends may search the whole records of the country, and it will be a matter of great astonishment to me if they shall be able to find that one human being three years ago had ever uttered the astounding sentiment that the term "all men" in the Declaration did not include the negro. Do not let me be misunderstood. I know that more than three years ago there were men who, finding this assertion constantly in the way of their schemes to bring about the ascendency and perpetuation of slavery, *denied the truth of it.* I know that Mr. Calhoun and all the politicians of his school denied the truth of the Declaration. I know that it ran along in the mouth of some Southern men for a period of years, ending at last in that shameful, though rather forcible, declaration of Pettit of Indiana, upon the floor of the United States Senate, that the Declaration of Independence was in that respect "a self-evident lie," rather than a self-evident truth. But I say, with a perfect knowledge of all this hawking at the Declaration without directly attacking it, that three years ago there never had lived a man who had ventured to assail it in the sneaking way of pretending to believe it, and then asserting it did not include the negro. I believe the first man who ever said it was Chief Justice Taney in the Dred Scott case, and the next to him was our friend Stephen A. Douglas. And now it has become the catchword of the entire party. I would like to call upon his friends everywhere to consider how they have come in so short a time to view this matter in a way so entirely different from their former belief; to ask whether they are not being borne along by an irresistible current,—whither, they know not.

In answer to my proposition at Galesburgh last week, I see that some man in Chicago has got up a letter, addressed to the Chicago *Times,* to show, as he professes, that somebody *had* said so before; and he signs himself "An Old-Line Whig," if I remember correctly. In the first place, I would say he *was not* an old-line Whig. I am somewhat acquainted with old-line Whigs from the origin to the end of that party; I became pretty well acquainted with them, and I know they always had some sense, whatever else you could ascribe to them. I know there never was one who had not more sense than to try to show by the evidence he produces that some men had, prior to the time I named, said that negroes were not included in the term "all men" in the Declaration of Independence. What is the evidence he produces? I will bring forward *his* evidence, and let you see what *he* offers by way of showing that somebody more than three years ago had said negroes were not included in the Declaration. He brings forward part of a speech from Henry Clay,—*the* part of *the* speech of Henry Clay which I used to bring forward to prove precisely the contrary. I guess we are surrounded to some extent to-day by the old friends of Mr. Clay, and they will be glad to hear anything from that authority. While he was in Indiana a man presented a petition to liberate his negroes, and he (Mr. Clay) made a speech in answer to it, which I suppose he carefully wrote out himself and caused to be published. I have before me an extract from that speech which constitutes the evidence this pretended "Old-Line Whig" at Chicago brought forward to show that Mr. Clay didn't suppose the negro was included in the Declaration of Independence. Hear what Mr. Clay said:

"And what is the foundation of this appeal to me in Indiana to liberate the slaves under my care in Kentucky? It is a general declaration in the act announcing to the world the independence of the thirteen American colonies, that all men are created equal. Now, as an abstract principle, *there is no doubt of the truth of that declaration;* and it is desirable, *in the original construction of society and in organized societies,* to keep it in view as a great fundamental principle. But, then, I apprehend that in no society that ever did exist, or ever shall be formed, was or can the equality asserted among the members of the human race be practically enforced and carried out. There are portions, large portions,—women, minors, insane, culprits, transient sojourners,—that will always probably remain subject to the government of another portion of the community.

"That declaration, whatever may be the extent of its import, was made by the delegations of the thirteen States. In most of them slavery existed, and had long existed, and was established by law. It was introduced and forced upon the colonies by the paramount law of England. Do you believe that in making that declaration the States that concurred in it intended that it should be tortured into a virtual emancipation of all the slaves within their respective limits? Would Virginia and other Southern States have ever united in a declaration which was to be interpreted into an abolition of slavery among them? Did any one of the thirteen colonies entertain such a design or expectation? To impute such a secret and unavowed purpose, would be to charge a political fraud upon the noblest band of patriots that ever assembled in council,—a fraud upon the Confederacy of the Revolution; a fraud upon the union of those States whose Constitution not only recognized the lawfulness of slavery, but permitted the importation of slaves from Africa until the year 1808."

This is the entire quotation brought forward to prove that somebody previous to three years ago had said the negro was not included in the term "all men" in the Declaration. How does it do so? In what way has it a tendency to prove that? Mr. Clay says *it is true as an abstract principle* that all men are created equal, but that we cannot practically apply it in all cases. He illustrates this by bringing forward the cases of females, minors, and insane persons, with whom it cannot be enforced; but he says it is true as an abstract principle in the organization of society as well as in organized society and it should be kept in view as a fundamental principle. Let me read a few words more before I add some comments of my own. Mr. Clay says, a little further on:

"I desire no concealment of my opinions in regard to the institution of slavery. I look upon it as a great evil, and deeply lament that we have derived it from the parental government and from our ancestors. I wish every slave in the United States was in the country of his ancestors. But here they are, and the question is, How can they be best dealt with? If a state of nature existed, and we were about to lay the foundations of society, *no man would be more strongly opposed than I should be to incorporate the institution of slavery amongst its elements.*"

Now, here in this same book, in this same speech, in this same extract, brought forward to prove that Mr. Clay held that the negro was not included in the Declaration of Independence, is no such statement on his part, but the declaration *that it is a great fundamental truth* which should be constantly kept in view in the organization of society and in societies already organized. But if I say a word about it; if I attempt, as Mr. Clay said all good men ought to do, to keep it in view; if, in this "organized society," I ask to have the public eye turned upon it; if I ask, in relation to the organization of new Territories, that the public eye should be turned upon it,—forthwith I am vilified as you hear me to-day. What have I done that I have not the license of Henry Clay's illustrious example here in doing? Have I done aught that I have not his authority for, while maintaining that in organizing new Territories and societies this fundamental principle should be regarded, and in organized society holding it up to the public view and recognizing what *he* recognized as the great principle of free government?

And when this new principle—this new proposition that no human being ever thought of three years ago—is brought forward, *I combat it* as having an evil tendency, if not an evil design. I combat it as having a tendency to dehumanize the negro, to take away from him the right of ever striving to be a man. I combat it as being one of the thousand things constantly done in these days to prepare the public mind to make property, and nothing but property, of the *negro in all the States of this Union.*

But there is a point that I wish, before leaving this part of the discussion, to ask attention to. I have read and I repeat the words of Henry Clay:

"I desire no concealment of my opinions in regard to the institution of slavery. I look upon it as a great evil, and deeply lament that we have derived it from the parental government and from our ancestors. I wish every slave in the United States was in the country of his ancestors. But here they are, and the question is, How can they best be dealt with? If a state of nature existed, and we were about to lay the foundations of society, no man would be more strongly opposed than I should be to incorporate the institution of slavery amongst its elements."

The principle upon which I have insisted in this canvass is in relation to laying the foundations of new societies. I have never sought to apply these principles to the old States for the purpose of abolishing slavery in those States. It is nothing but a miserable perversion of what I *have* said, to assume that I have declared Missouri, or any other slave State, shall emancipate her slaves; I have proposed no such thing. But when Mr. Clay says that in laying the foundations of society in our Territories where it does not exist, he would be opposed to the introduction of slavery as an element, I insist that we have *his warrant*—his license—for insisting upon the exclusion of that element which he declared in such strong and emphatic language *was most hateful to him.*

Judge Douglas has again referred to a Springfield speech in which I said "a house divided against itself cannot stand." The Judge has so often made the entire quotation from that speech that I can make it from memory. I used this language:

"We are now far into the fifth year since a policy was initiated with the avowed object and confident promise of putting an end to the slavery agitation. Under the operation of this policy, that agitation has not only not ceased, but has constantly augmented. In my opinion it will not cease until a crisis shall have been reached and passed. 'A house divided against itself cannot stand.' I believe this government cannot endure permanently, half slave and half free. I do not expect the house to fall, but I do expect it will cease to be divided. It will become all one thing, or all the other. Either the opponents of slavery will arrest the further spread of it, and place it where the public mind shall rest in the belief that it is in the course of ultimate extinction, or its advocates will push it forward till it shall become alike lawful in all the States,—old as well as new, North as well as South."

That extract and the sentiments expressed in it have been extremely offensive to Judge Douglas. He has warred upon them as Satan wars upon the Bible. His perversions upon it are endless. Here now are my views upon it in brief:

I said we were now far into the fifth year since a policy was initiated with the avowed object and confident promise of putting an end to the slavery agitation. Is it not so? When that Nebraska Bill was brought forward four years ago last January, was it not for the "avowed object" of putting an end to the slavery agitation? We were to have no more agitation in Congress; it was all to be banished to the Territories. By the way, I will remark here that, as Judge Douglas is very fond of complimenting Mr. Crittenden in these days, Mr. Crittenden has said there was a falsehood in that whole business, for there was *no slavery agitation at that time to allay*. We were for a little while *quiet* on the troublesome thing, and that very allaying plaster of Judge Douglas's stirred it up again. But was it not understood or intimated with the "confident promise" of putting an end to the slavery agitation? Surely it was. In every speech you heard Judge Douglas make, until he got into this "imbroglio," as they call it, with the Administration about the Lecompton Constitution, every speech on that Nebraska Bill was full of his felicitations that we were *just at the end* of the slavery agitation. The last tip of the last joint of the old serpent's tail was just drawing out of view. But has it proved so? I have asserted that under that policy that agitation "has not only not ceased, but has constantly augmented." When was there ever a greater agitation in Congress than last winter? When was it as great in the country as to-day?

There was a collateral object in the introduction of that Nebraska policy, which was to clothe the people of the

Territories with a superior degree of self-government, beyond what they had ever had before. The first object and the main one of conferring upon the people a higher degree of "self-government" is a question of fact to be determined by you in answer to a single question. Have you ever heard or known of a people anywhere on earth who had as little to do as, in the first instance of its use, the people of Kansas had with this same right of "self-government"? In its main policy and in its collateral object, *it has been nothing but a living, creeping lie from the time of its introduction till to-day.*

I have intimated that I thought the agitation would not cease until a crisis should have been reached and passed. I have stated in what way I thought it would be reached and passed. I have said that it might go one way or the other. We might, by arresting the further spread of it, and placing it where the fathers originally placed it, put it where the public mind should rest in the belief that it was in the course of ultimate extinction. Thus the agitation may cease. It may be pushed forward until it shall become alike lawful in all the States, old as well as new, North as well as South. I have said, and I repeat, my wish is that the further spread of it may be arrested, and that it may be placed where the public mind shall rest in the belief that it is in the course of ultimate extinction. I have expressed that as my wish. I entertain the opinion, upon evidence sufficient to my mind, that the fathers of this government placed that institution where the public mind *did* rest in the belief that it was in the course of ultimate extinction. Let me ask why they made provision that the source of slavery—the African slave-trade—should be cut off at the end of twenty years? Why did they make provision that in all the new territory we owned at that time slavery should be forever inhibited? Why stop its spread in one direction, and cut off its source in another, if they did not look to its being placed in the course of its ultimate extinction?

Again: the institution of slavery is only mentioned in the Constitution of the United States two or three times, and in neither of these cases does the word "slavery" or "negro race" occur; but covert language is used each time, and for a purpose full of significance. What is the language in regard to the prohibition of the African slave-trade? It runs in about this way: "The migration or importation of such persons as any of the States now existing shall think proper to admit, shall not be prohibited by the Congress prior to the year one thousand eight hundred and eight."

The next allusion in the Constitution to the question of slavery and the black race is on the subject of the basis of representation, and there the language used is:

"Representatives and direct taxes shall be apportioned among the several States which may be included within this Union, according to their respective numbers, which shall be determined by adding to the whole number of free persons, including those bound to service for a term of years, and excluding Indians not taxed,—three-fifths of all other persons."

It says "persons," not slaves, not negroes; but this "three-fifths" can be applied to no other class among us than the negroes.

Lastly, in the provision for the reclamation of fugitive slaves, it is said: "No person held to service or labor in one State, under the laws thereof, escaping into another, shall in consequence of any law or regulation therein be discharged from such service or labor, but shall be delivered up, on claim of the party to whom such service or labor may be due." There again there is no mention of the word "negro" or of slavery. In all three of these places, being the only allusions to slavery in the instrument, covert language is used. Language is used not suggesting that slavery existed or that the black race were among us. And I understand the contemporaneous history of those times to be that covert language was used with a purpose, and that purpose was that in our Constitution, which it was hoped and is still hoped will endure forever,—when it should be read by intelligent and patriotic men, after the institution of slavery had passed from among us,—there should be nothing on the face of the great charter of liberty suggesting that such a thing as negro slavery had ever existed among us. This is part of the evidence that the fathers of the government expected and intended the institution of slavery to come to an end. They expected and intended that it should be in the course of ultimate extinction. And when I say that I desire to see the further spread of it arrested, I only say I desire to see that done which the fathers have first done. When I say I desire to see it placed where the public mind will rest in the belief that it is in the course of ultimate extinction, I only say I desire to see it placed where they placed it. It is not true that our fathers, as Judge Douglas assumes, made this government part slave and part free. Understand the sense in which he puts it. He assumes that slavery is a rightful thing within itself,—was introduced by the framers of the Constitution. The exact truth is, that they found the institution existing among us, and they left it as they found it. But in making the government they left this institution with many clear marks of disapprobation upon it. They found slavery among them, and they left it among them because of the difficulty—the absolute impossibility—of its immediate removal. And when Judge Douglas asks me why we cannot let it remain part slave and part free, as the fathers of the government made it, he asks a question based upon an assumption which is itself a falsehood; and I turn upon him and ask him the question, when the policy that the fathers of the government had adopted in relation to this element among us was the best policy in the world, the only wise policy, the only policy that we can ever safely continue upon that will ever give us peace, unless this dangerous element masters us all and becomes a national institution,—*I turn upon him and ask him why he could not leave it alone.* I turn and ask him why he was driven to the necessity of introducing a *new policy* in regard to it. He has himself said he introduced a new policy. He said so in his speech on the 22d of March of the present year, 1858. I ask him why he could not let it remain where our fathers placed it. I ask, too, of Judge Douglas and his friends why we shall not again place this institution upon the basis on which the fathers left it. I ask you, when he infers that I am in favor of setting the free and slave States at war, when the institution was placed in that attitude by those who made the Constitution, *did they make any war?* If we had no war out of it when thus placed, wherein is the ground of belief that we shall have war out of it if we return to that policy?

Have we had any peace upon this matter springing from any other basis? I maintain that we have not. I have proposed nothing more than a return to the policy of the fathers.

I confess, when I propose a certain measure of policy, it is not enough for me that I do not intend anything evil in the result, but it is incumbent on me to show that it has not a *tendency* to that result. I have met Judge Douglas in that point of view. I have not only made the declaration that I do not *mean* to produce a conflict between the States, but I have tried to show by fair reasoning, and I think I have shown to the minds of fair men, that I propose nothing but what has a most peaceful tendency. The quotation that I happened to make in that Springfield Speech, that "a house divided against itself cannot stand," and which has proved so offensive to the Judge, was part and parcel of the same thing. He tries to show that variety in the democratic institutions of the different States is necessary and indispensable. I do not dispute it. I have no controversy with Judge Douglas about that. I shall very readily agree with him that it would be foolish for us to insist upon having a cranberry law here in Illinois, where we have no cranberries, because they have a cranberry law in Indiana, where they have cranberries. I should insist that it would be exceedingly wrong in us to deny to Virginia the right to enact oyster laws, where they have oysters, because we want no such laws here. I understand, I hope, quite as well as Judge Douglas or anybody else, that the variety in the soil and climate and face of the country, and consequent variety in the industrial pursuits and productions of a country, require systems of law conforming to this variety in the natural features of the country. I understand quite as well as Judge Douglas that if we here raise a barrel of flour more than we want, and the Louisianians raise a barrel of sugar more than they want, it is of mutual advantage to exchange. That produces commerce, brings us together, and makes us better friends. We like one another the more for it. And I understand as well as Judge Douglas, or anybody else, that these mutual accommodations are the cements which bind together the different parts of this Union; that instead of being a thing to "divide the house,"—figuratively expressing the

Union,—they tend to sustain it; they are the props of the house, tending always to hold it up.

But when I have admitted all this, I ask if there is any parallel between these things and this institution of slavery? I do not see that there is any parallel at all between them. Consider it. When have we had any difficulty or quarrel amongst ourselves about the cranberry laws of Indiana, or the oyster laws of Virginia, or the pine-lumber laws of Maine, or the fact that Louisiana produces sugar, and Illinois flour? When have we had any quarrels over these things? When have we had perfect peace in regard to this thing which I say is an element of discord in this Union? We have sometimes had peace, but when was it? It was when the institution of slavery remained quiet where it was. We have had difficulty and turmoil whenever it has made a struggle to spread itself where it was not. I ask, then, if experience does not speak in thunder-tones telling us that the policy which has given peace to the country heretofore, being returned to, gives the greatest promise of peace again. You may say, and Judge Douglas has intimated the same thing, that all this difficulty in regard to the institution of slavery is the mere agitation of office-seekers and ambitious Northern politicians. He thinks we want to get "his place," I suppose. I agree that there are office-seekers amongst us. The Bible says somewhere that we are desperately selfish. I think we would have discovered that fact without the Bible. I do not claim that I am any less so than the average of men, but I do claim that I am not more selfish than Judge Douglas.

But is it true that all the difficulty and agitation we have in regard to this institution of slavery spring from office-seeking, from the mere ambition of politicians? Is that the truth? How many times have we had danger from this question? Go back to the day of the Missouri Compromise. Go back to the Nullification question, at the bottom of which lay this same slavery question. Go back to the time of the annexation of Texas. Go back to the troubles that led to the Compromise of 1850. You will find that every time, with the single exception of the Nullification question, they sprung from an endeavor to spread this institution. There never was a party in the history of this country, and there probably never will be, of sufficient strength to disturb the general peace of the country. Parties themselves may be divided and quarrel on minor questions, yet it extends not beyond the parties themselves. But does *not* this question make a disturbance outside of political circles? Does it not enter into the churches and rend them asunder? What divided the great Methodist Church into two parts, North and South? What has raised this constant disturbance in every Presbyterian General Assembly that meets? What disturbed the Unitarian Church in this very city two years ago? What has jarred and shaken the great American Tract Society recently, not yet splitting it, but sure to divide it in the end? Is it not this same mighty, deep-seated power that somehow operates on the minds of men, exciting and stirring them up in every avenue of society,—in politics, in religion, in literature, in morals, in all the manifold relations of life? Is this the work of politicians? Is that irresistible power, which for fifty years has shaken the government and agitated the people, to be stilled and subdued by pretending that it is an exceedingly simple thing, and we ought not to talk about it? If you will get everybody else to stop talking about it, I assure you I will quit before they have half done so. But where is the philosophy or statesmanship which assumes that you can quiet that disturbing element in our society which has disturbed us for more than half a century, which has been the only serious danger that has threatened our institutions,—I say, where is the philosophy or the statesmanship based on the assumption that we are to quit talking about it, and that the public mind is all at once to cease being agitated by it? Yet this is the policy here in the North that Douglas is advocating,—that we are to care nothing about it! I ask you if it is not a false philosophy. Is it not a false statesmanship that undertakes to build up a system of policy upon the basis of caring nothing about *the very thing that everybody does care the most about*—a thing which all experience has shown we care a very great deal about?

The Judge alludes very often in the course of his remarks to the exclusive right which the States have to decide the whole thing for themselves. I agree with him very readily that the different States have that right. He is but fighting a man of straw when he assumes that I am contending against the right of the States to do as they please about it. Our controversy with him is in regard to the new Territories. We agree that when the States come in as States they have the right and the power to do as they please. We have no power as citizens of the free States, or in our Federal capacity as members of the Federal Union through the General Government, to disturb slavery in the States where it exists. We profess constantly that we have no more inclination than belief in the power of the government to disturb it; yet we are driven constantly to defend ourselves from the assumption that we are warring upon the rights of the *States*. What I insist upon is, that the new Territories shall be kept free from it while in the Territorial condition. Judge Douglas assumes that we have no interest in them,—that we have no right whatever to interfere. I think we have some interest. I think that as white men we have. Do we not wish for an outlet for our surplus population, if I may so express myself? Do we not feel an interest in getting to that outlet with such institutions as we would like to have prevail there? If *you* go to the Territory opposed to slavery, and another man comes upon the same ground with his slave, upon the assumption that the things are equal, it turns out that he has the equal right all his way, and you have no part of it your way. If he goes in and makes it a slave Territory, and by consequence a slave State, is it not time that those who desire to have it a free State were on equal ground? Let me suggest it in a different way. How many Democrats are there about here ["A thousand"] who have left slave States and come into the free State of Illinois to get rid of the institution of slavery? [Another voice: "A thousand and one."] I reckon there are a thousand and one. I will ask you, if the policy you are now advocating had prevailed when this country was in a Territorial condition, where would you have gone to get rid of it? Where would you have found your free State or Territory to go to? And when hereafter, for any cause, the people in this place shall desire to find new homes, if they wish to be rid of the institution, where will they find the place to go to?

Now, irrespective of the moral aspect of this question as to whether there is a right or wrong in enslaving a negro, I am still in favor of our new Territories being in such a condition that white men may find a home,—may find some spot where they can better their condition; where they can settle upon new soil and better their condition in life. I am in favor of this, not merely (I must say it here as I have elsewhere) for our own people who are born amongst us, but as an outlet for *free white people everywhere*—the world over—in which Hans, and Baptiste, and Patrick, and all other men from all the world, may find new homes and better their conditions in life.

I have stated upon former occasions, and I may as well state again, what I understand to be the real issue in this controversy between Judge Douglas and myself. On the point of my wanting to make war between the free and the slave States, there has been no issue between us. So, too, when he assumes that I am in favor of producing a perfect social and political equality between the white and black races. These are false issues, upon which Judge Douglas has tried to force the controversy. There is no foundation in truth for the charge that I maintain either of these propositions. The real issue in this controversy—the one pressing upon every mind—is the sentiment on the part of one class that looks upon the institution of slavery *as a wrong*, and of another class that *does not* look upon it as a wrong. The sentiment that contemplates the institution of slavery in this country as a wrong is the sentiment of the Republican party. It is the sentiment around which all their actions, all their arguments, circle, from which all their propositions radiate. They look upon it as being a moral, social, and political wrong; and while they contemplate it as such, they nevertheless have due regard for its actual existence among us, and the difficulties of getting rid of it in any satisfactory way, and to all the constitutional obligations thrown about it. Yet, having a due regard for these, they desire a policy in regard to it that looks to its not creating any more danger. They insist that it should, as far as may be, *be treated* as a wrong; and one of the methods of treating it as a wrong is to *make provision that it shall grow no larger*. They also desire a policy that looks to a peaceful end of slavery at some time, as being wrong. These are the views they entertain in regard to it as I understand them; and all their sentiments, all their arguments and propositions, are brought within this range. I have said, and I repeat it here, that if there be a man amongst us who does not think that the institution of slavery is wrong in any one of the aspects of which I have spoken, he is misplaced, and ought not to be with us. And if there be a man amongst us who is so impatient of it as a wrong as to disregard its actual presence among us and the difficulty of getting rid of it suddenly in a satisfactory way, and to disregard the constitutional obligations thrown about it, that man is misplaced if he is on our platform. We disclaim sympathy with him in practical action. He is not placed properly with us.

On this subject of treating it as a wrong, and limiting its spread, let me say a word. Has anything ever threatened the existence of this Union save and except this very institution of slavery? What is it that we hold most dear amongst us? Our own liberty and prosperity. What has ever threatened our liberty and prosperity, save and except this institution of slavery? If this is true, how do you propose to improve the condition of things by enlarging slavery,—by spreading it out and making it bigger? You may have a wen or cancer upon your person, and not be able to cut it out, lest you bleed to death; but surely it is no way to cure it, to engraft it and spread it over your whole body. That is no proper way of treating what you regard a wrong. You see this peaceful way of dealing with it as a wrong,—restricting the spread of it, and not allowing it to go into new countries where it has not already existed. That is the peaceful way, the old-fashioned way, the way in which the fathers themselves set us the example.

On the other hand, I have said there is a sentiment which treats it as *not* being wrong. That is the Democratic sentiment of this day. I do not mean to say that every man who stands within that range positively asserts that it is right. That class will include all who positively assert that it is right, and all who, like Judge Douglas, treat it as indifferent and do not say it is either right or wrong. These two classes of men fall within the general class of those who do not look upon it as a wrong. And if there be among you anybody who supposes that he, as a Democrat, can consider himself "as much opposed to slavery as anybody,"

I would like to reason with him. You never treat it as a wrong. What other thing that you consider as a wrong do you deal with as you deal with that? Perhaps you *say* it is wrong, *but your leader never does, and you quarrel with anybody who says it is wrong*. Although you pretend to say so yourself, you can find no fit place to deal with it as a wrong. You must not say anything about it in the free States, *because it is not here*. You must not say anything about it in the slave States, *because it is there*. You must not say anything about it in the pulpit, because that is religion, and has nothing to do with it. You must not say anything about it in politics, *because that will disturb the security of "my place."* There is no place to talk about it as being a wrong, although you say yourself it is a wrong. But, finally, you will screw yourself up to the belief that if the people of the slave States should adopt a system of gradual emancipation on the slavery question, you would be in favor of it. You would be in favor of it. You say that is getting it in the right place, and you would be glad to see it succeed. But you are deceiving yourself. You all know that Frank Blair and Gratz Brown, down there in St. Louis, undertook to introduce that system in Missouri. They fought as valiantly as they could for the system of gradual emancipation which you pretend you would be glad to see succeed. Now, I will bring you to the test. After a hard fight they were beaten, and when the news came over here, you threw up your hats and *hurrahed for Democracy*. More than that, take all the argument made in favor of the system you have proposed, and it carefully excludes the idea that there is anything wrong in the institution of slavery. The arguments to sustain that policy carefully exclude it. Even here to-day you heard Judge Douglas quarrel with me because I uttered a wish that it might sometime come to an end. Although Henry Clay could say he wished every slave in the United States was in the country of his ancestors, I am denounced by those pretending to respect Henry Clay for uttering a wish that it might sometime, in some peaceful way, come to an end. The Democratic policy in regard to that institution will not tolerate the merest breath, the slightest hint, of the least degree of wrong about it. Try it by some of Judge Douglas's arguments. He says he "don't care whether it is voted up or voted down" in the Territories. I do not care myself, in dealing with that expression, whether it is intended to be expressive of his individual sentiments on the subject, or only of the national policy he desires to have established. It is alike valuable for my purpose. Any man can say that who does not see anything wrong in slavery; but no man can logically say it who does see a wrong in it, because no man can logically say he don't care whether a wrong is voted up or voted down. He may say he don't care whether an indifferent thing is voted up or down, but he must logically have a choice between a right thing and a wrong thing. He contends that whatever community wants slaves has a right to have them. So they have, if it is not a wrong. But if it is a wrong, he cannot say people have a right to do wrong. He says that upon the score of equality slaves should be allowed to go in a new Territory, like other property. This is strictly logical if there is no difference between it and other property. If it and other property are equal, this argument is entirely logical. But if you insist that one is wrong and the other right, there is no use to institute a comparison between right and wrong. You may turn over everything in the Democratic policy from beginning to end, whether in the shape it takes on the statute book, in the shape it takes in the Dred Scott decision, in the shape it takes in conversation, or the shape it takes in short maxim-like arguments,—it everywhere carefully excludes the idea that there is anything wrong in it.

That is the real issue. That is the issue that will continue in this country when these poor tongues of Judge Douglas and myself shall be silent. It is the eternal struggle between these two principles—right and wrong—throughout the world. They are the two principles that have stood face to face from the beginning of time, and will ever continue to struggle. The one is the common right of humanity, and the other the divine right of kings. It is the same principle in whatever shape it develops itself. It is the same spirit that says, "You work and toil and earn bread, and I'll eat it." No matter in what shape it comes, whether from the mouth of a king who seeks to bestride the people of his own nation and live by the fruit of their labor, or from one race of men as an apology for enslaving another race, it is the same tyrannical principle. I was glad to express my gratitude at Quincy, and I re-express it here, to Judge Douglas,—*that he looks to no end of the institution of slavery*. That will help the people to see where the struggle really is. It will hereafter place with us all men who really do wish the wrong may have an end. And whenever we can get rid of the fog which obscures the real question, when we can get Judge Douglas and his friends to avow a policy looking to its perpetuation,—we can get out from among that class of men and bring them to the side of those who treat it as a wrong. Then there will soon be an end of it, and that end will be its "ultimate extinction." Whenever the issue can be distinctly made, and all extraneous matter thrown out so that men can fairly see the real difference between the parties, this controversy will soon be settled, and it will be done peaceably too. There will be no war, no violence. It will be placed again where the wisest and best men of the world placed it. Brooks of South Carolina once declared that when this Constitution was framed its framers did not look to the institution existing until this day. When he said this, I think he stated a fact that is fully borne out by the history of the times. But he also said they were better and wiser men than the men of these days, yet the men of these days had experience which they had not, and by the invention of the cotton-gin it became a necessity in this country that slavery should be perpetual. I now say that, willingly or unwillingly, purposely or without purpose, Judge Douglas has been the most prominent instrument in changing the position of the institution of slavery,—which the fathers of the government expected to come to an end ere this,—*and putting it upon Brooks's cotton-gin basis;* placing it where he openly confesses he has no desire there shall ever be an end of it.

I understand I have ten minutes yet. I will employ it in saying something about this argument Judge Douglas uses, while he sustains the Dred Scott decision, that the people of the Territories can still somehow exclude slavery. The first thing I ask attention to is the fact that Judge Douglas constantly said, before the decision, that whether they could or not, *was a question for the Supreme Court*. But after the court had made the decision he virtually says it is *not* a question for the Supreme

Court, but for the people. And how is it he tells us they can exclude it? He says it needs "police regulations," and that admits of "unfriendly legislation." Although it is a right established by the Constitution of the United States to take a slave into a Territory of the United States and hold him as property, yet unless the Territorial Legislature will give friendly legislation, and more especially if they adopt unfriendly legislation, they can practically exclude him. Now, without meeting this proposition as a matter of fact, I pass to consider the real constitutional obligation. Let me take the gentleman who looks me in the face before me, and let us suppose that he is a member of the Territorial Legislature. The first thing he will do will be to swear that he will support the Constitution of the United States. His neighbor by his side in the Territory has slaves and needs Territorial legislation to enable him to enjoy that constitutional right. Can he withhold the legislation which his neighbor needs for the enjoyment of a right which is fixed in his favor in the Constitution of the United States which he has sworn to support? Can he withhold it without violating his oath? And, more especially, can he pass unfriendly legislation to violate his oath? Why, this is a *monstrous* sort of talk about the Constitution of the United States! *There has never been as outlandish or lawless a doctrine from the mouth of any respectable man on earth.* I do not believe it is a constitutional right to hold slaves in a Territory of the United States. I believe the decision was improperly made and I go for reversing it. Judge Douglas is furious against those who go for reversing a decision. But he is for legislating it out of all force while the law itself stands. I repeat that there has never been so monstrous a doctrine uttered from the mouth of a respectable man.

I suppose most of us (I know it of myself) believe that the people of the Southern States are entitled to a Congressional Fugitive Slave law,—that is a right fixed in the Constitution. But it cannot be made available to them without Congressional legislation. In the Judge's language, it is a "barren right," which needs legislation before it can become efficient and valuable to the persons to whom it is guaranteed. And as the right is constitutional, I agree that the legislation shall be granted to it,—and that not that we like the institution of slavery. We profess to have no taste for running and catching niggers,—at least, I profess no taste for that job at all. Why then do I yield support to a Fugitive Slave law? Because I do not understand that the Constitution, which guarantees that right, can be supported without it. And if I believed that the right to hold a slave in a Territory was equally fixed in the Constitution with the right to reclaim fugitives, I should be bound to give it the legislation necessary to support it. I say that no man can deny his obligation to give the necessary legislation to support slavery in a Territory, who believes it is a constitutional right to have it there. No man can, who does not give the Abolitionists an argument to deny the obligation enjoined by the Constitution to enact a Fugitive State law. Try it now. It is the strongest Abolition argument ever made. I say if that Dred Scott decision is correct, then the right to hold slaves in a Territory is equally a constitutional right with the right of a slaveholder to have his runaway returned. No one can show the distinction between them. The one is express, so that we cannot deny it. The other is construed to be in the Constitution, so that he who believes the decision to be correct believes in the right. And the man who argues that by unfriendly legislation, in spite of that constitutional right, slavery may be driven from the Territories, cannot avoid furnishing an argument by which Abolitionists may deny the obligation to return fugitives, and claim the power to pass laws unfriendly to the right of the slaveholder to reclaim his fugitive. I do not know how such an argument may strike a popular assembly like this, but I defy anybody to go before a body of men whose minds are educated to estimating evidence and reasoning, and show that there is an iota of difference between the constitutional right to reclaim a fugitive and the constitutional right to hold a slave, in a Territory, provided this Dred Scott decision is correct, I defy any man to make an argument that will justify unfriendly legislation to deprive a slaveholder of his right to hold his slave in a Territory, that will not equally, in all its length, breadth, and thickness, furnish an argument for nullifying the Fugitive Slave law. Why, there is not such an Abolitionist in the nation as Douglas, after all!

Mr. Douglas's Reply

MR. LINCOLN has concluded his remarks by saying that there is not such an Abolitionist as I am in all America. If he could make the Abolitionists of Illinois believe that, he would not have much show for the Senate. Let him make the Abolitionists believe the truth of that statement, and his political back is broken.

His first criticism upon me is the expression of his hope that the war of the Administration will be prosecuted against me and the Democratic party of this State with vigor. He wants that war prosecuted with vigor; I have no doubt of it. His hopes of success and the hopes of his party depend solely upon it. They have no chance of destroying the Democracy of this State except by the aid of Federal patronage. He has all the Federal office-holders here as his allies, running separate tickets against the Democracy to divide the party, although the leaders all intend to vote directly the Abolition ticket, and only leave the green-horns to vote this separate ticket who refuse to go into the Abolition camp. There is something really refreshing in the thought that Mr. Lincoln is in favor of prosecuting one war vigorously. It is the first war that I ever knew him to be in favor of prosecuting. It is the first war that I ever knew him to believe to be just or constitutional. When the Mexican War was being waged, and the American army was surrounded by the enemy in Mexico, he thought that war was unconstitutional, unnecessary, and unjust. He thought it was not commenced on the right *spot*.

When I made an incidental allusion of that kind in the joint discussion over at Charleston some weeks ago, Lincoln, in reply-ing, said that I, Douglas, had charged him with voting against supplies for the Mexican War, and then he reared up, full length, and swore that he never voted against the supplies; that it was a slander; and caught hold of Ficklin, who sat on the stand, and said, "Here, Ficklin, tell the people that it is a lie." Well, Ficklin, who had served in Congress with him, stood up and told them all that he recollected about it. It was when George Ashmun, of Massachusetts, brought forward a resolu-tion declaring the war unconstitutional, unnecessary, and unjust, that Lincoln had voted for it. "Yes," said Lincoln, "I did." Thus he confessed that he voted that the war was wrong, that our country was in the wrong, and consequently that the Mexicans were in the right; but charged that I had slandered him by saying that he voted against the supplies. I never charged him with voting against the supplies in my life, because I knew that he was not in Congress when they were voted. The war was commenced on the 13th day of May, 1846, and on that day we appropriated in Congress ten millions of dollars and fifty thousand men to prosecute it. During the same session we voted more men and more money, and at the next session we voted more men and more money, so that by the time Mr. Lincoln entered Congress we had enough men and enough money to carry on the war, and had no occasion to vote for any more. When he got into the House, being opposed to the war, and not being able to stop the supplies, because they had all gone forward, all he could do was to follow the lead of Corwin, and prove that the war was not begun on the right spot, and that it was unconstitutional, unnecessary, and wrong. Remember, too, that this he did after the war had been begun. It is one thing to be opposed to the declaration of a war, another and very different thing to take sides with the enemy against your own country after the war has been commenced. Our army was in Mexico at the time, many battles had been fought; our citizens, who were defending the honor of their country's flag, were surrounded by the daggers, the guns, and the poison of the enemy. Then it was that Corwin made his speech in which he declared that the American soldiers ought to be welcomed by the Mexicans with bloody hands and hospitable graves; then it was that Ashmun and Lincoln voted in the House of Representatives that the war was unconstitutional and unjust; and Ashmun's resolution, Corwin's speech, and Lincoln's vote were sent to Mexico and read at the head of the Mexican army, to prove to them that there was a Mexican party in the Congress of the United States who were doing all in their power to aid them. That a man who takes sides with the common enemy against his own country in time of war should rejoice in a war being made on me now, is very natural. And, in my opinion, no other kind of a man would rejoice in it.

Mr. Lincoln has told you a great deal to-day about his being an old-line Clay Whig. Bear in mind that there are a great many old Clay Whigs down in this region. It is more agreeable, therefore, for him to talk about the old Clay Whig party than it is for him to talk Abolitionism. We did not hear much about the old Clay Whig party up in the Abolition districts. How much of an old-line Henry Clay Whig was he? Have you read General Singleton's speech at Jacksonville? You know that General Singleton was for twenty-five years the confidential friend of Henry Clay in Illinois, and he testified that in 1847, when the Constitutional Convention of this State was in session, the Whig members were invited to a Whig caucus at the house of Mr. Lincoln's brother-in-law, where Mr. Lincoln proposed to throw Henry Clay overboard and take up General Taylor in his place, giving as his reason that if the Whigs did not take up General Taylor the Democrats would. Singleton testifies that Lincoln in that speech urged as another reason for throwing Henry Clay overboard that the Whigs had fought long enough for principle and ought to begin to fight for success. Singleton also testifies that Lincoln's speech did have the effect of cutting Clay's throat, and that he (Singleton) and others withdrew from the caucus in indignation. He further states that when they got to Philadelphia to attend the National Convention of the Whig party, that Lincoln was there, the bitter and deadly enemy of Clay, and that he tried to keep him (Singleton) out of the Convention because he insisted on voting for Clay, and Lincoln was determined to have Taylor. Singleton says that Lincoln rejoiced with very great joy when he found the mangled remains of the murdered Whig statesman lying cold before him. Now, Mr. Lincoln tells you that he is an old-line Clay Whig! General Singleton testifies to the facts I have narrated, in a public speech which has been printed and circulated broadcast over the State for weeks, yet not a lisp have we heard from Mr. Lincoln on the subject, except that he is an old Clay Whig.

What part of Henry Clay's policy did Lincoln ever advocate? He was in Congress in 1848–9, when the Wilmot Proviso warfare disturbed the peace and harmony of the country, until it shook the foundation of the Republic from its centre to its circumference. It was that agitation that brought Clay forth from his retirement at Ashland again to occupy his seat in the Senate of the United States, to see if he could not, by his great wisdom and experience, and the renown of his name, do something to restore peace and quiet to a disturbed country. Who got up that sectional strife that Clay had to be called upon to quell? I have heard Lincoln boast that he voted forty-two times for the Wilmot Proviso, and that he would have voted as many times more if he could. Lincoln is the man, in connection with Seward, Chase, Giddings, and other Abolitionists, who got up that strife that I helped Clay to put down. Henry Clay came back to the Senate in 1849, and saw that he must do something to restore peace to the country. The Union Whigs and the Union Democrats welcomed him, the moment he arrived, as the man for the occasion. We believed that he, of all men on earth, had been preserved by Divine Providence to guide us out of our difficulties, and we Democrats rallied under Clay then, as you Whigs in Nullification time rallied under the banner of old Jackson, forgetting party when the country was in danger, in order that we might have a country first, and parties afterwards.

And this reminds me that Mr. Lincoln told you that the slavery question was the only thing that ever disturbed the peace and harmony of the Union. Did not Nullification once raise its head and disturb the peace of this Union in 1832? Was that the slavery question, Mr. Lincoln? Did not disunion raise its monster head during the last war with Great Britain? Was that the slavery question, Mr. Lincoln? The peace of this country has been disturbed three times, once during the war with Great Britain, once on the tariff question, and once on the slavery question. His argument, therefore, that slavery is the only question that has ever created dissension in the Union falls to the ground. It is true that agitators are enabled now to use this slavery question for the purpose of sectional strife. He admits that in regard to all things else, the principle that I advocate, making each State and Territory free to decide for itself, ought to prevail. He instances the cranberry laws and the oyster laws, and he might have gone through the whole list with the same effect. I say that all these laws are local and domestic, and that local and domestic concerns should be left to each State and each Territory to manage for itself. If agitators would acquiesce in that principle, there never would be any danger to the peace and harmony of the Union.

Mr. Lincoln tries to avoid the main issue by attacking the truth of my proposition that our fathers made this government divided into free and slave States, recognizing the right of each to decide all its local questions for itself. Did they not thus make it? It is true that they did not establish slavery in any of the States, or abolish it in any of them; but finding thirteen States, twelve of which were slave and one free, they agreed to form a government uniting them together as they stood, divided into free and slave States, and to guarantee forever to each State the right to do as it pleased on the slavery question. Having thus made the government, and conferred this right upon each State forever, I assert that this government can exist as they made it, divided into free and slave States, if any one State chooses to retain slavery. He says that he looks forward to a time when slavery shall be abolished everywhere. I look forward to a time when each State shall be allowed to do as it pleases. If it chooses to keep slavery forever, it is not my business, but its own; if it chooses to abolish slavery, it is its own business,—not mine. I care more for the great principle of self-government, the right of the people to rule, than I do for all the negroes in Christendom. I would not endanger the perpetuity of this Union, I would not blot out the great inalienable rights of the white man, for all the negroes that ever existed. Hence, I say, let us maintain this government on the principles that our fathers made it, recognizing the right of each State to keep slavery as long as its people determine, or to abolish it when they please. But Mr. Lincoln says that when our fathers made this government they did not look forward to the state of things now existing, and therefore he thinks the doctrine was wrong; and he quotes Brooks of South Carolina to prove that our fathers then thought that probably slavery would be abolished by each State acting for itself before this time. Suppose they did; suppose they did not foresee what has occurred,—does that change the principles of our government? They did not, probably, foresee the telegraph that transmits intelligence by lightning, nor did they foresee the railroads that now form the bonds of union between the different States, or the thousand mechanical inventions that have elevated mankind. But do these things change the principles of the government? Our fathers, I say, made this government on the principle of the right of each State to do as it pleases in its own domestic affairs, subject to the Constitution, and allowed the people of each to apply to every new change of circumstances such remedy as they may see fit to improve their condition. This right they have for all time to come.

Mr. Lincoln went on to tell you that he does not at all desire to interfere with slavery in the States where it exists, nor does his party. I expected him to say that down here. Let me ask him, then, how he expects to put slavery in the course of ultimate extinction everywhere, if he does not intend to interfere with it in the States where it exists? He says that he will prohibit it in all Territories, and the inference is, then, that unless they make free States out of them he will keep them out of the Union; for, mark you, he did not say whether or not he would vote to admit Kansas with slavery or not, as her people might apply (he forgot that, as usual, etc.): he did not say whether or not he was in favor of bringing the Territories now in existence into the Union on the principle of Clay's Compromise measures on the slavery question. I told you that he would not. His idea is that he will prohibit slavery in all the Territories and thus force them all to become free States, surrounding the slave States with a cordon of free States, and hemming them in, keeping the slaves confined to their present limits whilst they go on multiplying, until the soil on which they live will no longer feed them, and he will thus be able to put slavery in a course of ultimate extinction by starvation. He will extinguish slavery in the Southern States as the French general exterminated the Algerines when he smoked them out. He is going to extinguish slavery by surrounding the slave States, hemming in the slaves, and starving them out of existence, as you smoke a fox out of his hole. He intends to do that in the name of humanity and Christianity, in order that we may get rid of the terrible crime and sin entailed upon our fathers of holding slaves. Mr. Lincoln makes out that line of policy, and appeals to the moral sense of justice and to the Christian feeling of the community to sustain him. He says that any man who holds to the contrary doctrine is in the position of the king who claimed to govern by divine right. Let us examine for a moment and see what principle it was that overthrew the divine right of George the Third to govern us. Did not these colonies rebel because the British Parliament had no right to pass laws concerning our property and domestic and private institutions without our consent? We demanded that the British Government should not pass such laws unless they gave us representation in the body passing them; and this the British Government insisting on doing, we went to war, on the principle that the home government should not control and govern distant colonies without giving them a representation. Now, Mr. Lincoln proposes to govern the Territories without giving them a representation, and calls on Congress to pass laws controlling their property and domestic concerns without their consent and against their will. Thus, he asserts for his party the identical principle asserted by George III and the Tories of the Revolution.

I ask you to look into these things, and then tell me whether the Democracy or the Abolitionists are right. I hold that the people of a Territory, like those of a State (I use the language of Mr. Buchanan in his Letter of Acceptance), have the right to decide for themselves whether slavery shall or shall not exist within their limits. The point upon which Chief Justice Taney expresses his opinion is simply this, that slaves, being property, stand on an equal footing with other property, and consequently that the owner has the same right to carry that property into a Territory that he has any other, subject to the same conditions. Suppose that one of your merchants was to take fifty or one hundred thousand dollars' worth of liquors to Kansas. He has a right to go there, under that decision; but when he gets there he finds the Maine l iquor law in force, and what can he do with his property after he gets it there? He cannot sell it, he cannot use it; it is subject to the local law, and that law is against him, and the best thing he can do with it is to bring it back into Missouri or Illinois and sell it. If you take negroes to Kansas, as Colonel

Jefferson Davis said in his Bangor speech, from which I have quoted to-day, you must take them there subject to the local law. If the people want the institution of slavery, they will protect and encourage it; but if they do not want it, they will withhold that protection, and the absence of local legislation protecting slavery excludes it as completely as a positive prohibition. You slaveholders of Missouri might as well understand, what you know practically, that you cannot carry slavery where the people do not want it. All you have a right to ask is that the people shall do as they please: if they want slavery, let them have it; if they do not want it, allow them to refuse to encourage it.

My friends, if, as I have said before, we will only live up to this great fundamental principle, there will be peace between the North and the South. Mr. Lincoln admits that, under the Constitution, on all domestic questions, except slavery, we ought not to interfere with the people of each State. What right have we to interfere with slavery any more than we have to interfere with any other question? He says that this slavery question is now the bone of contention. Why? Simply because agitators have combined in all the free States to make war upon it. Suppose the agitators in the States should combine in one half of the Union to make war upon the railroad system of the other half? They would thus be driven to the same sectional strife. Suppose one section makes war upon any other peculiar institution of the opposite section, and the same strife is produced. The only remedy and safety is that we shall stand by the Constitution as our fathers made it, obey the laws as they are passed, while they stand the proper test, and sustain the decisions of the Supreme Court and the constituted authorities.

A CATALOG OF SELECTED
DOVER BOOKS
IN ALL FIELDS OF INTEREST

A CATALOG OF SELECTED DOVER
BOOKS IN ALL FIELDS OF INTEREST

CONCERNING THE SPIRITUAL IN ART, Wassily Kandinsky. Pioneering work by father of abstract art. Thoughts on color theory, nature of art. Analysis of earlier masters. 12 illustrations. 80pp. of text. 5⅜ x 8½. 23411-8

ANIMALS: 1,419 Copyright-Free Illustrations of Mammals, Birds, Fish, Insects, etc., Jim Harter (ed.). Clear wood engravings present, in extremely lifelike poses, over 1,000 species of animals. One of the most extensive pictorial sourcebooks of its kind. Captions. Index. 284pp. 9 x 12. 23766-4

CELTIC ART: The Methods of Construction, George Bain. Simple geometric techniques for making Celtic interlacements, spirals, Kells-type initials, animals, humans, etc. Over 500 illustrations. 160pp. 9 x 12. (Available in U.S. only.) 22923-8

AN ATLAS OF ANATOMY FOR ARTISTS, Fritz Schider. Most thorough reference work on art anatomy in the world. Hundreds of illustrations, including selections from works by Vesalius, Leonardo, Goya, Ingres, Michelangelo, others. 593 illustrations. 192pp. 7⅛ x 10¼. 20241-0

CELTIC HAND STROKE-BY-STROKE (Irish Half-Uncial from "The Book of Kells"): An Arthur Baker Calligraphy Manual, Arthur Baker. Complete guide to creating each letter of the alphabet in distinctive Celtic manner. Covers hand position, strokes, pens, inks, paper, more. Illustrated. 48pp. 8¼ x 11. 24336-2

EASY ORIGAMI, John Montroll. Charming collection of 32 projects (hat, cup, pelican, piano, swan, many more) specially designed for the novice origami hobbyist. Clearly illustrated easy-to-follow instructions insure that even beginning papercrafters will achieve successful results. 48pp. 8¼ x 11. 27298-2

THE COMPLETE BOOK OF BIRDHOUSE CONSTRUCTION FOR WOODWORKERS, Scott D. Campbell. Detailed instructions, illustrations, tables. Also data on bird habitat and instinct patterns. Bibliography. 3 tables. 63 illustrations in 15 figures. 48pp. 5¼ x 8½. 24407-5

BLOOMINGDALE'S ILLUSTRATED 1886 CATALOG: Fashions, Dry Goods and Housewares, Bloomingdale Brothers. Famed merchants' extremely rare catalog depicting about 1,700 products: clothing, housewares, firearms, dry goods, jewelry, more. Invaluable for dating, identifying vintage items. Also, copyright-free graphics for artists, designers. Co-published with Henry Ford Museum & Greenfield Village. 160pp. 8¼ x 11. 25780-0

HISTORIC COSTUME IN PICTURES, Braun & Schneider. Over 1,450 costumed figures in clearly detailed engravings—from dawn of civilization to end of 19th century. Captions. Many folk costumes. 256pp. 8⅜ x 11¾. 23150-X

STICKLEY CRAFTSMAN FURNITURE CATALOGS, Gustav Stickley and L. & J. G. Stickley. Beautiful, functional furniture in two authentic catalogs from 1910. 594 illustrations, including 277 photos, show settles, rockers, armchairs, reclining chairs, bookcases, desks, tables. 183pp. 6½ x 9¼.   23838-5

AMERICAN LOCOMOTIVES IN HISTORIC PHOTOGRAPHS: 1858 to 1949, Ron Ziel (ed.). A rare collection of 126 meticulously detailed official photographs, called "builder portraits," of American locomotives that majestically chronicle the rise of steam locomotive power in America. Introduction. Detailed captions. xi+ 129pp. 9 x 12.   27393-8

AMERICA'S LIGHTHOUSES: An Illustrated History, Francis Ross Holland, Jr. Delightfully written, profusely illustrated fact-filled survey of over 200 American light-houses since 1716. History, anecdotes, technological advances, more. 240pp. 8 x 10¾.
                                          25576-X

TOWARDS A NEW ARCHITECTURE, Le Corbusier. Pioneering manifesto by founder of "International School." Technical and aesthetic theories, views of industry, economics, relation of form to function, "mass-production split" and much more. Profusely illustrated. 320pp. 6⅛ x 9¼. (Available in U.S. only.)   25023-7

HOW THE OTHER HALF LIVES, Jacob Riis. Famous journalistic record, exposing poverty and degradation of New York slums around 1900, by major social reformer. 100 striking and influential photographs. 233pp. 10 x 7⅞.   22012-5

FRUIT KEY AND TWIG KEY TO TREES AND SHRUBS, William M. Harlow. One of the handiest and most widely used identification aids. Fruit key covers 120 deciduous and evergreen species; twig key 160 deciduous species. Easily used. Over 300 photographs. 126pp. 5⅜ x 8½.   20511-8

COMMON BIRD SONGS, Dr. Donald J. Borror. Songs of 60 most common U.S. birds: robins, sparrows, cardinals, bluejays, finches, more—arranged in order of increasing complexity. Up to 9 variations of songs of each species.
                                          Cassette and manual 99911-4

ORCHIDS AS HOUSE PLANTS, Rebecca Tyson Northen. Grow cattleyas and many other kinds of orchids—in a window, in a case, or under artificial light. 63 illustrations. 148pp. 5⅜ x 8½.   23261-1

MONSTER MAZES, Dave Phillips. Masterful mazes at four levels of difficulty. Avoid deadly perils and evil creatures to find magical treasures. Solutions for all 32 exciting illustrated puzzles. 48pp. 8¼ x 11.   26005-4

MOZART'S DON GIOVANNI (DOVER OPERA LIBRETTO SERIES), Wolfgang Amadeus Mozart. Introduced and translated by Ellen H. Bleiler. Standard Italian libretto, with complete English translation. Convenient and thoroughly portable—an ideal companion for reading along with a recording or the performance itself. Introduction. List of characters. Plot summary. 121pp. 5¼ x 8½.   24944-1

TECHNICAL MANUAL AND DICTIONARY OF CLASSICAL BALLET, Gail Grant. Defines, explains, comments on steps, movements, poses and concepts. 15-page pictorial section. Basic book for student, viewer. 127pp. 5⅜ x 8½.   21843-0

THE CLARINET AND CLARINET PLAYING, David Pino. Lively, comprehensive work features suggestions about technique, musicianship, and musical interpretation, as well as guidelines for teaching, making your own reeds, and preparing for public performance. Includes an intriguing look at clarinet history. "A godsend," *The Clarinet,* Journal of the International Clarinet Society. Appendixes. 7 illus. 320pp. 5⅜ x 8½. 40270-3

HOLLYWOOD GLAMOR PORTRAITS, John Kobal (ed.). 145 photos from 1926-49. Harlow, Gable, Bogart, Bacall; 94 stars in all. Full background on photographers, technical aspects. 160pp. 8⅜ x 11¼. 23352-9

THE ANNOTATED CASEY AT THE BAT: A Collection of Ballads about the Mighty Casey/Third, Revised Edition, Martin Gardner (ed.). Amusing sequels and parodies of one of America's best-loved poems: Casey's Revenge, Why Casey Whiffed, Casey's Sister at the Bat, others. 256pp. 5⅜ x 8½. 28598-7

THE RAVEN AND OTHER FAVORITE POEMS, Edgar Allan Poe. Over 40 of the author's most memorable poems: "The Bells," "Ulalume," "Israfel," "To Helen," "The Conqueror Worm," "Eldorado," "Annabel Lee," many more. Alphabetic lists of titles and first lines. 64pp. 5$\frac{3}{16}$ x 8¼. 26685-0

PERSONAL MEMOIRS OF U. S. GRANT, Ulysses Simpson Grant. Intelligent, deeply moving firsthand account of Civil War campaigns, considered by many the finest military memoirs ever written. Includes letters, historic photographs, maps and more. 528pp. 6⅛ x 9¼. 28587-1

ANCIENT EGYPTIAN MATERIALS AND INDUSTRIES, A. Lucas and J. Harris. Fascinating, comprehensive, thoroughly documented text describes this ancient civilization's vast resources and the processes that incorporated them in daily life, including the use of animal products, building materials, cosmetics, perfumes and incense, fibers, glazed ware, glass and its manufacture, materials used in the mummification process, and much more. 544pp. 6⅛ x 9¼. (Available in U.S. only.) 40446-3

RUSSIAN STORIES/RUSSKIE RASSKAZY: A Dual-Language Book, edited by Gleb Struve. Twelve tales by such masters as Chekhov, Tolstoy, Dostoevsky, Pushkin, others. Excellent word-for-word English translations on facing pages, plus teaching and study aids, Russian/English vocabulary, biographical/critical introductions, more. 416pp. 5⅜ x 8½. 26244-8

PHILADELPHIA THEN AND NOW: 60 Sites Photographed in the Past and Present, Kenneth Finkel and Susan Oyama. Rare photographs of City Hall, Logan Square, Independence Hall, Betsy Ross House, other landmarks juxtaposed with contemporary views. Captures changing face of historic city. Introduction. Captions. 128pp. 8¼ x 11. 25790-8

AIA ARCHITECTURAL GUIDE TO NASSAU AND SUFFOLK COUNTIES, LONG ISLAND, The American Institute of Architects, Long Island Chapter, and the Society for the Preservation of Long Island Antiquities. Comprehensive, well-researched and generously illustrated volume brings to life over three centuries of Long Island's great architectural heritage. More than 240 photographs with authoritative, extensively detailed captions. 176pp. 8¼ x 11. 26946-9

NORTH AMERICAN INDIAN LIFE: Customs and Traditions of 23 Tribes, Elsie Clews Parsons (ed.). 27 fictionalized essays by noted anthropologists examine religion, customs, government, additional facets of life among the Winnebago, Crow, Zuni, Eskimo, other tribes. 480pp. 6⅛ x 9¼. 27377-6

FRANK LLOYD WRIGHT'S DANA HOUSE, Donald Hoffmann. Pictorial essay of residential masterpiece with over 160 interior and exterior photos, plans, elevations, sketches and studies. 128pp. 9¼ x 10¾. 29120-0

THE MALE AND FEMALE FIGURE IN MOTION: 60 Classic Photographic Sequences, Eadweard Muybridge. 60 true-action photographs of men and women walking, running, climbing, bending, turning, etc., reproduced from rare 19th-century masterpiece. vi + 121pp. 9 x 12. 24745-7

1001 QUESTIONS ANSWERED ABOUT THE SEASHORE, N. J. Berrill and Jacquelyn Berrill. Queries answered about dolphins, sea snails, sponges, starfish, fishes, shore birds, many others. Covers appearance, breeding, growth, feeding, much more. 305pp. 5¼ x 8¼. 23366-9

ATTRACTING BIRDS TO YOUR YARD, William J. Weber. Easy-to-follow guide offers advice on how to attract the greatest diversity of birds: birdhouses, feeders, water and waterers, much more. 96pp. 5³⁄₁₆ x 8¼. 28927-3

MEDICINAL AND OTHER USES OF NORTH AMERICAN PLANTS: A Historical Survey with Special Reference to the Eastern Indian Tribes, Charlotte Erichsen-Brown. Chronological historical citations document 500 years of usage of plants, trees, shrubs native to eastern Canada, northeastern U.S. Also complete identifying information. 343 illustrations. 544pp. 6½ x 9¼. 25951-X

STORYBOOK MAZES, Dave Phillips. 23 stories and mazes on two-page spreads: Wizard of Oz, Treasure Island, Robin Hood, etc. Solutions. 64pp. 8¼ x 11. 23628-5

AMERICAN NEGRO SONGS: 230 Folk Songs and Spirituals, Religious and Secular, John W. Work. This authoritative study traces the African influences of songs sung and played by black Americans at work, in church, and as entertainment. The author discusses the lyric significance of such songs as "Swing Low, Sweet Chariot," "John Henry," and others and offers the words and music for 230 songs. Bibliography. Index of Song Titles. 272pp. 6½ x 9¼. 40271-1

MOVIE-STAR PORTRAITS OF THE FORTIES, John Kobal (ed.). 163 glamor, studio photos of 106 stars of the 1940s: Rita Hayworth, Ava Gardner, Marlon Brando, Clark Gable, many more. 176pp. 8⅜ x 11¼. 23546-7

BENCHLEY LOST AND FOUND, Robert Benchley. Finest humor from early 30s, about pet peeves, child psychologists, post office and others. Mostly unavailable elsewhere. 73 illustrations by Peter Arno and others. 183pp. 5⅜ x 8½. 22410-4

YEKL and THE IMPORTED BRIDEGROOM AND OTHER STORIES OF YIDDISH NEW YORK, Abraham Cahan. Film Hester Street based on *Yekl* (1896). Novel, other stories among first about Jewish immigrants on N.Y.'s East Side. 240pp. 5⅜ x 8½. 22427-9

SELECTED POEMS, Walt Whitman. Generous sampling from *Leaves of Grass*. Twenty-four poems include "I Hear America Singing," "Song of the Open Road," "I Sing the Body Electric," "When Lilacs Last in the Dooryard Bloom'd," "O Captain! My Captain!"–all reprinted from an authoritative edition. Lists of titles and first lines. 128pp. 5³⁄₁₆ x 8¼. 26878-0

THE BEST TALES OF HOFFMANN, E. T. A. Hoffmann. 10 of Hoffmann's most important stories: "Nutcracker and the King of Mice," "The Golden Flowerpot," etc. 458pp. 5⅜ x 8½. 21793-0

FROM FETISH TO GOD IN ANCIENT EGYPT, E. A. Wallis Budge. Rich detailed survey of Egyptian conception of "God" and gods, magic, cult of animals, Osiris, more. Also, superb English translations of hymns and legends. 240 illustrations. 545pp. 5⅜ x 8½. 25803-3

FRENCH STORIES/CONTES FRANÇAIS: A Dual-Language Book, Wallace Fowlie. Ten stories by French masters, Voltaire to Camus: "Micromegas" by Voltaire; "The Atheist's Mass" by Balzac; "Minuet" by de Maupassant; "The Guest" by Camus, six more. Excellent English translations on facing pages. Also French-English vocabulary list, exercises, more. 352pp. 5⅜ x 8½. 26443-2

CHICAGO AT THE TURN OF THE CENTURY IN PHOTOGRAPHS: 122 Historic Views from the Collections of the Chicago Historical Society, Larry A. Viskochil. Rare large-format prints offer detailed views of City Hall, State Street, the Loop, Hull House, Union Station, many other landmarks, circa 1904-1913. Introduction. Captions. Maps. 144pp. 9⅜ x 12¼. 24656-6

OLD BROOKLYN IN EARLY PHOTOGRAPHS, 1865-1929, William Lee Younger. Luna Park, Gravesend race track, construction of Grand Army Plaza, moving of Hotel Brighton, etc. 157 previously unpublished photographs. 165pp. 8⅞ x 11¾. 23587-4

THE MYTHS OF THE NORTH AMERICAN INDIANS, Lewis Spence. Rich anthology of the myths and legends of the Algonquins, Iroquois, Pawnees and Sioux, prefaced by an extensive historical and ethnological commentary. 36 illustrations. 480pp. 5⅜ x 8½. 25967-6

AN ENCYCLOPEDIA OF BATTLES: Accounts of Over 1,560 Battles from 1479 B.C. to the Present, David Eggenberger. Essential details of every major battle in recorded history from the first battle of Megiddo in 1479 B.C. to Grenada in 1984. List of Battle Maps. New Appendix covering the years 1967-1984. Index. 99 illustrations. 544pp. 6½ x 9¼. 24913-1

SAILING ALONE AROUND THE WORLD, Captain Joshua Slocum. First man to sail around the world, alone, in small boat. One of great feats of seamanship told in delightful manner. 67 illustrations. 294pp. 5⅜ x 8½. 20326-3

ANARCHISM AND OTHER ESSAYS, Emma Goldman. Powerful, penetrating, prophetic essays on direct action, role of minorities, prison reform, puritan hypocrisy, violence, etc. 271pp. 5⅜ x 8½. 22484-8

MYTHS OF THE HINDUS AND BUDDHISTS, Ananda K. Coomaraswamy and Sister Nivedita. Great stories of the epics; deeds of Krishna, Shiva, taken from puranas, Vedas, folk tales; etc. 32 illustrations. 400pp. 5⅜ x 8½. 21759-0

THE TRAUMA OF BIRTH, Otto Rank. Rank's controversial thesis that anxiety neurosis is caused by profound psychological trauma which occurs at birth. 256pp. 5⅜ x 8½. 27974-X

A THEOLOGICO-POLITICAL TREATISE, Benedict Spinoza. Also contains unfinished Political Treatise. Great classic on religious liberty, theory of government on common consent. R. Elwes translation. Total of 421pp. 5⅜ x 8½. 20249-6

MY BONDAGE AND MY FREEDOM, Frederick Douglass. Born a slave, Douglass became outspoken force in antislavery movement. The best of Douglass' autobiographies. Graphic description of slave life. 464pp. 5⅜ x 8½. 22457-0

FOLLOWING THE EQUATOR: A Journey Around the World, Mark Twain. Fascinating humorous account of 1897 voyage to Hawaii, Australia, India, New Zealand, etc. Ironic, bemused reports on peoples, customs, climate, flora and fauna, politics, much more. 197 illustrations. 720pp. 5⅜ x 8½. 26113-1

THE PEOPLE CALLED SHAKERS, Edward D. Andrews. Definitive study of Shakers: origins, beliefs, practices, dances, social organization, furniture and crafts, etc. 33 illustrations. 351pp. 5⅜ x 8½. 21081-2

THE MYTHS OF GREECE AND ROME, H. A. Guerber. A classic of mythology, generously illustrated, long prized for its simple, graphic, accurate retelling of the principal myths of Greece and Rome, and for its commentary on their origins and significance. With 64 illustrations by Michelangelo, Raphael, Titian, Rubens, Canova, Bernini and others. 480pp. 5⅜ x 8½. 27584-1

PSYCHOLOGY OF MUSIC, Carl E. Seashore. Classic work discusses music as a medium from psychological viewpoint. Clear treatment of physical acoustics, auditory apparatus, sound perception, development of musical skills, nature of musical feeling, host of other topics. 88 figures. 408pp. 5⅜ x 8½. 21851-1

THE PHILOSOPHY OF HISTORY, Georg W. Hegel. Great classic of Western thought develops concept that history is not chance but rational process, the evolution of freedom. 457pp. 5⅜ x 8½. 20112-0

THE BOOK OF TEA, Kakuzo Okakura. Minor classic of the Orient: entertaining, charming explanation, interpretation of traditional Japanese culture in terms of tea ceremony. 94pp. 5⅜ x 8½. 20070-1

LIFE IN ANCIENT EGYPT, Adolf Erman. Fullest, most thorough, detailed older account with much not in more recent books, domestic life, religion, magic, medicine, commerce, much more. Many illustrations reproduce tomb paintings, carvings, hieroglyphs, etc. 597pp. 5⅜ x 8½. 22632-8

SUNDIALS, Their Theory and Construction, Albert Waugh. Far and away the best, most thorough coverage of ideas, mathematics concerned, types, construction, adjusting anywhere. Simple, nontechnical treatment allows even children to build several of these dials. Over 100 illustrations. 230pp. 5⅜ x 8½. 22947-5

THEORETICAL HYDRODYNAMICS, L. M. Milne-Thomson. Classic exposition of the mathematical theory of fluid motion, applicable to both hydrodynamics and aerodynamics. Over 600 exercises. 768pp. 6⅛ x 9¼. 68970-0

SONGS OF EXPERIENCE: Facsimile Reproduction with 26 Plates in Full Color, William Blake. 26 full-color plates from a rare 1826 edition. Includes "The Tyger," "London," "Holy Thursday," and other poems. Printed text of poems. 48pp. 5¼ x 7. 24636-1

OLD-TIME VIGNETTES IN FULL COLOR, Carol Belanger Grafton (ed.). Over 390 charming, often sentimental illustrations, selected from archives of Victorian graphics—pretty women posing, children playing, food, flowers, kittens and puppies, smiling cherubs, birds and butterflies, much more. All copyright-free. 48pp. 9¼ x 12¼. 27269-9

PERSPECTIVE FOR ARTISTS, Rex Vicat Cole. Depth, perspective of sky and sea, shadows, much more, not usually covered. 391 diagrams, 81 reproductions of drawings and paintings. 279pp. 5⅜ x 8½. 22487-2

DRAWING THE LIVING FIGURE, Joseph Sheppard. Innovative approach to artistic anatomy focuses on specifics of surface anatomy, rather than muscles and bones. Over 170 drawings of live models in front, back and side views, and in widely varying poses. Accompanying diagrams. 177 illustrations. Introduction. Index. 144pp. 8⅜ x11¼. 26723-7

GOTHIC AND OLD ENGLISH ALPHABETS: 100 Complete Fonts, Dan X. Solo. Add power, elegance to posters, signs, other graphics with 100 stunning copyright-free alphabets: Blackstone, Dolbey, Germania, 97 more–including many lower-case, numerals, punctuation marks. 104pp. 8⅛ x 11. 24695-7

HOW TO DO BEADWORK, Mary White. Fundamental book on craft from simple projects to five-bead chains and woven works. 106 illustrations. 142pp. 5⅜ x 8.
20697-1

THE BOOK OF WOOD CARVING, Charles Marshall Sayers. Finest book for beginners discusses fundamentals and offers 34 designs. "Absolutely first rate . . . well thought out and well executed."–E. J. Tangerman. 118pp. 7¾ x 10⅝. 23654-4

ILLUSTRATED CATALOG OF CIVIL WAR MILITARY GOODS: Union Army Weapons, Insignia, Uniform Accessories, and Other Equipment, Schuyler, Hartley, and Graham. Rare, profusely illustrated 1846 catalog includes Union Army uniform and dress regulations, arms and ammunition, coats, insignia, flags, swords, rifles, etc. 226 illustrations. 160pp. 9 x 12. 24939-5

WOMEN'S FASHIONS OF THE EARLY 1900s: An Unabridged Republication of "New York Fashions, 1909," National Cloak & Suit Co. Rare catalog of mail-order fashions documents women's and children's clothing styles shortly after the turn of the century. Captions offer full descriptions, prices. Invaluable resource for fashion, costume historians. Approximately 725 illustrations. 128pp. 8⅜ x 11¼. 27276-1

THE 1912 AND 1915 GUSTAV STICKLEY FURNITURE CATALOGS, Gustav Stickley. With over 200 detailed illustrations and descriptions, these two catalogs are essential reading and reference materials and identification guides for Stickley furniture. Captions cite materials, dimensions and prices. 112pp. 6½ x 9¼. 26676-1

EARLY AMERICAN LOCOMOTIVES, John H. White, Jr. Finest locomotive engravings from early 19th century: historical (1804–74), main-line (after 1870), special, foreign, etc. 147 plates. 142pp. 11⅜ x 8¼. 22772-3

THE TALL SHIPS OF TODAY IN PHOTOGRAPHS, Frank O. Braynard. Lavishly illustrated tribute to nearly 100 majestic contemporary sailing vessels: Amerigo Vespucci, Clearwater, Constitution, Eagle, Mayflower, Sea Cloud, Victory, many more. Authoritative captions provide statistics, background on each ship. 190 black-and-white photographs and illustrations. Introduction. 128pp. 8⅞ x 11¾.
27163-3

LITTLE BOOK OF EARLY AMERICAN CRAFTS AND TRADES, Peter Stockham (ed.). 1807 children's book explains crafts and trades: baker, hatter, cooper, potter, and many others. 23 copperplate illustrations. 140pp. 4⅝ x 6.   23336-7

VICTORIAN FASHIONS AND COSTUMES FROM HARPER'S BAZAR, 1867–1898, Stella Blum (ed.). Day costumes, evening wear, sports clothes, shoes, hats, other accessories in over 1,000 detailed engravings. 320pp. 9⅜ x 12¼. 22990-4

GUSTAV STICKLEY, THE CRAFTSMAN, Mary Ann Smith. Superb study surveys broad scope of Stickley's achievement, especially in architecture. Design philosophy, rise and fall of the Craftsman empire, descriptions and floor plans for many Craftsman houses, more. 86 black-and-white halftones. 31 line illustrations. Introduction 208pp. 6½ x 9¼.   27210-9

THE LONG ISLAND RAIL ROAD IN EARLY PHOTOGRAPHS, Ron Ziel. Over 220 rare photos, informative text document origin (1844) and development of rail service on Long Island. Vintage views of early trains, locomotives, stations, passengers, crews, much more. Captions. 8⅞ x 11¾.   26301-0

VOYAGE OF THE LIBERDADE, Joshua Slocum. Great 19th-century mariner's thrilling, first-hand account of the wreck of his ship off South America, the 35-foot boat he built from the wreckage, and its remarkable voyage home. 128pp. 5⅜ x 8½.
40022-0

TEN BOOKS ON ARCHITECTURE, Vitruvius. The most important book ever written on architecture. Early Roman aesthetics, technology, classical orders, site selection, all other aspects. Morgan translation. 331pp. 5⅜ x 8½.   20645-9

THE HUMAN FIGURE IN MOTION, Eadweard Muybridge. More than 4,500 stopped-action photos, in action series, showing undraped men, women, children jumping, lying down, throwing, sitting, wrestling, carrying, etc. 390pp. 7⅞ x 10⅝.
20204-6 Clothbd.

TREES OF THE EASTERN AND CENTRAL UNITED STATES AND CANADA, William M. Harlow. Best one-volume guide to 140 trees. Full descriptions, woodlore, range, etc. Over 600 illustrations. Handy size. 288pp. 4½ x 6⅜.   20395-6

SONGS OF WESTERN BIRDS, Dr. Donald J. Borror. Complete song and call repertoire of 60 western species, including flycatchers, juncoes, cactus wrens, many more–includes fully illustrated booklet.   Cassette and manual 99913-0

GROWING AND USING HERBS AND SPICES, Milo Miloradovich. Versatile handbook provides all the information needed for cultivation and use of all the herbs and spices available in North America. 4 illustrations. Index. Glossary. 236pp. 5⅜ x 8½.
25058-X

BIG BOOK OF MAZES AND LABYRINTHS, Walter Shepherd. 50 mazes and labyrinths in all–classical, solid, ripple, and more–in one great volume. Perfect inexpensive puzzler for clever youngsters. Full solutions. 112pp. 8⅛ x 11.   22951-3

PIANO TUNING, J. Cree Fischer. Clearest, best book for beginner, amateur. Simple repairs, raising dropped notes, tuning by easy method of flattened fifths. No previous skills needed. 4 illustrations. 201pp. 5⅜ x 8½. 23267-0

HINTS TO SINGERS, Lillian Nordica. Selecting the right teacher, developing confidence, overcoming stage fright, and many other important skills receive thoughtful discussion in this indispensible guide, written by a world-famous diva of four decades' experience. 96pp. 5⅜ x 8½. 40094-8

THE COMPLETE NONSENSE OF EDWARD LEAR, Edward Lear. All nonsense limericks, zany alphabets, Owl and Pussycat, songs, nonsense botany, etc., illustrated by Lear. Total of 320pp. 5⅜ x 8½. (Available in U.S. only.) 20167-8

VICTORIAN PARLOUR POETRY: An Annotated Anthology, Michael R. Turner. 117 gems by Longfellow, Tennyson, Browning, many lesser-known poets. "The Village Blacksmith," "Curfew Must Not Ring Tonight," "Only a Baby Small," dozens more, often difficult to find elsewhere. Index of poets, titles, first lines. xxiii + 325pp. 5⅝ x 8¼. 27044-0

DUBLINERS, James Joyce. Fifteen stories offer vivid, tightly focused observations of the lives of Dublin's poorer classes. At least one, "The Dead," is considered a masterpiece. Reprinted complete and unabridged from standard edition. 160pp. 5³⁄₁₆ x 8¼. 26870-5

GREAT WEIRD TALES: 14 Stories by Lovecraft, Blackwood, Machen and Others, S. T. Joshi (ed.). 14 spellbinding tales, including "The Sin Eater," by Fiona McLeod, "The Eye Above the Mantel," by Frank Belknap Long, as well as renowned works by R. H. Barlow, Lord Dunsany, Arthur Machen, W. C. Morrow and eight other masters of the genre. 256pp. 5⅜ x 8½. (Available in U.S. only.) 40436-6

THE BOOK OF THE SACRED MAGIC OF ABRAMELIN THE MAGE, translated by S. MacGregor Mathers. Medieval manuscript of ceremonial magic. Basic document in Aleister Crowley, Golden Dawn groups. 268pp. 5⅜ x 8½. 23211-5

NEW RUSSIAN-ENGLISH AND ENGLISH-RUSSIAN DICTIONARY, M. A. O'Brien. This is a remarkably handy Russian dictionary, containing a surprising amount of information, including over 70,000 entries. 366pp. 4½ x 6⅛. 20208-9

HISTORIC HOMES OF THE AMERICAN PRESIDENTS, Second, Revised Edition, Irvin Haas. A traveler's guide to American Presidential homes, most open to the public, depicting and describing homes occupied by every American President from George Washington to George Bush. With visiting hours, admission charges, travel routes. 175 photographs. Index. 160pp. 8¼ x 11. 26751-2

NEW YORK IN THE FORTIES, Andreas Feininger. 162 brilliant photographs by the well-known photographer, formerly with *Life* magazine. Commuters, shoppers, Times Square at night, much else from city at its peak. Captions by John von Hartz. 181pp. 9¼ x 10¾. 23585-8

INDIAN SIGN LANGUAGE, William Tomkins. Over 525 signs developed by Sioux and other tribes. Written instructions and diagrams. Also 290 pictographs. 111pp. 6⅛ x 9¼. 22029-X

ANATOMY: A Complete Guide for Artists, Joseph Sheppard. A master of figure drawing shows artists how to render human anatomy convincingly. Over 460 illustrations. 224pp. 8⅜ x 11¼. 27279-6

MEDIEVAL CALLIGRAPHY: Its History and Technique, Marc Drogin. Spirited history, comprehensive instruction manual covers 13 styles (ca. 4th century through 15th). Excellent photographs; directions for duplicating medieval techniques with modern tools. 224pp. 8⅜ x 11¼. 26142-5

DRIED FLOWERS: How to Prepare Them, Sarah Whitlock and Martha Rankin. Complete instructions on how to use silica gel, meal and borax, perlite aggregate, sand and borax, glycerine and water to create attractive permanent flower arrangements. 12 illustrations. 32pp. 5⅜ x 8½. 21802-3

EASY-TO-MAKE BIRD FEEDERS FOR WOODWORKERS, Scott D. Campbell. Detailed, simple-to-use guide for designing, constructing, caring for and using feeders. Text, illustrations for 12 classic and contemporary designs. 96pp. 5⅜ x 8½. 25847-5

SCOTTISH WONDER TALES FROM MYTH AND LEGEND, Donald A. Mackenzie. 16 lively tales tell of giants rumbling down mountainsides, of a magic wand that turns stone pillars into warriors, of gods and goddesses, evil hags, powerful forces and more. 240pp. 5⅜ x 8½. 29677-6

THE HISTORY OF UNDERCLOTHES, C. Willett Cunnington and Phyllis Cunnington. Fascinating, well-documented survey covering six centuries of English undergarments, enhanced with over 100 illustrations: 12th-century laced-up bodice, footed long drawers (1795), 19th-century bustles, 19th-century corsets for men, Victorian "bust improvers," much more. 272pp. 5⅜ x 8¼. 27124-2

ARTS AND CRAFTS FURNITURE: The Complete Brooks Catalog of 1912, Brooks Manufacturing Co. Photos and detailed descriptions of more than 150 now very collectible furniture designs from the Arts and Crafts movement depict davenports, settees, buffets, desks, tables, chairs, bedsteads, dressers and more, all built of solid, quarter-sawed oak. Invaluable for students and enthusiasts of antiques, Americana and the decorative arts. 80pp. 6½ x 9¼. 27471-3

WILBUR AND ORVILLE: A Biography of the Wright Brothers, Fred Howard. Definitive, crisply written study tells the full story of the brothers' lives and work. A vividly written biography, unparalleled in scope and color, that also captures the spirit of an extraordinary era. 560pp. 6⅛ x 9¼. 40297-5

THE ARTS OF THE SAILOR: Knotting, Splicing and Ropework, Hervey Garrett Smith. Indispensable shipboard reference covers tools, basic knots and useful hitches; handsewing and canvas work, more. Over 100 illustrations. Delightful reading for sea lovers. 256pp. 5⅜ x 8½. 26440-8

FRANK LLOYD WRIGHT'S FALLINGWATER: The House and Its History, Second, Revised Edition, Donald Hoffmann. A total revision–both in text and illustrations–of the standard document on Fallingwater, the boldest, most personal architectural statement of Wright's mature years, updated with valuable new material from the recently opened Frank Lloyd Wright Archives. "Fascinating"–*The New York Times*. 116 illustrations. 128pp. 9¼ x 10¾. 27430-6

PHOTOGRAPHIC SKETCHBOOK OF THE CIVIL WAR, Alexander Gardner. 100 photos taken on field during the Civil War. Famous shots of Manassas Harper's Ferry, Lincoln, Richmond, slave pens, etc. 244pp. 10⅝ x 8¼.   22731-6

FIVE ACRES AND INDEPENDENCE, Maurice G. Kains. Great back-to-the-land classic explains basics of self-sufficient farming. The one book to get. 95 illustrations. 397pp. 5⅜ x 8½.   20974-1

SONGS OF EASTERN BIRDS, Dr. Donald J. Borror. Songs and calls of 60 species most common to eastern U.S.: warblers, woodpeckers, flycatchers, thrushes, larks, many more in high-quality recording.   Cassette and manual 99912-2

A MODERN HERBAL, Margaret Grieve. Much the fullest, most exact, most useful compilation of herbal material. Gigantic alphabetical encyclopedia, from aconite to zedoary, gives botanical information, medical properties, folklore, economic uses, much else. Indispensable to serious reader. 161 illustrations. 888pp. 6½ x 9¼. 2-vol. set. (Available in U.S. only.)   Vol. I: 22798-7
Vol. II: 22799-5

HIDDEN TREASURE MAZE BOOK, Dave Phillips. Solve 34 challenging mazes accompanied by heroic tales of adventure. Evil dragons, people-eating plants, blood-thirsty giants, many more dangerous adversaries lurk at every twist and turn. 34 mazes, stories, solutions. 48pp. 8¼ x 11.   24566-7

LETTERS OF W. A. MOZART, Wolfgang A. Mozart. Remarkable letters show bawdy wit, humor, imagination, musical insights, contemporary musical world; includes some letters from Leopold Mozart. 276pp. 5⅜ x 8½.   22859-2

BASIC PRINCIPLES OF CLASSICAL BALLET, Agrippina Vaganova. Great Russian theoretician, teacher explains methods for teaching classical ballet. 118 illustrations. 175pp. 5⅜ x 8½.   22036-2

THE JUMPING FROG, Mark Twain. Revenge edition. The original story of The Celebrated Jumping Frog of Calaveras County, a hapless French translation, and Twain's hilarious "retranslation" from the French. 12 illustrations. 66pp. 5⅜ x 8½.
22686-7

BEST REMEMBERED POEMS, Martin Gardner (ed.). The 126 poems in this superb collection of 19th- and 20th-century British and American verse range from Shelley's "To a Skylark" to the impassioned "Renascence" of Edna St. Vincent Millay and to Edward Lear's whimsical "The Owl and the Pussycat." 224pp. 5⅜ x 8½.
27165-X

COMPLETE SONNETS, William Shakespeare. Over 150 exquisite poems deal with love, friendship, the tyranny of time, beauty's evanescence, death and other themes in language of remarkable power, precision and beauty. Glossary of archaic terms. 80pp. 5³⁄₁₆ x 8¼.   26686-9

THE BATTLES THAT CHANGED HISTORY, Fletcher Pratt. Eminent historian profiles 16 crucial conflicts, ancient to modern, that changed the course of civilization. 352pp. 5⅜ x 8½.   41129-X

THE WIT AND HUMOR OF OSCAR WILDE, Alvin Redman (ed.). More than 1,000 ripostes, paradoxes, wisecracks: Work is the curse of the drinking classes; I can resist everything except temptation; etc. 258pp. 5⅜ x 8½. 20602-5

SHAKESPEARE LEXICON AND QUOTATION DICTIONARY, Alexander Schmidt. Full definitions, locations, shades of meaning in every word in plays and poems. More than 50,000 exact quotations. 1,485pp. 6½ x 9¼. 2-vol. set.
Vol. 1: 22726-X
Vol. 2: 22727-8

SELECTED POEMS, Emily Dickinson. Over 100 best-known, best-loved poems by one of America's foremost poets, reprinted from authoritative early editions. No comparable edition at this price. Index of first lines. 64pp. 5³⁄₁₆ x 8¼. 26466-1

THE INSIDIOUS DR. FU-MANCHU, Sax Rohmer. The first of the popular mystery series introduces a pair of English detectives to their archnemesis, the diabolical Dr. Fu-Manchu. Flavorful atmosphere, fast-paced action, and colorful characters enliven this classic of the genre. 208pp. 5³⁄₁₆ x 8¼. 29898-1

THE MALLEUS MALEFICARUM OF KRAMER AND SPRENGER, translated by Montague Summers. Full text of most important witchhunter's "bible," used by both Catholics and Protestants. 278pp. 6⅝ x 10. 22802-9

SPANISH STORIES/CUENTOS ESPAÑOLES: A Dual-Language Book, Angel Flores (ed.). Unique format offers 13 great stories in Spanish by Cervantes, Borges, others. Faithful English translations on facing pages. 352pp. 5⅜ x 8½. 25399-6

GARDEN CITY, LONG ISLAND, IN EARLY PHOTOGRAPHS, 1869–1919, Mildred H. Smith. Handsome treasury of 118 vintage pictures, accompanied by carefully researched captions, document the Garden City Hotel fire (1899), the Vanderbilt Cup Race (1908), the first airmail flight departing from the Nassau Boulevard Aerodrome (1911), and much more. 96pp. 8⅞ x 11¾. 40669-5

OLD QUEENS, N.Y., IN EARLY PHOTOGRAPHS, Vincent F. Seyfried and William Asadorian. Over 160 rare photographs of Maspeth, Jamaica, Jackson Heights, and other areas. Vintage views of DeWitt Clinton mansion, 1939 World's Fair and more. Captions. 192pp. 8⅞ x 11. 26358-4

CAPTURED BY THE INDIANS: 15 Firsthand Accounts, 1750-1870, Frederick Drimmer. Astounding true historical accounts of grisly torture, bloody conflicts, relentless pursuits, miraculous escapes and more, by people who lived to tell the tale. 384pp. 5⅜ x 8½. 24901-8

THE WORLD'S GREAT SPEECHES (Fourth Enlarged Edition), Lewis Copeland, Lawrence W. Lamm, and Stephen J. McKenna. Nearly 300 speeches provide public speakers with a wealth of updated quotes and inspiration–from Pericles' funeral oration and William Jennings Bryan's "Cross of Gold Speech" to Malcolm X's powerful words on the Black Revolution and Earl of Spenser's tribute to his sister, Diana, Princess of Wales. 944pp. 5⅜ x 8⅜. 40903-1

THE BOOK OF THE SWORD, Sir Richard F. Burton. Great Victorian scholar/adventurer's eloquent, erudite history of the "queen of weapons"–from prehistory to early Roman Empire. Evolution and development of early swords, variations (sabre, broadsword, cutlass, scimitar, etc.), much more. 336pp. 6⅛ x 9¼.
25434-8

AUTOBIOGRAPHY: The Story of My Experiments with Truth, Mohandas K. Gandhi. Boyhood, legal studies, purification, the growth of the Satyagraha (nonviolent protest) movement. Critical, inspiring work of the man responsible for the freedom of India. 480pp. 5⅜ x 8½. (Available in U.S. only.)   24593-4

CELTIC MYTHS AND LEGENDS, T. W. Rolleston. Masterful retelling of Irish and Welsh stories and tales. Cuchulain, King Arthur, Deirdre, the Grail, many more. First paperback edition. 58 full-page illustrations. 512pp. 5⅜ x 8½.   26507-2

THE PRINCIPLES OF PSYCHOLOGY, William James. Famous long course complete, unabridged. Stream of thought, time perception, memory, experimental methods; great work decades ahead of its time. 94 figures. 1,391pp. 5⅜ x 8½. 2-vol. set.
Vol. I: 20381-6   Vol. II: 20382-4

THE WORLD AS WILL AND REPRESENTATION, Arthur Schopenhauer. Definitive English translation of Schopenhauer's life work, correcting more than 1,000 errors, omissions in earlier translations. Translated by E. F. J. Payne. Total of 1,269pp. 5⅜ x 8½. 2-vol. set.   Vol. 1: 21761-2   Vol. 2: 21762-0

MAGIC AND MYSTERY IN TIBET, Madame Alexandra David-Neel. Experiences among lamas, magicians, sages, sorcerers, Bonpa wizards. A true psychic discovery. 32 illustrations. 321pp. 5⅜ x 8½. (Available in U.S. only.)   22682-4

THE EGYPTIAN BOOK OF THE DEAD, E. A. Wallis Budge. Complete reproduction of Ani's papyrus, finest ever found. Full hieroglyphic text, interlinear transliteration, word-for-word translation, smooth translation. 533pp. 6½ x 9¼.   21866-X

MATHEMATICS FOR THE NONMATHEMATICIAN, Morris Kline. Detailed, college-level treatment of mathematics in cultural and historical context, with numerous exercises. Recommended Reading Lists. Tables. Numerous figures. 641pp. 5⅜ x 8½.
24823-2

PROBABILISTIC METHODS IN THE THEORY OF STRUCTURES, Isaac Elishakoff. Well-written introduction covers the elements of the theory of probability from two or more random variables, the reliability of such multivariable structures, the theory of random function, Monte Carlo methods of treating problems incapable of exact solution, and more. Examples. 502pp. 5⅜ x 8½.   40691-1

THE RIME OF THE ANCIENT MARINER, Gustave Doré, S. T. Coleridge. Doré's finest work; 34 plates capture moods, subtleties of poem. Flawless full-size reproductions printed on facing pages with authoritative text of poem. "Beautiful. Simply beautiful."–*Publisher's Weekly.* 77pp. 9¼ x 12.   22305-1

NORTH AMERICAN INDIAN DESIGNS FOR ARTISTS AND CRAFTSPEOPLE, Eva Wilson. Over 360 authentic copyright-free designs adapted from Navajo blankets, Hopi pottery, Sioux buffalo hides, more. Geometrics, symbolic figures, plant and animal motifs, etc. 128pp. 8⅜ x 11. (Not for sale in the United Kingdom.)   25341-4

SCULPTURE: Principles and Practice, Louis Slobodkin. Step-by-step approach to clay, plaster, metals, stone; classical and modern. 253 drawings, photos. 255pp. 8⅛ x 11.
22960-2

THE INFLUENCE OF SEA POWER UPON HISTORY, 1660–1783, A. T. Mahan. Influential classic of naval history and tactics still used as text in war colleges. First paperback edition. 4 maps. 24 battle plans. 640pp. 5⅜ x 8½.   25509-3

THE STORY OF THE TITANIC AS TOLD BY ITS SURVIVORS, Jack Winocour (ed.). What it was really like. Panic, despair, shocking inefficiency, and a little heroism. More thrilling than any fictional account. 26 illustrations. 320pp. 5⅜ x 8½.
20610-6

FAIRY AND FOLK TALES OF THE IRISH PEASANTRY, William Butler Yeats (ed.). Treasury of 64 tales from the twilight world of Celtic myth and legend: "The Soul Cages," "The Kildare Pooka," "King O'Toole and his Goose," many more. Introduction and Notes by W. B. Yeats. 352pp. 5⅜ x 8½.
26941-8

BUDDHIST MAHAYANA TEXTS, E. B. Cowell and others (eds.). Superb, accurate translations of basic documents in Mahayana Buddhism, highly important in history of religions. The Buddha-karita of Asvaghosha, Larger Sukhavativyuha, more. 448pp. 5⅜ x 8½.
25552-2

ONE TWO THREE . . . INFINITY: Facts and Speculations of Science, George Gamow. Great physicist's fascinating, readable overview of contemporary science: number theory, relativity, fourth dimension, entropy, genes, atomic structure, much more. 128 illustrations. Index. 352pp. 5⅜ x 8½.
25664-2

EXPERIMENTATION AND MEASUREMENT, W. J. Youden. Introductory manual explains laws of measurement in simple terms and offers tips for achieving accuracy and minimizing errors. Mathematics of measurement, use of instruments, experimenting with machines. 1994 edition. Foreword. Preface. Introduction. Epilogue. Selected Readings. Glossary. Index. Tables and figures. 128pp. 5⅜ x 8½. 40451-X

DALÍ ON MODERN ART: The Cuckolds of Antiquated Modern Art, Salvador Dalí. Influential painter skewers modern art and its practitioners. Outrageous evaluations of Picasso, Cézanne, Turner, more. 15 renderings of paintings discussed. 44 calligraphic decorations by Dalí. 96pp. 5⅜ x 8½. (Available in U.S. only.)
29220-7

ANTIQUE PLAYING CARDS: A Pictorial History, Henry René D'Allemagne. Over 900 elaborate, decorative images from rare playing cards (14th–20th centuries): Bacchus, death, dancing dogs, hunting scenes, royal coats of arms, players cheating, much more. 96pp. 9¼ x 12¼.
29265-7

MAKING FURNITURE MASTERPIECES: 30 Projects with Measured Drawings, Franklin H. Gottshall. Step-by-step instructions, illustrations for constructing handsome, useful pieces, among them a Sheraton desk, Chippendale chair, Spanish desk, Queen Anne table and a William and Mary dressing mirror. 224pp. 8⅛ x 11¼.
29338-6

THE FOSSIL BOOK: A Record of Prehistoric Life, Patricia V. Rich et al. Profusely illustrated definitive guide covers everything from single-celled organisms and dinosaurs to birds and mammals and the interplay between climate and man. Over 1,500 illustrations. 760pp. 7½ x 10⅛.
29371-8